INTERNATIONAL
Great Meals
IN MINUTES

INTERNATIONAL
Great Meals
IN MINUTES

LITTLE, BROWN AND COMPANY
BOSTON TORONTO

Selections from *Great Meals in Minutes* series, reprinted by arrangement with Time-Life Books. *Great Meals in Minutes* was created by Rebus, Inc.

Rebus, Inc.

Publisher: Rodney Friedman
Editorial Director: Shirley Tomkievicz

Editor: Marya Dalrymple
Art Director: Ronald Gross
Managing Editors: Brenda Goldberg, Frederica A. Harvey
Senior Editors: Charles Blackwell, Cara De Silva, Ruth A. Peltason, Barbara Benton
Assistant Managing Editor: Cynthia Villani
Food Editor and Food Stylist: Grace Young
Photographer: Steven Mays
Prop Stylists: Cathryn Schwing, Zazel Wilde Lovén
Staff Writer: Alexandra Greeley
Associate Editors: Ann M. Harvey, Jordan Verner, Bonnie J. Slotnick
Editorial Assistants: Joan Michel, Jennifer Mah, Michael Flint
Assistant Food Stylists: Karen Hatt, Nancy Leland Thompson
Photography Assistants: Glenn Maffei, Lars Klove
Recipe Tester: Gina Palombi Barclay
Production Assistants: Lorna Bieber, Lisa Young
Editorial Board: Angelica Cannon, Sally Dorst, Lilyan Glusker, Kim MacArthur, Kay Noble, Joan Whitman
Introduction this edition written and adapted by Camille Cusumano

Library of Congress Cataloging-in-Publication Data
International great meals in minutes.
    "Selections from the Great meals in minutes series"—
P. facing t.p.
    Includes index.
    1. Cookery, International.   I. Time-Life Books.
TX725.A1I43   1986   641.5′55   86–7455
ISBN 0–316–85091–8

Time-Life Books Inc.
is a wholly owned subsidiary of
Time Incorporated
Founder: Henry R. Luce 1898–1967

Editor-in-Chief: Henry Anatole Grunwald
President: J. Richard Munro
Chairman of the Board: Ralph P. Davidson
Corporate Editor: Ray Cave
Group Vice President, Books: Reginald K. Brack Jr.
Vice President, Books: George Artandi

Time-Life Books Inc.

Editor: George Constable
Director of Design: Louis Klein
Editorial General Manager: Neal Goff
Director of Editorial Resources: Phyllis K. Wise
Acting Text Director: Ellen Phillips
Editorial Board: Dale M. Brown, Roberta Conlan, Thomas H. Flaherty, Donia Ann Steele, Rosalind Stubenberg, Kit van Tulleken, Henry Woodhead
Director of Photography and Research: John Conrad Weiser

President: Reginald K. Brack Jr.
Executive Vice Presidents: John M. Fahey Jr., Christopher T. Linen
Senior Vice President: James L. Mercer
Vice Presidents: Stephen L. Bair, Edward Brash, Ralph J. Cuomo, Juanita T. James, Robert J. Passantino, Robert H. Smith, Paul R. Stewart, Leopoldo Toralballo

SERIES CONSULTANT
Margaret E. Happel is the author of *Ladies' Home Journal Adventures in Cooking,* *Ladies Home Journal Handbook of Holiday Cuisine,* and other best-selling cookbooks, as well as the translator and adapter of Rebecca Hsu Hiu Min's *Delights of Chinese Cooking.* A food consultant based in New York City, she has been director of the food department of *Good Housekeeping* and editor of *American Home* magazine.

WINE CONSULTANT
Tom Maresca combines a full-time career teaching English literature with writing about and consuming fine wines. He is the author of *Mastering Wine.*

Cover: Bernice Hunt's fresh melon with prosciutto, cartwheels with mixed vegetables, fennel salad vinaigrette, and cheese pie. See pages 42–45.

Contents

Introduction

When it comes to appreciating good food, Americans are truly cosmopolitan. Many of us have traveled or lived abroad and enjoy re-creating the tantalizing dishes experienced in foreign countries. Others of us travel vicariously, utilizing high-quality imported ingredients to produce meals from countries we'd like to visit. Today almost no cuisine is off limits to the home cook; once-exotic foods are now widely available, and we can be as adventurous as our culinary imaginations allow.

International Great Meals in Minutes is tailored for the busy cook—novice or expert—who wants to savor another culture through its native cooking without spending hours in the kitchen. In this volume twenty-nine talented and respected cooks contribute seventy-eight international menus for all occasions. Many of the cooks have spent time in the countries whose menus they present, learning the details and nuances of food selection and preparation that make each cuisine unique. They have visited the marketplaces where fresh produce is sold, they have dined in the restaurants where skilled chefs work their magic, and they have watched home cooks prepare unwritten recipes handed down through generations. The menus these cooks offer integrate their experiences abroad with ingredients and techniques accessible to us; yet each menu retains its ethnic integrity.

In addition, every menu, which serves four, is planned for ease and efficiency, and all can be prepared *in an hour or less*. The cooks provide shopping lists, utensils lists, and a step-by-step format that assures impressive results each time you prepare a meal.

In *International Great Meals in Minutes* every recipe uses fresh produce. The other ingredients (vinegars, spices, herbs, and so on) are all widely available in supermarkets or occasionally in specialty food stores or ethnic markets. Alternative ingredients are generally suggested for those that may be difficult to find. The cooks and the test kitchen staff have planned and tested the meals for appearance as well as taste, as the accompanying photographs show: The vegetables are brilliant and fresh, the visual combinations appetizing. The table settings feature bright colors, simple flower arrangements, and attractive serving dishes.

For each menu, the Editors, with advice from the cooks, suggest wines and other beverages. And there are Added Touches, which are extra recipes for appetizers, side dishes, and desserts, as well as ideas for using leftovers.

BEFORE YOU START

International Great Meals in Minutes will work best for you if you follow these suggestions:

1. Read the guidelines on the following pages for selecting ingredients.

2. Review the cooking techniques. They will quickly become second nature and will help you produce professional-quality international meals in minutes.

3. Read the menus before you shop. Each lists the ingredients you will need, in the order you would expect to find them in the supermarket. Many items will already be on your pantry shelf.

4. Check the equipment list on page 17. Good, sharp knives and pots and pans of the right shape and material are essential for making great meals in minutes. This may be the time to buy some new pieces.

5. Set out everything you need before you start to cook: The lists at the beginning of each menu tell just what is required. To save effort, always keep your ingredients in the same place so you can reach for them instinctively.

6. Follow the start-to-finish steps provided with each menu. That way, you will be sure to have the entire meal ready in an hour.

The menus in this volume are grouped according to their country of origin. The majority of the menus were selected from the four cuisines most popular with Americans—Italian, Oriental, French, and Mexican. Read the information that follows about each of these cuisines, then try several of the menus from each section; you will quickly discover the variety of dishes to be found within a country and how different cooking techniques and treatment of ingredients help define each cuisine.

The last section of the book—More International Menus—allows you to visit less well known parts of the gastronomical globe. You will find menus from Hungary, Turkey, Portugal, Morocco, and India, among other countries, and will discover that making *falafel* "cutlets," sauerkraut-bean soup, or *couscous* can be just as easy as preparing a meal of steak and potatoes.

Awaiting preparation, opposite, the ingredients that form the foundation of Mediterranean cooking. Clockwise from top left: fish and shellfish, bulgur and couscous, extra-virgin olive oil, lamb and fresh mint, olives, cinnamon and coffee, saffron and bay leaves, fresh and dried fruits, nuts, ginger, and perfectly ripe melons.

ITALIAN MENUS IN MINUTES

The boot-shaped peninsula of Italy is segmented into 20 regions, which are subdivided into 94 provinces. Every region and province is idiosyncratic about its cooking, and even the towns within the provinces have distinct culinary quirks. Nevertheless, it is the basic differences between the cooking of the north and the south that really divide Italian cuisine. Cooks in the prosperous industrial north, which is also dairy country, use butter as well as olive oil, and prefer fresh egg-based pastas such as tagliatelli, lasagna, and ravioli. In the poorer south, cooks use less luxurious ingredients—olive oil and dried tubular pastas such as macaroni and spaghetti, which are made solely from flour and water.

Despite regional differences, Italian cooks do have some things in common: a passion for pasta, which is served at practically every meal throughout the country, and an insistence on using only the very freshest ingredients, purchased daily at local markets.

Beginning on page 22, five talented cooks offer dishes from a number of prominent regions, provinces, and cities in Italy including:

Liguria and Genoa: The crescent-shaped region called Liguria, also known as the Italian Riviera, is located in northern Italy on the Ligurian Sea. Its principal port, Genoa, influences the cooking of the entire region, with its focus on freshly caught seafood combined with aromatic herbs grown on the nearby hillsides. Basil, the best known of these Genoese herbs, is the basis for *pesto Genovese*, a cheese, garlic, pine nut, and herb paste usually spooned into soups or tossed with pasta. On pages 22–31, Susan DeRege offers three menus inspired by the many meals she has enjoyed beside the Gulf of Genoa. In her Menu 3, she features a unique lasagna, in which the flat noodles are layered with pesto and béchamel sauce.

Lombardy: The fertile region of Lombardy, which stretches from the Alps in the north to the Po Valley in the south, has a rich, diverse cuisine. This is dairy country, and Lombardian cooks make lavish use of butter and cheese. A specialty is *fitascetta con peperoni*, a ring-shaped flat bread that is one of the oldest styles of pizza in Italy. On page 61, Evelyne Slomon tops her version of this pizza with Fontina and sautéed peppers.

Istria: Cooks Felice and Lidia Bastianich, both born in Istria, offer three menus that preserve the unpretentious cooking traditions of this region, once part of northern Italy and now governed by Yugoslavia. Istria is known for its seafood and game dishes flavored with onions, garlic, and olive oil. In their Menu 1, pages 50–53, the Bastianichs prepare scampi with quick risotto, and in Menu 2, pages 54–55, quail with polenta.

Basilicata: Situated at the southernmost tip of Italy, Basilicata has a limited but hearty cuisine based on locally raised goats, lamb, pigs, and small game. Sausages, vegetables (particularly artichokes, cabbage, and hot peppers), local cheeses such as Provolone and *caciocavallo*, and sweet pastries are also part of the diet. On pages 34–35, Nancy Barr offers braised duck with black olives, a

PIZZA

Pizza evolved from the hearth-baked flatbreads of ancient times, but the Italians have refined it and elaborated upon it. Today, the varieties are endless: Flat, rolled, folded, or stuffed, pizzas can have almost any kind of filling.

Evelyne Slomon, whose recipes for food-processor pizza dough appear on pages 58–67, has provided the following traditional method for making the dough.

Pizza Dough by Hand

1 cup hot tap water
1 package active dry yeast
3½ cups all-purpose white flour, approximately
½ teaspoon salt
Vegetable oil for greasing bowl

1. In medium-size mixing bowl, combine hot tap water with yeast, stirring gently with fork until yeast has dissolved and liquid turns light beige.
2. Add 1 cup flour and salt, and stir with a wooden spoon to combine. Add another cup of flour and mix until dough starts to pull away from sides of bowl and begins to form a soft, sticky mass.
3. Sprinkle some flour over work surface and flour your hands generously. Remove dough from bowl and knead in another cup of flour, one-quarter cup at a time.
4. With heel of one hand (or both hands, if you wish), push dough across floured work surface. Grab dough with one hand and twist and fold it over. Scrape up any moist dough that sticks to work surface. Working quickly, repeat this action, adding only as much of remaining flour as it takes to keep dough from sticking to your hands.
5. To test, push the heel of your hand into dough for 10 seconds. If your hand comes up clean, the dough is ready; if it is sticky, a bit more kneading will be necessary. Be careful not to overwork the dough; continue kneading only until it is smooth and elastic, about 5 to 10 minutes.
6. Clean the bowl and lightly grease it with vegetable oil. Place dough in bowl and turn dough until evenly coated with a thin film of oil. Cover bowl securely with plastic wrap.
7. Let dough rise 30 to 45 minutes in a warm, draft-free place, preferably in a gas oven with a pilot light or in an electric oven preheated to 200 degrees and then turned off.
8. Once dough has doubled in bulk, punch it down with your fist and turn it onto a lightly floured surface and knead it for another minute. Follow your recipe for what to do next.

Advance Preparation of Pizza Dough
Refrigerated rising: To prepare pizza dough a day ahead, follow the recipe above through step 6, and refrigerate dough. The next morning, punch dough down and knead it for 1 minute. Return dough to bowl, reseal, and refrigerate. Be sure to remove dough from refrigerator at least 30 minutes before rolling it out.

Freezing: After step 6 above, press dough into ½-inch-thick disk, wrap in plastic, and freeze. Defrost dough for 6 to 8 hours in refrigerator or set it in a warm place for 2 hours. Use the dough as soon as it is warm enough to handle. Although the dough will not be double in bulk, follow step 8.

specialty of the region.

Sicily: Sicilians love food and eat with gusto, utilizing all that their farms and the seas provide. On this sun-washed isle, cooks prepare breads at home and favor tubular pastas with strongly seasoned sauces. On page 63, Evelyne Slomon makes a Sicilian-style pizza called *scacciata,* which she accompanies with a salad scented with lemon and cinnamon. And on page 49, Bernice Hunt presents steamed broccoli with a flourish of lemon juice and olive oil, a dish often found on Sicilian tables.

ORIENTAL MENUS IN MINUTES

On pages 70–111, four prominent cooks present six Japanese and six Chinese menus.

Japanese Menus

Japanese cuisine is like no other. Although Japanese cooks have a number of things in common with Chinese cooks—a deceptively subtle approach to ingredients, an eye for beautiful food presentation, a keen aptitude for mixing tastes and textures, and a mastery of quick cooking techniques—Japanese cooks strive to preserve the intrinsic properties of each ingredient in a way that is uniquely their own.

Although the influence of the Western world has modified Japanese eating habits, certain traditions prevail. The eating of meat, once a Buddhist taboo, has not diminished the importance of fish in the Japanese diet. And other staples have survived the Western onslaught: rice, a short-grain type, cooked to a slightly sticky texture; seaweed; tofu (bean curd); and vegetables such as *daikon* (a giant white radish), Chinese cabbage, and bamboo shoots.

Cooks Warren Mah and Connie Handa Moore show that Japanese menus can be easy and quick to prepare. Warren Mah's Menu 1, pages 80–83, features pork and scallion rolls with a *teriyaki* sauce, accompanied by stir-fried vegetables. His presentation dazzles the eye as well as the palate. And all three of Connie Handa Moore's menus, pages 70–79, present salads that utilize such readily available Oriental ingredients as miso and tofu.

Chinese Menus

Thousands of years before Americans turned fast food into a national passion, Chinese cooks had mastered the art of preparing great meals quickly—and easily. Their invention was born of necessity. The family kitchen usually consisted of nothing more than a small container of coals. Fuel was scarce and, because there was often not enough land or rain to bring crops to maturity, so was food. The Chinese learned that young, tender vegetables and meats, sliced, diced, minced, or shredded, cooked faster than big pieces and, therefore, required less cooking fuel. The cook needed only a chopping surface, a sharp knife, a pan, and a pair of chopsticks for stirring.

For today's cook with little time to spend in the kitchen, the Chinese way with food is still one of the fastest and most economical for delicious, nourishing family meals as well as for memorable dinners for guests.

Like Italy, China has a fascinating variety of regional cooking styles primarily influenced by the climate, which ranges from sub-Arctic to tropical. The cuisine of eastern China often goes by the name Shanghai, the prominent seaport of the region. Rice, fish, pork, and beef are staples here, and Shanghai cooks often braise meats in a liquid comprised of soy sauce, sugar, and spices, a technique known as "red-cooking."

Peking is the dominant influence in the north. Because frigid winter temperatures make rice cultivation impossi-

---

A GUIDE TO OLIVE OILS

Olive oils differ with the variety of olives, the climate and soil in which the olives are grown, and the method by which they are processed. The color of olive oil may vary from pale gold to jade green, but it is not an indication of quality. Any good oil, however, will have a distinct olive-like bouquet. Designations of quality vary from one country to another, and oil from the same producer may differ from year to year. Taste a number of oils and decide for yourself what you like. You may find you prefer a fruity Sicilian oil, a lighter Tuscan product, or perhaps one of the French, Greek, Spanish, or American oils. In any case, always choose a product labeled 100% OLIVE OIL, and look for one that is pressed where the olives are grown.

Traditionally, EXTRA-VIRGIN is the designation for olive oil of the highest quality. Although criteria vary, extra-virgin usually means that the oil is from the first cold pressing—without heat or further refining—of the finest hand-picked olives. Extra-virgin oil is low in acidity and therefore gentle on the palate. It is expensive but worth the price.

The less expensive grades of oil—SUPERFINE VIRGIN and FINE VIRGIN—are good for everyday use and better for cooking than extra-virgin since they stand up better to heat. A general rule is to use the finest oils for salad dressings and delicate, uncooked dishes, or as an addition to cooked dishes such as soups, but only after they are removed from the heat. Use fuller flavored oils for robust sauces, meat dishes, and highly spiced foods.

Extra-virgin olive oil's fine flavor, low smoking point, and high cost make it unsuitable for frying. However, the lower grades of oil (those labeled simply PURE) are more refined and can safely be heated to about 400 degrees; this makes them usable for sautéing and even for deep frying. Remember, though, that olive oil will always add a distinctive flavor to the food cooked in it. In Italy today, the trend is to use olive oil only when it will noticeably enhance the food; if the oil's flavor will be negligible or overpowered by stronger seasonings, Italian cooks prefer to use a neutral vegetable oil.

Olive oil keeps well—for up to a year—if stored in a cool, dark place. Leave it in its original bottle or tin, tightly capped, or, if you prefer, decant a small amount into a smaller glazed ceramic or glass container (a half-size wine bottle is good) and keep it accessible for daily use. Do not use plastic containers, which may alter the taste of the oil. It is not desirable to refrigerate olive oil, as it will thicken and become difficult to pour.

ble, wheat is the staple crop, and wheat-based products such as noodles, dumplings, and pancakes form the basis of northern cooking.

Szechwan and Hunan—which Americans usually (and rightly) associate with beef dishes and peppery sauces—are the provincial cuisines best known in the West. Indeed, cooks from those provinces are fond of spices, particularly fiery chili peppers.

Canton and British-ruled Hong Kong dominate the south, where rice, fish, pork, and fresh vegetables are staples and the emphasis is on minimal cooking time. Cantonese cooks favor crisp, fresh ingredients seasoned with delicate spices and flavorings, and southern cooking is subtle rather than fiery.

On pages 90–101, Barbara Tropp features the robust dishes of northern China and the spicy hot foods of Szechwan and Hunan in the west. Her menus include such dishes as spicy Hunan beef with scallions and sweet red peppers, hoisin-explosion shrimp, and steamed spicy fish. Cook Karen Lee is more eclectic, offering her own versions of such Chinese classics as chili shrimp, page 104, and orange chicken, page 107. In preparing their dishes, both cooks utilize a number of classic Chinese cutting techniques as well as stir frying. You may find the cutting techniques require a little practice before you can do them quickly (see below); stir frying simply requires a wok or a heavy-bottomed pan. For details on the wok, see opposite; for information on stir frying, see pages 15–16.

Cutting Techniques

Precision cutting is fundamental to Chinese cooking. Food must be both uniformly and beautifully cut for even, quick cooking and for artistic presentation. The Chinese have designed a versatile three-way tool—the cleaver—which has a razor-sharp edge for cutting, a blunt top edge for pounding, and broad sides for flattening and scooping up food pieces.

Two basic tips: To cut anything quickly and uniformly, you must keep it steady on the cutting board. Carrots, garlic, onions, and other round vegetables will roll. Therefore, except when you are roll cutting (see below), start by slicing these vegetables in half lengthwise or crosswise to create a flat surface. Then put the flat surface downward and finish the work. Meats cut more easily when they are cold: Try chilling meat for half an hour in the freezer before you dice it, but take it out before it freezes. By keeping your knife or cleaver razor-sharp, you will need very little muscle power to accomplish the following cutting techniques.

Slicing: Place the food on the cutting board. Hold it firmly with the fingertips of one hand. Using an easy back-and-forth motion, but not a strenuous sawing motion, with just the weight of the knife and your hand for pressure, cut off pieces in even strips, according to recipe specifications.

Dicing: Begin by slicing. Then, while holding the slices together in a stack, slice again, leaving about ¼ to ½ inch between cuts. Finally, turn the food or the cutting board 180 degrees and slice once more at ¼- to ½-inch intervals. For fine dice, begin by cutting the food in half horizontally. Keep it stacked, then slice it two more times.

Mincing: Proceed with dicing. Then, using the blade of your knife or cleaver, push the pieces into a tight pile. With your cutting hand, grasp the knife by the handle and take the pointed end between the thumb and forefinger of the other hand. Hold down the pointed end firmly on the cutting board and, using quick, vertical motions of the handle, chop across the pile in one direction and then the other, pausing now and then to push the pieces into a pile again. If you are using a cleaver, grasp the handle only and keep reforming the pile with the blade.

Julienning: Proceed as though you were dicing. But after stacking the slices, instead of cutting the food into small squares, slice the stack into long, thin pieces about the size and shape of a wooden kitchen match.

Shredding: Follow the procedure for julienning. Then, holding the knife tip on the board with one hand and the handle in the other, keep cutting lengthwise through the pieces until they are as fine as you can make them.

Roll Cutting: This special method is used for long, cylindrical vegetables such as carrots, asparagus, or zucchini. First, peel the vegetable if the recipe so directs. Then make a sharp, diagonal cut, perhaps an inch from one end, trying for about a 45-degree angle. Then roll the vegetable a quarter turn and slice again at the same angle,

---

RICE

Rice is the customary accompaniment to most Chinese meals and the simplest of all side dishes to cook. Once you have mastered the technique, you will not need a recipe.

The Chinese eat many types of rice—long-grained, short-grained, round, and flat—but long-grain white rice cooks up drier and fluffier, with each cooked grain remaining separate, and is also less starchy than other kinds. The directions on whatever brand you buy will no doubt advise against rinsing the rice before cooking. A Chinese chef, nevertheless, always rinses rice thoroughly in cold water, not once but five or six times, on the theory that rice tastes fresher and less starchy when rinsed. If you buy a standard American long-grain rice, uncoated with any kind of additive, you may skip the rinsing without sacrificing either quality or cleanliness.

One cup of uncooked rice yields slightly less than four cups of cooked—the amount specified for the menus in this volume. When a menu calls for rice, you will be referred to the following recipe.

Perfect Rice

2 cups cold water
1 cup raw long-grain rice

1. Add the water and rice to a medium-size saucepan. Heat uncovered until water comes to a full boil.
2. Turn heat to low and cover. Simmer rice for 20 minutes without stirring.
3. Remove pot from heat and let it stand 5 to 10 minutes.
4. Remove cover and fluff rice with a fork before serving.

about an inch from the first cut. Continue until you have sliced the whole length. Because the diagonal slices expose more of the insides of the vegetables, they will cook faster and absorb more flavor than will conventional slices.

The Wok
The typical wok is a large spun-steel pan, either round- or flat-bottomed, with high sloping sides and two handles, which may or may not conduct heat (wear mitts to guard against burning yourself). A round-bottomed wok works best on the open flame of a gas range. The flame will heat the bottom and sides of the wok quickly and uniformly, and the flame is adjustable. Because it can tip over on a flat burner coil, a round-bottomed pan is dangerous on an electric range; use a flat-bottomed wok or a large, heavy skillet if you have an electric range. Either will conduct heat more efficiently.

Electric woks are used for steaming (see page 16) but not for stir frying, as you cannot maneuver the wok to regulate the flow of heat. Avoid woks or skillets coated with Teflon, Silverstone, or other nonstick linings for stir frying because they are useless at the high heats required for this technique and will quickly lose their nonstick properties.

Before stir frying in a new wok, you must clean and season it. The "seasoning" is a coat of oil permanently baked onto the interior to prevent food from sticking to the surface. Because most woks come from the manufacturer with a machine-oil coating, first wash the wok inside and out with hot water and detergent, and dry it before seasoning.

To season the wok, pour a tablespoon of liquid cooking oil (corn, peanut, or any vegetable oil) into a small bowl and set out a pastry brush or a wadded paper towel. Place the wok over very high heat, making sure it heats all over, right up to the rim. Dip the pastry brush or paper towel into the oil and coat the interior of the wok carefully and thoroughly. Wipe off any excess oil. Remove the wok from the heat to cool for about 10 minutes. Then repeat the heating, oiling, and cooling process once or twice more until a black spot appears in the bottom of the wok. You are now ready to cook with it. Be sure to wipe out the wok with a sponge dipped in hot water immediately after using it for the first time. Eventually, through repeated use, the whole interior of the wok should turn a lustrous black.

FRENCH MENUS IN MINUTES
French contributions to gastronomy are characterized by a profound respect for superior ingredients; an extensive, codified repertoire of recipes; and a wealth of culinary knowledge perpetuated by chefs exhaustively trained in the art of cooking. Indeed, French chefs are such perfectionists that several are reputed to have committed suicide because, in their opinion, they could not live up to their reputations. In short, the French take their food seriously.

Many people associate French cuisine with elaborate sauces, subtle seasonings, expensive ingredients, and

---

CHOPSTICKS
You may prefer to eat your Chinese meals with a knife and fork. But chopsticks are perfectly designed for picking up small pieces of meat and vegetables from a plate or a soup bowl, as well as for bringing small bites of rice from bowl to mouth. They come in a variety of materials, from wood to ivory. The standard length is 12 inches. The illustration below shows the basic position for holding chopsticks with the fingers. The bottom stick braces, and the top one moves.

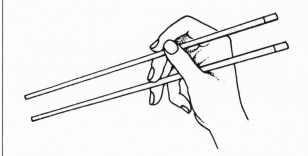

Chopsticks are the best possible tool not only for eating Chinese food but for stir frying or deep frying. For cooking use, buy 16-inch wooden chopsticks, two or three pairs at a minimum.

---

complicated kitchen procedures—the hallmarks of classic *haute cuisine.* However, it is the regional dishes, originating in restaurants and homes far from the kitchens of Paris, that are the heart and soul of French cooking.

Regional cooking, unlike *haute cuisine,* requires no highly technical cooking skills or rigid recipes; rather it is improvisational, relying on the indigenous foods—seasonal herbs and vegetables, eggs and cheese, poultry, meats, and fresh fish—that give each region's cuisine its character. Although they take their cooking as seriously as the country's most sophisticated chefs, French regional cooks avoid complexity and pretension.

A French gastronome once observed that a dedicated eater could live to be 80 years old and not sample every French regional dish, even by eating a different one every day. There are in fact thousands of French regional recipes, characteristic of particular areas and cities. In this volume, five cooks present fifteen complete menus featuring dishes from several of France's renowned gastronomic areas.

Burgundy: The robust cuisine of Burgundy uses liberal amounts of garlic, Dijon mustard, purified lard, thick cream, and the region's famous wines. Foods prepared in the Burgundy style generally are cooked in a red wine sauce with mushrooms and onions, and often are garnished with lardoons (finely diced bacon). William Rice and Jill Van Cleave have re-created several Burgundy-style dishes, including a first course of snails in wine sauce, which precedes pork chops with Dijon mustard. See pages 146–147.

Provence: Blessed with a hot, sunny climate, Provence is sometimes called the "market garden of France." As in other areas bordering the Mediterranean, the cooks of Provence have developed a cuisine based on olive oil, olives, garlic, tomatoes, saffron, sweet and hot peppers, and wild herbs. Lavender, rosemary, sage, thyme, savory, and basil grow profusely here and perfume the air.

Provençal cooking is simple and seasonal, utilizing fresh vegetables, including artichokes and eggplants, and fruit such as melons, figs, peaches, apricots, quinces, and cherries. For fish lovers, Provence is paradise, with hundreds of species indigenous to its waters. For their Menu 3, pages 141–143, Maria and Guy Reuge have created a Provençal fish stew that combines fish, shellfish, tomatoes, and cream.

Gascony: Gascony is a strip of land in the south of France lying between the Garonne River valley to the north and the Pyrenees to the south. This ancient province was home to D'Artagnan, one of the swashbuckling musketeers created by Alexandre Dumas. Gascony boasts rolling hills and pine forests that shelter small game; lagoons and streams teeming with fish; and soil that produces grapes, potatoes, cabbage, and corn. Gourmets praise Gascony's fine cuisine—its goose, duck, chicken, and game-bird dishes—as well as its Armagnac, the local vintage brandy. William Rice and Jill Van Cleave present a Gascony-style main course, broiled duck breast served with prunes in Armagnac, on pages 152–153.

Périgord: The hilly Périgord region of southwest France is primarily agricultural. Its land yields an abundance of grains, vegetables, fruits, and nuts, and supports cattle, pigs, chickens, and the plump Toulouse geese. Périgord is known for two local commodities that have substantially enhanced cooking in the rest of France: *foie gras* from the Toulouse geese, and black truffles, walnut-sized fungi with a delicate, musky flavor that makes them one of the most sought-after of ingredients.

Dennis Gilbert offers his version of a *tourte à la périgourdine* (chicken-filled pie) on pages 116–117. And Danièle Delpeuch adapts three Périgord menus for the American kitchen, all featuring either turkey or duck, on pages 124–133.

Auvergne: The Auvergne, located on the once-volcanic central plateau of France, suffers from long winters. To stave off the cold, the peasants here have developed a hearty and highly caloric cuisine. Cabbage soup and the potato and cheese casserole called *aligot* are two of the Auvergne's notable dishes. Dennis Gilbert's Menus 2 and 3 illustrate Auvergnat cooking: In Menu 2, pages 118–120, he prepares sautéed boneless chicken breasts with parsnips and carrots accompanied by *aligot*. And in Menu 3, pages 121–123, veal with saffron and apples is the featured dish.

MEXICAN MENUS IN MINUTES

Mexican food is infinitely more diverse than the taco, tortilla, or fiery bowl of *chili con carne* it signifies to most Americans. It can be as simple as the familiar Indian tamales (cornmeal dough with a savory filling baked in corn husks) or as elegant as the national dish, *mole poblano* (a chili-and-chocolate-based turkey stew, said to have been created by sixteenth-century Spanish nuns in Mexico). Mexican cooking, with all its complex and exotic flavors, ranks with French, Chinese, Japanese, and Italian cuisines as one of the most sophisticated in the world.

The cuisine of Mexico owes its extraordinary diversity to a blending of two cultures. When Cortés and his Spanish soldiers marched into the Aztec capital of Tenochtitlán (now Mexico City) in 1519, they were dazzled by a strange Indian civilization. The Aztecs, a fierce, once-nomadic tribe that had settled in the central valley of Mexico in the 1300s, had become a powerful political force, conquering many lesser tribes and ruling much of the land.

The Spaniards were captivated by the Indians' sumptuous cuisine, concocted from ingredients carried into the capital from every part of Mexico. Many of these foods were hitherto unknown to Europeans: corn, beans, squash, peanuts, chocolate, vanilla, eggplant, and chilies among them. The Spaniards gradually assimilated these novel foods, but the culinary exchange was not one-sided. The conquistadors contributed much to the Indian larders: wine, hogs, cattle, chickens, onions, garlic, citrus fruits, almonds, dairy products, cinnamon, olive oil, rice, and wheat. Spanish cooks also taught the Aztecs how to fry foods. Today's Mexican food, still a mix of Indian and Spanish, also reflects other European influences, includ-

A good stock is the foundation for many dishes in this volume, and is also an excellent base for sauces and gravies. Although canned stock or broth is acceptable to use when you are short on time, homemade stock has a rich flavor that is hard to match. Moreover, canned products are likely to be overly salty. Homemade stock is not difficult to make. The following pointers will ensure a rich, clear stock, no matter which type you make.

Use a large nonaluminum stockpot or saucepan. Stir the stock as little as possible to prevent clouding. Watch carefully to make sure the stock stays at a simmer but does not boil. Cooking chicken stock a half hour more or less will not affect its flavor significantly; however, if fish stock is cooked for more than 30 minutes, it may acquire an unpleasant taste. Once cooked, cool the stock as quickly as possible, preferably by placing the pan in a sinkful of cold water. Do not cover it as it cools, and refrigerate it as soon as it has cooled. After several hours of refrigeration, the fat will congeal at the top of the stock; it may be removed or left as a protective covering. At this point, transfer the stock to jars or freezer containers (1-cup sizes are convenient); it will keep for up to three days in the refrigerator and up to three months in the freezer.

Chicken Stock

Save chicken parts as they accumulate and freeze them. The yellow onion skin adds color; the optional veal bone adds extra flavor and richness.

3 pounds bony chicken parts, such as wings,
   back, and neck
1 veal knuckle (optional)
Yellow onion, unpeeled and stuck with 2 whole cloves
2 stalks celery with leaves, halved
12 peppercorns
2 carrots, peeled and cut into 2-inch lengths
4 sprigs parsley
1 bay leaf
1 tablespoon chopped fresh thyme, or 1 teaspoon dried
Salt

1. Wash chicken parts, and veal knuckle if using, and drain. Place in stockpot with remaining ingredients (except salt) and add 3 quarts cold water. Cover pot and bring to a boil over medium heat.
2. Reduce heat and simmer stock, partially covered, 2 to 3 hours, skimming foam and scum from surface several times. Add salt to taste after stock has cooked 1 hour.
3. Strain stock through fine sieve placed over large bowl. Discard solids. Let stock cool uncovered; refrigerate when completely cool.

Chinese Chicken Stock

An authentic Chinese stock uses a whole chicken for flavoring. The stock cooks for 4 hours, but if you wish to save time, you may disjoint the chicken and obtain a perfectly good stock in just 2 hours. Be sure to include the neck, gizzard, and liver for a richer flavor.

1 whole roasting chicken (about 2½ pounds)
1 whole scallion
1 small chunk fresh ginger, sliced into quarter-sized rounds
2 slices Chinese dried orange peel (optional)
Salt

1. Clean chicken, removing excess fat. Rinse well to rid it of any clinging connective tissue or blood clots.
2. Place chicken in stockpot filled with 2 quarts water or water to cover.
3. Trim off scallion root and add scallion, ginger, and orange peel if using, to pot.
4. Bring stock to a boil, then lower heat and cover. Simmer 4 hours, stirring occasionally.
5. If you have time, allow stock to cool before straining. Place a colander or strainer lined with a triple thickness of cheesecloth or strong paper towels over a large pot. Pour in the stock and discard the bones and chicken.
6. Season to taste but sparingly; the stock may be the base of a sauced stir-fry dish that does not need salt.
7. To remove accumulated fat, use a broad spoon tilted at an angle or paper towels to carefully skim the surface until the broth is clear.
8. Let stock cool uncovered; refrigerate when completely cool. Before using, reheat stock and allow to boil 2 minutes.

Fish Stock

Ask your fish dealer to provide you with some trimmings. You may want to request them a day in advance.

2 pounds fish bones, heads, and tails
½ cup sliced carrots
½ cup sliced onions or shallots
½ cup sliced celery
1 bay leaf
5 or 6 sprigs parsley
8 peppercorns
2 cups white wine (optional)
Salt

1. Remove gills from heads, if necessary. Rinse fish under cold running water and cut or break into chunks.
2. Place fish in stockpot with vegetables, seasonings, and wine, if using. Do not add salt at this point. Add 6 cups cold water if using wine, 8 cups if not. Bring to a boil over high heat. Reduce heat and simmer stock, uncovered, 30 minutes, skimming as necessary. Stock should reduce by about half.
3. Strain stock through fine sieve set over large bowl. If not sufficiently reduced, return strained stock to pot and bring to a boil over high heat. Reduce heat and simmer stock, uncovered, until reduction is complete. Add salt to taste.
4. Let stock cool uncovered; refrigerate when completely cool.

ing French, Austrian, and Italian.

Certain dishes, with minor local variations, are standard throughout Mexico. Some familiar examples include tacos, tortillas, and enchiladas. But for the most part Mexican cooking varies considerably from region to region, largely because of topography and climate. In the arid north—cattle and wheat country—dried beef, cheese-based dishes, wheat tortillas, and barbecued foods abound, while in central Mexico, where the Aztecs thrived and developed their corn-based cuisine, tamales and enchiladas are more common and tortilla-based casseroles, freshwater fish and seafood, pork, goat, chicken, and venison take the place of beef. The most distinctive of all Mexican regional foods comes from the Yucatán, the southeastern peninsula noted for its tropical fruits, seafood, and meat and fowl dishes called *pibil* (in which the food is rubbed with a seasoning paste, wrapped in banana leaves, then steamed in a pit). Rick Bayless prepares dishes in the Yucatecan style in his Menu 3, pages 189–191, which features black bean *tostadas* and chicken in *escabeche*, a spicy "pickling" sauce.

In this country, Mexican-American cooking is an amalgam of foods handed down by Spanish and other European settlers, Mexican immigrants, and American Indians. It differs widely from state to state in the Southwest and West.

Tex-Mex cooking, for example, has its roots in northern Mexico–style cooking, and is generally characterized by the use of fresh and dried chilies, tortillas, barbecued meats, cheeses, tacos, and tamales. Texas cooks also take credit for inventing the first bowl of chili—cubes of beef in a spicy sauce. On page 173, Jane Butel offers a recipe for chili with no beans as an example of Tex-Mex cooking. And on pages 192–201, Lucinda Hutson does some interpretive

---

HANDLING CHILIES

The oils of chilies, concentrated in the seeds and ribs, contain a highly irritating substance, capsaicin, which, depending on the hotness of the chili, can cause a rash or even a burn. When handling all chilies—fresh, dried, canned, or powdered—take very great care to protect your skin. Work with whole chilies under cold running water (hot water can release irritating vapors). Wear thin rubber gloves or generously oil your hands. Do not touch your face, especially your eyes, until you have thoroughly washed your hands with soap and warm water. If you do touch your eyes, flush them with cold water immediately.

Tex-Mex cooking.

In New Mexico, the cuisine (sometimes called Santa Fe style) is more Spanish and Indian than Mexican and has strong peasant roots. It is simpler and less fatty than Tex-Mex cooking, featuring puffy breads, wild greens, a preponderance of chilies, and products made from the unique variety of blue corn indigenous to New Mexico. Elizabeth Schneider's recipe for green chili and cheese enchiladas, page 162, is representative of New Mexico cuisine.

Californians, too, have their own eclectic, more refined Mexican cuisine known as Cal-Mex. It is reminiscent of Italian and Oriental cooking, and fresh fruits and vegetables, seafood, mild chili sauces, and coriander predominate. On pages 175–181, Sue Huffman provides some Cal-Mex menus that are light, colorful, and flavorful.

Chilies

Most of the Mexican recipes in this volume recommend using fresh chilies. Although there are at least 100 varieties of chilies grown in Mexico, only a few of these varieties are available—fresh, dried, or canned—in some parts of the United States. For this reason, the cooks or the Editors frequently suggest substitutes for chilies in these recipes. The following fresh chilies are called for:

Anaheim: Also known as California green chilies, these bright green pods are 5 to 7 inches long and are usually very mild. They have firm, thick flesh and are abundant in the West and Southwest. Elsewhere, check Mexican groceries.

Serrano: These very small (about 1½ inches long and ½ inch wide) chilies are available in areas with large Mexican communities, but otherwise can be hard to find. You can substitute jalapeños.

Poblano: Triangular and about 4½ inches long and 2½ inches wide, these chilies are dark green and variably hot. They are not widely available, except in groceries in Mexican communities. Allowing for subtle differences in flavor and hotness, you can use poblano and Anaheim chilies interchangeably.

Jalapeño: These very hot chilies are dark green to greenish black and about 2 inches long. They are available in Mexican markets and many greengrocers.

MARGARITAS

Refreshing fruit-flavored drinks are perfect adjuncts to spicy Mexican food. At cocktail time, offer margaritas ("daisies"), a slightly tart blend of tequila, crushed ice, lime juice, and Triple Sec, an orange-flavored liqueur. Classically, margaritas are served in chilled salt-rimmed cocktail glasses. Several sources claim credit for having created this cocktail, but whatever its origin, the margarita has been popular for many years.

Juice of 1 lime
Table salt
4 ice cubes, crushed
1½ ounces tequila
½ ounce Triple Sec or other orange-flavored liqueur

1. Fill a small bowl ½ inch full with salt.
2. Rub the rim of a chilled cocktail glass with a slice of lime and press the rim into the salt. Set aside.
3. Combine remaining ingredients in a cocktail shaker, cover, and shake vigorously. Strain the mixture into the prepared glass.

Yield: 1 cocktail

When you buy fresh chilies, select those that are firm, plump, and smooth, with shiny and unblemished skin. Whole chilies will keep, refrigerated, for up to two weeks if wrapped in paper towels and then placed in a paper bag. They should never be tightly wrapped in plastic, as moisture causes them to decay. They will keep, frozen, up to a year if they are first boiled or roasted.

Roasting Chilies

A number of the recipes in this book call for roasting fresh chilies, which enhances their flavor and helps to remove the tough outer skins. (Jalapeños and serranos need to be roasted only if you are going to freeze them.)

Before roasting, pierce the chilies a couple of times with a toothpick or sharp knife. Spear the chilies with a fork or skewer and hold them directly over the flame of a gas stove, or place them on a rack over an electric burner or on a foil-lined baking sheet approximately 4 inches from the heat source in a gas or electric broiler. Turn the chilies often to char the skins evenly. They should be thoroughly blistered and somewhat blackened, but not burned through. Place the chilies in a paper bag and allow them to steam for 10 to 20 minutes to loosen the skins. If you plan to use the chilies immediately, remove them from the bag and peel off the skins with a sharp paring knife or rub under cold water (the skins should slip off easily). After peeling the chilies, remove the stems, unless you are making a dish that requires the chilies to hold their shape. Seed and derib carefully, remembering that most of the hotness is in the seeds.

Roasted chilies freeze well. Do not peel them before freezing, as they will hold their shape better when thawed. Freeze a number of chilies in a plastic bag. As the chilies thaw you can peel off the skins.

Chili Powders

Some recipes in this volume call for "pure" chili powder, which contains chilies only, as distinct from powders that are a blend of chilies, cumin, oregano, onion, garlic, or salt. Other recipes simply call for "chili powder," indicating the blended type. Several recipes call for "California" (mild) or "New Mexico" (hot) chili powder, which can be found in Mexican groceries or specialty stores. Buy powder that is bright orange-red to dark red. A yellowish color indicates age or inferior quality.

GENERAL COOKING TECHNIQUES

Mastering the following cooking techniques will help you prepare many of the main courses and side dishes in this volume.

Sautéing

Sautéing is a form of quick frying with no cover on the pan. In French, *sauter* means "to jump," which is what vegetables or small pieces of food do when you shake the sauté pan. The purpose of sautéing is to brown the food lightly and seal in the juices—sometimes before further cooking. The technique has three critical elements: the pan, the fat, and maintaining the proper temperature.

The pan: A proper sauté pan is 10 to 12 inches in diameter and has 2- to 3-inch straight sides to allow you to turn the food and keep the fat from spattering. It has a heavy bottom that can be moved back and forth easily across a burner.

The best material is tin-lined copper because it is a superior heat conductor. Heavy-gauge cast aluminum works well but will discolor acidic food like tomatoes. Another option is a heavy-duty sauté pan made of strong, heat-conducting aluminum alloys. Be sure the pan has a handle that is long and comfortable to hold, and a tight-fitting cover, since many recipes call for covered cooking following the initial sautéing.

Use a sauté pan large enough to hold the food without crowding, or sauté in two batches. Use a wooden spoon or tongs to keep the food moving in the pan as you shake the pan over the burner. If the food sticks, as it occasionally will, a metal spatula will loosen it best. Turn the food so that all surfaces come into contact with the hot fat. Do not use a fork when sautéing meat; piercing the meat will allow the juices to escape, causing the meat to become tough and dry.

The fat: Half butter and half vegetable oil is perfect for most sautéing. It heats to high temperatures without burning, yet imparts a rich buttery flavor. For cooking, unsalted butter tastes best and adds no unwanted salt to the recipe. Some recipes in this book call for olive oil, which imparts a delicious and distinctive flavor of its own (see box on olive oil, page 9). Nevertheless, even the finest olive oil has some residue of fruit pulp, which will occasionally scorch. Watch carefully when you sauté in olive oil; discard any scorched oil and start with fresh, if necessary.

To sauté properly, heat the fat until it is hot but not smoking. When you see small bubbles on top of the fat, lower the heat because the fat is on the verge of smoking. When using butter and oil together, add butter to the hot oil. After the foam from the melting butter subsides, you are ready to sauté. If the temperature of the fat is just right for sautéing, the food will sizzle when you put it in the pan.

Stir Frying

A basic technique of Chinese cooking is stir frying: quickly cooking bite-size chopped foods in small amounts of oil over high heat. The purpose of stir frying is to cook food until just done—never to overcook it—and to infuse it with seasonings, which are first added to the hot oil. To keep the food from scorching, you must keep it in motion both by shaking the pan slightly and by stirring with a pair of 16-inch chopsticks or a wooden spatula or long-handled spoon. Because the oil must be very hot but not smoking, part of the technique is to adjust the heat up and down from time to time so that the temperature of the oil remains constant. A Chinese wok or a heavy skillet will both work well for this purpose (see page 11).

Corn, peanut, and safflower oils have just the right clean aroma and taste for stir frying foods. Butter and olive oil are unacceptable because they burn at high temperatures, and like shortening, are not traditional Chinese ingredients. To help create a smooth, nonstick cooking surface, first heat the wok or skillet before adding the oil. When a drop of water sizzles on contact, add the oil. Then wait 30 to 90 seconds, depending on your stove, and put a sliver of food in the pan. If it foams at once, you are ready to stir fry.

Deep Frying

Use the same oil for deep frying as you would for stir frying. Proper deep frying will yield food that is crisp on the outside and cooked through within. The temperature of the oil is critical, so a deep-fat thermometer is a must—at least until you have enough experience to gauge the temperature of the oil by appearance. At 275 degrees, the oil has small swirls and subsurface eddies, but is not bubbling, and food dropped in will sink to the bottom and begin cooking at once. At 375 degrees, the oil gives off a slight haze, and food added at this time will rise to the top, surrounded by bubbles. At 400 degrees—the temperature for a very quick fry—the oil is just below the smoking point and gives off a thicker haze. A piece of food will rise quickly to the surface, covered by white foam, and will brown immediately. Do not linger, or the oil may burn. Begin cooking at once.

Searing

Heat the oil until it is very hot, then brown the meat over high heat for a minute or two on each side. A metal spatula is essential, for the meat will tend to stick. Wait until the meat is very brown on one side before you turn it to the other side.

Pan Frying

The food cooks, uncovered, in a small amount of fat, which has been preheated in a heavy skillet. Pan frying is a quick cooking method suitable for thin-cut chops, steaks, and other foods.

Braising

Braising is simmering meats or vegetables in a relatively small amount of liquid, usually for a long period of time. Sometimes the food is browned or parboiled before braising. You may flavor the braising liquid with herbs, spices, and aromatic vegetables, or use wine, stock, or tomato sauce.

Deglazing

Deglazing is an easy way to create a sauce for sautéed, braised, or roasted food. To deglaze a pan, pour off all but one or two tablespoons of the fat in which the food has been cooked. Add liquid—water, wine, or stock—and reduce the sauce over medium heat, using a wooden spoon to scrape up the concentrated juices and brown bits of food clinging to the bottom of the pan.

Glazing

Glazing vegetables in their cooking liquid, butter, and a little sugar gives them a slight sheen as the butter and sugar reduce to a syrupy consistency. Glazing enhances the vegetables' flavor and appearance, and they need no additional sauce.

Steaming

Steaming is a nutritious way to cook vegetables and other food. Bring water to a boil in a saucepan. Place the food in a steamer or on a rack over the liquid and cover the pan, periodically checking the water level. Keeping the food above the liquid preserves vitamins and minerals often lost in other methods of cooking.

Blanching

Also called parboiling, blanching is an invaluable technique. Immerse whole or cut vegetables for a few moments in boiling water, then "refresh" them—that is, plunge them into cold water to stop their cooking and set their colors. Blanching softens or tenderizes dense or crisp vegetables, often as a preliminary to further cooking by another method, such as stir frying.

Poaching

You poach meat, fish, chicken, fruit, and eggs in very hot liquid in a pan on top of the stove. You can use water or, better still, beef, chicken, or fish stock, a combination of stock and white wine, or even cream as the poaching liquid. Bring the liquid to the simmering point and add the food. Be prepared to lower the heat if the liquid begins to boil.

Flambéing

Flambéing requires igniting an already warm, but not close to boiling, liqueur in the pan with already cooked hot food. Be sure to remove the pan from the heat first; then avert your face and ignite the liqueur with a lighted match. A quiet flame will burn for a few seconds. Allow about an ounce of liqueur per person; the taste remains, but the alcohol burns off.

Roasting and Baking

Roasting is a dry-heat process (usually used for large cuts of meat and poultry) that cooks food by exposing it to heated air in an oven or, perhaps, a covered barbecue. For more even circulation of heat, the food should be placed in a shallow pan or on a rack in a pan. For greater moisture retention, baste the food with its own juices, fat, or a flavorful marinade.

Baking applies to the dry-heat cooking of foods such as casseroles; small cuts of meat, fish, and poultry; vegetables; and, of course, breads and pastries. Some foods are baked tightly covered to retain their juices and flavors; others, such as breads, cakes, and cookies, are baked in open pans to release moisture.

Broiling and Grilling

These are two relatively fast ways to cook meat, poultry, and fish, giving food a crisp exterior while leaving the inside juicy. Whether broiling or grilling, brush the food with melted fat, a sauce, or marinade before you cook it. This adds flavor and moisture.

In broiling, the food cooks directly under the heat source. In grilling, the food cooks either directly over an open fire or on a well-seasoned griddle placed directly over a burner.

Equipment

Proper cooking equipment makes the work light and is a good cook's most prized possession. You can cook expertly without a store-bought steamer or even a food processor, but basic pans, knives, and a few other items are indispensable. Below are the things you need—and some attractive options—for preparing the menus in this volume.

Pots and pans
Stockpot with cover
3 skillets (large, medium, small) with covers; one with oven-proof handle
Large sauté pan with cover
3 saucepans with covers (1-, 2-, and 4-quart capacities)
  Choose heavy-gauge enameled cast-iron, plain cast-iron, aluminum-clad stainless steel, or aluminum (but you need at least one saucepan that is not aluminum). Best—but very expensive—is tin-lined copper.
Wok with cover
Broiler pan with rack
2-quart baking dish
13 x 9-inch baking dish
8 x 8-inch baking dish
2 baking sheets, 17 x 11-inch and 15 x 10-inch
9-inch pie pan
Jelly-roll pan
1½-quart flameproof casserole with cover
Large heatproof platter
Four 8- to 12-ounce ovenproof ramekins or small custard cups
Salad bowl

Knives
A carbon-steel knife takes a sharp edge but tends to rust. You must wash and dry it after each use; otherwise it can blacken foods and counter tops. Good-quality stainless-steel knives, frequently honed, are less trouble and will serve just as well in the home kitchen. Never put a fine knife in the dishwasher. Rinse it, dry it, and put it away—but not loose in a drawer. Knives will stay sharp if they have their own storage rack.
Small paring knife
10-inch chef's knife
Chinese cleaver
Bread knife (serrated edge)
Sharpening steel

Other cooking tools
2 sets of mixing bowls in graduated sizes, one set preferably glass or stainless steel
Colander with a round base (stainless steel, aluminum, or enamel)
2 sets of measuring cups and spoons in graduated sizes
  One for dry ingredients, another for shortenings and liquids.
2 strainers, coarse and fine mesh
Cooking spoon
Slotted spoon
Long-handled wooden spoons
Ladle
2 metal spatulas or turners (for lifting hot foods from pans)
Slotted spatula
Chinese metal wok spatula
16-inch chopsticks
Rubber or vinyl spatula (for folding in ingredients)
Rolling pin
Grater (metal, with several sizes of holes)
  A rotary grater is handy for hard cheese.
Long metal or bamboo skewers
Large and small wire whisks
Pair of metal tongs
Wooden board
Garlic press
Vegetable peeler
Vegetable brush
Stiff scrubbing brush
Collapsible vegetable steamer
Mortar and pestle
Pastry brush for basting (a small, new paintbrush that is not nylon serves well)
Potato masher
Melon baller
Kitchen shears
Kitchen timer
Cheesecloth
Aluminum foil

Paper towels
Plastic wrap
Waxed paper
Kitchen string
Small paper bag
Oven mitts or potholders
Thin rubber gloves

Electric appliances
Food processor or blender
  A blender will do most of the work required in this volume, but a food processor will do it more quickly and in larger volume. A food processor should be considered a necessity, not a luxury, for anyone who enjoys cooking.
Electric mixer

Optional cooking tools
Salad spinner
Small jar with tight-fitting lid
Spice grinder
Salad servers
Citrus juicer
  Inexpensive glass kind from the dime store will do.
Deep-fat thermometer
Nutmeg grater
Pastry blender
Roll of masking tape or white paper tape for labeling and dating

Pantry

A well-stocked, properly organized pantry is essential for preparing great meals in the shortest time possible. Whether your pantry consists of a small refrigerator and two or three shelves over the sink, or a large freezer, refrigerator, and entire room just off the kitchen, you must protect staples from heat and light.

In maintaining your pantry, follow these rules:

1. Store staples by kind and date. Canned goods, canisters, and spices need a separate shelf, or a separate spot on a shelf. Date all staples—shelved, refrigerated, or frozen—by writing the date directly on the package or on a bit of masking tape. Then put the oldest ones in front to be sure you use them first.

2. Store flour, sugar, and other dry ingredients in canisters or jars with tight lids. Glass and clear plastic allow you to see at a glance how much remains.

3. Keep a running grocery list so that you can note when a staple is half gone, and be sure to stock up.

ON THE SHELF:

Anchovies
Anchovy fillets, both flat and rolled, come oil-packed, in tins. If you buy whole, salt-packed anchovies, they must be cleaned under running water, skinned, and boned. To bone, separate the fish with your fingers and slip out the backbone.

Baking powder

Capers
Capers are usually packed in vinegar and less frequently in salt. If you use the latter, you should rinse them under cold water before using them.

Chili paste

Chilies, canned
mild green chilies

Cornstarch
Less likely to lump than flour, cornstarch is an excellent thickener for sauces. Substitute in the following proportions: 1 tablespoon cornstarch to 2 of flour.

Dried fruit
golden raisins

Flour
all-purpose, bleached or
    unbleached
cornmeal

Garlic
Store in a cool, dry, well-ventilated place. Garlic powder and garlic salt are not adequate substitutes for fresh garlic.

Herbs and spices
The flavor of fresh herbs is much better than that of dried. Fresh herbs should be refrigerated and used as soon as possible. The following herbs are perfectly acceptable dried, but buy in small amounts, store airtight in dry area away from heat and light, and use as quickly as possible. In measuring herbs, remember that one part dried will equal three parts fresh. Crushing dried herbs brings out their flavor: Use a mortar and pestle or sandwich the herbs between 2 sheets of waxed paper and crush with a rolling pin. *Note:* Dried chives and parsley should not be on your shelf, since they have little or no flavor; frozen chives are acceptable. Buy whole spices rather than ground, as they keep their flavor much longer. Grind spices at home and store as directed for herbs.

basil
bay leaves
caraway seeds
Cayenne pepper
chili powder
cinnamon
coriander, whole and
    ground
cumin, whole and ground
curry powder
dill
fennel seeds
ginger
marjoram
mustard (powdered)
nutmeg, whole and ground
oregano
paprika, sweet Hungarian
pepper
    black peppercorns
    These are unripe peppercorns dried in their husks. Grind with a pepper mill for each use.
    white peppercorns
    These are the same as the black variety, but are picked ripe and husked. Use them in pale sauces when black pepper specks would spoil the appearance.
red pepper flakes (also
    called crushed red
    pepper)
rosemary
saffron
    Made from the dried stigmas of a species of crocus, this spice—the most costly of all seasonings—adds both color and flavor. Use sparingly.
salt
    Use coarse salt—commonly available as kosher or sea—for its superior flavor, texture, and purity. Kosher salt and sea salt are less salty than table salt. Substitute in the following proportions: three-quarters teaspoon table salt equals just under one teaspoon kosher or sea salt.
tarragon
thyme

Honey

Hot pepper sauce

Mushrooms, Chinese
    dried black

Nuts and seeds
almonds
pine nuts (pignoli)
sesame seeds
walnuts

Oils
corn, safflower, peanut,
    or vegetable
    Because these neutral-tasting oils have high smoking points, they are good for high-heat sautéing.
olive oil
    Olive oil ranges in color from pale yellow to dark green and in taste from mild and delicate to rich and fruity. Different olive oils can be used for different purposes: For example, use stronger ones for cooking, lighter ones for salads. The finest quality olive oil is labeled extra-virgin or virgin.
Oriental sesame oil
    Flavorful dark amber-colored oil; for seasoning.
walnut oil
    Rich and nutty tasting. It turns rancid easily, so keep it in a tightly closed container in the refrigerator.

Olives
    California pitted black
    olives

Onions
Store all dry-skinned onions in a cool, dry, well-ventilated place.
red or Italian onions
    Zesty tasting and generally eaten raw. The perfect salad onion.
shallots
    The most subtle member of the onion family, the shallot has a delicate garlic flavor.

yellow onions
All-purpose cooking onions, strong in taste.

Pimientos

Potatoes, boiling and baking
"New" potatoes are not a particular kind of potato, but any potato that has not been stored.

Rice

long-grain white rice
Slender grains that become light and fluffy when cooked and are best for general use.

Soy sauce, Chinese and Japanese

Stock, chicken
For optimal flavor and quality, your own stock is best (see recipe page 13), but canned stock, or broth, is convenient to have on hand.

Sugar

granulated sugar
brown sugar

Tomatoes

Italian plum tomatoes
Canned plum tomatoes (preferably imported) are an acceptable substitute for fresh.

Tomato paste

Vinegars

apple cider vinegar
balsamic vinegar
distilled white vinegar
red and white wine vinegars
rice vinegar

Wines and spirits

Chinese rice wine
sherry, dry
white wine, dry

Worcestershire sauce

Yeast

IN THE REFRIGERATOR:

Basil
Though fresh basil is widely available only in summer, try to use it whenever possible to replace dried; the flavor is markedly superior. Stand the stems, preferably with roots intact, in a jar of water, and loosely cover leaves with a plastic bag.

Bread crumbs
You need never buy bread crumbs. To make fresh crumbs, use fresh or day-old bread and process in food processor or blender. For dried, toast bread 30 minutes in preheated 250-degree oven, turning occasionally to prevent slices from browning. Proceed as for fresh. Store bread crumbs in an airtight container: fresh crumbs in the refrigerator and dried crumbs in a cool, dry place. Either type may also be frozen for several weeks in a tightly sealed plastic bag.

Butter
Many cooks prefer unsalted butter because of its finer flavor and because it does not burn as easily as salted.

Cheese

Cheddar, sharp
A firm cheese, ranging in color from nearly white to yellow. Cheddar is a versatile cooking cheese.

Monterey Jack
From California—a mild cheese made from skim, partly skim, or whole milk.

Mozzarella
A mild cheese, most commonly made from cow's milk. Fresh mozzarella is far superior to packaged and can generally be found in Italian grocery stores.

Parmesan
Avoid the pre-grated packaged variety; it is very expensive and almost flavorless. Buy Parmesan by the piece and grate as needed: 4 ounces produces about one cup of grated cheese.

Ricotta
A soft fresh cheese resembling cottage cheese. Available as a whole- or skimmed-milk product.

Romano
This sharp Italian grating cheese may be made from sheep's milk (pecorino Romano) or cow's milk.

Chilies, fresh

Chives
Refrigerate fresh chives wrapped in plastic. You may also buy small pots of growing chives—keep them on a windowsill and snip as needed.

Coriander
Also called *cilantro* or Chinese parsley, its pungent leaves resemble flat-leaf parsley. Keep in a glass of water covered with a plastic bag.

Cream

half and half
heavy cream
sour cream

Eggs
Will keep 4 to 5 weeks in refrigerator. For best results, bring to room temperature before using, except when separating.

Ginger, fresh
Found in the produce section. Wrap in a paper towel, then in plastic, and refrigerate; it will keep for about 1 month, but should be checked weekly for mold. Or, if you prefer, store it in the freezer, where it will last about 3 months. Firm, smooth-skinned ginger need not be peeled.

Lemons
In addition to its many uses in cooking, a slice of lemon rubbed over cut apples and pears will keep them from discoloring. Do not substitute bottled juice or lemon extract.

Limes

Milk

Mint
Fresh mint will keep for a week if wrapped in a damp paper towel and enclosed in a plastic bag.

Mustard
The recipes in this book usually call for Dijon or coarse-grained mustard.

Parsley
The two most commonly available kinds of parsley are flat-leaf and curly; they can be used interchangeably when necessary. Flat-leaf parsley has a more distinctive flavor and is generally preferred in cooking. Curly parsley wilts less easily and is excellent for garnishing. Store parsley in a glass of water and cover loosely with a plastic bag. It will keep for a week in the refrigerator. Or wash and dry it, and refrigerate in a small plastic bag with a dry paper towel inside to absorb any moisture.

Scallions
Also called green onions. Mild flavor. Use the white bulbs as well as the fresh green tops. Wrap in plastic and store in the refrigerator, or chop coarsely, wrap in plastic, and freeze.

Yogurt

ITALIAN MENUS

Susan DeRege

S usan DeRege teaches Italian cooking in New York City in the winter and travels to Italy in the summer to collect regional recipes. No visit is complete without stops along the Italian Riviera in such towns as Portofino, Santa Margherita, Recco, and Camogli. The three menus she offers here are inspired by the many meals she has enjoyed beside the Gulf of Genoa.

Menu 1 features a number of Genoese staples: fresh fish, eggplant, zucchini, bell peppers, and herbs such as rosemary, basil, and parsley. The herbed vegetable dish can be served with the fish main course or presented as a tempting appetizer. Susan DeRege likes to toss the potatoes in a fine virgin olive oil, preferably one produced in Liguria, the region that encompasses the Riviera.

A meal fit for company, Menu 2 features a rich and creamy pasta dish favored in Recco. Walnuts, pine nuts, heavy cream, butter, Parmesan cheese, garlic, and basil are the principal ingredients in the sauce. With the pasta the cook serves tuna steaks, which are marinated and then grilled.

Menu 3 offers an interesting lasagna, in which the flat noodles are layered with two sauces—pesto and béchamel. The accompanying light seafood salad of shrimp and squid (known in Italy as *insalata di frutti di mare*) is served chilled with a mustardy vinaigrette.

Casual pottery underscores the simplicity of this Mediterranean meal: wine-braised red snapper with plum tomatoes, herbed vegetables, and new red potatoes tossed with basil and olive oil.

Braised Red Snapper
Herbed Mixed Vegetables
New Potatoes with Basil

Braised whole red snapper, redolent of rosemary, is the focal point of this meal. If you cannot find snapper, sea bass, red mullet, ocean perch, or grouper would also be good.

For the best flavor contrast in the herbed vegetable recipe, be sure to follow the suggested order of layering the vegetables. You can assemble this dish early in the day, cover and refrigerate it, then bake it at dinner time.

WHAT TO DRINK

This menu demands a crisp white wine, preferably one with lots of fruit and acid. A Pinot Grigio or an Italian Sauvignon Blanc is an excellent choice.

SHOPPING LIST AND STAPLES

2- to 2½-pound whole fresh red snapper, cleaned and
   gutted
12 small new red potatoes (about 1¾ pounds total weight)
2 medium-size onions (about 1 pound total weight)
2 small Italian eggplants (about ½ pound total weight)
4 fresh plum tomatoes (about ¾ pound total weight), or
   16-ounce can plum tomatoes
Medium-size zucchini (about ½ pound)
Medium-size red bell pepper
Medium-size yellow bell pepper
2 small cloves garlic
Small bunch arugula (optional)
Small bunch fresh parsley
Small bunch fresh rosemary, or 1 teaspoon dried
Small bunch fresh basil, or 1 tablespoon dried
1 lemon (optional)
2 ounces Parmesan cheese
¾ cup good-quality olive oil, preferably virgin
2-ounce jar capers
¼ cup all-purpose flour
1 teaspoon dried oregano
4 bay leaves
Salt
Freshly ground black pepper
½ cup dry white wine

UTENSILS

Food processor or grater
Large heavy-gauge skillet
Small skillet
Shallow 15 x 10-inch glass or ceramic baking dish
11 x 7-inch baking dish
Medium-size saucepan with cover
Small strainer
Measuring cups and spoons
Chef's knife
Paring knife
Wooden spoon
2 wide metal spatulas
Vegetable brush
Vegetable peeler

START-TO-FINISH STEPS

1. Wash parsley, and fresh basil and rosemary if using, and dry with paper towels. Trim stems and discard. Chop enough parsley to measure 1 tablespoon for red snapper recipe and, if *not* using fresh basil, chop enough parsley to measure 2 tablespoons for potatoes recipe. If using fresh basil, set aside 2 sprigs for garnish, if desired, and chop enough leaves to measure ¼ cup for potatoes recipe. If using fresh rosemary, set aside 6 sprigs for red snapper recipe. Reserve remaining fresh herbs for another use. Crush dried oregano for vegetables recipe, and dried rosemary, if using, for red snapper recipe. Peel and mince enough garlic to measure 1 teaspoon each for red snapper and vegetables recipes.
2. Follow vegetables recipe steps 1 through 8.
3. Follow red snapper recipe steps 1 through 9.
4. While fish is baking, follow vegetables recipe steps 9 through 11.
5. While fish and vegetables are baking, follow potatoes recipe steps 1 through 3 and red snapper recipe steps 10 and 11.
6. Follow potatoes recipe step 4, red snapper recipe step 12, vegetables recipe step 12, and serve.

RECIPES

Braised Red Snapper

2- to 2½-pound whole fresh red snapper, cleaned and
   gutted
¼ cup good-quality olive oil, preferably virgin
¼ cup all-purpose flour
1 bay leaf

1 tablespoon capers
4 fresh plum tomatoes (about ¾ pound total weight), or
    16-ounce can plum tomatoes
½ cup dry white wine
1 teaspoon minced garlic
6 sprigs fresh rosemary, or 1 teaspoon dried, crushed
1 tablespoon chopped fresh parsley
Salt and freshly ground black pepper
3 sprigs arugula for garnish (optional)
1 lemon for garnish (optional)

1. Rinse cavity and outside of fish under cold running water, and pat fish dry with paper towels; set aside.
2. Heat oil over medium-high heat in heavy-gauge skillet large enough to accommodate the fish.
3. While oil is heating, place flour on large sheet of waxed paper and lightly dredge fish in flour.
4. When oil is hot but not smoking, carefully place fish in pan and cook about 1½ to 2 minutes on one side, or until lightly browned.
5. Using 2 wide metal spatulas, turn fish and cook another 1½ to 2 minutes.
6. Transfer fish to shallow 15 x 10-inch glass or ceramic baking dish and place bay leaf in cavity of fish.
7. Turn capers into small strainer and rinse under cold running water; set aside to drain.
8. If using fresh tomatoes, wash and dry with paper towels. If using canned, drain well, reserving juice for another use. Quarter tomatoes or, if large, cut into sixths and arrange around fish.
9. Pour wine over fish; sprinkle with capers, garlic, rosemary, parsley, ½ teaspoon salt, and pepper to taste. Cover baking dish with foil and bake in preheated 450-degree oven 25 to 35 minutes, or until fish is firm and flakes easily when tested with a toothpick.
10. If using arugula, wash, dry, and set aside.
11. If using lemon, wash and dry. Halve lengthwise and then cut one half into thin wedges; set aside. Reserve remaining half for another use.
12. Using 2 wide metal spatulas, transfer fish to serving platter. Arrange tomato wedges around fish and pour pan liquid around fish and over tomatoes. Serve garnished with arugula and lemon wedges, if desired.

Herbed Mixed Vegetables

2 small Italian eggplants (about ½ pound total weight)
Salt
1 each medium-size red and yellow bell pepper
Medium-size zucchini (about ½ pound)
2 medium-size onions (about 1 pound total weight)
2 ounces Parmesan cheese
¼ cup plus 1 tablespoon good-quality olive oil, preferably
    virgin
1 teaspoon minced garlic
1 teaspoon dried oregano, crushed
Freshly ground black pepper
1 tablespoon chopped fresh parsley
3 bay leaves

1. Preheat oven to 450 degrees.
2. Wash and dry eggplants. Remove stem ends from eggplants and discard. Cut enough eggplant crosswise into ¼-inch-thick rounds to measure 3 cups.
3. Arrange a single layer of eggplant slices on platter and sprinkle generously with salt. Cover with double thickness of paper towels and repeat with remaining eggplant. Top with another platter and place bag of flour or other weight on platter; set eggplant aside 10 minutes to allow salt to extract bitter juices.
4. Meanwhile, wash peppers and dry with paper towels. Slice off tops; core, seed, and remove membranes. Cut peppers crosswise into ¼-inch-thick rings; stack rings and cut into quarters. Measure 1 cup mixed peppers; set aside.
5. Scrub zucchini under cold running water and dry with paper towel. Trim ends and discard; do *not* peel. Cut enough zucchini crosswise into ¼-inch-thick slices to measure 1 cup; set aside.
6. Peel onions and cut enough crosswise into ¼-inch-thick slices to measure 2 cups; set aside.
7. Using food processor fitted with steel blade, or grater, grate enough Parmesan to measure 3 tablespoons.
8. Grease 11 x 7-inch baking dish with 1 tablespoon olive oil; set aside.
9. Rinse eggplant slices and pat dry with paper towels. Scatter eggplant over bottom of prepared baking dish. Top with onion slices, then cover with zucchini slices. Sprinkle with red and yellow peppers; set aside.
10. Heat remaining ¼ cup oil in small skillet over medium heat. Add garlic and sauté about 2 minutes, or until slightly golden.
11. Sprinkle vegetables with grated Parmesan, oregano, ¼ teaspoon salt, pepper to taste, parsley, and bay leaves. Drizzle with oil and garlic from skillet and bake, uncovered, 25 to 30 minutes, or until vegetables are tender.
12. Remove dish from oven, discard bay leaves, and serve.

New Potatoes with Basil

12 small new red potatoes (about 1¾ pounds total weight)
1 teaspoon salt
3 tablespoons good-quality olive oil, preferably virgin
¼ cup chopped fresh basil, or 1 tablespoon dried plus 2
    tablespoons chopped fresh parsley
2 sprigs fresh basil for garnish (optional)

1. Scrub potatoes under cold running water. Using vegetable peeler or paring knife, remove strip of peel from circumference of each potato to prevent splitting while cooking.
2. Combine potatoes, salt, and enough cold water to cover in medium-size saucepan, cover pan, and bring water to a boil over high heat.
3. When water boils, remove cover, reduce heat to medium-high, and cook potatoes 20 minutes, or until they can be easily pierced with tip of knife.
4. Drain water from pan. Add oil and chopped fresh basil, or dried basil and parsley, and toss. Transfer potatoes to serving dish and garnish with basil sprigs, if desired.

Grilled Tuna Steaks
Pasta with Walnut Sauce
Tomatoes with Basil Vinaigrette

For the pasta dish, use imported packaged *fusilli* or *tagliatelle*. Or, if you have the time, the cook recommends making fresh *trenette*. This eggless pasta, in the form of ½-inch-wide ribbons, is cut on one side with a knife and on the other with a crimped pasta cutter.

When preparing the tuna steaks, use a ridged cast-iron griddle or skillet, or a stove-top grill. If using a stove-top grill, do not pour the marinade over the fish while it is on the grill; rather, keep the marinade warm, then pour it over the fish at serving time.

Grilled tuna steaks with capers and pasta with walnut sauce are two classic Ligurian dishes. Serve the salad of sliced tomatoes and fresh basil vinaigrette with the meal or offer it as an appetizer.

WHAT TO DRINK

The cook suggests a fine Frascati to accompany this menu, but a top quality Orvieto or Soave would serve as well.

SHOPPING LIST AND STAPLES

Four ½- to ¾-inch-thick fresh tuna steaks (1 to 1¼ pounds total weight)
3 medium-size ripe tomatoes (about 1 pound total weight)
Small head escarole
2 small cloves garlic
Medium-size shallot
Small bunch fresh basil, or 2½ teaspoons dried plus small bunch fresh parsley

Small bunch fresh rosemary, or ½ teaspoon dried
2 lemons, plus 1 lemon (optional)
3 tablespoons milk
1 pint heavy cream
4 tablespoons salted butter
¼ pound Parmesan cheese, preferably imported
⅔ cup good-quality olive oil, approximately, preferably virgin
2 teaspoons corn oil
2 tablespoons red wine vinegar
2-ounce jar capers
¾ pound dried fusilli or tagliatelle, or fresh trenette
1 slice firm home-style white bread
4-ounce can walnut pieces
2-ounce jar pine nuts
Freshly grated nutmeg
Salt and freshly ground black pepper

UTENSILS

Food processor or blender
Nonaluminum stockpot
Large cast-iron skillet or griddle with ridges
13 x 9 x 2-inch glass or ceramic baking dish
Small heavy-gauge nonaluminum saucepan
Small bowl
Colander
Small strainer
Measuring cups and spoons
Chef's knife
Paring knife
2 wooden spoons
Metal spatula
Rubber spatula
Basting brush
Small jar with tight-fitting lid
Grater, if not using food processor

START-TO-FINISH STEPS

1. Wash and dry fresh basil or parsley, and fresh rosemary if using. Trim stem ends and discard. Chop enough rosemary to measure 1 teaspoon for tuna recipe. Chop enough basil to measure 2 tablespoons each for pasta and tomatoes recipes, or, if using dried basil, chop enough parsley to measure 1 tablespoon for pasta recipe. Reserve remaining herbs for another use. If *not* using fresh basil or rosemary, crush enough dried basil to measure ½ teaspoon for pasta recipe and 2 teaspoons for tomatoes recipe, and enough dried rosemary to measure ½ teaspoon for tuna recipe. Squeeze enough lemon juice to measure 2 tablespoons each for tuna and tomatoes recipes. Peel and mince

garlic for tuna and pasta recipes. Peel and mince shallot for tomatoes recipe.

2. Follow pasta recipe step 1 and tuna recipe steps 1 through 3.

3. Follow tomatoes recipe steps 1 through 3.

4. Follow pasta recipe steps 2 through 6.

5. Follow tuna recipe steps 4 through 7.

6. Follow pasta recipe steps 7 and 8.

7. While pasta is cooking, follow tuna recipe step 8.

8. Follow pasta recipe steps 9 and 10, tuna recipe step 9, tomatoes recipe step 4, and serve.

RECIPES

Grilled Tuna Steaks

1 tablespoon capers
Four ½- to ¾-inch-thick fresh tuna steaks (1 to 1¼ pounds total weight)
¼ cup good-quality olive oil, preferably virgin
2 tablespoons freshly squeezed lemon juice
1 teaspoon minced garlic
1 teaspoon chopped fresh rosemary, or ½ teaspoon dried, crushed
Salt and freshly ground black pepper
2 teaspoons corn oil
1 lemon for garnish (optional)

1. Rinse capers in small strainer under cold water; drain.

2. Rinse tuna steaks and dry with paper towels.

3. Combine capers, olive oil, lemon juice, garlic, rosemary, ½ teaspoon salt, and pepper to taste in 13 x 9 x 2-inch glass or ceramic baking dish. Arrange tuna steaks in a single layer in dish and set aside to marinate 30 minutes, turning steaks every 10 minutes.

4. Brush cast-iron skillet or griddle with oil and place over medium-high heat. Preheat oven to 200 degrees.

5. Place 4 dinner plates in oven to warm.

6. When oil begins to smoke, place tuna steaks on skillet or griddle, reserving marinade, and cook 4 minutes, or until fish pales at edges and bottoms of steaks are seared.

7. Meanwhile, wash and dry lemon, if using for garnish. Halve lengthwise, then cut one half into 4 wedges; set aside. Reserve remaining half for another use.

8. With metal spatula, carefully turn tuna steaks. Pour marinade over steaks and cook another 4 minutes.

9. Transfer tuna steaks to dinner plates and top each steak with pan drippings. Garnish each plate with a lemon wedge, if desired.

Pasta with Walnut Sauce

1 slice firm home-style white bread
3 tablespoons milk
1 cup walnut pieces
1 tablespoon pine nuts
1 tablespoon good-quality olive oil, preferably virgin
4 tablespoons salted butter
½ teaspoon minced garlic

Salt
1¼ cups heavy cream
Pinch of freshly grated nutmeg
Freshly ground black pepper
¼ pound Parmesan cheese, preferably imported
¾ pound dried fusilli or tagliatelle, or fresh trenette
2 tablespoons chopped fresh basil, or ½ teaspoon dried, crushed basil plus 1 tablespoon chopped fresh parsley

1. Trim crusts from bread and discard. Place bread in small bowl, add milk, and set aside for a few minutes.

2. Bring 5 quarts of water to a boil in nonaluminum stockpot over high heat.

3. Meanwhile, combine walnuts and pine nuts in food processor fitted with steel blade or in blender and process until finely chopped.

4. Squeeze milk out of bread and tear bread into bits. Add bread, oil, butter, garlic, and ½ teaspoon salt to chopped nuts, and process until pastelike.

5. Transfer mixture to small heavy-gauge nonaluminum saucepan. Stir in heavy cream, nutmeg, and pepper to taste, and cook over medium heat, stirring occasionally, 15 minutes. Rinse and dry food processor container.

6. Grate enough Parmesan to measure ¾ cup; set aside. Reserve remaining Parmesan for another use.

7. Add ½ cup Parmesan to saucepan and stir briefly; reduce heat to low and keep sauce warm.

8. Add 1 tablespoon salt and pasta to boiling water, and stir to separate pasta. Cook fusilli 7 minutes, tagliatelle 6 minutes, or fresh trenette 45 seconds, or until *al dente*.

9. Turn pasta into colander and drain.

10. Return pasta to stockpot, add fresh basil, or dried basil and parsley, and toss to combine. Add sauce and toss until pasta is evenly coated. Divide pasta among 4 dinner plates and serve with remaining cheese on the side.

Tomatoes with Basil Vinaigrette

Small head escarole
3 medium-size ripe tomatoes (about 1 pound total weight)
2 tablespoons red wine vinegar
2 tablespoons freshly squeezed lemon juice
1 teaspoon minced shallot
2 tablespoons chopped fresh basil, or 2 teaspoons dried, crushed
Salt and freshly ground black pepper
⅓ cup good-quality olive oil, preferably virgin

1. Wash and dry escarole. Stack several leaves, roll up lengthwise, and cut crosswise to measure 2 cups shreds. Divide shreds among 4 salad plates.

2. Wash and dry tomatoes. Core tomatoes and cut crosswise into ¼-inch-thick slices. Divide slices among escarole-lined plates, cover with plastic wrap, and refrigerate.

3. Combine vinegar, lemon juice, shallot, basil, ¼ teaspoon salt, and pepper to taste in small jar with tight-fitting lid, and shake well. Add oil and shake until well blended.

4. Just before serving, shake dressing to recombine and pour equal amount over each salad.

Seafood Salad
Lasagna with Pesto and Béchamel

Serve family or friends a delicious dinner of baked lasagna layered with béchamel and pesto and a chilled seafood salad tossed with lemon and mustard dressing. Garnish each plate with lemon wedges and parsley, if desired.

Seafood salad is a traditional favorite of fishermen along the Italian Riviera, who often prepare it fresh for lunch. For this salad, purchase precleaned fresh or frozen squid or, if you prefer, clean the squid yourself at home. To do this, hold the head of the squid with one hand, the body with the other, and firmly pull the head away from the body. Cut away the tentacles and discard the remainder of the head. Pull the transparent quill-like piece out of the body sac and discard it. Wash the squid thoroughly inside and out, and peel the skin away from the body and fins. If you buy fresh squid the day before you plan to use it, refrigerate it in cold salted water, but cook it within 24 hours of purchase.

Pesto (a blend of fresh basil, olive oil, pine nuts, and cheese) is a popular Ligurian sauce for pasta. Here the pesto alternates with a delicate cheese-enriched béchamel (white sauce) between layers of lasagna. If you like, use fresh lasagna, but remember that the fresh noodles will cook through in less than a minute. To save time, you can prepare the sauces a day ahead of serving, and assemble and bake the lasagna at mealtime.

WHAT TO DRINK

Greco di Tufo, a distinctive, full-flavored white wine from around Naples, is a good first choice here. Or try an Italian Pinot Bianco.

SHOPPING LIST AND STAPLES

1 pound medium-size squid, cleaned
¾ pound medium-size shrimp, peeled and deveined
Small head leaf lettuce
Small bunch celery
Small red bell pepper
3 large cloves garlic
Large bunch fresh basil
Small bunch fresh parsley
2 lemons, plus 1 lemon (optional)
3 cups milk
4 tablespoons unsalted butter
½ pound Parmesan cheese
2 ounces Sardo or Pecorino Romano cheese
1 cup good-quality olive oil, preferably virgin
1 tablespoon Dijon mustard
¾ pound dried lasagna
2-ounce jar pine nuts

3 tablespoons all-purpose flour
1 bay leaf
Freshly grated nutmeg
Salt
Freshly ground black and white pepper
5 whole black peppercorns

UTENSILS

Food processor or blender
Large stockpot with cover
Large saucepan
2 medium-size saucepans, 1 heavy-gauge nonaluminum
13 x 9 x 2-inch glass or ceramic baking dish
Large nonaluminum bowl
Medium-size bowl
Small nonaluminum bowl
Colander
Measuring cups and spoons
Chef's knife
Paring knife
2 wooden spoons
Whisk
Metal spatula
Rubber spatula
Grater (if not using food processor)

START-TO-FINISH STEPS

1. Grate enough Parmesan cheese to measure 1¼ cups and enough Sardo or Pecorino Romano to measure 3 table-spoons for lasagna recipe; set aside separately. Prepare fresh herbs for all recipes.
2. Follow seafood salad recipe steps 1 through 6.
3. Follow lasagna recipe steps 1 through 7.
4. While lasagna is cooking, follow seafood salad recipe steps 7 through 10.
5. Follow lasagna recipe steps 8 through 13.
6. While lasagna is baking, follow seafood salad recipe steps 11 through 17.
7. Follow lasagna recipe step 14, seafood salad recipe step 18, and serve.

RECIPES

Seafood Salad

1 pound medium-size squid, cleaned and with tentacles
    separated
Salt
1 bay leaf
5 whole black peppercorns
¾ pound medium-size shrimp, peeled and deveined
2 stalks celery
Small red bell pepper
2 lemons, plus 1 lemon for garnish (optional)
1 tablespoon Dijon mustard
Freshly ground black pepper
½ cup good-quality olive oil, preferably virgin

3 tablespoons chopped fresh parsley, plus 4 sprigs for
    garnish (optional)
Small head leaf lettuce

1. Rinse squid thoroughly under cold running water, then cut crosswise into ½-inch-thick slices. Chop tentacles coarsely. Place in medium-size bowl with 1 tablespoon salt and enough cold water to cover; set aside.
2. Combine 1 quart water, bay leaf, and peppercorns in medium-size saucepan and bring to a boil over high heat.
3. Meanwhile, bring 2 quarts water to a boil in large saucepan over high heat.
4. Add 1 teaspoon salt and shrimp to boiling water in medium-size saucepan, return to a boil, and cook 2 min-utes, or just until shrimp turn pink.
5. Meanwhile, add 1 teaspoon salt and squid to boiling water in large saucepan, reduce heat to medium, and simmer 15 minutes, or just until tender. Do *not* overcook or squid will become tough.
6. Turn shrimp into colander and place under cold running water to cool.
7. Transfer shrimp to double thickness of paper towels and pat dry.
8. Turn squid into colander and set under cold running water to cool.
9. Wash and dry celery. Cut enough celery crosswise into ¼-inch-thick slices to measure 1 cup; set aside.
10. Wash and dry bell pepper. Halve, core, and seed pep-per. Cut lengthwise into ¼-inch-wide strips; set aside.
11. Squeeze enough lemon juice to measure ⅓ cup.
12. Combine lemon juice, mustard, ½ teaspoon salt, and pepper to taste in small nonaluminum bowl, and whisk until blended.
13. Whisking continuously, slowly add olive oil and whisk until dressing is blended and smooth; set aside.
14. Transfer squid to double thickness of paper towels and pat dry.
15. Combine squid, shrimp, celery, bell pepper, and chopped parsley in large nonaluminum bowl. Add dress-ing and toss to combine. Cover with plastic wrap and refrigerate until ready to serve.
16. Meanwhile, wash and dry lettuce. Remove and discard any bruised or discolored leaves. Using 1 or 2 large leaves for each, form beds for salad on 4 dinner plates. Reserve remaining lettuce for another use.
17. If using lemon for garnish, wash and dry with paper towel. Halve lengthwise, then cut each half into 4 wedges.
18. Just before serving, top lettuce with equal portions of chilled salad and garnish each serving with lemon wedges and a sprig of parsley, if desired.

Lasagna with Pesto and Béchamel

1 tablespoon salt
¾ pound dried lasagna

Pesto:
3 large cloves garlic
3 cups firmly packed fresh basil leaves

3 tablespoons pine nuts
½ cup virgin olive oil, approximately
1 tablespoon unsalted butter
½ teaspoon each salt and freshly ground black pepper
¾ cup freshly grated Parmesan cheese
3 tablespoons freshly grated Sardo or Pecorino Romano cheese

Béchamel:
3 tablespoons unsalted butter
3 tablespoons all-purpose flour
3 cups milk
Pinch of salt
Pinch of freshly grated nutmeg
½ teaspoon freshly ground white pepper
½ cup freshly grated Parmesan cheese

1. Bring 4½ quarts water to a boil in large covered stockpot over high heat.
2. Meanwhile, prepare pesto: Crush garlic under flat blade of chef's knife; remove peels and discard.
3. In food processor fitted with steel blade or in blender, chop basil leaves, turning machine on and off a few times.
4. With machine running, add garlic and process until finely chopped. Add pine nuts and continue to process. Add oil, butter, salt, and pepper, and process until mixture is smooth and pastelike.
5. Stir in cheeses. If using processor, quickly blend in cheeses to maintain pastelike consistency; set pesto aside.
6. Add 1 tablespoon salt to boiling water in stockpot, add lasagna, and cook about 7 minutes, or until *al dente*.
7. Fill 13 x 9 x 2-inch glass or ceramic baking dish half full with cold water; set aside.
8. Drain lasagna in colander and carefully transfer to baking dish of cold water to prevent sticking. Arrange cooled lasagna in single layer on damp kitchen towel or jelly-roll pan and set aside. Dry baking dish; set aside.
9. Preheat oven to 450 degrees.
10. For béchamel, melt butter in medium-size heavy-gauge nonaluminum saucepan over medium heat. Whisk in flour and bring to a gentle simmer, whisking continuously. Simmer 2 minutes; do *not* allow to brown.
11. Add milk and seasonings, and whisk until blended. Increase heat to medium-high and, whisking continuously, bring mixture to a boil. Reduce heat and simmer, whisking occasionally, 5 minutes. Remove pan from heat.
12. Add ¼ cup Parmesan to béchamel and whisk until blended. Cover surface of sauce with plastic wrap to prevent skin from forming; set aside.
13. Butter baking dish. Cover bottom of prepared dish with a single layer of lasagna (about 6 strips). Spread half of the béchamel over lasagna, then top with another layer of lasagna. Spread pesto evenly over lasagna, then cover with another layer of lasagna. Top with remaining béchamel, sprinkle evenly with remaining ¼ cup Parmesan, and bake in center of oven 15 to 20 minutes, or until béchamel is golden and lasagna is heated through.
14. Cut lasagna into squares and, using metal spatula, transfer to dinner plates.

ADDED TOUCH
The rich fruity flavor of amaretto, an Italian almond liqueur, enhances this delightful dessert.

Peach Cake with Toasted Almonds

4 ripe freestone peaches (about 1½ pounds total weight), or 1-pound can sliced peaches
¼ cup sliced blanched almonds
Large lemon

Batter:
⅓ cup unsalted butter, at room temperature
⅔ cup granulated sugar
⅔ cup milk
1 tablespoon amaretto or other almond-flavored liqueur
1 teaspoon vanilla extract
2 eggs, at room temperature
1 teaspoon baking powder
1½ cups all-purpose flour
Pinch of salt

1 tablespoon granulated sugar
1 tablespoon unsalted butter, cut into bits

1. Preheat oven to 375 degrees.
2. If using fresh peaches, bring 1 quart water to a boil in medium-size saucepan over high heat.
3. Meanwhile, butter 1-quart round baking dish or 9-inch pie pan; set aside.
4. Spread almonds in baking dish and toast in oven, shaking dish occasionally to prevent scorching, 8 to 10 minutes, or until almonds are light golden.
5. Plunge peaches into boiling water and blanch 1 minute to loosen skins. Turn into colander and cool under cold running water.
6. Wash lemon and dry with paper towel. Grate enough rind, avoiding white pith as much as possible, to measure 2 teaspoons; set aside. Halve lemon and squeeze juice; set aside.
7. Remove almonds from oven and set aside to cool.
8. Remove skins from peaches and discard. Halve each peach lengthwise and twist halves to separate. Remove pits and discard. Cut peaches lengthwise into ½-inch-thick slices and place in medium-size nonaluminum bowl. Sprinkle with lemon juice to prevent discoloration and toss gently until evenly coated; set aside. If using canned sliced peaches, turn into strainer set over medium-size bowl and set aside to drain.
9. Combine butter and sugar in medium-size mixing bowl and cream together until light and fluffy.
10. Add remaining batter ingredients and stir until well blended.
11. Turn batter into prepared baking pan and smooth top. Top batter with peaches, arranging them in a decorative pattern, and then top with almonds. Sprinkle cake evenly with sugar and butter, and bake 30 to 35 minutes, or until firm to the touch. Serve directly from pan.

Nancy Verde Barr

MENU 1 (Right)
Braised Duck with Black Olives
Penne with Mushroom Sauce

MENU 2
Piquant Chicken
Baked Stuffed Tomatoes

MENU 3
Zucchini Soup
Lamb Catanzaro-style
Broccoli Rabe

Nancy Barr is particularly interested in recipes from southern Italy, which was her paternal grandparents' home. As a cooking teacher, her ambition is to familiarize Americans with the diversity of southern Italian food. "I want people to know that southerners eat so many more dishes than pizza, lasagna, spaghetti, and meatballs!" she says.

Her Menus 1 and 3 introduce easy but relatively unfamiliar southern Italian dishes. In Menu 1, she serves pasta with a highly seasoned tomato sauce from the region of Calabria and couples it with braised duck and black olives from nearby Basilicata. Menu 3 features a zucchini soup from Naples, lamb chops cooked with mushrooms (a dish popular in Calabria's province of Catanzaro), and broccoli rabe sautéed with olive oil and garlic.

For a change of pace, in Menu 2 Nancy Barr prepares a simple meal from the region of Abruzzo, where pickled vegetables are often cooked with chicken or veal. The tomatoes are stuffed with a mixture of bread crumbs, capers, anchovies, and *soppressata*, a hard Italian salami.

For this informal dinner, present the pieces of browned duck on a large serving platter, then spoon the olives and other sauce ingredients over the top. Penne in a spicy tomato sauce is a traditional southern Italian partner for duck.

Braised Duck with Black Olives
Penne with Mushroom Sauce

Most supermarkets sell frozen whole ducks, but because they are increasingly in demand, you can often find them fresh as well. The skin of fresh ducks should be elastic, free of pinfeathers, and should feel well padded with fat. Keep fresh duck loosely wrapped in the coldest part of the refrigerator for up to three days. Frozen ducks should be securely wrapped in sturdy, unbroken plastic wrap. They can be stored frozen for up to three months. Thaw them in the plastic wrap in the refrigerator 24 to 36 hours before cooking; or, if you are in a hurry, put the frozen duck, still wrapped in waterproof plastic, in a pan of cold water and it will be ready for cooking in about three hours.

The *penne*, or quill-shaped pasta, is served with a simple sauce sparked with hot pepper flakes. Start with a small amount of the flakes, and adjust the seasoning to your taste. If fresh hot chilies are available, try them in place of the pepper flakes. Begin with half a small hot pepper, and increase the amount, if desired. To remove the seeds, wear rubber gloves to protect your hands. The more seeds you leave in, the hotter the flavor.

WHAT TO DRINK

A southern Italian red wine such as the dry and flavorful Taurasi or Aglianico del Vulture complements the strong flavors of the duck.

SHOPPING LIST AND STAPLES

5-pound duckling
¼ pound prosciutto, unsliced
¾ pound mushrooms
2 small onions (about ½ pound total weight)
Small bunch celery
Small bunch carrots
Large clove garlic
1 bunch fresh parsley
Small bunch fresh oregano, or 2 teaspoons dried
¼ pound pecorino Romano or Parmesan cheese
32-ounce can Italian plum tomatoes
6-ounce can pitted black olives
6 tablespoons olive oil
¾ pound penne or similarly shaped pasta
¼ teaspoon red pepper flakes, approximately
1 bay leaf
Salt

Freshly ground black pepper
1 cup dry white wine

UTENSILS

Food processor (optional)
Stockpot
Large sauté pan with cover
Medium-size sauté pan
Broiler rack and pan
Medium-size bowl
Large heatproof serving bowl
Large heatproof serving platter
Colander
Strainer
Measuring cups and spoons
Cleaver
Chef's knife
Paring knife
Wooden spoon
Metal tongs
Grater (if not using processor)
Skewer (optional)
Vegetable peeler (optional)

START-TO-FINISH STEPS

1. Wash parsley and fresh oregano, if using, and dry with paper towels. Chop enough parsley to measure ½ cup for duck recipe and ¼ cup for pasta recipe; chop enough oregano to measure 2 tablespoons for pasta recipe. Peel and chop onions for duck and pasta recipes.
2. Follow duck recipe steps 1 through 6.
3. While duck is broiling, follow pasta recipe steps 1 and 2.
4. Follow duck recipe step 7.
5. While duck is cooking, follow pasta recipe steps 3 through 5.
6. Follow duck recipe steps 8 and 9, and pasta recipe steps 6 through 10.
7. Follow duck recipe step 10 and pasta recipe step 11, and serve together.

RECIPES

Braised Duck with Black Olives

5-pound duckling
Small celery stalk

Small carrot
¼ pound prosciutto, unsliced
1 cup pitted black olives
3 tablespoons olive oil
Small onion, peeled and chopped
1 cup dry white wine
½ cup chopped parsley
1 bay leaf
Salt
Freshly ground black pepper

1. Preheat broiler.
2. Remove any excess fat from cavity of duck. Trim off neck skin. Chop off wing tips and reserve with neck and gizzards for another use. With cleaver, quarter duck: Turn duck skin-side up on cutting surface and cut through the breastbone. Turn duck over, push back breast halves, and cut backbone in two. Next, place each half skin-side up and, feeling for end of rib cage, cut pieces in half just below ribs. Turn quarters skin-side down and, with sharp knife, trim excess skin and any visible fat from each piece.

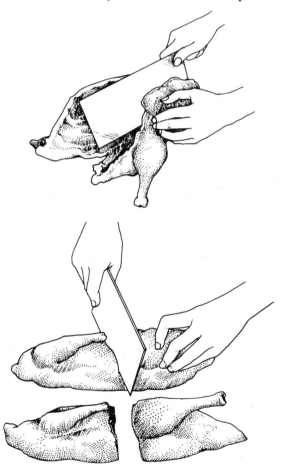

3. Wash celery, dry, and dice enough to measure ¼ cup. Peel and finely dice enough carrot to measure ¼ cup. Chop prosciutto into ¼-inch dice. Slice olives in half; set aside.
4. Place rack in broiler pan. Place duck skin-side up on rack and broil 6 inches away from heating element for 5 minutes.
5. Meanwhile, heat olive oil in large sauté pan over medium heat. Add onion, celery, carrot, and prosciutto and sauté, stirring occasionally, about 10 minutes, or until onion is golden.
6. After duck has broiled 5 minutes, prick skin all over with skewer or tip of paring knife to release fat, being careful not to penetrate meat. Broil another 5 minutes, pricking skin once more during this time. Turn duck and broil another 5 minutes.
7. Transfer duck to sauté pan with vegetables and prosciutto, add wine, and bring to a boil over high heat. Reduce oven temperature to 200 degrees, leaving door ajar if necessary. Seal pan with sheet of foil, place cover over foil, and cook duck over medium heat 15 minutes.
8. Remove cover and foil, add parsley, bay leaf, olives, and salt and pepper to taste. Reseal pan with foil, re-cover, and cook another 20 minutes, or until tender.
9. Meanwhile, place large heatproof serving platter in oven to warm.
10. When duck is done, transfer to warm platter, top with sauce, and serve.

Penne with Mushroom Sauce

Large clove garlic
¾ pound mushrooms
32-ounce can Italian plum tomatoes
3 tablespoons olive oil
Small onion, peeled and chopped
Salt
¼ cup chopped parsley
2 tablespoons chopped fresh oregano, or
    2 teaspoons dried
¼ teaspoon red pepper flakes, approximately
¼ pound pecorino Romano or Parmesan cheese
¾ pound penne or similarly shaped pasta

1. Peel and coarsely chop garlic. Wipe mushrooms clean with damp paper towels and chop coarsely.
2. In strainer set over medium-size bowl, drain tomatoes; reserve juice. Coarsely chop tomatoes; set aside.
3. Heat oil in medium-size sauté pan over medium heat. Add onion and garlic, and sauté, stirring occasionally, 3 to 4 minutes, or until onions are soft and translucent.
4. Raise heat to high, add mushrooms, and salt to taste; sauté 2 to 3 minutes, or until mushrooms exude liquid.
5. Reduce heat to medium. Add tomatoes, ½ cup reserved tomato juice, parsley, oregano, red pepper flakes, and salt to taste, and simmer 25 minutes, adding more tomato juice if sauce becomes too thick.
6. Bring 2 to 3 quarts salted water to a boil in stockpot over high heat.
7. Meanwhile, in food processor or with grater, grate enough cheese to make 1 cup and set aside.
8. Place large heatproof serving bowl in 200-degree oven to warm.
9. Add penne to boiling water and cook according to package directions until *al dente*.
10. Drain pasta in colander.
11. Turn sauce into warm serving bowl, add drained pasta, and toss to combine. Serve with grated cheese.

Piquant Chicken
Baked Stuffed Tomatoes

For the chicken main dish, the cook suggests butterflying a whole fryer: splitting the bird in half, removing the backbone, and opening the chicken flat. Cooking the chicken this way makes it juicier. Or, have your butcher butterfly the chicken, or substitute a cut-up fryer.

WHAT TO DRINK

A white Lacryma Christi or a top-quality Orvieto would be fine here, or try a California Sauvignon Blanc.

The aromas of the piquant chicken enhance this meal. Spoon some of the sauce with pickled sweet peppers and artichoke hearts over the chicken quarters, and offer a whole baked tomato with each helping.

SHOPPING LIST AND STAPLES

1 frying chicken (about 3 pounds)
¼ pound soppressata or other hard salami
4 medium-size tomatoes (about 1½ pounds total weight)
Small bunch parsley
2 large cloves garlic
9-ounce package frozen artichoke hearts
7 tablespoons olive oil, approximately
12-ounce jar Italian pickled sweet peppers
3½-ounce jar capers
2-ounce tin anchovy fillets
3 slices stale bread, approximately
Salt

Freshly ground black pepper
½ cup dry white wine

UTENSILS

Food processor (optional)
Large heavy-gauge nonaluminum skillet with cover
1½-quart shallow baking dish
Small bowl (if not using processor)
Cake rack
Small strainer
Measuring cups and spoons
Chef's knife
Paring knife
Wooden spoon
Serrated teaspoon (optional)
Metal tongs
Poultry shears (optional)
Grater (if not using processor)

START-TO-FINISH STEPS

One hour ahead: Set out artichoke hearts to thaw for chicken recipe.

1. Follow tomatoes recipe steps 1 and 2.

2. Follow chicken recipe steps 1 through 6.
3. While ehicken is cooking, follow tomatoes recipe step 3.
4. Follow chicken recipe step 7 and tomatoes recipe steps 4 through 6.
5. Follow chicken recipe step 8 and tomatoes recipe steps 7 and 8.
6. Follow chicken recipe steps 9 through 12, and serve with tomatoes.

RECIPES

Piquant Chicken

1 frying chicken (about 3 pounds)
2 large cloves garlic
¼ cup olive oil
1 cup Italian pickled sweet peppers, without liquid
½ cup dry white wine
9-ounce package frozen artichoke hearts, thawed
Salt

1. Rinse chicken under cold water and dry with paper towels. To butterfly chicken: Place chicken on cutting surface, breast-side down, with legs pointing toward you. Using poultry shears or chef's knife, cut along each side of backbone as close to the bone as possible. Remove backbone and discard. Turn bird breast-side up and flatten by

striking breastbone with the heel of your hand. Cut off wing tips and tuck wings under.

2. Bruise garlic by placing cloves under flat blade of chef's knife; peel.

3. Heat olive oil in large skillet over medium-low heat. Add garlic and sauté, stirring occasionally, 4 to 6 minutes, or until golden. Discard garlic.

4. Place chicken skin-side down in skillet. Raise heat to medium-high and cook about 8 minutes, or until chicken skin is nicely browned.

5. Meanwhile, cut peppers into ½-inch-wide by 2-inch-long strips; set aside.

6. Turn chicken skin-side up and cook another 7 minutes.

7. Pour off all but 1 tablespoon fat from skillet. Add wine and bring to a boil over high heat; boil 15 seconds. Reduce heat to medium, cover, and cook 15 minutes.

8. Add pepper strips, artichoke hearts, and salt to taste to skillet. Cover and cook another 15 to 20 minutes, or until juices run clear when chicken is pierced with a sharp knife.

9. Toward end of cooking time, place 4 dinner plates under hot running water to warm.

10. When chicken is cooked, remove from pan to cutting surface. With poultry shears or chef's knife, cut chicken into quarters. Dry plates and transfer chicken pieces to them.

11. Raise heat under skillet to high and boil pan juices, stirring to scrape up any browned bits clinging to bottom of pan, until juices are slightly thickened and glossy, 2 to 4 minutes. There should be about ¼ cup of pan juices.

12. Top each serving of chicken with a spoonful of pan juices and some vegetables.

Baked Stuffed Tomatoes

4 medium-size tomatoes (about 1½ pounds total weight)
Salt
3 slices stale bread, approximately
Small bunch parsley
3½-ounce jar capers
2 to 4 anchovy fillets
¼ pound soppressata or other hard salami
3 tablespoons olive oil, approximately
Freshly ground black pepper

1. Preheat oven to 375 degrees.

2. Cut ½-inch-thick slice from tops of tomatoes. Turn each tomato upside down and squeeze gently to remove seeds and juice. Using serrated or regular teaspoon, remove any remaining seeds and enough pulp to make room for stuffing. Sprinkle insides of tomatoes lightly with salt and place upside down on paper-towel-covered cake rack to drain.

3. Trim off crusts from bread and discard. Using food processor or grater, grate enough bread to measure 1 cup crumbs.

4. Rinse parsley and dry with paper towels; finely chop enough to measure ¼ cup. Drain 1 tablespoon capers in small strainer and rinse under cold running water; chop

finely. Drain anchovies; chop finely. Finely chop soppressata to make about 1 cup.

5. Combine parsley, capers, anchovies, soppressata, and bread crumbs in small bowl. Add 1 tablespoon olive oil to mixture and stir until blended. Add pepper to taste but *no* salt; the capers and anchovies provide sufficient saltiness.

6. Divide stuffing among tomato shells.

7. Lightly grease shallow baking dish with some of the remaining oil. Place tomatoes upright in dish and drizzle with 1 or 2 teaspoons olive oil.

8. Bake 20 minutes, or until tomatoes are lightly browned on top.

ADDED TOUCH

Pumate, or dried Italian plum tomatoes, are used in this pasta dish—here in their oil-packed form. Add them sparingly because their concentrated tomato flavor can be overpowering. The richly flavored oil makes a good seasoning for salad dressings or garlic bread.

Linguine with Onions

3 medium-size onions (about ¾ pound total weight)
½ cup plus 3 tablespoons olive oil
2 tablespoons fresh oregano, preferably, or other fresh herb such as marjoram or parsley
9½-ounce jar sun-dried tomatoes in olive oil
¼ pound Kalamata olives
3 slices bread
Salt and freshly ground black pepper
¾ pound linguine, preferably imported

1. Peel and halve onions, then cut crosswise into thin semicircles.

2. Heat ½ cup oil in medium-size sauté pan over medium-low heat. Add onions, cover, and cook until completely softened, about 30 minutes. Do *not* allow onions to brown.

3. Meanwhile, wash fresh oregano and pat dry with paper towels. Coarsely chop enough oregano to measure 2 tablespoons. Cut enough sun-dried tomatoes into ¼-inch-wide strips to measure ½ cup. Pit olives and cut lengthwise into quarters.

4. Trim off crusts from bread and discard. In food processor or with grater, grate enough bread to measure 1 cup crumbs.

5. When onions are ready, stir in oregano, tomatoes, olives, and salt and freshly ground pepper to taste, and cook gently, uncovered, 10 minutes.

6. Meanwhile, in stockpot, bring 3 quarts salted water to a boil over high heat.

7. Heat remaining 3 tablespoons olive oil in small skillet over high heat. Add bread crumbs and toss with fork until golden and toasted, about 4 minutes. Set aside.

8. Transfer onion mixture to large serving bowl.

9. Add linguine to boiling water and cook according to package directions until *al dente*.

10. Drain linguine in colander, turn into bowl with onion mixture, and toss to combine. Sprinkle with toasted bread crumbs and serve.

Zucchini Soup
Lamb Catanzaro-style
Broccoli Rabe

The zucchini soup can precede the main course of broccoli rabe and lamb chops topped with mushrooms and onions.

Whole beaten eggs thicken the zucchini soup. To prevent the eggs from coagulating, first add a small portion of soup to the beaten eggs, stirring continuously. Then blend the warmed eggs into the soup. If the eggs scramble slightly despite this measure, the flavor of the soup will not be affected.

The two-step cooking technique for the broccoli rabe is used throughout Italy. Blanching the vegetable before sautéing it eliminates any bitterness. You may substitute turnip, beet, or mustard greens, but cooking times for these greens vary, so check for doneness.

WHAT TO DRINK

A light red wine would best suit this menu. Choose a young Chianti, Valpolicella, or Bardolino, or a domestic Beaujolais-style Zinfandel.

SHOPPING LIST AND STAPLES

Eight ¾-inch-thick rib lamb chops (about 2¼ pounds total weight)
4 medium-size zucchini (about 1¾ pounds total weight)
1½ pounds broccoli rabe or turnip, beet, or mustard greens
½ pound mushrooms
2 medium-size onions (about ½ pound each)
Small bunch fresh parsley
Small bunch fresh oregano, or 2 teaspoons dried
2 medium-size cloves garlic
2 lemons
2 large eggs
2 ounces pecorino Romano or imported Parmesan cheese
3½ cups beef stock, preferably homemade, or 13¾-ounce can each chicken and beef stock, or 3 cups water
1 cup plus 1 tablespoon olive oil
2 tablespoons lard
2-ounce tin anchovy fillets
3½-ounce jar capers
Four ¾-inch-thick slices Italian bread
¼ cup all-purpose flour, approximately
Salt
Freshly ground black pepper
½ cup dry white wine

UTENSILS

Food processor (optional)
Stockpot
Large heavy-gauge skillet
Medium-size nonaluminum skillet or sauté pan with cover
Large heavy-gauge saucepan
Small saucepan
Large sauté pan with cover
13 x 9-inch baking sheet
Heatproof platter
Medium-size bowl
9-inch pie pan or flat shallow dish
Colander
Small strainer
Measuring cups and spoons
Chef's knife
Paring knife
Wooden spoon
Slotted metal spatula
Ladle
Metal tongs
Grater (if not using processor)

START-TO-FINISH STEPS

1. Follow soup recipe steps 1 through 10.
2. Follow lamb recipe steps 1 through 6.
3. Follow broccoli rabe recipe steps 1 and 2.
4. Follow lamb recipe steps 7 and 8.
5. Follow broccoli rabe recipe steps 3 through 6.
6. Follow lamb recipe step 9 and broccoli rabe recipe step 7.
7. While broccoli rabe cooks, follow soup recipe steps 11 and 12, and serve.
8. Follow lamb recipe steps 10 through 12 and broccoli rabe recipe step 8, and serve.

RECIPES

Zucchini Soup

Small bunch fresh parsley
Small bunch fresh oregano, or 2 teaspoons dried
4 medium-size zucchini (about 1¾ pounds total weight)
Medium-size onion (about ½ pound)
2 ounces pecorino Romano or Parmesan cheese
Four ¾-inch-thick slices Italian bread
2 tablespoons lard
2 tablespoons olive oil
3½ cups beef stock, or 13¾-ounce can each chicken and beef stock, or 3 cups water
Salt
Freshly ground black pepper
2 large eggs

1. Preheat oven to 350 degrees.
2. Wash parsley and fresh oregano and dry with paper towels. Chop enough parsley to measure ¼ cup. Chop enough oregano to measure 2 tablespoons. Wash zucchini, dry, and trim off ends. Cut zucchini into ½-inch slices. Peel and slice onion crosswise into thin rounds.
3. In food processor or with grater, grate enough cheese to measure ⅓ cup; set aside.
4. Arrange bread in single layer on baking sheet and toast in oven 5 minutes.
5. While bread is toasting, combine lard and olive oil in large heavy-gauge saucepan over medium heat. Add onion and sauté, stirring occasionally, 4 to 5 minutes, or until soft and translucent.

6. Turn bread and toast on other side another 5 minutes.

7. Meanwhile, bring stock to a gentle simmer in small saucepan over medium heat.

8. Add zucchini to onion and toss to combine. Add hot stock and salt and pepper to taste, and simmer gently 15 to 20 minutes, or until zucchini are tender.

9. Meanwhile, remove bread from oven and set aside. Reduce oven temperature to 200 degrees.

10. In medium-size bowl, combine eggs, grated cheese, and chopped herbs, and beat until blended; set aside.

11. Beating continuously with wooden spoon, slowly add 1 cup of hot soup to egg mixture; then gradually add egg mixture to soup, stirring continuously until blended. Heat soup just to a simmer; do *not* boil.

12. Place a slice of toasted bread in each of 4 soup bowls. Divide soup among bowls, and serve.

Lamb Catanzaro-style

Medium-size onion (about ½ pound)
½ pound mushrooms
3½-ounce jar capers
2-ounce tin anchovy fillets
½ cup plus 3 tablespoons olive oil
¼ cup all-purpose flour, approximately
Eight ¾-inch-thick rib lamb chops (about 2¼
   pounds total weight)
Salt
Freshly ground black pepper
½ cup dry white wine

1. Peel and finely chop enough onion to measure ¼ cup. Wipe mushrooms clean with damp paper towels and cut into ⅛-inch-thick slices.

2. Rinse 2 tablespoons capers in small strainer under cold running water and drain. Rinse 3 anchovy fillets under cold running water and dry with paper towels. Coarsely chop capers and anchovies.

3. Heat 3 tablespoons olive oil in medium-size non-aluminum skillet over medium heat. Add onion and sauté, stirring occasionally, 5 to 8 minutes, or until onion is golden.

4. Meanwhile, place flour in pie pan or flat shallow dish. Trim off excess fat from lamb chops and dust chops lightly with flour.

5. Heat remaining ½ cup olive oil in large heavy-gauge skillet over medium-high heat. Add chops and brown 5 to 6 minutes on one side.

6. While chops are cooking, add mushrooms, and salt and pepper to taste to onions, and sauté, stirring occasionally, 3 to 5 minutes, or until mushrooms release their juices.

7. Using metal tongs, turn chops and brown on other side another 5 to 6 minutes.

8. Cover onion-mushroom mixture, remove pan from heat, and set aside.

9. With slotted metal spatula, transfer chops to heatproof platter, sprinkle with salt and pepper, and place in 200 degree oven.

10. Pour off all but 2 tablespoons of fat from skillet. Return skillet to high heat, add wine and any juices that have accumulated around lamb chops, and bring to a boil, scraping up any browned bits clinging to bottom of pan. Continue boiling 2 to 3 minutes, or until liquid is reduced by half.

11. Add reduced pan juices to onion-mushroom mixture and stir to combine. Reheat briefly over medium heat.

12. Divide lamb chops among 4 dinner plates and top each serving with some of the onion-mushroom mixture.

Broccoli Rabe

Salt
1½ pounds broccoli rabe or turnip, beet, or
   mustard greens
2 medium-size cloves garlic
2 lemons
¼ cup olive oil
Freshly ground black pepper

1. Bring 2 quarts of lightly salted water to a boil in stockpot over high heat.

2. Meanwhile, remove tough outer leaves from broccoli rabe and discard. With paring knife, peel stems and wash broccoli rabe thoroughly under cold running water. Cut each stalk into thirds.

Broccoli rabe

3. Add broccoli rabe to boiling water and cook 3 minutes.

4. While broccoli rabe is cooking, bruise garlic under flat blade of chef's knife and peel. Rinse 1 lemon, dry, and cut into 8 wedges; set aside. Halve remaining lemon. Squeeze juice of one half and set aside; reserve other half for another use.

5. Turn broccoli rabe into colander, refresh under cold running water, and drain. Wrap in clean kitchen towel or paper towels to dry.

6. Heat olive oil in large sauté pan over medium heat. Add garlic and sauté 2 to 3 minutes, or until lightly golden.

7. Add broccoli rabe, and salt and pepper to taste, cover pan, and cook 10 to 12 minutes, or until broccoli rabe is fork-tender.

8. Remove garlic and discard. Sprinkle broccoli rabe with lemon juice, divide among 4 dinner plates, and serve with lemon wedges.

Bernice Hunt

MENU 1 (Left)
Fresh Figs or Melon with Prosciutto
Cartwheels with Mixed Vegetables

MENU 2
Carrot Soup
Fusilli with Chicken and Rosemary

MENU 3
Mushroom Salad
Fettuccine alla Carbonara
Steamed Broccoli with Lemon Juice and Olive Oil

B ernice Hunt, a New York author, not only writes about food, but also loves to cook for both family and friends. Many of her recipes are inspired by northern Italian cooking, which she grew to love after numerous trips to Bologna, the gastronomic center of northern Italy. There, the emphasis is on using cheeses, cured hams, delicate pasta, and quality raw ingredients. As all good cooks do, Bernice Hunt emphasizes using fresh natural ingredients and rarely plans a meal until she visits her local greengrocer. She has not let a busy career interfere with her cooking, but in order to have the time she needs for kitchen creativity, she has learned an economy of motion, making every recipe direct and simple. The menus she presents reflect her no-fuss, Italian-style approach to cooking.

In Menu 1, a light spring or summer meal from northern Italy—and loved throughout that country—fresh figs or melon with sliced prosciutto balance the main pasta course of cartwheels with a sauce replete with chunks of vegetables. The key to the success of this menu is to use fresh, seasonal produce.

By contrast, Menu 2 and Menu 3 require fresh, but not strictly seasonal, produce—such as the carrots for the soup and the mushrooms for the salad in Menu 2, and the broccoli for the vegetable platter in Menu 3. This way you can serve these two meals any time of the year.

Casual pottery serving pieces underline the informality of canta-loupe wedges with prosciutto and cartwheels tossed with bite-size vegetables and Parmesan cheese—a meal best served buffet style, with the cheese grater handy. Fill out the meal with a green salad, if you wish.

43

Fresh Figs or Melon with Prosciutto
Cartwheels with Mixed Vegetables

This classic Italian appetizer pairs sliced salty prosciutto with fresh, sweet melon slices or whole figs. Italian cooks use a type of cantaloupe that thrives in northern Italy, but Cranshaw or honeydew melons are also delicious with prosciutto. Fresh figs are very perishable and are luxury items in most American markets. If you can find fresh figs, select those that are soft but not mushy and that have unbroken skins. Store them in the refrigerator and use them as soon as possible. For peak flavor, serve figs at room temperature.

Bernice Hunt's version of pasta with vegetables calls for cartwheel-shaped pasta, which is widely available in most supermarkets, sometimes in spinach and carrot varieties as well as plain. A medley of fresh vegetables—leeks, mushrooms, summer-ripe zucchini, and regular or cherry tomatoes—are combined with cream and grated Parmesan cheese to serve as a sauce for the cartwheels. This wheel-shaped pasta is sturdy enough to hold the vegetable-laden sauce. But you can also vary the pasta by using elbows or shells instead; if you do, they should be bite-size for easy eating.

WHAT TO DRINK

You could serve a red or white wine here. For red, select a full-bodied Chianti Classico *reserva* or a Barbaresco. For white, choose a bright fruity Italian Pinot Grigio, or a dry California Riesling.

SHOPPING LIST AND STAPLES

8 slices prosciutto
2 medium-size leeks
2 medium-size zucchini
¼ pound fresh mushrooms
1 large ripe tomato, or 5 to 7 cherry tomatoes
1 bunch watercress, arugula, or parsley (optional)
8 fresh figs, or 1 ripe cantaloupe or melon
4 tablespoons butter
1 to 1½ cups light cream or half-and-half
¼ pound Parmesan cheese
1 pound cartwheels or pasta shells
Salt and pepper

UTENSILS

Large stockpot or kettle with cover
Large skillet
Small bowl
Colander
Measuring cups and spoons
Chef's knife
All-purpose knife
Grater

START-TO-FINISH STEPS

1. Follow pasta recipe steps 1 through 5.
2. As pasta cooks, follow fruit and prosciutto recipe step 1 if using figs or steps 2 and 3 if using melon.
3. Grate Parmesan cheese for pasta recipe and follow pasta recipe steps 6 through 9.
4. Serve fruit and prosciutto.
5. Follow pasta recipe steps 10 and 11.

RECIPES

Fresh Figs or Melon with Prosciutto

8 fresh figs, or 1 ripe melon
8 slices prosciutto
1 bunch watercress, arugula, or parsley for garnish
  (optional)

1. Wash figs and pat them dry. Put 2 on each of 4 serving plates and arrange 2 slices of prosciutto alongside. The perfect garnish is fresh fig leaves, but they are not often included with the figs. Brighten up plate with sprigs of watercress, arugula, or parsley, if desired.
2. If using melon, cut in half, remove seeds, and peel.
3. With cut side up, slice each half into uniform crescents about ½ inch thick. Attractively arrange several slices on individual plates—slightly overlapping—and drape 2 slices of prosciutto across top. Garnish with sprigs of watercress, arugula, or parsley, if desired.

Cartwheels with Mixed Vegetables

Salt
2 medium-size leeks
4 tablespoons butter
1 medium-size zucchini
¼ pound fresh mushrooms
1 large ripe tomato, or 5 to 7 cherry tomatoes
1 pound cartwheels or pasta shells
1 to 1½ cups light cream or half-and-half

1 cup freshly grated Parmesan cheese
Freshly ground black pepper

1. Heat water and 1 tablespoon salt in stockpot or kettle for pasta.
2. Clean leeks (see drawing), separating segments to wash out all sand and grit. Finely chop both white and green parts, discarding only tough ends.

3. Melt butter in skillet. Add chopped leeks and sauté over medium heat about 10 minutes, stirring several times.
4. Scrub and slice zucchini. Wipe mushrooms and slice them. Wash and chop tomato.
5. Add pasta to boiling water and cook until just tender, about 15 minutes.
6. Add zucchini, mushrooms, and tomato to leeks and stir fry over fairly high heat until zucchini is barely tender; it should remain bright green.
7. Add 1 cup of the cream, ½ cup of the grated cheese, and salt and pepper to taste. Just before mixture comes to a boil, turn off heat.
8. When pasta is just tender, drain in colander and return to stockpot.
9. Pour half of the sauce over pasta and stir well; cover and reserve until after appetizer course.
10. When ready to serve, add the remaining sauce to pasta and toss well. Heat briefly over high heat, stirring constantly. If pasta has absorbed too much sauce, add the additional ½ cup of cream.
11. Serve and pass the remaining grated cheese at table.

ADDED TOUCHES

A salad of delicately flavored, slightly sweet fennel seasoned with a tangy vinaigrette makes a quick-to-prepare addition to this warm-weather meal.

Fennel Salad Vinaigrette

1 bunch fennel
Salt
Freshly ground black pepper
4 teaspoons red wine vinegar
6 tablespoons olive oil
1 bunch watercress

1. Cut tops off fennel and trim base. Rinse well. Cut fennel bulb into thin slices.
2. Put salt, pepper, and vinegar in small bowl. Blend well and add oil, beating with fork or whisk to blend.
3. Arrange watercress on individual plates and put fennel on top. Spoon dressing over.

A rich creamy pie baked in a nut pastry shell goes well as dessert.

Cheese Pie

The nut pastry shell:
½ cup finely chopped unsalted almonds
1 cup flour
Pinch of salt
5 tablespoons butter, softened
1 teaspoon water

The filling:
1½ pounds ricotta cheese (3 cups)
3 eggs
⅓ cup granulated sugar
1 teaspoon vanilla
¼ pound chopped toasted almonds (optional)
2 teaspoons grated lemon or orange rind
Pinch of confectioners' sugar

1. Preheat oven to 375 degrees.
2. Make pie shell first by putting pastry ingredients into 8-inch pie tin and mixing with fingertips until thoroughly blended. Crumble mixture over bottom of pan and up sides, pressing it down smoothly. Crimp edge with fork or your fingers.
3. For filling: put cheese, eggs, granulated sugar, and vanilla into medium-size bowl and beat with wooden spoon or electric beater until mixture is well blended.
4. Spoon filling into pastry shell and sprinkle grated rind over top. Bake about 45 to 55 minutes or until custard sets and is firm. Cool on wire rack. Before serving, sprinkle top of pie with confectioners' sugar.

Carrot Soup
Fusilli with Chicken and Rosemary

Tangerine-colored carrot soup introduces the entrée of fusilli, *which is topped with a creamy rosemary, cheese, and chicken sauce.*

In Menu 2, the tangerine-colored soup will delight your guests, and you will be surprised that a soup so elegant can be so simple to prepare. This creamy carrot soup serves as both a first course and a vegetable. When you serve the soup, Bernice Hunt suggests that you garnish each bowl with chopped fresh chives or curly parsley.

Spiral-shaped *fusilli* has grooves that pick up the cubed chicken and rosemary-flavored sauce. You can substitute any other grooved pasta, such as *ziti, rigatoni,* or *rotelle.*

The herb rosemary enhances lamb, beef, and poultry, but it has an intense, pungent flavor, so use it cautiously. For maximum flavor, crumble the leaves before using.

To round out this meal, serve a tossed salad and an Italian dessert, *zuccotto mandorlo* (see the ADDED TOUCH), which is chocolaty rich and fun to make.

WHAT TO DRINK

These rich flavors need a full-bodied white wine: a California Chardonnay, an Italian Cortese, or a French Mâcon. Whichever you choose, serve it lightly chilled.

SHOPPING LIST AND STAPLES

1 pound skinless, boneless chicken breasts
1 bunch carrots (about 1 pound)
1 large shallot
1 clove garlic
2 tablespoons chopped fresh chives (optional)
1 bunch fresh parsley (optional)
3 to 4 cups milk
1 to 1½ cups light cream or half-and-half
¼ pound Parmesan cheese
4 tablespoons butter
1 pound fusilli
1 cup chicken broth
1½ teaspoons chopped fresh rosemary,
    or ½ teaspoon dried
Salt and pepper

UTENSILS

Food processor or blender
Large stockpot or kettle with cover
Large skillet with cover
Medium-size saucepan with cover
Colander
Measuring cups and spoons
All-purpose knife
Grater
Vegetable peeler

START-TO-FINISH STEPS

1. Follow soup recipe steps 1 through 5.
2. Cut garlic into quarters, chop rosemary, and grate cheese for pasta recipe. Follow pasta recipe steps 1 through 6.
3. Chop chives or parsley for soup recipe, if using either, and follow soup recipe step 6.
4. Follow pasta recipe steps 7 through 9. Serve.

RECIPES

Carrot Soup

1 bunch carrots (about 1 pound)
1 large shallot
1 cup chicken broth
3 to 4 cups milk
Freshly ground black pepper
Salt
2 tablespoons chopped fresh chives or fresh parsley for garnish (optional)

1. Trim and peel carrots. Cut into thin slices.
2. Peel and slice shallot.
3. Put chicken broth into saucepan. Add sliced carrots and shallot and bring to a boil. Lower heat and simmer until carrots are tender, about 15 minutes.
4. Puree mixture in blender or food processor, adding 1 to 2 cups milk until smooth.
5. Return puree to saucepan and thin to desired consistency with milk. Do not make soup too thin; it should have consistency of heavy cream or thick vichyssoise. Add salt and pepper to taste.
6. Ladle soup into individual bowls and sprinkle with chopped chives or parsley, if desired.

Fusilli with Chicken and Rosemary

1 tablespoon salt
1 pound skinless, boneless chicken breasts
4 tablespoons butter
1 clove garlic, cut into quarters
1½ teaspoons chopped fresh rosemary, or ½ teaspoon dried
1 to 1½ cups light cream or half-and-half
1 cup freshly grated Parmesan cheese
Salt

Freshly ground black pepper
1 pound fusilli

1. Bring water and 1 tablespoon salt to a boil for pasta in stockpot or kettle.
2. Rinse chicken breasts in cold water and pat dry with paper towels. Trim and discard all fat and cut breasts into small pieces, about ½ inch square.
3. Melt butter in skillet and add garlic. Press garlic with back of wooden spoon and rub over surface of pan. Cook until garlic is nut brown, then remove and discard.
4. Turn heat to high and add chicken. Stir and toss constantly to brown all sides quickly, about 1 to 2 minutes.
5. Add rosemary and 1 cup of the cream and bring to a simmer.
6. Stir in ½ cup of the cheese, taste, then add salt and pepper as needed. Turn off heat and cover pan.
7. Cook fusilli in boiling water until just tender but not mushy. Drain well.
8. When ready to serve, warm sauce over medium heat. If sauce is too thick, add additional ½ cup cream.
9. Put sauce on pasta at table and serve additional grated cheese and pass pepper mill.

ADDED TOUCH

This dessert needs to set for a day in the refrigerator.

Zuccotto Mandorlo

1 package ladyfingers, separated into single layers (12 to 16)
3 tablespoons light rum
2 tablespoons Marsala
2½ ounces unsweetened chocolate
½ cup blanched and toasted almonds, coarsely chopped
1½ cups heavy cream
¾ cup confectioners' sugar
1 teaspoon vanilla extract
2 teaspoons unsweetened cocoa

1. Line 1½-quart soufflé or straight-sided dish with a double layer of aluminum foil, which should extend several inches above rim of bowl. This helps to remove dessert for unmolding.
2. Cover bottom of bowl with a layer of the ladyfingers, arranging them artistically to make attractive pattern. Stand the remaining ladyfingers upright around sides of bowl. Reserve any extra.
3. Mix rum and Marsala and sprinkle over ladyfingers so slightly moistened. Grate chocolate and almonds in container of blender or food processor. Set aside.
4. Whip cream until it begins to thicken, then add sugar and vanilla and continue beating until very stiff. Fold in chocolate and nuts and spoon mixture into ladyfinger-lined dish. If you have extra ladyfingers, arrange them on top.
5. Cover bowl tightly with plastic wrap or foil and refrigerate overnight. At serving time, unmold *zuccotto* onto plate and peel off foil. Sprinkle top with cocoa pressed through small sieve.

Mushroom Salad
Fettuccine alla Carbonara
Steamed Broccoli with Lemon Juice and Olive Oil

A classic Roman dish is *spaghetti* (*fettuccine* in this version) *alla carbonara*, which is seasoned with bacon and cheese. Take care to add the beaten eggs, cheese, and cream mixture slowly to the hot pasta; otherwise the eggs cook too quickly and scramble. You can use smoked American bacon—but for an authentic flavor, it is worth buying *pancetta*, a mild unsmoked Italian bacon.

You can serve the broccoli stalks as in the photo below, arranged cartwheel fashion, and insert curled, thinly sliced lemon wedges in the hub.

WHAT TO DRINK

This subtle combination of simple ingredients will match either a white or a red wine. An ideal white would be a dry (*secco*) Orvieto or a California Sauvignon Blanc; an ideal red, a young Chianti.

SHOPPING LIST AND STAPLES

⅓ pound bacon
1 bunch broccoli

Steamed broccoli with a delicate lemon and olive oil dressing is a perfect partner for fettuccine alla carbonara and a mushroom and watercress salad.

½ pound fresh mushrooms
1 bunch watercress
1 bunch fresh parsley
2 lemons plus 1 lemon (optional)
1 to 1½ cups light cream or half-and-half
5 tablespoons butter
2 eggs
¼ pound Romano cheese
1 pound fettuccine
⅓ cup plus 3 tablespoons olive oil
Salt and pepper

UTENSILS

Large stockpot or kettle with cover
Large skillet
Small saucepan
Vegetable steamer
2 small bowls
Colander
Measuring cups and spoons
All-purpose knife
Grater

1. Follow pasta recipe steps 1 through 3.
2. Chop parsley and juice lemon for salad recipe and follow salad recipe steps 1 and 2.
3. Grate Romano cheese for pasta recipe and follow pasta recipe steps 4 and 5.
4. Follow broccoli recipe steps 1 and 2. Juice lemon for broccoli recipe and follow broccoli recipe step 3.
5. Follow pasta recipe steps 6 and 7.
6. Follow salad recipe step 3, and serve.
7. Follow pasta recipe step 8, broccoli recipe step 4, and serve both.

RECIPES

Mushroom Salad

½ pound fresh mushrooms
⅓ cup olive oil
2 tablespoons fresh lemon juice
Salt and freshly ground black pepper
1 bunch watercress
2 tablespoons chopped fresh parsley

1. Rinse and trim mushrooms. Do not peel or remove stems. Thinly slice mushrooms.
2. Mix olive oil and lemon juice in bowl and add salt and pepper to taste. Add mushrooms and toss gently.
3. Place watercress on 4 serving plates and top with mushrooms. Sprinkle with chopped parsley.

Fettuccine alla Carbonara

⅓ pound bacon
2 eggs
1 to 1½ cups light cream or half-and-half
½ cup freshly grated Romano cheese

1 pound fettuccine
5 tablespoons butter

1. Bring salted water to a boil in stockpot or kettle.
2. Fry bacon in skillet until crisp. Drain on paper towels; then cut into small pieces.
3. Break eggs into bowl and beat lightly. Set aside.
4. Heat 1 cup of the cream and cheese in saucepan, stirring to combine until warmed through.
5. Stir fettuccine into boiling salted water and stir again. It should not cook more than 2 minutes if you are using fresh fettuccine, 5 to 7 minutes if using dried.
6. Drain pasta in colander and return it to stockpot. Stir in butter.
7. Add half of the warmed cheese and cream and toss well. Cover.
8. After serving mushroom salad, turn on heat under pasta and add eggs, bacon, and remaining cream-and-cheese mixture. Toss well until heated through. If pasta seems dry, add the remaining ½ cup of cream.

Steamed Broccoli with Lemon Juice and Olive Oil

1 bunch broccoli
Salt and freshly ground black pepper
3 tablespoons olive oil
3 tablespoons fresh lemon juice
Lemon wedges for garnish (optional)

1. Wash and trim broccoli. If stalks are large, split lengthwise into 2 or 3 pieces.
2. Place broccoli in vegetable steamer over boiling water and steam until barely tender, 5 to 7 minutes. Remove from heat and put in warm serving bowl.
3. Sprinkle with salt, pepper, olive oil, and lemon juice.
4. Serve with lemon wedges as garnish, if desired.

Felice and Lidia Bastianich

Cooking comes naturally to Felice and Lidia Bastianich. As a youth he worked at his father's small northern Italian inn, and from the age of 14, she cooked for her entire family. Advocates of using only top-quality ingredients, the Bastianiches plan meals—both at home and in their restaurant—around what is best in the marketplace, then fill in with their own homemade prosciutto and pasta. By adhering to the unpretentious cooking traditions of their native Istria, the Bastianiches serve meals that are simple and nourishing. As Lidia Bastianich says, "We want our customers and guests to be able to duplicate our recipes, so we stick to uncomplicated foods and methods."

Istrian simplicity underlies each of the menus they present here. The sautéed shrimp of Menu 1 are lightly seasoned with garlic, lemon juice, and white wine, and are served on a bed of risotto. The asparagus spears are broiled with a light coating of melted butter and grated Parmesan.

In Istria, where game is abundant, cooks often serve polenta with wild fowl. Menu 2 offers quail in a tomato sauce flavored with bay leaves, rosemary, and cloves, presented on a platter with polenta. A green bean and bacon salad adds color and texture to this cold-weather meal.

Chicken is the entrée for Menu 3. The breasts are dredged with flour, dipped in parsley and grated Parmesan, and then sautéed in stock with wine and lemon juice. A substantial dish of Swiss chard and potatoes complements the fowl.

A heaping platter of risotto topped with whole shrimp in a garlic and parsley sauce is a delightful entrée for an informal spring dinner. The crisp-tender asparagus spears should be served on a warmed platter.

51

Scampi with Quick Risotto
Asparagus Gratinati

When buying raw shrimp, select those that are plump and odor-free; avoid any with meat that has shrunk away from the shell, which indicates that the shrimp have been frozen and thawed. If the shrimp do not have the shells and veins removed, follow step 1 of the recipe. Because they are highly perishable, shrimp should be purchased at the last minute. If you must store them, do so in a covered container in the coldest part of the refrigerator. After cooking, the shrimp should be firm and crisp.

WHAT TO DRINK

A well-chilled fruity white wine such as an Italian Chardonnay or Vernaccia, or a California Sauvignon Blanc or Riesling, goes well with the scampi.

SHOPPING LIST AND STAPLES

24 large shrimp (about 1¼ pounds total weight)
16 medium-size asparagus spears (about 1 pound total weight)
Medium-size yellow onion
4 cloves garlic
Small bunch parsley
1 lemon
3 to 4 cups chicken stock, preferably homemade (see page 13), or canned
1 stick plus 2 tablespoons unsalted butter
6 ounces Parmesan cheese, preferably imported
¼ cup plus 2 tablespoons olive oil
2 cups long-grain rice
3 tablespoons dry bread crumbs
Salt and freshly ground black pepper
½ cup dry white wine

UTENSILS

Food processor (optional)
Stockpot or large saucepan with cover
Large heavy-gauge skillet
Large heavy-gauge saucepan with cover
Small heavy-gauge saucepan or butter warmer
13 x 9-inch flameproof baking dish
Large serving platter
Colander
Measuring cups and spoons
Chef's knife
Paring knife
2 wooden spoons
Metal tongs
Grater (if not using processor)
Juicer
Kitchen string

START-TO-FINISH STEPS

1. Grate enough Parmesan to measure 1 cup for risotto recipe and ½ cup for asparagus recipe.
2. Follow scampi recipe steps 1 and 2.
3. Follow asparagus recipe steps 1 through 3 and scampi recipe step 3.
4. Follow asparagus recipe step 4 and risotto recipe steps 1 through 3.
5. Follow asparagus recipe steps 5 through 7.
6. Follow risotto recipe steps 4 and 5, and scampi recipe steps 4 through 6.
7. Follow asparagus recipe step 8 and scampi recipe step 7.
8. Follow risotto recipe step 6, scampi recipe step 8, and serve with asparagus.

RECIPES

Scampi with Quick Risotto

24 large shrimp (about 1¼ pounds total weight)
4 cloves garlic
Small bunch parsley
1 lemon
¼ cup olive oil
4 tablespoons unsalted butter
½ cup dry white wine
Salt and freshly ground black pepper
3 tablespoons dry bread crumbs
Quick Risotto (see following recipe)

1. Pinch off legs of shrimp, several at a time, then bend back and snap off sharp, beaklike pieces of shell just above tail. Remove shell and discard. Using sharp paring knife, make shallow incision along back of each shrimp, exposing digestive vein. Extract vein and discard (see illustration on next page).
2. Place shrimp in colander, rinse under cold running water, drain, and dry with paper towels. Set aside.
3. Peel and finely chop garlic. Rinse parsley, dry, and chop enough to measure 3 tablespoons. Squeeze enough lemon juice to measure 2 teaspoons; set aside.
4. In large heavy-gauge skillet, heat olive oil over

medium-high heat. Add shrimp and sauté, stirring, about 2 minutes, or until slightly golden.

5. Stir in garlic and sauté 3 minutes, or until golden.

6. Add butter, lemon juice, white wine, and salt and pepper to taste, and cook about 5 minutes, or until shrimp begin to curl and turn opaque.

7. Sprinkle shrimp with parsley and bread crumbs, and cook another minute.

8. Turn shrimp and sauce onto platter with risotto.

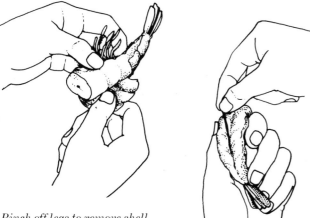

Pinch off legs to remove shell.

Extract digestive vein with your fingers.

Quick Risotto

Medium-size yellow onion
2 tablespoons olive oil
2 cups long-grain rice
4 tablespoons unsalted butter
3 to 4 cups chicken stock
Salt and freshly ground black pepper
1 cup freshly grated Parmesan cheese

1. Peel and chop onion.

2. In large heavy-gauge saucepan, heat oil over medium-high heat. Add onion and sauté 5 minutes, or until golden.

3. Stir in rice, butter, 3 cups chicken stock, and salt and pepper to taste. Reduce heat to low, cover, and cook, stirring occasionally, 10 minutes. If rice sticks to pan, add small amounts of stock, stirring after each addition until incorporated.

4. After 10 minutes, remove cover and allow excess stock to boil off; or, if rice seems too dry, add small amounts of stock, cover, and continue simmering another 5 to 10 minutes, or until rice is tender and all liquid is absorbed. Keep pan covered until ready to serve.

5. Meanwhile, place serving platter under hot running water to warm.

6. When ready to serve, dry platter. Add Parmesan to rice and stir until combined. Turn out onto warm platter.

Asparagus Gratinati

16 medium-size asparagus spears (about 1 pound total weight)

2 tablespoons unsalted butter
½ cup freshly grated Parmesan cheese

1. In stockpot or large saucepan, bring 1 quart of water to a boil over high heat.

2. Meanwhile, rinse asparagus under cold running water and drain. Trim off woody stems and, if desired, peel.

3. Using kitchen string, tie asparagus into 2 bundles. Stand upright in pot, cover, and cook over high heat 6 minutes, or until crisp-tender.

4. With tongs, transfer bundles to colander, untie, and let cool.

5. In small heavy-gauge saucepan or butter warmer, melt butter over low heat.

6. In flameproof baking dish, arrange asparagus spears side by side in single layer and drizzle with melted butter. Sprinkle with Parmesan and set aside.

7. Preheat broiler.

8. Before serving, broil asparagus about 4 inches from heating element 3 to 5 minutes, or just until cheese turns light golden.

ADDED TOUCH

When you ignite the warmed brandy and Grand Marnier for flambéing the strawberries, the flames may be high at first but should die down quickly. If they do not subside, simply put a cover on the skillet.

Flamed Strawberries

1 pint fresh strawberries
Large orange
½ pint heavy cream
¼ cup sugar
2 tablespoons Grand Marnier or other orange liqueur
2 tablespoons brandy
1 pint vanilla ice cream

1. Place medium-size bowl and beaters in freezer to chill.

2. Rinse strawberries and pat dry with paper towels. With sharp paring knife, hull berries and set aside.

3. Rinse orange and dry. Grate enough rind to measure about 3 tablespoons. Cut orange in half. Squeeze juice from one half, reserving remaining half for another use.

4. Pour heavy cream into chilled bowl and whip with electric mixer at high speed until stiff. Cover and refrigerate.

5. In small heavy-gauge skillet, heat sugar over medium heat, stirring, until melted and golden, about 5 minutes.

6. Stir orange rind into sugar and cook about 2 minutes, or until sugar is light brown and syrupy.

7. Add strawberries, orange juice, Grand Marnier, and brandy, and stir to combine. Simmer gently, turning berries to coat with syrup, another 3 minutes.

8. Remove skillet from heat and, averting your face, ignite syrup. When flames have subsided, set skillet aside.

9. Place a generous spoonful of whipped cream in center of each of 4 dessert plates. Top each with a scoop of ice cream and surround "islands" with strawberries. Spoon remaining syrup over ice cream and serve.

Quail with Polenta
Green Bean, Red Onion, and Bacon Salad

Arrange the sautéed quail attractively around the polenta and garnish with a sprig of parsley, if desired; extra sauce may be served on the side. Bacon and red onion rings add color to the green beans.

A popular game bird considered a delicacy throughout the world, quail has pale-colored flesh that tastes like a gamy version of dark-meat chicken. Fresh quail are now available year-round at many butchers, but can also be ordered through the mail. When buying quail, select those that are plump and silky-skinned with no discoloration. Small Rock Cornish hens can be substituted for quail. They are larger than quail, so you will need only one hen per serving.

WHAT TO DRINK

For this cold-weather meal, the cooks suggest a full-bodied red Barolo or Barbaresco from the Italian Piedmont or a Merlot from Friuli. California Merlot is a good domestic alternative.

SHOPPING LIST AND STAPLES

8 quail (about 3½ pounds total weight), or 4 small
   Rock Cornish hens (about ¾ pound each)
6 slices bacon
1 pound green beans
2 medium-size yellow onions (about 1 pound total weight)
Small red onion
Small bunch fresh rosemary, or ½ teaspoon dried
3 tablespoons unsalted butter
2 ounces Parmesan cheese (optional)
2 cups chicken stock, preferably homemade
   (see page 13), or canned
6-ounce can tomato paste
1 cup olive or vegetable oil, approximately
3 tablespoons white or red wine vinegar
1 cup imported coarsely ground cornmeal or 1⅓ cups regular yellow cornmeal
8 bay leaves, approximately
4 cloves
Salt and freshly ground black pepper
1 cup dry white wine

UTENSILS

Food processor (optional)
Large heavy-gauge skillet
Small skillet
Large heavy-gauge saucepan
Medium-size saucepan with cover

Large heatproof serving platter
Large bowl
Small bowl
Sauceboat or small serving bowl
Colander
Strainer
Rubber spatula
Measuring cups and spoons
Chef's knife
2 wooden spoons
Grater (if not using processor)

START-TO-FINISH STEPS

1. Coarsely chop bacon for quail and salad recipes.
2. Follow salad recipe steps 1 through 3.
3. Follow quail recipe steps 1 and 2.
4. Follow salad recipe step 4 and polenta recipe steps 1 and 2.
5. Follow quail recipe steps 3 through 5.
6. While quail browns, follow salad recipe steps 5 through 8.
7. Follow quail recipe steps 6 and 7.
8. Follow polenta recipe steps 3 through 5, if cooking quail; if cooking hens, wait 10 minutes before beginning polenta recipe step 3, and then proceed through step 5.
9. Follow quail recipe step 8 and serve with polenta and salad.

RECIPES

Quail with Polenta

2 medium-size yellow onions (about 1 pound total weight)
Small bunch fresh rosemary, or ½ teaspoon dried
½ cup olive or vegetable oil
2 slices bacon, coarsely chopped
4 cloves
3 bay leaves
Salt
Freshly ground black pepper
8 quail (about 3½ pounds total weight), or 4 small Rock Cornish hens (about ¾ pound each)
2 ounces Parmesan cheese (optional)
2 teaspoons tomato paste
1 cup dry white wine
2 cups chicken stock
Polenta (see following recipe)

1. Peel and dice onions. Rinse fresh rosemary and pat dry with paper towels. Chop enough to measure 1 teaspoon.
2. In large heavy-gauge skillet, heat oil over medium heat. Add onions, rosemary, bacon, cloves, bay leaves, and salt and pepper to taste, and sauté, stirring occasionally, 5 to 10 minutes, or until onions are nicely browned.
3. Add quail or hens and brown 8 to 10 minutes on one side.
4. If using Parmesan, grate enough in food processor or with grater to measure ¼ cup; set aside.
5. Turn birds and cook another 8 to 10 minutes on other side, or until evenly browned.

6. In small bowl, blend tomato paste and wine. Add mixture to skillet and stir into pan juices until blended, basting birds as you stir. Raise heat to medium-high and simmer until liquid has almost evaporated, about 12 minutes.
7. Add stock and simmer another 15 minutes for quail, or 25 to 30 minutes for hens, or until tip of knife easily penetrates breast and juices run clear.
8. Transfer birds to platter with polenta. Pour sauce through strainer set over sauceboat or small bowl, extruding as much liquid as possible with back of spoon. Spoon sauce over each bird and around polenta. Sprinkle birds with cheese, if using, and serve with remaining sauce.

Polenta

1 cup imported coarsely ground cornmeal or 1⅓ cups regular yellow cornmeal
½ teaspoon salt
3 tablespoons unsalted butter
4 or 5 bay leaves

1. Preheat oven to 200 degrees.
2. In large heavy-gauge saucepan, bring 4 cups water to a boil over high heat.
3. Place serving platter in oven to warm.
4. Reduce heat under saucepan to medium and add cornmeal in a very slow, steady stream, stirring constantly with wooden spoon. Add salt, butter, and bay leaves, and continue stirring until polenta thickens and pulls away from sides of pan, about 15 minutes.
5. Remove bay leaves and discard. With rubber spatula, turn out polenta into middle of warm platter.

Green Bean, Red Onion, and Bacon Salad

1 pound green beans
Small red onion
4 slices bacon, coarsely chopped
3 tablespoons white or red wine vinegar
3 tablespoons olive or vegetable oil, approximately
Salt and freshly ground black pepper

1. In medium-size saucepan, bring 2 quarts of water to a boil over high heat.
2. Meanwhile, trim beans. Peel red onion and cut into thin slices. Separate into rings and set aside.
3. Add beans to boiling water, lower heat to medium, cover, and cook 5 minutes, or just until crisp-tender.
4. Turn beans into colander and refresh under cold running water. Drain and set aside to cool.
5. In small skillet, cook bacon over medium heat, stirring occasionally, 5 minutes, or until crisp.
6. Meanwhile, transfer beans to large bowl.
7. Remove skillet from heat and pour off bacon fat. Add vinegar, stir, and return to heat for 1 minute.
8. Pour bacon and vinegar mixture over beans, add oil and salt and pepper to taste, and toss until combined. Adjust seasoning, toss again, and arrange on serving platter. Top with onion rings and set aside until ready to serve.

Chicken Felice
Swiss Chard and Potatoes

Crisp golden chicken breasts topped with a lemon and wine sauce are accompanied by Swiss chard mashed with potatoes.

The lemony, cheese-encrusted boneless chicken breasts are simple to prepare and are an impressive dinner for company. The vegetable dish of Swiss chard and coarsely mashed potatoes can be varied if you wish: Substitute spinach or savoy cabbage for the chard.

For the best flavor, you should always buy Parmesan cheese by the chunk and grate it at home as needed; a quarter pound produces one cup of grated cheese. Slice off the rind before grating. If you are using a food processor to grate the cheese, cut the cheese into ½-inch cubes before grating with the steel blade.

WHAT TO DRINK

A dry, lightly acidic white Pinot Grigio, Gavi, or Verdicchio would be good here, or choose a domestic Sauvignon Blanc or fully dry Chenin Blanc.

SHOPPING LIST AND STAPLES

4 skinless, boneless chicken breasts (about 1½ pounds total weight), halved and pounded ¼ inch thick

2 bunches Swiss chard (about 4 pounds total weight)
3 medium-size potatoes (about 1¼ pounds total weight)
Small bunch parsley
4 cloves garlic
3 lemons
2½ cups chicken stock, preferably homemade (see page 13), or canned
4 eggs
¼ cup milk
7 tablespoons unsalted butter
2 ounces Parmesan cheese
¼ cup olive oil
½ cup vegetable oil
1 cup all-purpose flour
Salt and freshly ground black pepper
1 cup dry white wine

UTENSILS

Food processor (optional)
Stockpot or large kettle
Large heavy-gauge skillet

Large heavy-gauge saucepan
Large heatproof platter
9-inch pie pan
Large heatproof bowl
Medium-size bowl
Colander
Measuring cups and spoons
Chef's knife
Paring knife
2 wooden spoons
Potato masher
Vegetable peeler (optional)
Metal tongs
Grater (if not using processor)
Juicer

START-TO-FINISH STEPS

1. Follow Swiss chard recipe steps 1 through 4.
2. Follow chicken recipe steps 1 through 3.
3. Follow Swiss chard recipe step 5.
4. Follow chicken recipe steps 4 through 6.
5. Follow Swiss chard recipe step 6.
6. Follow chicken recipe steps 7 through 10.
7. Follow Swiss chard recipe steps 7 through 10.
8. Follow chicken recipe steps 11 and 12 and Swiss chard recipe step 11.
9. Follow chicken recipe steps 13 and 14, and serve with Swiss chard and potatoes.

RECIPES

Chicken Felice

4 tablespoons unsalted butter
Small bunch parsley
2 ounces Parmesan cheese
4 skinless, boneless chicken breasts (about 1½ pounds total weight), halved and pounded ¼ inch thick
4 eggs
¼ cup milk
Salt and freshly ground black pepper
½ cup vegetable oil
1 cup all-purpose flour
3 lemons
1 cup dry white wine
2½ cups chicken stock

1. Preheat oven to 200 degrees. Set out butter to reach room temperature.
2. Wash and dry parsley; chop enough to measure 2 tablespoons and refrigerate remainder for another use. In food processor fitted with steel blade, or with grater, grate enough cheese to measure ½ cup; set aside.
3. Rinse chicken and dry with paper towels.
4. Beat eggs in medium-size bowl. Add milk, grated cheese, chopped parsley, and salt and pepper to taste, and stir to combine.
5. In large heavy-gauge skillet, heat vegetable oil over medium-high heat until hot but not smoking.

6. Place flour in pie pan. One by one, dredge each breast lightly with flour, shake off excess, and dip in egg and cheese mixture, letting excess mixture drip off into bowl. Place coated breasts in skillet and fry 5 minutes on one side, or until golden.
7. Meanwhile, line heatproof platter with double thickness of paper towels. Rinse 2 lemons and dry. Cut each lemon into rounds, then halve, and set aside. Squeeze enough juice from remaining lemon to measure 2 tablespoons.
8. With tongs, turn breasts and fry another 5 minutes on other side, or until golden.
9. Transfer chicken to paper-towel-lined platter, loosely cover with foil, and keep warm in oven.
10. Pour off oil from skillet. Add wine, lemon juice, stock, and salt and pepper to taste to skillet and bring to a boil over medium-high heat. Continue boiling until sauce is reduced to about 1 cup, about 10 to 15 minutes.
11. Place 4 dinner plates in oven to warm.
12. Reduce heat under skillet to medium. Return chicken to skillet and simmer 15 minutes.
13. Transfer chicken to warm plates. Add butter, 1 tablespoon at a time, to liquid in pan, swirling after each addition until butter is incorporated.
14. Remove pan from heat. Top each breast with a generous spoonful of sauce and garnish with lemon slices.

Swiss Chard and Potatoes

2 bunches Swiss chard (about 4 pounds total weight)
3 medium-size potatoes (about 1¼ pounds total weight)
4 cloves garlic
¼ cup olive oil
3 tablespoons unsalted butter
Salt and freshly ground black pepper

1. In stockpot or large kettle, bring 6 quarts of water to a boil over high heat.
2. Meanwhile, trim off lower (stem) half of Swiss chard. Cut leaf tops into 1-inch pieces and wash thoroughly in several changes of cold water to remove all traces of grit.
3. Peel and quarter potatoes.
4. Add potatoes to boiling water and cook 5 minutes.
5. Add Swiss chard to potatoes and cook another 10 minutes.
6. Transfer vegetables to colander and drain.
7. Bruise garlic cloves with flat side of knife blade and peel.
8. In large heavy-gauge saucepan, heat oil over medium heat. Add garlic and sauté, stirring occasionally, until browned, 2 to 3 minutes.
9. Add Swiss chard, potatoes, butter, and salt and pepper to taste, and mash coarsely.
10. Cook mixture, stirring constantly with wooden spoon, 5 minutes.
11. Remove garlic cloves and discard. Turn vegetables into large heatproof bowl and keep warm in 200-degree oven until ready to serve.

Evelyne Slomon

MENU 1 (Left)
Antipasto
Hearty Vegetable Soup
Home-style Pizza with Peppers

MENU 2
Sicilian Pizza
Escarole, Chicory, and Radicchio Salad
Fresh Fennel and Oranges

MENU 3
Calzoni with Three Cheeses
Stuffed Eggplant Fans
Arugula and Leaf Lettuce Salad

E velyne Slomon believes in pizza. "When made with cheese, vegetables, and perhaps some meat on a homemade crust, pizza is a nutritionally complete meal," she says. It requires no special equipment—only an oven, a bowl, and a flat baking sheet—and can be assembled in no time using a food processor to knead the dough. Even if you prepare the dough by hand, it does not take long (for details on making pizza dough by hand, see page 8).

In Italy, pizza varies markedly from one region to another. Evelyne Slomon's three menus demonstrate the adaptability of this dish. The home-style pizza of Menu 1 is known in Lombardy as *fitascetta*. This ring-shaped flat bread is usually topped with onions, but here it is covered with cheese and sautéed strips of red, yellow, and green pepper. *Fitascetta* is normally served as a bread, not as a main course, so the cook has added an antipasto platter and a soup to the meal.

Menu 2 offers the doughy deep-dish Sicilian pizza called *scacciata*, which is excellent hot or cold. This substantial pie, typical of the earthy fare of Sicily, has a thick, chewy crust and a topping of sautéed eggplant, anchovies, tomatoes, cheese, and olives. It is accompanied by two salads: one of escarole, chicory, and radicchio, and the other made with fennel and orange slices sweetened and dusted with cinnamon.

Neapolitan *calzoni*, or individual pizza turnovers enclosing a savory filling, are the main course of Menu 3. The cook uses an herb-seasoned blend of three cheeses to fill the *calzoni*, and serves them with stuffed eggplant fans and a tossed salad.

Topped with cheese and bell pepper strips, the pizza ring is good served hot or at room temperature. Offer it with a tureen of richly textured vegetable soup and a colorful antipasto platter.

Antipasto
Hearty Vegetable Soup
Home-style Pizza with Peppers

The antipasto can be prepared several hours in advance, covered with plastic wrap, and refrigerated. If you do so, remove the antipasto from the refrigerator 20 minutes before serving to bring it to room temperature.

To vary the pizza ring, use any combination of bell peppers you wish, and substitute some other mild cheese for the Fontina. Or fill the pizza sandwich-style: Split the ring in half, place a layer of arugula or lettuce leaves on the bottom ring, and top with slices of salami and a layer of sliced tomatoes. Drizzle a mild vinaigrette over the filling, replace the top ring, and cut the pizza into wedges. As a substitute for the spinach in the soup, try broccoli rabe, dandelion greens, escarole, or Swiss chard.

WHAT TO DRINK

A fruity red Dolcetto or Barbera is an excellent choice with this menu.

SHOPPING LIST AND STAPLES

¼ pound thinly sliced Genoa salami or other good-quality salami
2 ounces pancetta, prosciutto, or bacon
1 pound spinach
1 pint cherry tomatoes
3 small bell peppers, preferably 1 green, 1 red, and 1 yellow
Medium-size onion
Small bunch fresh parsley
2 cloves garlic, approximately
1 cup chicken stock, preferably homemade (see page 13), or canned
½ pound Italian Fontina cheese or other mild cheese
¼ pound Bel Paese cheese or other mild cheese
2 ounces Parmesan cheese, preferably imported
28-ounce can whole plum tomatoes
15-ounce can cannellini or other white or red beans
¼ cup plus 3 tablespoons olive oil
1 tablespoon vegetable oil, approximately
12-ounce jar medium-hot pickled peppers
7½-ounce jar oil-cured black olives or other Mediterranean olives
3½ cups all-purpose flour, preferably unbleached, approximately
1 package active dry yeast
Salt and freshly ground black pepper

UTENSILS

Food processor or blender
Large skillet with cover
Large heavy-gauge saucepan with cover
15-inch round pizza pan or 17 x 11-inch cookie sheet
Strainer
Measuring cups and spoons
Chef's knife
Serrated bread knife or pizza wheel
Paring knife
2 wooden spoons or spatulas
Grater (if not using processor)

START-TO-FINISH STEPS

1. Follow antipasto recipe steps 1 through 7.
2. Follow pizza recipe steps 1 through 8.
3. Follow soup recipe steps 1 through 4.
4. Follow pizza recipe steps 9 through 11.
5. Follow soup recipe steps 5 and 6.
6. Follow pizza recipe step 12 and soup recipe step 7.
7. While pizza is baking and soup is simmering, serve antipasto.
8. Follow soup recipe step 8 and serve with pizza.

RECIPES

Antipasto

12-ounce jar medium-hot pickled peppers
¼ pound Bel Paese cheese or other mild cheese
¼ pound thinly sliced Genoa salami or other good-quality salami
1 pint cherry tomatoes
6 sprigs parsley for garnish
2 dozen oil-cured black olives or other Mediterranean olives

1. Drain pickled peppers. Slit each pepper open by inserting point of paring knife ¼ inch below stem and cutting lengthwise down through tip. Remove seeds with tip of knife and discard.
2. Cut cheese into 2-inch-long by ¼-inch-thick pieces. Insert 1 piece of cheese into each pepper.
3. Overlap salami along outer edge of serving platter.
4. Arrange stuffed peppers over salami slices with tips facing outward.

5. Wash cherry tomatoes and dry with paper towels, leaving stems on if desired. Place tomatoes in center of platter.
6. Rinse parsley and dry with paper towels.
7. Scatter olives over platter and garnish with parsley.

Hearty Vegetable Soup

1 pound spinach
Medium-size onion
1 or 2 cloves garlic
2 ounces pancetta, prosciutto, or bacon
2 ounces Parmesan cheese
28-ounce can whole plum tomatoes
15-ounce can cannellini or other white or red beans
¼ cup olive oil
1 cup chicken stock
Salt and freshly ground pepper

1. Wash spinach thoroughly in several changes of cold water. Remove tough stems and discard. Coarsely chop spinach to make about 4 cups.
2. Peel and chop onion. Peel and finely mince 1 or 2 cloves garlic, according to taste. Cut pancetta into ½-inch cubes.
3. Using food processor or grater, grate Parmesan to make ½ cup; set aside.
4. Purée tomatoes with their juice in two batches in food processor or blender. Turn beans into strainer and rinse under cold running water; set aside.
5. Heat oil in large heavy-gauge saucepan over medium-high heat. Add onion and pancetta, and sauté 2 to 3 minutes, or until onion wilts and pancetta begins to brown.
6. Stir in spinach and garlic. Raise heat to high and cook, stirring, until spinach is wilted, about 2 minutes.
7. Add puréed tomatoes, beans, and stock, and bring to a boil. Lower heat and simmer, stirring occasionally, 10 to 15 minutes.
8. Add salt and pepper to taste and turn soup into tureen. Top with a generous spoonful of Parmesan and serve with remaining cheese.

Home-style Pizza with Peppers

1 package active dry yeast
3½ cups all-purpose flour, preferably unbleached, approximately
Salt
1 tablespoon vegetable oil, approximately
3 small bell peppers, preferably 1 green, 1 red, and 1 yellow
3 tablespoons olive oil
½ pound Italian Fontina cheese or other mild cheese
Freshly ground black pepper

1. Preheat oven to 450 degrees.
2. If not using food processor, prepare dough by hand (see page 8) and then proceed to step 4. If using processor, fit with dough blade or steel blade and pour in 1 cup hot tap water. Sprinkle in yeast and pulse machine on and off once or twice to dissolve yeast.
3. With processor running, add 3 cups flour, and ½ teaspoon salt; continue to process 10 to 15 seconds, or until

dough forms a ball. (With the steel blade, the dough often does not form a ball but forms a layer under or over the blade. This is fine.) Test consistency of dough by squeezing a small portion in your hand. If it sticks, add a bit more flour and process until no longer sticky; if dough is dry, add water, 1 tablespoon at a time, and process until smooth and elastic. Let dough rise in processor bowl 10 minutes.
4. Meanwhile, grease pizza pan or cookie sheet with vegetable oil and set aside.
5. Wash peppers and dry with paper towels. Halve, core, and seed peppers; cut into ¼-inch-thick strips.
6. Heat olive oil in large skillet over high heat. Add peppers and cook, covered, 3 to 4 minutes, stirring occasionally to prevent sticking.
7. Meanwhile, cut cheese into ⅛-inch-thick slices.
8. Remove peppers from heat and season with salt and pepper to taste; set aside.
9. Transfer dough to lightly floured work surface and knead briefly. Shape into 12-inch circle, pressing down with your fingertips. Push your fist down into center of circle to form 4-inch hole (like a large doughnut).
10. Transfer dough ring to prepared pan and reshape it if necessary.
11. Cover dough with cheese slices, top with peppers and their accumulated liquid, and let stand in a warm place 5 minutes.
12. Bake 15 to 20 minutes, or until golden and crusty.

ADDED TOUCH

This refreshing, creamy sherbet mixes quickly and does not require an ice-cream maker. You can substitute lime, orange, or grapefruit juice for the lemon juice and, if fresh raspberries are out of season, use whole frozen berries packed in heavy syrup.

Lemon Sorbetto with Raspberries

¾ cup freshly squeezed lemon juice
¾ cup superfine sugar
¾ cup heavy cream
1 cup fresh raspberries or whole frozen raspberries in heavy syrup
4 sprigs fresh mint for garnish (optional)
4 tablespoons Sambuca

1. Combine lemon juice and sugar in medium-size mixing bowl and stir until sugar is completely dissolved.
2. Stir in heavy cream.
3. Pour mixture into metal ice-cube tray (without sections) and freeze about 6 hours, or until solid.
4. One or two hours before serving, divide sherbet among individual bowls and return to freezer until ready to serve.
5. If using fresh raspberries, rinse gently in cold water and pat dry with paper towels.
6. Wash mint, if using, and dry.
7. Just before serving, remove sherbet from freezer. Top each serving with berries, drizzle with Sambuca, and garnish with a mint sprig, if desired.

Sicilian Pizza
Escarole, Chicory, and Radicchio Salad
Fresh Fennel and Oranges

For a family-style meal, serve a wedge of deep-dish pizza, a tossed salad, and sliced fennel and oranges.

When you make pizza, you learn that there are no hard and fast rules for what to use as a topping or filling. In this recipe, you can vary the topping by substituting two or three slices of fresh Italian sweet or hot sausages for the anchovies and capers. Use Provolone instead of *caciocavallo* cheese, or substitute chunks of zucchini for the eggplant. You can also season this pizza with oregano, fresh mint, and thyme.

The refreshing slices of raw fennel and orange sections are garnished with *pignoli*, or pine nuts. These slender, cream-colored nuts are popular throughout Italy in sweet and savory dishes. They come from a variety of Mediterra-

nean pine tree and have a delicate flavor. Because they turn rancid quickly, refrigerate any unused nuts in an airtight container. Pine nuts are sold in gourmet shops, health food stores, and many supermarkets. Use toasted almonds as a substitute, if necessary.

WHAT TO DRINK

To match the flavors of this meal, serve your guests a good dry red Sicilian wine such as Corvo Rosso or Etna Rosso. A good California Gamay is a fine domestic alternative.

Small eggplant (about 1 pound)
1 pound fresh tomatoes, or 28-ounce can whole tomatoes
Small head chicory
Small head escarole
Small head radicchio
Large fennel bulb with leaves, or small bunch celery
3 cloves garlic
2 small bunches parsley, or small bunch parsley plus
    small bunch basil
Medium-size lemon
4 large navel oranges
Medium-size juice orange
¾ pound mozzarella cheese
2 ounces caciocavallo or imported Provolone cheese
2-ounce tin anchovies
¾ cup olive oil, approximately
1 tablespoon vegetable oil, approximately
2 tablespoons red wine vinegar
2-ounce jar capers
7½-ounce jar oil-cured black olives
3½ cups all-purpose flour, approximately
2 tablespoons sugar or honey
1 package active dry yeast
2-ounce jar pignoli (pine nuts)
Small hot dried chili pepper
Pinch of cinnamon
Salt and freshly ground black pepper

UTENSILS

Food processor (optional)
Large skillet
15-inch round pizza pan, or 17 x 11-inch jelly-roll pan
13 x 9-inch cookie sheet
Large salad bowl
Medium-size bowl
2 small bowls
Salad spinner (optional)
Strainer
Measuring cups and spoons
Chef's knife
Serrated bread knife or pizza wheel
Paring knife
Wooden spoon
Spatula
Juicer (optional)
Grater (if not using processor)
Rolling pin

START-TO-FINISH STEPS

1. Wash and dry parsley and basil, if using. Mince enough parsley to measure 2 tablespoons for pizza recipe and enough parsley or basil to measure 2 tablespoons for escarole salad recipe. Peel garlic; mince 2 cloves for pizza recipe and crush 1 clove for escarole salad recipe.
2. Follow pizza recipe steps 1 through 11.

3. While pizza is baking, follow fennel and oranges recipe steps 1 through 7.
4. Follow pizza recipe step 12.
5. Follow escarole salad recipe step 1 and remove pizza from oven.
6. Follow escarole salad recipe steps 2 and 3, and serve with pizza and fennel and oranges.

RECIPES

Sicilian Pizza

1 package active dry yeast
½ cup olive oil
3½ cups all-purpose flour, approximately
Salt
1 tablespoon vegetable oil, approximately
Small hot dried chili pepper
Small eggplant (about 1 pound)
2-ounce tin anchovies
2 tablespoons capers
1 pound fresh tomatoes, or 28-ounce can whole tomatoes
2 cloves garlic, peeled and minced
2 tablespoons minced parsley
2 ounces caciocavallo or imported Provolone cheese
¾ pound mozzarella cheese
5 oil-cured black olives

1. Preheat oven to 450 degrees.
2. If not using food processor, prepare dough by hand (see page 8) and proceed to step 4. If using processor, fit with dough blade or steel blade and pour in ¾ cup hot tap water. Sprinkle in yeast and pulse machine on and off once or twice to dissolve the yeast.
3. With processor running, add ¼ cup olive oil, 3 cups flour, and ¼ teaspoon salt, and continue to process until dough forms a ball. (With the steel blade, the dough often does not form a ball but forms a layer under or over the blade. This is fine.) Test consistency of dough by squeezing a small portion in your hand. If it sticks to your palm, add a bit more flour and process until no longer sticky; if dough is dry, add water, 1 tablespoon at a time, and process until smooth and elastic.
4. Grease pizza or jelly-roll pan with vegetable oil and press dough over bottom and up 1 inch of sides with your fingertips. Or, you can use a rolling pin to roll dough out on a lightly floured surface and then fit it into pan in same manner, pressing 1 inch of dough up sides. Let dough rise in pan while you prepare filling.
5. Prepare dried chili pepper: Place pepper between 2 sheets of waxed paper and, using a rolling pin, bruise pepper for a spicy flavor, or pulverize it if you like a fiery taste.
6. Trim, peel, and coarsely chop eggplant into ½-inch dice to make 4 cups. Drain anchovies and capers.
7. Heat remaining ¼ cup olive oil in large skillet over medium heat. Add eggplant, season with chili pepper and salt to taste, and cook, stirring occasionally to prevent sticking, 5 minutes.

8. Meanwhile, if using fresh tomatoes, core, halve, seed, and coarsely chop to measure about 2 cups. If using canned tomatoes, drain and coarsely chop.

9. Add garlic and parsley to skillet and cook another 2 to 3 minutes, or until eggplant is tender.

10. Meanwhile, using food processor or grater, grate caciocavallo cheese to make ½ cup. Cut mozzarella into ¼-inch-thick slices; set aside.

11. Spread eggplant over dough and top with 1 layer each of anchovies, capers, tomatoes, caciocavallo cheese, and olives. Bake 20 minutes, or just until dough is golden.

12. Top with mozzarella and bake another 5 minutes, or until cheese is melted and bubbly. Cut into wedges or slices and serve.

Escarole, Chicory, and Radicchio Salad

Small head escarole
Small head chicory
Small head radicchio
2 tablespoons minced parsley or basil, or combination of both
2 tablespoons red wine vinegar
1 clove garlic, peeled and crushed
Salt and freshly ground black pepper
¼ cup olive oil, approximately

1. Wash escarole, chicory, and radicchio and discard bruised or discolored leaves. Dry in salad spinner or with paper towels. Combine greens, radicchio, and herbs in large salad bowl, cover with plastic wrap, and refrigerate until ready to serve.

2. Combine vinegar, garlic, and salt and pepper to taste in small bowl; beat with fork until salt dissolves. While beating with fork, add olive oil in a slow, steady stream and continue beating until dressing thickens.

3. Pour dressing over salad and toss until evenly coated. Divide among 4 dinner plates and serve.

Radicchio

Fresh Fennel and Oranges

¼ cup pignoli (pine nuts)
4 large navel oranges
Large fennel bulb with leaves, or small bunch celery
Medium-size juice orange
Medium-size lemon
2 tablespoons sugar or honey
Pinch of cinnamon

1. Place pignoli on cookie sheet and toast in 450-degree oven, shaking pan once or twice to prevent scorching, 3 to 5 minutes, or until golden.

2. Remove pignoli from oven and set aside to cool.

3. Using sharp paring knife, peel navel oranges over small bowl to catch juice. Reserve juice for dressing. Remove all traces of pith. Cut oranges crosswise into very thin rounds and set aside.

4. Trim off tops and bottom of fennel and cut bulb crosswise into thin slices. Reserve top leaves for garnish, if desired.

5. Squeeze enough juice from remaining orange to measure ¼ cup when combined with reserved juice in bowl. Juice lemon.

6. In medium-size bowl, combine orange and lemon juice with sugar and cinnamon to taste, and stir to combine. Add fennel slices and toss until well coated.

7. Divide orange slices among dinner plates. Top orange slices with fennel, sprinkle with toasted pignoli, and garnish with fennel leaves, if using, and a light dusting of cinnamon. Set aside until ready to serve.

ADDED TOUCH

This vegetable salad goes well not only with pizza but also with roasted or grilled chicken. Or, by adding blanched carrots, zucchini, green beans, and thinly sliced raw onions, you can expand this salad into a main course.

Sicilian Vegetable Salad

Small head broccoli (about 1 pound)
Small head cauliflower (about 1 pound)
Large red bell pepper
Small bunch parsley or basil (optional)
Medium-size lemon
2-ounce tin anchovies
1½ tablespoons capers
1 clove garlic
3½-ounce can imported oil-packed tuna
½ cup olive oil

1. Bring 3 quarts lightly salted water to a boil in large saucepan or stockpot over medium-high heat.

2. Meanwhile, trim broccoli and cauliflower, and cut into florets. Rinse bell pepper and dry. Core, halve, and seed pepper; cut into ¼-inch-thick slices. Wash parsley or basil, if using, dry with paper towels, and chop enough to measure 2 tablespoons. Juice lemon. Drain anchovies and capers.

3. Peel garlic and chop in food processor fitted with steel blade or in blender. Add half the anchovies, reserving remainder for another use. Add capers, tuna, tuna oil, lemon juice, and olive oil, and process until smooth.

4. Add broccoli and cauliflower to boiling water and blanch 3 to 5 minutes, or just until crisp-tender.

5. Transfer broccoli and cauliflower to colander, refresh under cold running water, and drain.

6. Arrange the broccoli, cauliflower, and pepper slices in large shallow bowl. Pour dressing over vegetables and garnish with chopped parsley or basil, if desired.

Calzoni with Three Cheeses
Stuffed Eggplant Fans
Arugula and Leaf Lettuce Salad

A basket of calzoni, *eggplant fans with sausage and tomato stuffing, and a green salad are perfect buffet fare.*

For the eggplant fans, select eggplants that are firm and shiny with fresh green tops. Baby eggplants have fewer seeds than mature ones, are less likely to be bitter, and need not be pared. To retain the eggplants' moisture, wrap them unwashed in a plastic bag and refrigerate until ready to use.

Goat cheese provides a tangy contrast to the bland mozzarella and ricotta in the filling for the *calzoni*. Young goat cheese is creamy and melts easily. Look for Italian *caprini di capra,* French log-shaped Montrachet (without the ash coating), Bûcheron, or a mild domestic goat cheese with herbs.

WHAT TO DRINK

A crisp white Vernaccia, a soft red Dolcetto, or a simple Sienese Chianti would go well with *calzoni*.

SHOPPING LIST AND STAPLES

4 Italian-style sweet sausages (about ¾ pound total weight)
4 small eggplants (about ¼ pound each)
4 small tomatoes (about 1 pound total weight)
Small head leaf lettuce
Small bunch arugula
Small yellow bell pepper
Medium-size sweet white onion
Small sweet red onion
Small bunch each fresh parsley, chives, and basil, or small bunch of any one of these
Small bunch fresh marjoram or oregano, or 1 teaspoon dried
2 cloves garlic
½ pound mozzarella cheese
½ pound ricotta
½ pound herbed goat cheese
3-ounce can walnut pieces
1¼ cups olive oil
1 tablespoon vegetable oil, approximately
2 tablespoons balsamic vinegar
3½ cups all-purpose flour, approximately
1 package active dry yeast
Salt
Coarsely ground black pepper

UTENSILS

Food processor (optional)
Two 17 x 11-inch baking pans
9 x 17-inch baking sheet (optional)
Large bowl
Medium-size bowl
Small bowl
Salad spinner (optional)
Measuring cups and spoons
Chef's knife
Paring knife
Wide metal spatula
Pastry brush
Rolling pin
Grater

START-TO-FINISH STEPS

1. Wash fresh herbs and pat dry. Chop enough parsley, basil, and chives to measure 1 tablespoon each for calzoni recipe, or chop 3 tablespoons of any one of these herbs. If using parsley, reserve 4 sprigs for garnish for eggplant recipe. If using fresh marjoram or oregano, mince enough to measure 2 teaspoons for eggplant recipe.
2. Follow calzoni recipe steps 1 through 3.
3. Follow eggplant recipe steps 1 through 7.
4. While eggplants are baking, follow calzoni recipe steps 4 through 11.
5. Follow salad recipe steps 1 through 4.
6. Follow eggplant recipe step 8.
7. Follow salad recipe steps 5 through 7 and serve with calzoni and eggplant.

RECIPES

Calzoni with Three Cheeses

1 package active dry yeast
3½ cups all-purpose flour, approximately
½ teaspoon salt
1 teaspoon coarsely ground black pepper
1 tablespoon vegetable oil, approximately
2 cloves garlic
½ pound mozzarella cheese
½ pound herbed goat cheese
½ pound ricotta
1 tablespoon each of minced fresh parsley, chives, and basil, or 3 tablespoons of any one of these
½ cup olive oil

1. Preheat oven to 500 degrees.
2. If not using food processor, prepare dough by hand (see page 8) and proceed to step 4. If using processor, fit with dough blade or steel blade and pour in 1 cup hot tap water. Sprinkle in yeast and pulse machine on and off once or twice to dissolve yeast.
3. With processor running, add 3 cups flour and the salt and pepper, and continue to process 10 to 15 seconds, or until dough forms a ball. (With the steel blade, the dough often does not form a ball but forms a layer under or over the blade. This is fine.) Test consistency of dough by squeezing a small portion of it in your hand. If it sticks to your palm, add a bit more flour and process until no longer sticky; if dough is dry, add water, 1 tablespoon at a time, and process until smooth and elastic. Let dough rise in processor bowl 10 minutes.
4. Grease large baking pan with vegetable oil.
5. Peel and mince garlic.
6. Using grater, coarsely shred mozzarella; crumble goat cheese by hand.

7. In medium-size mixing bowl, combine ricotta and goat cheese and blend with fork. Fold in garlic and herbs, being careful not to overmix or herbs will impart a greenish tinge. Fold in mozzarella.

8. Transfer dough to lightly floured work surface and knead briefly. Pat into ball and divide into quarters.

9. Using rolling pin and dusting with flour, if necessary, roll out each piece of dough into an 8-inch circle about ⅛ inch thick.

10. Place one fourth of filling on lower half of each circle, leaving a 1-inch border. Brush edges of dough with cold water and fold top half of circle over filling. Then fold border back to double seal, and crimp edges with tines of fork or with your fingers.

11. Using wide metal spatula, transfer calzoni to prepared baking pan. Brush with olive oil and bake on bottom rack of oven about 15 minutes, or until puffed and golden.

Stuffed Eggplant Fans

4 small eggplants (about ¼ pound each)
4 small tomatoes (about 1 pound total weight)
Medium-size sweet white onion
4 Italian-style sweet sausages (about ¾ pound total weight)
½ cup olive oil
2 teaspoons minced fresh marjoram or oregano, or 1 teaspoon dried
Salt and coarsely ground black pepper
4 parsley sprigs for garnish (optional)

1. Wash eggplants and dry with paper towels; do *not* trim off stem ends. Halve each eggplant lengthwise. With eggplant half cut-side down, make three lengthwise cuts, starting 1 inch below stem and slicing down through bottom. Repeat with remaining halves.

2. Wash tomatoes and dry with paper towels. Core and halve each tomato; cut each half into thirds.

3. Peel and quarter onion. Cut each quarter lengthwise into slivers.

4. Remove sausage meat from casings.

5. Grease large baking pan with 1 tablespoon oil and arrange eggplant fans cut-side down in a single layer.

6. Spread each fan open and stuff about 1 tablespoon sausage meat into each section. Cover meat with 1 tomato wedge and stuff any remaining spaces with onion slivers. Drizzle eggplant with remaining oil and sprinkle with marjoram or oregano, and salt and pepper to taste.

7. Place baking pan on top rack in 500-degree oven and bake eggplant 20 to 30 minutes, or just until tender. If fans begin to burn, cover loosely with foil and continue baking until tender.

8. With wide metal spatula, carefully transfer eggplant fans to serving platter and garnish with parsley, if desired.

Arugula and Leaf Lettuce Salad

½ cup walnut pieces
2 tablespoons balsamic vinegar
Salt and coarsely ground black pepper
¼ cup olive oil
Small bunch arugula
Small head leaf lettuce
Small yellow bell pepper
Small sweet red onion

1. Coarsely chop walnuts. Place on small baking sheet or on sheet of heavy-duty foil and roast in 500-degree oven 3 to 5 minutes, or until nicely browned.

2. While nuts are roasting, prepare dressing: Combine vinegar and salt and pepper to taste in small bowl, and stir with fork until salt dissolves. While beating with fork, add olive oil in a slow, steady stream and continue beating until dressing thickens slightly.

3. Stir hot walnuts into dressing and set aside.

4. Wash arugula and lettuce, and dry in salad spinner or with paper towels. Discard any wilted or bruised leaves; tear lettuce into bite-size pieces. Place greens in large bowl.

5. Wash bell pepper and dry. Halve, core, and seed pepper; cut into ¼-inch-thick strips.

6. Peel onion and slice thinly; separate into rings.

7. Just before serving, stir dressing to recombine, if necessary. Pour dressing over greens and toss until evenly coated. Top with pepper strips and onion rings.

ADDED TOUCH

Fresh or canned peaches steeped in red wine and topped with crumbled Italian macaroons are an easy dessert. For a delicious variation, serve the fruit over a generous portion of fresh *mascarpone*, a delicate, moist Italian cheese sometimes layered with Provolone or mixed with Gorgonzola.

Peaches in Red Wine

4 fresh sweet peaches, or 8 canned peach halves
Sugar
3 cups dry red wine
1 cup amaretti cookies or macaroons

1. If using macaroons, preheat oven to 350 degrees.

2. If using fresh peaches, wash under cold running water and dry with paper towels. Halve peaches and remove pits; do not peel. If using canned peaches, drain. Cut fresh or canned peaches into ½-inch-thick slices and place in serving bowl. If fresh peaches are not sweet enough, sprinkle with sugar to taste and toss gently until evenly coated.

3. Add wine to peaches. Set aside at room temperature for at least 4 hours, or cover with plastic wrap and refrigerate overnight.

4. Crumble amaretti or macaroons. If using macaroons, place crumbs on cookie sheet and toast 10 minutes, or until golden.

5. Remove macaroons from oven and set aside until ready to serve.

6. Divide peaches among individual bowls and sprinkle each serving with amaretti or macaroon crumbs.

ORIENTAL MENUS

JAPANESE · CHINESE

Connie Handa Moore

MENU 1 (Right)
Peasant-style Miso Soup
Ham, Vegetable, and Noodle Salad
Strawberries with Frosted Ladyfingers

MENU 2
Shrimp and Vegetable Rice
Japanese Orange Mousse

MENU 3
Glazed Beef and Mushrooms
with Shredded Cabbage
Baked Tomato Pudding

The art of Japanese cooking involves treating all foods with respect—never overcooking them and paying careful attention to the way dishes are presented. "Because we Japanese eat with our eyes," says Connie Handa Moore, "we want our meals to be aesthetically pleasing." Her three Oriental-style salad menus are in keeping with this time-honored tradition.

Menu 1 is a three-course meal that starts with a soup brimming with diced vegetables, tofu, and scallions, and flavored with *miso*. The soup whets the palate for the salad of vegetables, ham, and noodles on crisp spinach leaves. Fresh whole strawberries and ladyfingers frosted with whipped cream and nuts are the tempting dessert.

The beautiful salad of Menu 2 makes a good luncheon or a light dinner. Large shrimp and ribbons of egg crêpe are arranged on a mixture of rice, peas, and *shiitake* mushrooms. The colorful shrimp complement the orange mousse dessert, which can be placed on the table with the main course for visual appeal.

Presentation is again the key in Menu 3. Here strips of beef and mushrooms are stir fried briefly, then placed on a contrasting bed of crisp shredded cabbage coated with a light vinaigrette. Tomato pudding, topped with rings of green bell pepper, is the bright side dish.

The miso *soup garnished with scallions is served in lidded bowls to retain heat. It precedes the ham, vegetable, and noodle salad with strips of cucumber and zucchini, and the light dessert of fresh strawberries with frosted ladyfingers.*

70

Peasant-style Miso Soup
Ham, Vegetable, and Noodle Salad
Strawberries with Frosted Ladyfingers

Bamboo shoots are a main ingredient in the soup. Most often associated with Chinese cookery, these tender young shoots of tropical bamboo plants have a slightly sweet taste and a crisp texture. They are sold whole or sliced in cans and have the best flavor when packed in water rather than brine.

WHAT TO DRINK

Enjoy a firm, dry white wine with this menu. Sancerre and Pouilly-Fumé would both be excellent, as would their California cousin Sauvignon Blanc.

SHOPPING LIST AND STAPLES

1¼ pounds imported Danish ham
6 ounces firm tofu
Small bunch large-leaf spinach (about ½ pound)
1 pint cherry tomatoes
Large carrot, or small daikon radish (about ¼ pound)
Medium-size cucumber
Medium-size zucchini
Large red onion
Small bunch scallions
Medium-size lemon
1 to 2 pints strawberries, preferably with stems,
    or raspberries
4 cups chicken stock, preferably homemade (see page 13),
    or two 10¾-ounce cans condensed chicken broth
8-ounce can bamboo shoots
½ pint heavy cream
1 pound fresh Chinese egg noodles, or ¾ pound dried
    capellini or spaghettini
½ cup plus 1 tablespoon vegetable oil
½ cup white vinegar
5 tablespoons white miso paste
¾ cup granulated sugar
¼ cup confectioners' sugar
1 package ladyfingers
4-ounce can walnut pieces
Salt
Freshly ground pepper

UTENSILS

Large saucepan or stockpot
Medium-size saucepan with cover
Medium-size bowl
2 small bowls
Colander
Measuring cups and spoons
Chef's knife
Paring knife
Wooden spoon
Rubber spatula
Vegetable brush
Vegetable peeler
Juicer
Electric mixer

START-TO-FINISH STEPS

1. Follow strawberries recipe steps 1 through 5.
2. Follow salad recipe steps 1 through 12.
3. Follow soup recipe steps 1 through 8 and strawberries recipe step 6.
4. Follow soup recipe step 9 and serve as first course.
5. Follow salad recipe step 13 and serve.
6. Follow strawberries recipe step 7 and serve.

RECIPES

Peasant-style Miso Soup

4 cups chicken stock, preferably homemade, or two
    10¾-ounce cans condensed chicken broth
Large carrot, or small daikon radish (about ¼ pound)
8-ounce can bamboo shoots
5 tablespoons white miso paste
6 ounces firm tofu
1 scallion

1. Place chicken stock in medium-size saucepan. Or, if using canned chicken broth, skim fat from surface and pour defatted broth plus 2 cans of water into pan. Cover and bring to a boil over medium heat.
2. While stock is heating, peel and trim carrot or daikon. Cut into ¼-inch dice to measure ½ cup.
3. Turn bamboo shoots into colander, rinse under cold running water, and drain. Coarsely chop enough bamboo shoots to measure 1 cup.
4. Add vegetables to stock and return to a boil. Reduce heat, cover, and gently simmer vegetables about 5 minutes, or until crisp-tender.
5. While soup is simmering, measure miso into small

bowl. Add 1 tablespoon hot tap water and stir until thoroughly blended. Set aside.

6. Rinse tofu under cold running water; pat dry with paper towel. Cut tofu into ¼-inch dice; set aside.

7. Rinse scallion and dry with paper towel. Trim ends and discard. Cut on diagonal into ¼-inch slices; set aside.

8. Turn miso into soup and stir until blended. Raise heat to medium-high and bring soup to a boil.

9. As soon as soup comes to a boil, remove pan from heat. Add tofu to soup and divide among individual bowls. Sprinkle with sliced scallion and serve.

Ham, Vegetable, and Noodle Salad

Small bunch large-leaf spinach (about ½ pound)
Large red onion
1 pint cherry tomatoes
Medium-size cucumber
Medium-size zucchini
1¼ pounds imported Danish ham
½ cup plus 1 tablespoon vegetable oil
1 pound fresh Chinese egg noodles, or ¾ pound dried
    capellini or spaghettini
Medium-size lemon
¾ cup granulated sugar
Salt and freshly ground pepper
½ cup white vinegar

1. In large saucepan or stockpot, bring 4 quarts of water to a rapid boil.

2. Meanwhile, remove and discard any bruised or discolored spinach leaves. Wash remaining leaves in several changes of cold water; remove tough stems. Shake leaves and drain in colander; set aside.

3. Peel and halve red onion. Cut into thin slices. Cut slices in half and separate into strips; set aside.

4. Wash and dry cherry tomatoes. Remove stems.

5. Wash and dry cucumber. Trim ends and discard. Halve cucumber crosswise and then halve each piece lengthwise. Cut quarters lengthwise into ¼-inch julienne.

6. Under cold running water, scrub zucchini with vegetable brush to remove sand; dry with paper towel. Cut zucchini into ¼-inch julienne; set aside.

7. Cut ham into ¼-inch julienne; set aside.

8. Add 1 tablespoon oil to boiling water to prevent noodles from sticking together. Add noodles, stir with wooden spoon to separate, and cook 2 to 3 minutes for fresh, or according to package directions for dried.

9. Squeeze lemon to measure 2 tablespoons juice.

10. Turn noodles into colander and rinse under cold running water; set aside to drain.

11. For dressing, combine sugar, 2 teaspoons salt, ½ teaspoon pepper, vinegar, lemon juice, and ½ cup oil in small bowl and beat with fork until blended; set aside.

12. Divide spinach among 4 dinner plates. Divide noodles among plates, mounding them in center. Top noodles with cucumber, zucchini, and onion. Arrange cherry tomatoes and ham strips decoratively around noodles; cover and set aside until ready to serve.

13. Just before serving, stir dressing to recombine and serve with salads.

Strawberries with Frosted Ladyfingers

1 to 2 pints strawberries, preferably with stems,
    or raspberries
¼ to ½ cup walnut pieces
½ pint heavy cream
4 to 8 ladyfingers
¼ cup confectioners' sugar

1. Place medium-size bowl and beaters for whipping cream in freezer to chill.

2. Leave stems on strawberries and gently rinse berries under cold running water. Transfer to double thickness of paper towels and pat dry. Divide berries among 4 dessert plates; set aside.

3. Coarsely chop walnuts; set aside.

4. Pour cream into chilled bowl. Using electric mixer, whip cream until soft peaks form.

5. Separate ladyfingers into single sections and spread each half with a layer of whipped cream. Sprinkle with walnuts and divide ladyfingers among plates with berries. Cover each serving with plastic wrap and refrigerate.

6. Twenty minutes before serving, remove plates from refrigerator.

7. When ready to serve, place confectioners' sugar in small bowl and serve separately with strawberries and ladyfingers.

ADDED TOUCH

For an impressive appetizer or *hors d'oeuvre*, sculpture cucumber sections into attractive cups to hold slices of smoked salmon.

Cucumber Cups with Gravlax and Capers

1 head Bibb lettuce
Small lemon
1 large English hothouse cucumber (about 16 inches long)
12 thin slices gravlax or Nova lox
4 teaspoons capers, rinsed and drained

1. Wash and dry lettuce. Remove any bruised or discolored leaves. Divide among 4 salad plates; set aside.

2. Wash and dry lemon. Cut crosswise into four ¼-inch-thick slices; set aside.

3. Wash and dry cucumber. Trim ends and discard. With sharp paring knife, cut cucumber crosswise into approximately 4-inch quarters. Cut 1-inch-deep triangles around one end of each quarter to form crown shape. Using melon baller or teaspoon, scoop out inside, leaving ¼ inch of flesh at bottom, to form cup for filling.

4. Stuff each cucumber cup with two slices of gravlax and top with 1 teaspoon capers.

5. Divide cucumber cups among lettuce-lined plates. Fold remaining slices of gravlax into cone shape and place one next to each cucumber cup. Garnish each plate with a lemon slice and serve.

Shrimp and Vegetable Rice
Japanese Orange Mousse

Golden ribbons of egg garnish this beautifully composed salad of shrimp, vegetables, and rice. The dessert is orange mousse.

Thin, delicate ribbons of egg make an unusual topping for the shrimp and vegetable rice salad. Before cooking, lightly grease the skillet with oil, heat the skillet, then slowly pour in just enough beaten egg mixture to form a paper-thin sheet. As you pour, rotate the hot skillet so the egg is evenly distributed. Do not allow the egg to brown; the finished egg strips should be pale yellow. Slice the cooked egg thinly—the thinner the slices, the more delicate they appear. You can vary the salad by substituting drained canned white-meat tuna or poached chicken slices for the cooked shrimp.

The foamy orange mousse is garnished with Mandarin orange, whipped cream, mint leaves, and slivers of crystallized ginger. Mandarin oranges originated in China and are similar to tangerines, which can be substituted. Crystallized, or candied, ginger is covered with sugar, so use it sparingly or the dessert will be too sweet.

WHAT TO DRINK

The cook recommends a fruity white wine with a touch of sweetness: Vouvray is the first choice, or try California Chenin Blanc or German Riesling.

SHOPPING LIST AND STAPLES

1¼ pounds large shrimp
Medium-size carrot
Small bunch mint
11-ounce can Mandarin oranges
8-ounce can whole water chestnuts
1 egg
½ pint heavy cream
1 pint vanilla ice cream
10-ounce package frozen peas
5 tablespoons white vinegar
⅓ cup mayonnaise, preferably homemade
1 tablespoon ketchup
2 teaspoons Japanese soy sauce
Hot pepper sauce
2 cups long-grain rice
8 dried shiitake mushrooms (about ¼ pound total weight), or ½ pound fresh button mushrooms
4-ounce can walnuts or almonds
Two 3-ounce packages orange-flavored gelatin
4¼-ounce package crystallized ginger
½ cup plus ½ teaspoon sugar
Salt
1 teaspoon dry white wine
2 tablespoons orange-flavored liqueur

UTENSILS

Large nonstick skillet
Stockpot or large saucepan
Medium-size heavy-gauge saucepan with cover
Small saucepan
2 large bowls
Medium-size bowl
4 small bowls
Colander
Large strainer
Measuring cups and spoons
Chef's knife
Paring knife
2 wooden spoons
Rubber spatula
Whisk
Vegetable peeler
Electric mixer

START-TO-FINISH STEPS

One hour ahead: Set out frozen peas to thaw at room temperature.

Thirty minutes ahead: Remove vanilla ice cream from freezer and set out until it has a semi-soft but still firm consistency.

1. Follow mousse recipe steps 1 through 8.
2. Follow rice recipe steps 1 through 20 and serve with mousse.

RECIPES

Shrimp and Vegetable Rice

2 cups long-grain rice
3 teaspoons salt
1¼ pounds large shrimp
8 dried shiitake mushrooms (about ¼ pound total weight), or ½ pound fresh button mushrooms
½ cup plus ½ teaspoon sugar
Medium-size carrot
8-ounce can whole water chestnuts
10-ounce package frozen peas, thawed
1 egg
¼ cup walnuts or almonds
5 tablespoons white vinegar
1 teaspoon dry white wine
⅓ cup mayonnaise
2 teaspoons Japanese soy sauce
1 tablespoon ketchup
Hot pepper sauce

1. In medium-size heavy-gauge saucepan, bring 3½ cups of water to a rapid boil over high heat. Add rice and 1 teaspoon salt, return to a boil, and stir rice with wooden spoon. Cover pan, reduce heat, and simmer 20 minutes.
2. While rice simmers, bring 4 quarts of water to a rapid boil in stockpot over high heat.
3. While water is heating, peel and devein shrimp: Pinch off legs of shrimp, several at a time, then bend back and snap off sharp, beaklike piece of shell just above tail. Remove shell and discard. Using sharp paring knife, make shallow incision along back of each shrimp, exposing black digestive vein. Extract black vein with your fingers and

discard. Place shrimp in colander, rinse under cold running water, and drain.

4. Add shrimp to boiling water in stockpot and cook 3 to 4 minutes, or until backs of shrimp turn opaque and begin to curl.

5. Fluff rice with fork and turn into large bowl; set aside to cool. Rinse saucepan.

6. Turn shrimp into colander and refresh under cold running water; set aside to cool.

7. Bring 3 cups of water to a boil in medium-size saucepan over high heat. If using button mushrooms, wipe clean with damp paper towels; leave whole. Add ¼ cup sugar, 1 teaspoon salt, and shiitake or button mushrooms to boiling water and stir. When water returns to a boil, cover pan, reduce heat, and simmer 15 minutes for shiitake or 5 minutes for button mushrooms.

8. While mushrooms are simmering, bring 1 cup of water to a boil in small saucepan over medium-high heat.

9. Meanwhile, peel and trim carrot. Halve crosswise and then halve each piece lengthwise. Cut quarters into 1-inch-long slivers. You should have about ¾ cup.

10. Add carrot to boiling water and blanch 1 minute. Turn into large strainer and refresh under cold running water. Transfer to small plate and set aside to cool.

11. Turn water chestnuts into strainer and rinse under cold running water; dry with paper towels. Cut into ⅛-inch-thick slices; set aside.

12. Turn thawed peas into strainer and drain. Transfer to small bowl and set aside.

13. Turn mushrooms into strainer and rinse under cold running water; drain. Transfer mushrooms to double thickness of paper towels and press to remove excess moisture. Remove and discard stems of shiitake and cut caps into ⅛-inch-thick slices; if using button mushrooms, leave whole. Set mushrooms aside.

14. Using paper towel that has been dipped in oil, grease large nonstick skillet and heat over medium-high heat until hot.

15. Meanwhile, crack egg into small bowl. Add ½ teaspoon sugar and 1 teaspoon water, and whisk until blended. Slowly pour just enough egg into pan to barely coat bottom and cook about 1 minute or until crêpe appears dry; do *not* allow to brown. When set, loosen edge of crêpe with rubber spatula and flip over onto clean work surface. Regrease pan, beat egg to recombine, and repeat until all egg mixture is used.

16. Stack crêpes and roll stack into cylinder. Using a sharp knife, cut crosswise into very thin strips. Transfer strips to a plate and toss to separate; set aside.

17. Coarsely chop walnuts; set aside.

18. For vinaigrette, combine white vinegar, ¼ cup sugar, 1 teaspoon salt, and white wine in small bowl and whisk until blended.

19. Combine mayonnaise, soy sauce, ketchup, and dash of hot pepper sauce in a small bowl and stir until blended. Turn into serving dish and set aside.

20. Add mushrooms, carrots, water chestnuts, and vinaigrette to rice and stir with wooden spoon to combine. Divide mixture among 4 dinner plates and sprinkle with drained peas. Top with equal portions of egg strips and arrange shrimp around border of each plate. Sprinkle with nuts and serve with spicy mayonnaise on the side.

Japanese Orange Mousse

Small bunch mint
⅓ cup crystallized ginger
11-ounce can Mandarin oranges
Two 3-ounce packages orange-flavored gelatin
2 tablespoons orange-flavored liqueur
1 pint vanilla ice cream, semi-soft
½ cup heavy cream

1. Place medium-size bowl and beaters for whipping cream in freezer to chill.

2. Rinse mint and dry with paper towels. Set aside 12 leaves for garnish; refrigerate remainder for another use.

3. Slice ginger into thin slivers; set aside.

4. Drain Mandarin oranges; set aside.

5. In small saucepan, bring 1 cup of water to a boil over high heat. Add orange-flavored gelatin and stir with wooden spoon until thoroughly dissolved.

6. Pour gelatin mixture into large bowl, add 3 ice cubes and liqueur, and stir until ice melts. Add ice cream and whisk by hand until light and fluffy. Cover mixture with plastic wrap and place in freezer.

7. Pour heavy cream into chilled bowl and beat with electric mixer until cream stands in soft peaks.

8. Divide mousse among 4 serving bowls or goblets and top each serving with a spoonful of whipped cream. Arrange orange slices and mint leaves decoratively around whipped cream. Garnish whipped cream with ginger slices. Cover desserts with plastic wrap and refrigerate until ready to serve.

Glazed Beef and Mushrooms
with Shredded Cabbage
Baked Tomato Pudding

For a quick family meal, serve beef and mushrooms on a bed of shredded cabbage coated with vinaigrette dressing. Baked tomato pudding garnished with green pepper rings is the vegetable side dish.

The stir-fried beef strips are glazed with a sauce seasoned with *mirin*, a sweet rice wine that is frequently used in Japanese cooking. Once opened, *mirin* lasts for several months on a pantry shelf and indefinitely in the refrigerator. If you cannot locate it in a specialty food store, you can make your own by combining equal parts sherry and sugar, then cooking the mixture over low heat until syrupy.

WHAT TO DRINK

The spiciness of a well-chilled California Gewürztraminer would enhance the varied flavors of this meal. An Alsatian or Italian Gewürztraminer is also good.

SHOPPING LIST AND STAPLES

1¼ to 1½ pounds boneless sirloin or other lean beef, cut into 2-inch-wide strips
8 medium-size mushrooms (about 6 ounces total weight)
Small head Chinese or Savoy cabbage (about 1 pound)
1 Italian green pepper
Small onion
Small bunch scallions
Large clove garlic
2-inch piece fresh ginger
Small bunch fresh basil, or 1 tablespoon dried
Small bunch fresh coriander for garnish (optional)
28-ounce can crushed tomatoes
2 tablespoons unsalted butter, approximately
9 tablespoons plus 1 teaspoon vegetable oil
¼ cup white vinegar
¼ cup Japanese soy sauce
16-ounce can large pitted black olives
1 slice firm white bread
2 tablespoons unseasoned bread crumbs
½ cup plus 2 tablespoons sugar
1 tablespoon cornstarch
2½-ounce jar sesame seeds
Salt
Freshly ground white and black pepper
2 tablespoons mirin

UTENSILS

Food processor (optional)
Large heavy-gauge skillet

77

Medium-size skillet
Small heavy-gauge skillet
Large bowl
Medium-size bowl
2 small bowls
Colander
Measuring cups and spoons
Chef's knife
Paring knife
Wooden spoon
Slotted spoon
Rubber spatula

START-TO-FINISH STEPS

1. Follow tomato pudding recipe steps 1 through 9.
2. While tomato pudding is baking, follow salad recipe steps 1 through 15.
3. Follow tomato pudding recipe step 10 and salad recipe steps 16 through 18.
4. Follow tomato pudding recipe steps 11 and 12, and serve with salad.

RECIPES

Glazed Beef and Mushrooms with Shredded Cabbage

2 tablespoons sesame seeds
¼ cup plus 3 tablespoons sugar
½ cup plus 1 tablespoon vegetable oil
¼ cup white vinegar
1 teaspoon salt
½ teaspoon freshly ground black pepper
Small bunch fresh coriander for garnish (optional)
Small head Chinese or Savoy cabbage (about 1 pound)
8 medium-size mushrooms (about 6 ounces total weight)
2 scallions
2-inch piece fresh ginger
Large clove garlic
1 tablespoon cornstarch
¼ cup Japanese soy sauce
2 tablespoons mirin
1¼ to 1½ pounds boneless sirloin or other lean beef, cut into 2-inch-wide strips
16-ounce can large pitted black olives

1. In small heavy-gauge skillet, toast sesame seeds over

medium heat, shaking skillet to prevent scorching. When seeds start to pop, remove skillet from heat. Set aside.
2. For vinaigrette, combine 3 tablespoons sugar, ½ cup oil, vinegar, salt, and pepper in small bowl and beat with fork until blended; set aside.
3. Wash coriander, if using, and dry with paper towels. Trim off root ends, leaving 2-inch-long sprigs. Wrap in paper towels and refrigerate until ready to serve.
4. Wash cabbage and dry with paper towels. Quarter cabbage; remove and discard core. Using food processor fitted with slicing disk, feed each quarter into tube, with core side at right angle to disk, and pulse until all cabbage is sliced. Or, thinly slice each quarter with chef's knife.
5. Place cabbage in large bowl and add enough ice water to cover; set aside.

Chinese cabbage

6. Wipe mushrooms clean with damp paper towels. Remove and discard stems. Cut caps into ⅛-inch-thick slices; set aside.
7. Wash scallions and dry with paper towels. Trim ends and discard. Thinly slice scallions; set aside.
8. Grate enough ginger to measure 2 teaspoons; set aside.

Fresh ginger

9. Peel and mince garlic; set aside.
10. Combine cornstarch, soy sauce, remaining sugar, mirin, and ginger in small bowl and stir to combine. Pour into medium-size skillet and heat over medium heat, stirring constantly with a wooden spoon, 1 to 2 minutes, or until sauce thickens and starts to bubble. Remove skillet from heat and set aside.
11. Transfer cabbage to colander and shake to drain as much water as possible. Dry large bowl. Return cabbage to bowl, cover with plastic wrap, and refrigerate.

12. Heat 1 tablespoon oil in large heavy-gauge skillet over high heat for 30 seconds. Reduce heat to medium-low, add garlic and scallions, and stir 1 minute. With slotted spoon, transfer garlic and scallions to measuring cup; set aside.
13. Using same skillet, quickly stir fry meat over medium-high heat about 3 minutes, or until it loses its pink color.
14. Add mushrooms to meat and cook another 30 seconds. Transfer meat and mushrooms to colander and drain.
15. Return meat and mushrooms to skillet, add sautéed scallions and garlic and sauce, and stir to combine. Remove pan from heat and set aside.
16. Drain olives; set aside.
17. Stir dressing to recombine. Remove cabbage from refrigerator, add dressing, and toss until evenly coated.
18. Divide cabbage among 4 dinner plates, making well in center of cabbage. Spoon meat and mushroom mixture into wells. Sprinkle cabbage with toasted sesame seeds. Garnish each serving with large black olives and sprigs of coriander, if desired.

Baked Tomato Pudding

1 teaspoon vegetable oil
28-ounce can crushed tomatoes
Small onion
Large fresh basil leaf, or 1 tablespoon dried
5 teaspoons unsalted butter
1 slice firm white bread
3 tablespoons sugar
Salt and freshly ground white pepper
2 tablespoons unseasoned bread crumbs
1 Italian green pepper for garnish

1. Preheat oven to 350 degrees. Set rack in top half of oven.
2. Grease four 1½-cup ramekins or ovenproof dishes with vegetable oil.
3. Pour tomatoes into medium-size bowl.
4. Peel and finely chop enough onion to measure ⅓ cup. Wash basil leaf, if using, and chop finely.
5. Melt 1 teaspoon butter in small heavy-gauge skillet over medium heat. Add onion and basil, and sauté, stirring occasionally, 3 to 5 minutes, or until onion is soft and translucent.
6. While onion is sautéing, cut bread slice into ½-inch cubes and add to tomatoes.
7. Add onion and basil mixture, sugar, salt, and a pinch of pepper to tomatoes; stir to combine. Rinse and dry skillet.

8. Divide tomato pudding mixture among prepared ramekins or dishes, leveling tops with spatula. Sprinkle bread crumbs lightly over puddings and dot each serving with 1 teaspoon of remaining butter.
9. Reduce oven temperature to 325 degrees and bake puddings in top half of oven 30 minutes.
10. Turn off heat and keep warm in oven until ready to serve.
11. Just before serving, wash pepper and dry with paper towel. Slice pepper into ⅛-inch-thick rings; remove and discard ribs and seeds.
12. Remove puddings from oven, garnish with pepper rings, and serve.

ADDED TOUCH

Soba noodles, snow peas, and scallions flavored with soy sauce and sesame oil make a substantial accompaniment for this salad.

Soba Noodles with Snow Peas and Scallions

¼ pound snow peas
3 scallions
10-ounce package soba noodles
3 tablespoons soy sauce
3 teaspoons sesame oil

1. Bring 3 quarts of water to a boil in stockpot over high heat. Bring 2 cups of water to a boil in small saucepan over medium-high heat.
2. Rinse snow peas under cold running water. Remove and discard strings. Add peas to small saucepan of boiling water. When water returns to a boil, turn peas into strainer and refresh under cold running water; set aside.
3. Wash and dry scallions. Trim ends and discard. Cut scallions crosswise into ¼-inch-thick slices; set aside.
4. Add noodles to stockpot of boiling water and stir with wooden spoon to separate. Cover pot to help water return to a boil; then remove cover and continue cooking noodles 6 minutes, stirring occasionally.
5. Turn noodles into colander and rinse under hot running water for 30 seconds to remove starch.
6. Turn noodles into large mixing bowl, add soy sauce and sesame oil, and toss until evenly coated.
7. Divide noodles among 4 plates, sprinkle with scallions and snow peas, and serve.

Warren V. Mah

MENU 1 (Right)
Pork and Scallion Rolls with Teriyaki Sauce
Stir-Fried Carrots, Snow Peas,
and Enoki Mushrooms
Steamed White Rice

MENU 2
Chicken Sukiyaki
Bean Sprout, Carrot, and Lettuce Salad
with Tofu Dressing

MENU 3
Miso and Watercress Soup
Shrimp and Vegetable Tempura

A specialist in Oriental cookery, Warren Mah has selected three traditional Japanese meals for this volume. "My menus show that Japanese cooking is not hard to do," he says, "even though the names of the recipes may sound complicated." All of his dishes are light, and the washing and chopping of the ingredients can be done well in advance of mealtime.

Menu 1 offers *teriyaki*, which translates as "shining broil." A *teriyaki* dish comprises meat, fish, poultry, or vegetables marinated in and then glazed with a soy-based sauce. *Teriyaki* foods may be broiled, boiled, steamed, or sautéed. For this meal, Warren Mah marinates and sautés scallion-filled pork rolls and accompanies them with stir-fried vegetables and bowls of white rice.

For Menu 2, he presents a main course of *sukiyaki* (pronounced *skee-yáh-kee*), which means "broiled on the blade of a plow." (In ancient times, Japanese farmers and hunters often killed wild animals and cooked the meat over an open fire with improvised utensils.) Today, *sukiyaki* is generally cooked at the table in restaurants, but at home it is best prepared in the kitchen for safety's sake. This *sukiyaki* features slices of chicken breast, tofu, noodles, and an assortment of vegetables, and is accompanied by a salad of bean sprouts, lettuce, and carrots tossed with a tart *tofu* dressing.

Menu 3 highlights *tempura*, or foods dipped in batter and then quickly fried. Here, the *tempura* is composed of shrimp and vegetables, and served with a delicious dipping sauce. A light *miso* and watercress soup introduces the meal.

Food prepared Japanese-style should please the eye as well as the palate: Arrange the pork rolls in a semicircle around the stir-fried vegetables and enoki *mushrooms. A bowl of white rice is the traditional accompaniment.*

80

Pork and Scallion Rolls with Teriyaki Sauce
Stir-Fried Carrots, Snow Peas, and Enoki Mushrooms
Steamed White Rice

Pork wrapped around scallions and marinated in a sweet gingered *teriyaki* sauce is called *butaniku-no-negimaki* in Japanese. In this recipe, the *teriyaki* sauce is used to flavor and tenderize the meat before cooking and to baste it during sautéing. The marinade is traditionally made with *mirin*—a sweet Japanese rice wine—but here the cook substitutes *sake*, a rice wine that is not as sweet. *Sake* is sold in most liquor stores and Oriental markets. If you prefer, you can barbecue the pork rolls, or substitute beef or chicken for the pork, with equally good results.

The bright vegetable combination includes *enoki* (or *enokitaki*) mushrooms—slender ivory-colored stalks that look like tiny umbrellas. These mushrooms are increasingly available in well-stocked supermarkets, specialty produce stores, and Oriental groceries. Refrigerate them in the original package, or wrapped in paper towels, and use them as soon as possible. Because *enoki* are fragile, cook them just long enough to heat them through. If they are not available, thinly slice ¼ pound large cultivated white mushrooms, and cook them as you would the *enoki*.

Rinsing rice until the water runs clear is a traditional Asian practice: A thorough rinsing not only removes any starchy residue left from milling but also produces cooked rice that is lighter and more tender. Swish the grains gently with your hands, taking care not to break them.

WHAT TO DRINK

Cold beer—especially a Japanese brand—goes well with the pork rolls. For a more exotic flavor, you could also serve warm *sake*.

SHOPPING LIST AND STAPLES

8 boneless pork loin cutlets, trimmed and pounded
    to ¼- to ⅛-inch thickness (about 1 pound
    total weight)
2 large carrots (about ½ pound total weight)
¼ pound snow peas
3½-ounce package enoki mushrooms
Large bunch scallions
1½-inch piece fresh ginger
2 tablespoons vegetable oil
½ teaspoon Oriental sesame oil, approximately
½ cup Japanese soy sauce

1 cup long-grain white rice (not converted)
¼ cup sugar, approximately
Salt
Freshly ground white pepper
2 tablespoons sake

UTENSILS

Large heavy-gauge skillet
Large sauté pan or wok
Steamer unit, or heavy-gauge saucepan large enough to
    accommodate bamboo steamer or other steamer insert
    with cover
Bamboo steamer or steamer insert (if not using steamer
    unit)
Small saucepan
Glass or ceramic baking dish
Heatproof platter
2 medium-size heatproof bowls
Small bowl
Strainer
Measuring cups and spoons
Chef's knife
Paring knife
2 wooden spoons
Metal tongs
Vegetable peeler
Kitchen string

START-TO-FINISH STEPS

1. Follow pork rolls recipe steps 1 through 6.
2. Follow rice recipe steps 1 through 3.
3. While rice is steaming, follow vegetables recipe steps 1 through 8.
4. Follow rice recipe step 4.
5. Follow pork rolls recipe steps 7 through 13 and serve with vegetables and rice.

RECIPES

Pork and Scallion Rolls with Teriyaki Sauce

1½-inch piece fresh ginger
½ cup Japanese soy sauce
¼ cup sugar
Large bunch scallions

2 tablespoons sake
8 boneless pork loin cutlets, trimmed
  and pounded to ¼- to ⅛-inch thickness (about 1 pound
  total weight)
1 tablespoon vegetable oil

1. Mince enough ginger to measure 2 tablespoons.
2. For marinade, combine soy sauce, sugar, and ginger in small saucepan and bring to a boil over medium-high heat. Reduce heat and simmer 5 minutes.
3. Meanwhile, rinse scallions under cold running water and dry with paper towels. Trim ends and discard. Halve scallions crosswise; set aside.
4. Remove marinade from heat, add sake, and set aside to cool.
5. Divide scallion halves into 8 equal bunches. Gather one bunch of scallion halves, place at edge of one short end of cutlet, and roll tightly. Using kitchen string, tie pork roll firmly, but not too tightly, in two places. Repeat with remaining cutlets.
6. Place pork rolls in glass or ceramic baking dish, add marinade, and set aside for 30 minutes, turning pork rolls every 10 minutes.
7. Remove pork rolls from dish and pat dry with paper towels. Pour marinade through strainer set over small bowl and reserve.
8. Place 4 dinner plates and platter in preheated 200-degree oven to warm.
9. Heat vegetable oil in large heavy-gauge skillet over medium-high heat until hot. Add pork rolls and sauté about 3 minutes, or until lightly brown on all sides.
10. Lower heat to medium and continue to cook, turning pork occasionally with tongs, 3 to 4 minutes.
11. Add about ¼ cup of reserved marinade to skillet and continue to cook pork, basting with sauce, another 2 to 3 minutes, or until pork is firm to the touch.
12. Transfer pork rolls to warm platter, remove string, and carefully cut each roll on the diagonal into 4 pieces.
13. Divide pork rolls among 4 warm dinner plates, arranging them decoratively around edges of plates. Top each serving with a spoonful of sauce and serve.

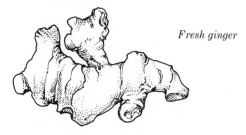

Fresh ginger

Stir-Fried Carrots, Snow Peas, and Enoki Mushrooms

2 large carrots (about ½ pound total weight)
¼ pound snow peas
3½-ounce package enoki mushrooms
1 tablespoon vegetable oil
½ teaspoon Oriental sesame oil, approximately

Pinch of sugar
Salt
Freshly ground white pepper

1. Preheat oven to 200 degrees.
2. Peel and trim carrots. Cut crosswise into 2-inch-long pieces. Halve each piece lengthwise, then cut lengthwise into ¼-inch julienne; set aside.
3. Place snow peas in colander and rinse under cold running water; drain and dry with paper towels. Trim ends and remove strings. Cut snow peas lengthwise into thin strips; set aside.

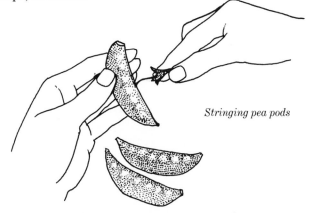

Stringing pea pods

4. Trim root ends of enoki mushrooms and discard; set mushrooms aside.
5. Heat vegetable oil in large sauté pan or wok over medium-high heat. When oil is hot, add carrots and stir fry, adding 1 to 2 tablespoons water to help speed cooking, 2 minutes.
6. Add snow peas and continue stir frying 1 minute.
7. Add mushrooms and stir fry another minute, or just until heated through.
8. Remove pan from heat. Season vegetables with sesame oil, sugar, and salt and pepper to taste. Turn into medium-size heatproof bowl and keep warm in oven until ready to serve.

Steamed White Rice

1 cup long-grain white rice (not converted)

1. Bring 2 cups water to a boil over medium heat in bottom of steamer unit or in saucepan large enough to accommodate bamboo steamer or steamer insert.
2. Meanwhile, place rice in bowl that will fit into steamer or pan when steamer or pan is covered, and add enough cold water to cover rice. With your hands, gently swish rice around until water becomes cloudy. Carefully pour off water, refill bowl with fresh water, and repeat process until water is clear.
3. Drain rice and add enough cold water to cover rice by ½ inch. Place bowl in steamer or pan, cover, and cook rice, without disturbing, 30 minutes.
4. Carefully remove bowl of cooked rice from steamer or pan and fluff rice with fork. Return bowl to steamer or pan and remove from heat. Cover to keep rice warm until ready to serve.

Chicken Sukiyaki
Bean Sprout, Carrot, and Lettuce Salad
with Tofu Dressing

A major ingredient in this *sukiyaki* is *shirataki* (meaning "white waterfall")—gelatinous, transparent noodles made from a yam-like tuber. Canned *shirataki* are sold in Oriental markets and some supermarkets. If you cannot locate them, substitute bean threads, slender translucent strands made from ground mung beans.

Shirataki need only a brief rinsing, but bean threads require soaking in either hot or boiling water, depending on where they are made: If the bean threads are from

Taiwan or Thailand, use hot water, because boiling water turns them gelatinous. If they are from the People's Republic of China, use boiling water. Do not remove the rubber band before soaking the bean threads, or they will become too unmanageable to cut. When pliable (after about 10 seconds), use scissors to cut through the looped ends or the center of the skein, thereby cutting the bean threads into manageable 4- to 5-inch lengths. Snip the rubber band and discard it, then swish the bean threads in the water to separate them. After another 10 to 15 seconds, when the bean threads are firm, rinse them briefly in cool water and drain again. Now they are ready for use according to recipe directions.

The cook suggests serving individual bowls of very fresh raw egg as an accompaniment to the *sukiyaki*. Tra-

Bring the sukiyaki *to the table steaming hot, and offer chopsticks for dipping the various morsels into individual bowls of raw egg, if desired. The bean sprout, carrot, and lettuce salad should be served on separate plates.*

ditionally, the diner beats the egg with chopsticks and then dips the hot food in the beaten egg. The egg cools the food and also seals in the juices.

WHAT TO DRINK

Japanese green tea, warm *sake*, or any type of cold beer would suit this Oriental meal.

SHOPPING LIST AND STAPLES

2 whole boneless, skinless chicken breasts, halved (about 1¼ pounds total weight)
3 blocks firm tofu (each about 10 ounces)
1 pound fresh bean sprouts
Small head romaine lettuce
Small bunch watercress
Small bunch scallions
Medium-size onion
Small carrot
1-inch piece fresh ginger
4 very fresh eggs (optional)
½ cup chicken stock, preferably homemade (see page 13), or canned
8-ounce can sliced bamboo shoots

8-ounce can shirataki, or 9-ounce package bean threads
2 tablespoons vegetable oil
2 tablespoons Oriental sesame oil
½ cup Japanese rice vinegar
¼ cup Japanese soy sauce
1-ounce package dried shiitake mushrooms
3-ounce jar sesame seeds
5 tablespoons sugar
Salt
Freshly ground white pepper
2 tablespoons sake

UTENSILS

Food processor or blender
Wok or large sauté pan
Small heavy-gauge skillet or sauté pan
Large saucepan
Large platter
Large salad bowl
2 small bowls
4 small serving bowls or cups (if serving raw eggs)
Salad spinner (optional)
Colander

Large strainer
Measuring cups and spoons
Chef's knife
Paring knife
2 wooden spoons or salad servers
Slotted spoon
Tongs or two 16-inch chopsticks
Vegetable peeler
Grater (if not using processor)

START-TO-FINISH STEPS

1. Follow sukiyaki recipe steps 1 through 11.
2. Follow salad recipe steps 1 through 10.
3. Follow sukiyaki recipe steps 12 through 14 and serve with salad.

RECIPES

Chicken Sukiyaki

1-ounce package dried shiitake mushrooms
2 whole boneless, skinless chicken breasts, halved (about 1¼ pounds total weight)
Medium-size onion
Small bunch scallions
Small bunch watercress
2 blocks firm tofu (each about 10 ounces)
8-ounce can sliced bamboo shoots
8-ounce can shirataki, or 9-ounce package bean threads
1-inch piece fresh ginger
½ cup chicken stock
¼ cup Japanese soy sauce
3 tablespoons sugar
2 tablespoons sake
2 tablespoons vegetable oil
4 very fresh eggs (optional)

1. Place 4 or 5 shiitake mushrooms in small bowl and add hot water to cover; set aside to soften at least 15 minutes.
2. Meanwhile, rinse and dry chicken. Remove and discard any excess fat and tendons. Cut breasts crosswise into ¼-inch-wide slices. Transfer to large platter and set aside.
3. Halve and peel onion. Cutting lengthwise, thinly slice enough onion to measure ½ cup; transfer to platter.
4. Wash and dry scallions. Cut enough scallions into 2-inch pieces to measure ½ cup; transfer to platter.
5. Wash and dry watercress. Trim ends and discard. Transfer watercress to platter.
6. Rinse and dry tofu. Halve, then cut halves crosswise into ½-inch-wide slices; transfer to platter.
7. Turn bamboo shoots into strainer and rinse under cold running water. Drain and transfer to platter.
8. If using shirataki, turn into large strainer and rinse under cold running water; drain. Cut shirataki into thirds; transfer to platter.
9. Rinse and dry mushrooms. Using paring knife, trim stems and discard. Cut caps into ¼-inch-wide slices; transfer to platter.

10. Mince enough ginger to measure 2 tablespoons.
11. Combine chicken stock, soy sauce, sugar, ginger, and sake in small bowl and stir to dissolve sugar; set aside.
12. Heat oil in wok or sauté pan over medium-high heat until a drop of water evaporates on contact. Add chicken and stir fry 2 to 3 minutes, or until it loses its raw look.
13. Move chicken to center of wok or sauté pan and surround it with separate mounds of ingredients from platter. Add stock mixture to pan and bring to a boil. Reduce heat to low and simmer, stirring and turning ingredients without mixing any together, 5 minutes.
14. Bring wok or sauté pan to table and let guests select whatever sukiyaki ingredients they like. Offer bowls of raw egg for dipping the sukiyaki morsels, if desired.

Bean Sprout, Carrot, and Lettuce Salad with Tofu Dressing

1 tablespoon sesame seeds
1 block firm tofu (about 10 ounces)
2 tablespoons Oriental sesame oil
½ cup Japanese rice vinegar
2 tablespoons sugar
½ teaspoon salt
¼ teaspoon freshly ground white pepper
1 pound fresh beansprouts
Small head romaine lettuce
Small carrot

1. Line plate with double thickness of paper towels. In small dry heavy-gauge skillet or sauté pan, toast sesame seeds over medium-low heat, shaking pan and stirring to prevent scorching, 30 seconds to 1 minute, or until lightly browned. Turn sesame seeds onto paper towels; set aside.
2. Rinse tofu and pat dry. Cut into small chunks.
3. For dressing, combine tofu and sesame oil in food processor or blender and purée.
4. With machine running, drizzle in just enough rice vinegar to make dressing of smooth, pourable consistency. (The amount of vinegar used will vary, depending on water content of tofu.) Add sugar, salt, and pepper, cover container, and refrigerate until ready to serve.
5. Place bean sprouts in colander and rinse under cold running water; set aside to drain.
6. Bring 3 quarts water to a boil in large saucepan.
7. Remove and discard any bruised or discolored outer leaves from lettuce. Wash lettuce and dry in salad spinner or with paper towels. Stack leaves and cut enough lettuce crosswise into thin strips to measure 3 to 4 cups; place in large salad bowl.
8. Peel and trim carrot. Using food processor or coarse side of grater, shred carrot; add to lettuce in bowl.
9. Plunge bean sprouts into boiling water for 15 seconds, turn into colander, and refresh under cold water. Drain, dry, add to salad bowl, and toss.
10. Turn processor or blender on and off once or twice to recombine dressing. Add 1 cup dressing to salad and toss until evenly coated; reserve remaining dressing for another use. Sprinkle salad with toasted sesame seeds.

Miso and Watercress Soup
Shrimp and Vegetable Tempura

Miso *and watercress soup is the perfect prelude to vegetable and shrimp* tempura, *served with rice vinegar and soy sauce for dipping.*

Properly prepared *tempura* should have a crisp and delicate crust that doesn't coat the food heavily: The color of the food should be visible through the coating. The trick is to make the batter just before it is needed so it does not become thick or gummy. It also helps to have the shrimp and vegetables well chilled, so prepare them in advance and refrigerate them. As the batter-dipped food is lowered into the hot oil, the coating should puff up. For best results, cook the *tempura* quickly, taking care not to overcrowd the food in the hot oil. If the pan is crowded, the temperature of the oil drops and slows the cooking, resulting in soggy food.

The recipes for the soup and the dipping sauce use *katsuo dashi*, a clear stock made from kelp, dried bonito shavings, and other seasonings. Available in an instant dried form in Oriental markets, *katsuo dashi* has a long shelf life. If it is unavailable, you can use half a cup each of hot water and clam juice.

Miso is a seasoning and soup base with a consistency similar to peanut butter produced by fermenting soybeans with rice or wheat. This versatile high-protein paste comes in a variety of colors and is sold in Oriental markets and health food stores. There is no substitute for its unique flavor.

WHAT TO DRINK

Beer or a crisp white wine, such as a California Sauvignon Blanc or a French Sancerre or Pouilly Fumé, would be good with this menu.

SHOPPING LIST AND STAPLES

1 pound large shrimp
Small bunch watercress
20 snow peas (about ¼ pound total weight)
8 medium-size mushrooms (about ½ pound total weight)
1 Italian eggplant (about 6 ounces)
Medium-size zucchini (about 6 ounces)
2 eggs
8 cups vegetable oil
1 tablespoon Japanese rice vinegar
½ teaspoon Japanese soy sauce
1 tablespoon miso paste
3 cups all-purpose flour, approximately
3 tablespoons cornstarch
2 teaspoons sugar
Two ½-ounce packets katsuo dashi
Salt and freshly ground white pepper

UTENSILS

Wok or large heavy-gauge saucepan
Small saucepan
2 large platters, 1 heatproof
Medium-size bowl
2 small bowls
Salad spinner (optional)
Colander
Measuring cups and spoons
Chef's knife
Paring knife
Wooden spoon
Chinese mesh strainer or slotted spoon
Small whisk
Vegetable brush
Deep-fat thermometer
Small brown paper bag

START-TO-FINISH STEPS

1. Follow tempura recipe steps 1 through 6.

2. Follow soup recipe steps 1 through 6 and serve as first course.
3. Follow tempura recipe steps 7 through 14 and serve.

RECIPES

Miso and Watercress Soup

Small bunch watercress
½-ounce packet (1 tablespoon) katsuo dashi
1 tablespoon miso paste

1. Bring 2 cups water to a boil in small saucepan over medium-high heat.
2. Meanwhile, wash watercress and dry in salad spinner or with paper towels. Trim stem ends and discard. Measure 2 cups loosely packed watercress and set aside; refrigerate remainder for another use.

Watercress

3. Add katsuo dashi to boiling water and return to a boil. Lower heat and simmer gently 2 to 3 minutes.
4. Meanwhile, combine miso paste and ¼ cup of the boiling broth in measuring cup and stir until blended.
5. Add miso mixture to saucepan and return just to the boiling point. Remove pan from heat immediately; further boiling will diminish the flavor of the miso.
6. Divide soup among 4 bowls, add an equal amount of watercress to each bowl, and serve.

Shrimp and Vegetable Tempura

1 pound large shrimp
Salt
Freshly ground white pepper
20 snow peas (about ¼ pound total weight)
1 Italian eggplant (about 6 ounces)
Medium-size zucchini (about 6 ounces)
8 medium-size mushrooms (about ½ pound total weight)
2 eggs

3 tablespoons cornstarch
3 cups all-purpose flour, approximately
8 cups vegetable oil

Dipping sauce:
½-ounce packet (1 tablespoon) katsuo dashi
2 teaspoons sugar
1 tablespoon Japanese rice vinegar
½ teaspoon Japanese soy sauce

1. Pinch off legs of shrimp, several at a time, then bend back and snap off sharp, beaklike piece of shell just above tail, leaving tail intact. Remove shell and discard. Using sharp paring knife, make shallow incision along back of each shrimp, exposing black digestive vein. Extract black vein and discard. Place shrimp in colander and rinse under cold running water; drain and dry with paper towels. Sprinkle shrimp with salt and pepper. Transfer shrimp to small bowl, cover with plastic wrap, and refrigerate.

2. Place snow peas in colander and rinse under cold running water; drain and dry with paper towels. Trim ends and remove strings; place snow peas on platter.

3. Trim and peel eggplant. Halve lengthwise, then cut crosswise into ½-inch-thick slices; place on platter with snow peas.

4. Scrub zucchini with vegetable brush under cold running water; dry with paper towel. Halve zucchini lengthwise, then cut crosswise into ½-inch-thick slices; place on platter with other vegetables.

5. Wipe mushrooms clean with damp paper towels. Trim stems and discard. Place mushrooms on platter with other vegetables, cover platter with plastic wrap, and refrigerate.

6. Preheat oven to 200 degrees.

7. Line large heatproof platter with double thickness of paper towels; set aside.

8. Separate eggs, placing yolks in medium-size bowl and reserving whites for another use.

9. Add 2 cups ice water to egg yolks, and beat with fork until well blended. Add cornstarch and stir until dissolved. Stir in 2 teaspoons salt. Add 1½ to 2 cups flour, a handful at a time, stirring gently with whisk to avoid beating in too much air, until flour is totally incorporated and mixture resembles pancake batter. The batter should have small lumps.

10. Heat oil in wok or large heavy-gauge saucepan over medium-high heat until it registers 375 degrees on deep-fat thermometer.

11. For dipping sauce, combine katsuo dashi, sugar, rice vinegar, soy sauce, and 1 cup hot tap water in small bowl, and stir with fork to dissolve katsuo dashi and sugar.

12. Place 1 cup flour in brown paper bag. If necessary, sprinkle vegetables with water before dredging them to help flour adhere. Place snow peas in bag, close bag, and shake to coat snow peas with flour. Add snow peas to batter. Using Chinese mesh strainer or slotted spoon, remove snow peas from batter, allowing excess batter to drip off. Carefully add snow peas to hot oil and fry, occasionally skimming off any particles of batter that float to surface of oil, 1 to 2 minutes, or until crisp and golden.

13. Using mesh strainer, transfer snow peas to towel-lined platter and keep warm in oven until ready to serve. Repeat process for remaining vegetables and shrimp, adding only as many as fit in pan without crowding.

14. Stir dipping sauce to recombine and divide among 4 small serving bowls. Divide shrimp and vegetables among 4 dinner plates and serve with dipping sauce.

ADDED TOUCH

After a *tempura* dinner, fresh oranges are an ideal dessert because the citrus flavor freshens the mouth.

Gingered Orange Slices

3 navel oranges
½ cup freshly squeezed orange juice
2 tablespoons ginger brandy, or 1 teaspoon crystallized ginger
1 teaspoon cornstarch
2 teaspoons slivered crystallized ginger

1. Using sharp paring knife, peel oranges, removing as much white pith as possible. Cut oranges crosswise into ½-inch-thick slices; set aside.

2. Combine orange juice with ginger brandy or 1 teaspoon crystallized ginger in large sauté pan and bring to a boil over medium heat.

3. Meanwhile, combine cornstarch and 1 tablespoon water in measuring cup, and stir until dissolved.

4. Add cornstarch mixture to pan and simmer, stirring, 1 minute, or until mixture thickens.

5. Add orange slices to pan and cook, turning slices to coat with sauce, 1 minute, or until heated through.

6. Divide orange slices among 4 dessert plates, sprinkle with slivered crystallized ginger, and serve.

Barbara Tropp

MENU 1 (Right)
Spicy Hunan Beef with Scallions
and Sweet Red Peppers
Warm Chinese Noodles with Sesame Oil
Hot and Sour Hunan Carrots

MENU 2
Hoisin-Explosion Shrimp
Home-style Spicy Eggplant
Spicy Cold Noodles with Sesame Sauce
and Toasted Sesame Seeds

MENU 3
Steamed Spicy Fish with Black Mushrooms
and Ham
Temple Fried Rice
Cold-Tossed Watercress with Sesame Seeds

As you sample an authentic Chinese meal, you will become aware of the delicate balance between one flavor and another, one texture and another. This balance derives from the Chinese philosophy of the duality of life—the *yin* and the *yang*, complementary opposites of human life, such as male and female, passive and active, sweet and sour. Barbara Tropp, a China scholar turned Chinese cook, brings this classic Chinese view of harmony to her cooking.

A native of New Jersey, Barbara Tropp spent two years in Taiwan, where she learned about Chinese food. After she returned to America, she became so homesick for Chinese cooking that she taught herself how to prepare Chinese meals. She has learned to adapt Chinese techniques to the fresh ingredients available in Western markets. Knowing that for most cooks speed is essential, she has revamped some of the lengthier traditional recipes to suit the often hectic pace of American life. She believes in practicality and economy—good taste above fancy presentation or lengthy preparation—so her menus do not require a large supply of expensive tools or ingredients.

Barbara Tropp favors the robust dishes of North China and the spicy hot foods of Szechwan and Hunan in the West. Menu 1 combines noodles with spicy beef—a popular northern dish—and hot and sour Hunan carrots. Menu 2, starring shrimp and eggplant, is a spicy Hunanese blend of chili, ginger, garlic, and scallions, and Menu 3 is multiregional.

Patterned china sets off this brilliant dinner, ideal for a winter evening. Add a sprig of parsley to the platter of hot and sour carrots and top the noodles with sesame seeds if desired. The bright beef dish needs no garnish.

90

Spicy Hunan Beef with Scallions and Sweet Red Peppers
Warm Chinese Noodles with Sesame Oil
Hot and Sour Hunan Carrots

Both the beef and the noodle recipes call for a common Chinese ingredient—sesame oil. This dark brown nutty oil—a pantry basic—is not for cooking but for seasoning. Buy only a Chinese or Japanese brand; the cold-pressed health food or Middle Eastern types will not do.

In the hot and sour Hunan carrots, red chilies provide the hot taste, vinegar the sour, while the sprinkling of sugar enhances the flavor without sweetening the dish.

For this menu, the first step is to marinate the beef in the morning. At cooking time, you use a common Chinese technique that "double cooks" an ingredient. You sear the beef quickly in hot oil, then stir fry the other ingredients. For the last few seconds of cooking, you return the beef strips to the pan and combine all the ingredients.

WHAT TO DRINK

This spicy menu calls for a light, fruity wine with a touch of sweetness, such as a California Zinfandel.

SHOPPING LIST AND STAPLES

1 pound round or flank steak, trimmed of fat and gristle
1½ pounds baby carrots
1 red bell pepper
2 bunches scallions
1½ tablespoons Chinese salted black beans
Fresh coriander or Italian parsley sprigs (optional)
Fresh ginger
5 cloves garlic
1½ tablespoons *hoisin* sauce
⅔ cup unsalted Chinese Chicken Stock (see page 13)
3 to 4 cups plus 3½ tablespoons corn or peanut oil
2 tablespoons plus ¾ teaspoon Oriental sesame oil
1½ tablespoons unseasoned Oriental rice vinegar
6 tablespoons light soy sauce
1 pound ¹⁄₁₆-inch-thin Chinese egg noodles, fresh or dried
6½ teaspoons cornstarch
2 tablespoons plus 1⅜ teaspoons sugar
Kosher salt
1¼ teaspoons dried red pepper flakes
3 tablespoons Chinese rice wine or dry sherry

UTENSILS

Wok with cover
   or Dutch oven (for frying beef)
   and 12-inch skillet (for completing beef; carrots)

Stockpot or kettle
2 large bowls
4 small bowls
Saucer
Metal colander (optional)
Measuring cups and spoons
Chinese cleaver or chef's knife
Paring knife
Metal wok spatula or large wooden spoon
Chinese mesh spoon or long-handled slotted metal spoon
   (if not using colander)
16-inch chopsticks or 2 long-handled wooden spoons
Vegetable peeler
Deep-fat thermometer

START-TO-FINISH STEPS

In the morning: Follow Hunan beef recipe steps 1 and 2.
1. Follow warm Chinese noodles recipe step 1. While water comes to a boil, follow Hunan beef recipe steps 3 through 5.
2. Prepare carrots for Hunan carrots recipe step 1.
3. Wipe out wok. Follow Hunan beef recipe step 6.
4. Follow Hunan carrots recipe steps 2 through 4.
5. Follow Hunan beef recipe steps 7 through 12.
6. Follow Hunan carrots recipe steps 5 through 7.
7. Follow warm Chinese noodles recipe steps 2 and 3.
8. Follow Hunan carrots recipe step 8 and noodles recipe steps 4 through 6.
9. Remove beef and carrots from oven, and serve with warm noodles.

RECIPES

Spicy Hunan Beef with Scallions and Sweet Red Peppers

1 pound round or flank steak, trimmed of fat and gristle

The marinade:
2 tablespoons light soy sauce
4 teaspoons cornstarch
1 teaspoon sugar
1 tablespoon corn or peanut oil

The sauce:
3 tablespoons Chinese rice wine or dry sherry
2 tablespoons light soy sauce
2 tablespoons sugar
1½ tablespoons *hoisin* sauce
¾ teaspoon sesame oil

8 whole scallions
1 red bell pepper, cored, seeded, and cut into thin strips
2 to 3 teaspoons finely minced garlic (about 3 cloves)
2 to 3 teaspoons finely minced fresh ginger
½ to ¾ teaspoon dried red pepper flakes
3 to 4 cups corn or peanut oil
⅛ teaspoon kosher salt
⅛ teaspoon sugar

1. Prepare beef and marinade. Holding cleaver or knife at angle, cut beef against grain into long strips about ⅛ inch thick and ½ inch wide. Cut strips crosswise into 2-inch lengths.
2. Using fork, blend marinade ingredients in large bowl until smooth. Add beef and toss well to coat each slice. Seal and refrigerate. Remove 1 hour before preparation.
3. In small bowl stir to combine sauce ingredients.
4. Trim wilted tops and root ends from scallions. Cut on sharp diagonal into thin ovals about 1 inch long.
5. Core and seed pepper. Cut lengthwise into thinnest possible strips.
6. Combine garlic, ginger, and dried red pepper flakes in another small bowl.
7. Heat wok or Dutch oven over high heat until hot enough to evaporate a bead of water on contact. Add oil and heat to 350 degrees on deep-fat thermometer, or until a slice of beef bubbles very slowly when added. While oil is heating, drain beef in metal colander nested in large bowl.
8. Stir beef once more, then gently slide slices into the oil. Carefully stir to separate beef slices and fry 15 seconds, just until beef is slightly gray.
9. Using pot holders, immediately pour beef and hot oil into metal colander. Or, working very fast, you may use a Chinese mesh spoon or long-handled slotted metal spoon to scoop out the beef, then drain on paper towels. Turn off heat and allow oil to cool before pouring it off. Reserve.
10. Wipe out wok, leaving thin film of oil. Heat wok or heavy skillet over high heat until a bead of water sizzles on contact. Add 2 tablespoons of the hot oil and swirl to coat pan. Reduce heat to medium. Add garlic, ginger, and pepper flakes, and stir about 10 seconds, adjusting heat so they do not brown.
11. Add red pepper strips and stir briskly to glaze them. Sprinkle with salt and sugar, then toss to combine, about 10 seconds in all. Drizzle in a bit more oil, if neccessary, to prevent sticking. Lower heat if peppers begin to scorch.
12. Stir sauce mixture, then add to pan, stirring to combine. Raise heat slightly to bring mixture to the bubbling point. Add beef and toss briskly to coat with sauce, about 5 seconds. Add scallions and toss briskly to combine and glaze with sauce, about 5 seconds. Do not let scallions wilt. Place in serving dish and keep warm in preheated 200-degree oven.

Warm Chinese Noodles with Sesame Oil

1 pound ¹⁄₁₆-inch-thin Chinese egg noodles, fresh or dried
2 teaspoons kosher salt

2 tablespoons sesame oil
Fresh coriander or Italian parsley for garnish (optional)

1. Bring 4 quarts unsalted water to a rolling boil in stockpot or kettle.
2. If using fresh noodles, fluff them and add to pot.
3. Using chopsticks or 2 long-handled wooden spoons, swish noodles gently back and forth several times to separate strands. Cook until a single strand tastes cooked but still firm to the bite.
4. Drain immediately in metal colander.
5. Return drained noodles to pot, combine with salt and sesame oil, and toss well to coat each strand.
6. Turn onto heated serving platter and garnish with fresh coriander or Italian parsley sprigs, if desired. Serve.

Hot and Sour Hunan Carrots

1½ pounds baby carrots
1½ tablespoons salted black beans, coarsely chopped
2½ teaspoons finely minced garlic (about 2 cloves)
2½ teaspoons finely minced fresh ginger
½ teaspoon dried red pepper flakes

The sauce:
½ cup unsalted Chinese Chicken Stock
2 tablespoons light soy sauce
1½ tablespoons unseasoned Oriental rice vinegar
¼ teaspoon sugar

2½ teaspoons cornstarch
1½ tablespoons Chinese Chicken Stock
2½ tablespoons corn or peanut oil

1. Peel and roll cut carrots (see page 10). There should be about 4 cups.
2. Combine black beans, garlic, ginger, and red pepper flakes in saucer.
3. Combine sauce ingredients in small bowl, stirring to dissolve sugar.
4. Blend cornstarch and broth until smooth. Set aside.
5. Heat wok or heavy skillet over high heat until hot enough to evaporate a bead of water on contact. Add oil, swirling to coat pan, then reduce heat to medium-high. Add black bean mixture and stir gently until fully fragrant, about 10 seconds.
6. Add carrots and toss briskly to combine and glaze each nugget with oil, drizzling in a bit more oil from side of pan, if necessary, to prevent sticking. Continue to toss until carrots feel hot to the touch, about 1 minute.
7. Stir sauce, then add to pan. Toss to combine it with the carrots, then raise heat to bring liquids to a simmer. Level the carrots, adjust heat to maintain a steady simmer, then cover pan. Cook 3 to 4 minutes, until carrots are tender-crisp and still a bit underdone. Taste sauce and adjust with an extra splash of vinegar or a dash of sugar.
8. Stir cornstarch and chicken broth mixture quickly to recombine, then add to pan. Stir until glossy and slightly thick, about 10 seconds. Remove to heated serving bowl and keep warm in preheated 200-degree oven.

Hoisin-Explosion Shrimp
Home-style Spicy Eggplant
Spicy Cold Noodles with Sesame Sauce and Toasted Sesame Seeds

Hoisin-explosion shrimp are fresh shrimp cooked in the shell with *hoisin* sauce and wine. The "explosion" comes during the stir fry, when the alcohol evaporates and the sauce bubbles on contact with hot metal, causing the fragrances and flavors of the shellfish, spices, and wine to reach their peak. This is a home-style meal,

Though both the shrimp and eggplant are peppery to the taste, they provide pleasing contrasts in texture and color, which you can carry out in your table setting.

spicy but well-balanced in taste. The combination of shrimp and eggplant, soy sauce and vinegar, garlic and scallion unifies the meal and gives it a Hunanese character.

Most shrimp marketed today as fresh have been previously frozen and then thawed out in the fish market, but if you can buy truly fresh shrimp from a reliable fish store, do so. Otherwise look for a firm flesh, an intact shell, and a clean smell. The color of the shell is not an indication of freshness; it varies depending on locality and may be gray or pink.

Cooking shrimp in the shell is a favorite Chinese method

because the shell protects the tender shrimp and keeps it from drying out. Before you cook the shrimp, devein it as directed in the recipe and shown in the diagram, being careful not to detach the shell. You and your guests will find it easy to shell the shrimp once the shell has been cut.

Oriental eggplants—either Japanese or Chinese—are smaller and sweeter than the Western ones, and their skins are edible. If these varieties are not available, choose small Western eggplants with smooth, unblemished skins, but do not peel them.

The spicy cold noodles, tossed with a piquant sesame sauce and garnished with toasted sesame seeds, are especially good tasting and fun to eat. Fresh Chinese egg noodles are delicious, but if they are not available, select an Italian or Spanish dried egg noodle rather than a Chinese dried noodle.

Chinese black vinegar—used here to season the eggplant—is difficult to find. The best brand, according to Barbara Tropp, is Narcissus. Two readily available substitutes are Italian balsamic vinegar or California barengo vinegar, which you should be able to buy in any specialty food store.

Fresh coriander has a very pungent smell, unpleasant to some people, delightful to others. If you or your family and guests do not care for it, omit it and use Italian parsley instead.

WHAT TO DRINK

Chilled white wine is the appropriate drink to accompany this menu. Choose a California Sauvignon Blanc or Fumé Blanc for roundness and relative fullness. The cook also recommends a full-flavored Gewürztraminer from California or, if you prefer, Japanese beer.

SHOPPING LIST AND STAPLES

1½ pounds large fresh shrimp in the shell (15 to 20 shrimp)
2 pounds firm young eggplant, preferably long slender Oriental or small Italian variety
1 bunch scallions
1 bunch fresh coriander (optional)
Fresh ginger

10 cloves garlic
2 tablespoons *hoisin* sauce
6 tablespoons Chinese sesame paste
½ cup plus 6 tablespoons corn or peanut oil
5 tablespoons plus 1¼ teaspoons Oriental sesame oil
2 tablespoons sesame chili oil
2 tablespoons unseasoned Oriental rice vinegar
2 teaspoons plus dash Chinese black or balsamic vinegar
8 tablespoons light soy sauce
¾ pound ⅟₁₆-inch-thin Chinese egg noodles, preferably
   fresh
3 tablespoons plus 2 teaspoons sugar
2 tablespoons plus 1 teaspoon brown sugar
1¼ teaspoons dried red pepper flakes
2 tablespoons sesame seeds
2 tablespoons Chinese rice wine or dry sherry

UTENSILS

Food processor or blender
Wok with cover
   or 12-inch skillet with cover (for shrimp; eggplant)
Stockpot
   or Dutch oven (for noodles)
Small skillet
3 medium-size bowls
2 small bowls
3 small plates
Metal colander
Measuring cups and spoons
Chinese cleaver or chef's knife
Paring knife
Metal wok spatula or wooden spoon
16-inch chopsticks or 2 long-handled wooden spoons
Small scissors, preferably embroidery type

START-TO-FINISH STEPS

1. Follow spicy cold noodles recipe step 1 and set aside.
2. Follow eggplant recipe step 1.
3. Follow shrimp recipe steps 1 and 2.
4. Trim scallions for shrimp recipe step 3; trim and slice scallions for eggplant recipe step 2.
5. Follow spicy cold noodles recipe steps 2 and 3.
6. Follow eggplant recipe steps 3 and 4.
7. Follow cold noodles recipe steps 4 through 8.
8. Follow eggplant recipe steps 5 through 8 and shrimp recipe step 4.
9. Wipe out wok. Complete shrimp, steps 5 through 8.
10. Complete eggplant recipe step 9 and cold noodles recipe step 9, and serve with shrimp.

RECIPES

Hoisin-Explosion Shrimp

1½ pounds large fresh shrimp in the shell (15 to 20
   shrimp)
2 scallions

1 tablespoon finely minced garlic (about 3 cloves)
½ to ¾ teaspoon dried red pepper flakes (optional)
The sauce:
2 tablespoons sugar
2 tablespoons *hoisin* sauce
2 tablespoons Chinese rice wine or dry sherry
2 tablespoons light soy sauce
½ teaspoon sesame oil
5 to 6 tablespoons corn or peanut oil
Fresh coriander sprigs for garnish (optional)

1. Using your fingers, pinch off legs of shrimp, several at a time, then bend back and snap off sharp, beaklike piece of shell just above tail. Using scissors with straight, thin blades, cut through shell along back of each shrimp all the way to the tail, taking care to expose black digestive vein. Extract black vein with point of scissors. Be careful not to loosen shell.

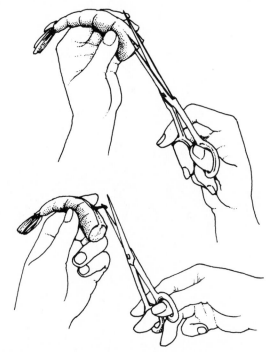

2. Put shrimp in colander, rinse briefly with cool water, then dry with paper towels. Remove to medium-size bowl and set aside.
3. Trim wilted green tops and roots from scallions. Cut scallions in half crosswise. Firmly grasp the pieces together and cut crosswise into ⅛-inch rings. Put aside ½ tablespoon for garnish if you are not using coriander. Put remaining scallion rings, garlic, and red pepper flakes side by side on small plate.
4. Stir to combine sauce ingredients in small bowl.
5. Heat wok or large heavy skillet over high heat until hot enough to evaporate a bead of water on contact. Add 5 tablespoons cooking oil, swirling to coat pan, then reduce heat to medium-high. Add garlic and stir so that it foams without browning. Add red pepper flakes and stir to combine. Then add scallion rings, again tossing several times to combine.
6. Add shrimp. Toss briskly 1 to 1½ minutes, until shrimp

turn pink and shells are evenly glazed with oil. Adjust heat so shrimp sizzle without scorching. Drizzle in more oil, if necessary, to keep shrimp and seasoning from sticking.

7. Stir sauce briefly to recombine, then add to pan. Raise heat to "explode" its fragrance (it will hiss and smell invitingly of wine), then toss briskly to combine. Toss until shrimp are evenly coated and sauce is slightly thick, about 10 seconds, then turn off heat.

8. Immediately transfer mixture to heated serving platter. Garnish with fresh coriander, if desired, or the reserved scallion rings.

Home-style Spicy Eggplant

2 pounds firm, young eggplant, preferably long slender
    Oriental or small Italian variety
2 scallions
5 to 6 teaspoons finely minced garlic (about 5 to 7 cloves)
4 teaspoons finely minced fresh ginger
½ teaspoon dried red pepper flakes

The sauce:
⅔ cup water
3 tablespoons light soy sauce
2 tablespoons plus 1 teaspoon brown sugar
2 teaspoons Chinese black or balsamic vinegar

½ cup corn or peanut oil
Dash black or balsamic vinegar
¾ teaspoon Oriental sesame oil

1. Trim stem ends and brown base of eggplant, then roll cut (see page 10). If using Western eggplant, cut into pieces about 1¼ inches long, 1 inch wide, and 1 inch thick. There should be about 8 cups. Put in medium-size bowl and set aside.

2. Trim wilted green tops and roots from scallions and cut scallions crosswise in half. Firmly grasp the pieces together and cut them crosswise into ¼-inch rings. There should be about ⅓ cup. Reserve 2 teaspoons green and white rings for garnish.

3. Put remaining scallion rings, garlic, ginger, and pepper flakes side by side on small plate.

4. Stir to combine sauce ingredients.

5. Heat wok or large heavy skillet over high heat until hot enough to evaporate a bead of water on contact. Add cooking oil, swirling to coat pan, then reduce heat to medium-high. Add scallion rings, garlic, and ginger. Stir to disperse them in the oil, adjusting heat so mixture foams without browning. Add pepper flakes. Stir gently about 10 seconds.

6. Add eggplant, tossing pieces to glaze them and pressing them gently against side of pan to encourage browning. Adjust heat so eggplant sizzles gently without scorching. As pan becomes dry, drizzle in another tablespoon of oil from the side. Continue tossing eggplant and pressing it against pan 3 to 4 minutes, until eggplant is brown-edged and a bit soft.

7. Briefly stir sauce ingredients and add them to pan. Toss gently to combine, then raise heat to bring liquids to a simmer. Cover tightly and adjust heat to maintain a lively

simmer. Cook about 3 minutes, until liquids are absorbed, shaking pan to prevent eggplant from sticking.

8. Remove cover and toss eggplant. Add dash vinegar, sprinkle with sesame oil, then toss to combine.

9. Turn into serving dish, cover, and keep warm. Serve garnished with a sprinkling of the reserved scallion rings.

Spicy Cold Noodles with Sesame Sauce and Toasted Sesame Seeds

The sauce:
6 tablespoons sesame paste, drained of oil
5 tablespoons sesame oil
3 tablespoons light soy sauce
2 tablespoons sesame chili oil
2 tablespoons unseasoned Oriental rice vinegar
1 tablespoon plus 2 teaspoons sugar
2 to 3 tablespoons finely chopped fresh coriander leaves
    and upper stems (optional)
4 tablespoons water, approximately

2 tablespoons sesame seeds
¾ pound ¹⁄₁₆-inch-thin Chinese egg noodles, preferably
    fresh

1. In food processor fitted with metal blade or in blender, combine sauce ingredients until smooth. Add enough water so that mixture will fall from a spoon in wide, silky ribbons. Adjust seasoning to taste. Transfer mixture to bowl and seal airtight. Set aside at room temperature. (This can be made several hours in advance or refrigerated overnight. Bring to room temperature before using.)

2. Bring 4 quarts unsalted water to a rolling boil in stockpot or Dutch oven.

3. Toast sesame seeds in small, heavy skillet over medium heat, stirring until golden, about 3 minutes. Remove to a plate to cool.

4. If using fresh noodles, fluff them to separate strands before adding to pot. Using wooden chopsticks or 2 long-handled wooden spoons, swish noodles gently back and forth several times to separate strands. Cook fresh noodles 1 to 2 minutes, until a single strand tastes cooked but still firm to the bite. Cook 4 to 8 minutes more if using dried noodles.

5. Drain immediately in colander and flush with cold running water until noodles are thoroughly chilled, tossing them gently to chill them quickly and evenly. Shake well to remove excess water.

6. Dry pot and return noodles to it.

7. Stir sauce. If it thickened when refrigerated, blend in a bit more water to achieve ribbony consistency. Do not thin sauce too much; it should cling to the noodles.

8. Pour half the sauce over the noodles and with your hands or wooden spoons toss gently to coat and separate each strand. Do not break the noodles (which to the Chinese are emblematic of long life). Pour remaining sauce into small bowl and serve separately.

9. Just before serving, toss noodles to redistribute sauce. Serve on individual plates or in shallow pasta bowls and sprinkle toasted sesame seeds on top.

Steamed Spicy Fish with Black Mushrooms and Ham
Temple Fried Rice
Cold-Tossed Watercress with Sesame Seeds

A long, oval platter makes the best setting for a whole steamed fish. Use a broad server, which both cuts and lifts, for slicing and serving the fish. Serve the watercress on individual plates, if you wish.

Ideal for a summer evening, this elegant meal of steamed fish, fried rice, and watercress salad depends (as do all the menus in this book) on fresh ingredients simply prepared. When you buy the fish, choose a whole one with bright red gills and glassy black eyes, as these are signs of freshness. Be sure to have the scales, fins, gills, and guts—including the air bladder—removed, but ask the fishmonger to leave the head and tail intact. If you cannot find a small, whole fish, use a two-pound section of a larger fish and have it cut in half lengthwise, through the backbone, so that you can lay it in the steamer skin side up as if it were two fish. Score the skin side only (see illustration, page 100).

Temple fried rice is a vegetarian dish, common to Buddhist temple kitchens. Since Buddhists are vegetarians who omit strongly flavored foods from their diets, this dish omits the meat, onions, and scallions that are typical ingredients in fried rice. Its unusual savoriness comes from celery heart, carrots, pine nuts, and eggs.

The watercress salad, briefly cooked, is a northern dish. Buy the crispest watercress you can find: good produce markets keep it standing in cold water or on shaved ice.

WHAT TO DRINK

Although Chinese foods usually call for a slightly sweet wine, a drier white would taste good here because of the savory rice and egg dish. Try either an Alsatian Sylvaner or a crisp Soave from Italy.

SHOPPING LIST AND STAPLES

3 pounds fresh whole fish (pompano, sea bass, porgy, flounder, or wall-eye), cleaned and gutted, with head and tail left on
1 ounce Smithfield ham or prosciutto, cut into paper-thin slices
4 bunches fresh watercress (about 1½ pounds)
2 medium-size carrots
1 bunch celery
1 red bell pepper (optional)
1 large scallion
6 to 8 Chinese dried black mushrooms
Fresh ginger
2 cloves garlic
3 large eggs
4½ to 5 tablespoons corn or peanut oil
7 teaspoons Oriental sesame oil

2 teaspoons unseasoned Oriental rice vinegar
4 tablespoons plus 2 teaspoons light soy sauce
1 cup uncooked rice
4¼ teaspoons sugar
Kosher salt
Dried red pepper flakes
4 ounces pine nuts
2 teaspoons raw or black sesame seeds
2 tablespoons plus 2 teaspoons Chinese rice wine or dry sherry

UTENSILS

Wok
    or 12-inch skillet (for completing rice)
Large stockpot
    or Dutch oven (for watercress)
Small heavy skillet
Medium-size saucepan with cover (for rice)
Fish steamer or large sauté pan with lid
Heatproof oval platter with sloping sides
Small flat plate
Large mixing bowl
4 small bowls
2 saucers
Metal colander
1-inch metal trivet (for steaming, if using sauté pan)
Measuring cups and spoons
Chinese cleaver or chef's knife
Metal wok spatula or long-handled wooden spoon
2 wooden spoons
Small whisk
Vegetable peeler
Scissors

START-TO-FINISH STEPS

1. For fried rice recipe, follow general rice recipe on page 10, steps 1 and 2.
2. Bring to a boil 1 cup water. Follow fish recipe step 1.
3. Follow fish recipe steps 2 and 3, and fried rice recipe steps 1 and 2.
4. Follow watercress recipe steps 2 and 3.
5. Follow watercress recipe step 4 and fried rice recipe step 3.
6. Follow watercress recipe steps 5 through 7.
7. Follow fish recipe steps 4 through 8.
8. Follow watercress recipe step 8.

9. Follow fish recipe steps 9 through 11.
10. Complete general rice recipe step 3.
11. Follow fish recipe step 12. While fish is steaming, beat eggs for fried rice recipe and follow step 4. Remove cover on cooked rice, step 4.
12. Follow fried rice recipe steps 5 through 8 and watercress recipe step 9.
13. Complete fried rice recipe steps 9 and 10, and fish recipe step 10. Serve at once.

RECIPES

Steamed Spicy Fish with Black Mushrooms and Ham

6 to 8 Chinese dried black mushrooms
3 pounds fresh whole fish (pompano, sea bass, porgy, flounder, or wall-eye), cleaned and gutted, with head and tail left on
1 ounce Smithfield ham or prosciutto, cut into paper-thin slices
2 teaspoons kosher salt
2 tablespoons Chinese rice wine or dry sherry
2 tablespoons light soy sauce
2 teaspoons sesame oil
¼ teaspoon sugar
2 teaspoons garlic, finely minced (about 2 cloves)
1½ teaspoons finely minced fresh ginger
½ teaspoon dried red pepper flakes
3 tablespoons thinly sliced scallion

1. Cover mushrooms with boiling water and allow to soak 20 to 30 minutes.
2. Trim fat from ham or prosciutto. Mince fat and reserve about 1 scant tablespoon. Cut ham into pieces about 1 inch square.
3. Rinse fish clean with water, inside and out. Shake to remove excess water, then pat fish dry inside and out with paper towels.
4. Holding cleaver or knife at a 45-degree angle, score fish at 1-inch intervals from neck to tail on both sides. Follow natural curve of collar and extend each cut from dorsal to ventral sides of fish (that is, from top to belly), cutting down nearly to the bone.
5. Sprinkle salt evenly over outside and inside of fish. Gently rub salt in score marks.
6. Put fish on heatproof oval platter about 1 inch smaller

than fish steamer or large sauté pan.
7. In small bowl, stir to combine wine, soy sauce, sesame oil, and sugar. Add garlic and ginger, and stir to blend. Pour mixture over fish.
8. In another bowl, combine reserved minced fat, red pepper flakes, and scallion rings. Sprinkle over fish.
9. Drain mushrooms and, using scissors, snip off stems and cut caps in half. Rinse caps under cold running water to dislodge any sand.
10. Neatly arrange ham and mushrooms along cuts in fish. Seal platter with plastic wrap.
11. Bring hot water to a gushing boil in covered steamer or large sauté pan. The water should not touch platter on which fish will steam.
12. Remove plastic wrap and put platter with fish on steaming rack or trivet. Wait until steam surges around fish, then reduce heat to medium-high and cover pan. Steam fish 10 to 15 minutes, depending on thickness of fish, or until flesh at base of score marks is white and firm. Do not overcook, as the fish will continue to cook from its own heat when it is removed from burner.
13. If fish was cooked in steamer, bring steamer directly to the table on a tray. Otherwise, lift out serving plate and place on serving trivet at the table.

Temple Fried Rice

2 medium-size carrots, peeled and trimmed
1 celery heart, plus several trimmed inner stalks
½ cup pine nuts
4½ to 5 tablespoons corn or peanut oil
3 large eggs, beaten
2 teaspoons Chinese rice wine or dry sherry
3½ cups cooked rice, at room temperature
1 teaspoon kosher salt or 2 tablespoons light soy sauce

1. Cut carrots lengthwise in half. Lay halves flat and cut lengthwise in half again. Firmly grasp the pieces together and cut crosswise into small, fan-shaped pieces, about ⅛ inch thick. Cut enough to measure about ⅔ cup. Put in small bowl.

2. Cut celery heart, leaves and all, into thin slices. Cut celery stalks lengthwise into fourths. Firmly grasp the pieces together in tight bunch and cut them crosswise into thin arcs. Measure out about ½ cup and reserve in small bowl.

3. Toast pine nuts in small heavy skillet until fragrant and lightly golden, about 2 to 3 minutes on medium to medium-high heat. Shake pan so nuts do not brown. Pour nuts into saucer and set aside.

4. Heat wok or skillet over high heat until hot enough to evaporate a bead of water on contact. Add 2½ tablespoons oil and swirl to coat pan. Reduce heat to medium-high and add beaten eggs to pan. They should puff and bubble immediately. Pause 2 to 3 seconds until a film of cooked egg sets on bottom, then tip pan toward you and with wooden spoon push cooked egg away. Pause about 2 seconds for a new film to set on bottom, then push it to far side of pan. Continue until there is no more flowing egg. Turn out soft mass onto flat plate and slice into dime-size bits or slivers. The egg should be moist, yellow, and loosely set. It will cook to doneness when combined with rice.

5. Heat wok or heavy skillet over medium-high heat until hot enough to evaporate a bead of water on contact. Add 2 tablespoons oil, swirling to coat bottom. When oil is hot, add carrots and stir fry briskly, about 15 seconds, in order to glaze pieces with oil and heat them through.

6. Add celery and toss briskly about 10 seconds. Scatter wine (or sherry) into pan and toss quickly just to mix.

7. Immediately add rice and toss briskly to combine. Lower heat if rice begins to scorch and drizzle in a bit more oil from the side if rice is sticking badly (it does tend to stick a little bit). Continue tossing until rice is heated through.

8. Sprinkle salt or soy sauce over rice and toss briskly to blend. Then taste, adding more seasoning if needed.

9. Return eggs to pan and toss gently 10 seconds just to combine and heat through.

10. Put rice in serving bowl and scatter in pine nuts. Toss gently to combine.

Cold-Tossed Watercress with Sesame Seeds

4 bunches fresh watercress (about 1½ pounds)

2 teaspoons raw or black sesame seeds
4 teaspoons sugar
5 teaspoons sesame oil
2 teaspoons light soy sauce
2 teaspoons unseasoned Oriental rice vinegar

1. Bring 4 quarts unsalted water to a boil in large stockpot or Dutch oven.

2. Cut watercress above band that joins each bunch and discard stems. Discard any wilted or discolored pieces from leafy tops.

3. Fill large mixing bowl with cold water and add watercress. Pump up and down with your hand to dislodge any dirt. Drain in colander, then shake off excess water. Dry bowl.

4. If using raw sesame seeds, toast them in small heavy skillet over medium heat, stirring until golden, about 3 minutes. Put seeds aside on saucer to cool. Black seeds do not require toasting.

5. Add watercress to the boiling water, pushing leaves beneath surface with spatula. Blanch 20 seconds, then drain immediately in colander and flush with cold running water until chilled.

6. Using your hands, press down gently but firmly to remove excess water, then sandwich watercress between two triple thicknesses of paper towels and pat dry.

7. Transfer watercress to the large mixing bowl. Fluff mass with your fingers and gently separate leaves.

8. Whisk sugar, sesame oil, soy sauce, and rice vinegar in small bowl, stirring briskly to thicken mixture. Taste and adjust with a bit more sugar, if desired. Pour sauce over watercress and with your fingers toss well to coat leaves. Cover with plastic wrap and chill.

9. Just before serving, toss watercress to redistribute seasonings. Mound on plate or in shallow bowl of contrasting color, then sprinkle sesame seeds on top.

ADDED TOUCH

For a fruit compote that will satisfyingly end this meal, peel and section one large grapefruit and four medium oranges, reserving their juice. Arrange the fruit in 4 serving dishes and drizzle the juice over them. Serve plain, or top with blueberries or whole strawberries, if in season. Sliced fresh kiwi fruit is also good, and you might combine it with lemon, lime, or tangerine sherbet.

Karen Lee

K aren Lee, a New York-based author and cooking teacher, describes Chinese cooking as "physically demanding—an action cuisine," which is actually both relaxing and fascinating when you know how to approach it. She emphasizes the importance of proper equipment—a sharp knife or cleaver and a good pan—because these make the work go quickly and produce the best results. For a successful stir fry, she prefers a flat-bottomed wok or heavy skillet. Remember that the essence of stir frying is speed, so prepare and organize all ingredients in the correct cooking order. Reheat oil between batches and quickly add the ingredients. The food cooks almost at once if the heat is high enough and if you do not overcrowd the pan.

Karen Lee was once the assistant of Grace Zia Chu, a famous Chinese cook, but she has developed her own cooking methods, which stress using little fat or salt. Her recipes are her own versions of Chinese classics and are based on homemade stocks and sauces and the freshest ingredients.

The three menus represent a mélange of Chinese regional fare, with contrasting tastes and colors. In Menu 1, the smoky taste of the bean sprouts offsets the fiery chili shrimp. The orange chicken in Menu 2 is spicy, aromatic, and sweet. Menu 3 features a northern Chinese favorite, barbecued lamb, served with braised turnips, which Eastern Chinese believe to have a medicinal effect, and Szechwan-style green beans flavored with dried shrimp and preserved vegetables.

This meal of shrimp, diced chicken, and bean sprouts comes to the table on serving dishes decorated with a delicate Chinese motif. Set off the shrimp by turning them out on a bed of lettuce leaves. Chopsticks and straw place mats will add attractive Oriental accents to this simple but authentic menu.

Chili Shrimp
Smoked Bean Sprouts
Diced Chicken with Fermented Black Beans / Rice

This chili shrimp dish is typical of Szechwan. Chinese chilies range from the firebrands used in sauces and oils to the larger, milder ones. Chinese cooks often use chilies stirred into a paste with garlic, as in this recipe.

The Chinese frequently cook shrimp with the shells still on, actually scorching the shells to intensify the shrimp flavor. This method has another benefit—it cuts down preparation time.

The smoked bean sprouts and diced chicken breasts are Cantonese. The fermented black beans in the chicken recipe are very pungent, so before using them you may wish to rinse them to remove some of the saltiness.

When buying bean sprouts, avoid the kind that are sold soaking in water. They will not scorch and thus will not take on the proper smoky flavor.

WHAT TO DRINK

Here you need a full-bodied, dry wine: a white Burgundy from Mâcon or an inexpensive California Chardonnay.

SHOPPING LIST AND STAPLES

1 pound skinless, boneless chicken breasts
16 large shrimp (about 1 pound)
1 bunch scallions
½ pound shallots (about 10 whole)
1 leek
¾ pound mung bean sprouts (not soaked in water)
4 Chinese dried black mushrooms
8-ounce package fermented black beans
Fresh ginger
2 cloves garlic
1 egg
2 tablespoons Chinese Chicken Stock (see page 13)
1 tablespoon oyster sauce
3 cups plus 4 tablespoons plus 2 teaspoons peanut oil
1 teaspoon Oriental sesame oil
2 tablespoons plus 1½ teaspoons dark soy sauce
3 teaspoons light soy sauce
1 teaspoon Chinese red rice vinegar or Western red wine vinegar
1 teaspoon chili paste
1 cup uncooked rice
2 tablespoons water chestnut powder, preferably, or cornstarch
1 tablespoon plus ½ teaspoon sugar
7 tablespoons dry sherry

UTENSILS

Wok
    or Dutch oven (for chicken)
    and 12-inch skillet (for shrimp; bean sprouts)
Medium-size saucepan with cover (for rice)
Large bowl
Medium-size bowl
4 small bowls
Metal colander
Strainer
Measuring cups and spoons
Chinese cleaver or chef's knife
Paring knife
Metal wok spatula
16-inch chopsticks or 2 long-handled wooden spoons
Deep-fat thermometer
Small scissors, preferably embroidery-type

START-TO-FINISH STEPS

1. Follow general rice recipe on page 10, step 1. Bring 1 cup water to a boil and follow bean sprouts recipe step 1.
2. Follow general rice recipe step 2.
3. Combine marinade ingredients in chicken recipe step 1 and follow steps 2 and 3. Preheat oven to 200 degrees.
4. Follow bean sprouts recipe steps 2 and 3.
5. Follow shrimp recipe steps 1 and 2.
6. Remove saucepan from heat in rice recipe step 3.
7. Follow bean sprouts recipe steps 4 through 6.
8. Follow chicken recipe steps 4 and 5.
9. Complete bean sprouts recipe steps 7 through 9 and keep warm in preheated oven, if desired.
10. Wipe out wok. Complete chicken, steps 6 through 11.
11. Wipe out wok (or skillet used for bean sprouts). Follow shrimp recipe steps 3 through 6; follow general rice recipe step 4.
12. Remove bean sprouts and chicken from oven. Serve together with shrimp and rice on the side.

RECIPES

Chili Shrimp

The seasoning sauce:
2 tablespoons dry sherry
1 tablespoon sugar
1 teaspoon Chinese red rice vinegar or Western red wine vinegar

1 tablespoon dark soy sauce
1½ teaspoons light soy sauce
2 tablespoons Chinese Chicken Stock
1 teaspoon chili paste
1 teaspoon water chestnut powder or cornstarch

16 large shrimp (about 1 pound)
2½ tablespoons plus 2 teaspoons peanut oil
2 whole scallions, chopped
2 teaspoons minced fresh ginger
1 clove garlic, minced
1 teaspoon sesame oil

1. Combine seasoning sauce ingredients in small bowl. Stir to dissolve water chestnut powder or cornstarch.
2. Using small pair of scissors, cut shell along back of shrimp, cutting into shrimp about halfway through. Do not remove shell. Remove dark vein with nose of scissors and pull off legs. Rinse shrimp under cold running water, drain in colander, and pat dry.
3. Heat wok or heavy skillet over high heat about 1 minute. Add 2½ tablespoons peanut oil and heat until hot but not smoking. Add shrimp and stir fry about 5 minutes, or until shrimp are almost cooked through. Shrimp will be charred and deep orange in color. Empty shrimp onto warm serving platter.
4. Return pan to high heat and add remaining 2 teaspoons peanut oil. Stir fry scallions, ginger, and garlic 30 seconds.
5. Stir seasoning sauce once more and add it all at once to wok or skillet, stirring until sauce thickens slightly.
6. Return shrimp to pan and stir another minute, or until shrimp are evenly coated with sauce. Turn off heat and swirl in sesame oil. Empty contents onto serving platter.

Smoked Bean Sprouts

4 Chinese dried black mushrooms
1 medium-size leek, white part only
¾ pound mung bean sprouts
1 teaspoon water chestnut powder or cornstarch
1 tablespoon oyster sauce
1½ teaspoons dark soy sauce
1 tablespoon dry sherry
1½ tablespoons peanut oil

1. Cover mushrooms with 1 cup boiling water and allow to soak 20 to 30 minutes.
2. Cut off root end of leek. Slice leek in half lengthwise and rinse under warm water to remove all sand. Cut into 3-inch lengths; then shred. Set aside in small bowl.
3. Place sprouts on layers of paper towels and pat dry.
4. Squeeze each mushroom over bowl. Using strainer lined with double thickness of cheesecloth or paper towels, strain and reserve 1 tablespoon of the liquid. Remove tough stems, rinse under cold water to get rid of any grit trapped in gills, and shred mushrooms. Add to leeks.
5. Combine water chestnut powder or cornstarch, oyster sauce, soy sauce, and sherry with the tablespoon of mushroom soaking liquid. Stir to dissolve.
6. Heat wok or skillet over high heat 2 minutes. Add bean sprouts, reserving a sprinkling for garnish, if desired. Stir fry without oil 2 or 3 minutes, or until sprouts begin to scorch. Transfer cooked sprouts to flat serving dish.
7. Return wok or skillet to high heat and add peanut oil. Immediately add mushrooms and leeks, and stir fry 2 minutes.
8. Stir oyster sauce mixture once more and add to the vegetables all at once, stirring until sauce thickens.
9. Add the cooked bean sprouts and mix briefly. Empty contents onto serving dish. This dish may be eaten hot or served at room temperature, garnished with a sprinkling of some fresh sprouts, if desired.

Diced Chicken with Fermented Black Beans

1 egg white
1 tablespoon water chestnut powder or cornstarch
1 tablespoon dry sherry
1 pound skinless, boneless chicken breasts

The seasoning sauce:
3 tablespoons dry sherry
1 tablespoon dark soy sauce
1½ teaspoons light soy sauce
½ teaspoon sugar
1 teaspoon water chestnut powder or cornstarch

¾ cup shallots (about 10 whole)
2 teaspoons minced fresh ginger
1 clove garlic, minced
1½ tablespoons fermented black beans
3 cups peanut oil

1. Combine egg white, water chestnut powder or cornstarch, and dry sherry in medium-size bowl and stir vigorously about 1 minute, or until marinade is smooth.
2. Remove any cartilage and fat from chicken. Cut into ¾-inch pieces and add to marinade, tossing well until chicken is evenly coated.
3. Combine seasoning sauce ingredients in small bowl. Stir to dissolve water chestnut powder or cornstarch.
4. Peel shallots and leave them whole.
5. Combine ginger, garlic, and black beans in small bowl.
6. Heat wok or Dutch oven over high heat about 1 minute. Pour in peanut oil and heat until oil reaches 350 degrees or until a sliver of garlic sizzles on contact.
7. Stir chicken in marinade. Turn heat to high and add mixture to pan all at once, stirring in circular motion about 1½ minutes, or until chicken turns opaque.
8. Turn off heat and carefully drain chicken and hot oil in metal colander set over large bowl.
9. Return 1 tablespoon of the oil to the wok or to a heavy skillet and add shallots. Stir occasionally over low heat about 3 minutes, or until shallots are cooked through.
10. Turn heat to high and add ginger, garlic, and black beans. Stir another minute.
11. Stir seasoning sauce and add it to the pan along with the cooked chicken. Stir another minute, or until chicken is evenly coated. Empty pan onto heated serving dish and keep warm in oven.

Orange Chicken
Stir-Fried Sugar Snap Peas
Stir-Fried Spinach with Fermented Bean Curd

Red peppers, scallion tops, and orange peel create an appetizing mélange of color with browned chicken thighs. The peas and stir-fried spinach add two more constrasting greens. Garnish the meal with semicircles of orange.

The crisp chicken dish in this menu is an excellent example of Szechwan cooking, successfully combining the sting of chilies in the chili paste with the mild aftertaste of the slightly sweet seasoning sauce. Orange peel, a favorite Szechwan flavoring, is also an ingredient. If you cannot find dried Chinese orange or tangerine peel, substitute fresh grated peel. Just be sure to grate the peel only; do not include any of the bitter white pith.

The sugar snap peas are likely to scorch, so stir fry them quickly over medium heat. Snow peas work equally well, and can be cooked the same way. If you must store them for a few days, wrap the unwashed peas in a plastic bag and refrigerate.

Both the chicken and the spinach recipes call for water chestnut powder as a thickening agent. Cornstarch is less expensive and perfectly adequate—and also more readily available—but use the chestnut powder if possible; it is lighter and gives a more luminous cast to foods. To remove any lumpiness, pulverize the powder in a blender and store it in an airtight jar. You will find water chestnut powder in Chinese groceries.

The fermented bean curd in the stir-fried spinach recipe has a strong, cheesy taste when mashed. Available in Chinese groceries as bottled cubes, it keeps indefinitely in the refrigerator. Several brands are seasoned with chili flakes. Buy one of these if you like extra spice. There are no Western equivalents. If you cannot find fermented bean curd, simply omit bean curd from the recipe; plain bean curd is not a substitute.

WHAT TO DRINK

Here, a medley of delicate flavors calls for an equally delicate wine with a light touch of sweetness. A German wine—say a Riesling Kabinett or, possibly, an Auslese (which is slightly sweeter than Kabinett) should be your first choice. Look for one from the Rheingau or the Rheinhessen.

SHOPPING LIST AND STAPLES

2 pounds chicken thighs
1½ pounds fresh spinach
¾ pound fresh sugar snap peas or snow peas
1 medium-size red bell pepper
1 orange (optional)
1 bunch scallions
Fresh ginger
3 cloves garlic
1 egg
2 tablespoons Chinese Chicken Stock (see page 13)
1 small jar fermented bean curd (optional)
3 cups plus 3 tablespoons peanut oil
3 teaspoons Oriental sesame oil
1 tablespoon dark soy sauce
1 tablespoon light soy sauce
1 teaspoon Chinese red rice vinegar
Dash white distilled vinegar

1 teaspoon chili paste
1 tablespoon plus 3 teaspoons water chestnut powder, preferably, or cornstarch
2 tablespoons plus 1 teaspoon sugar
Salt
1 ounce Chinese dried orange or tangerine peel, or 1 teaspoon grated fresh peel
5 tablespoons dry sherry

UTENSILS

Wok
    or Dutch oven (for chicken)
    and 12-inch skillet (for completing chicken; snow peas; spinach)
9-by-12-inch baking sheet
Large mixing bowl
3 small bowls
Salad spinner (optional)
Measuring cups and spoons
Chinese cleaver or chef's knife
Paring knife
Metal wok spatula
Chinese mesh spoon or long-handled slotted metal spoon
16-inch chopsticks or 2 long-handled wooden spoons
Deep-fat thermometer

START-TO-FINISH STEPS

1. Follow chicken recipe steps 1 and 2.
2. Follow spinach recipe steps 1 and 2, and snow peas recipe step 1.
3. Grate fresh orange or tangerine peel, if using, and follow chicken recipe steps 3 through 6.
4. Slice scallions in spinach recipe, step 3.
5. Complete chicken recipe, steps 7 through 16.
6. Wipe out wok. Complete spinach recipe steps 4 through 6. If you desire warm spinach, keep in oven with chicken while you finish preparing snow peas.
7. Wipe out wok or skillet for spinach. Follow snow peas recipe steps 2 and 3. Serve platter of chicken with snow peas and pass the spinach separately.

RECIPES

Orange Chicken

The chicken and marinade:
2 pounds chicken thighs
1 egg white
1 tablespoon plus 2 teaspoons water chestnut powder or cornstarch
1 tablespoon dry sherry

The seasoning sauce:
1 teaspoon water chestnut powder or cornstarch
3 tablespoons dry sherry
1 tablespoon dark soy sauce
1 tablespoon light soy sauce
2 tablespoons Chinese Chicken Stock

2 tablespoons sugar
1 teaspoon chili paste
1 teaspoon Chinese red rice vinegar

1 medium-size red bell pepper
3 whole scallions
3 pieces Chinese dried orange or tangerine peel, approximately 1½ by 2 inches, or 1 teaspoon grated fresh peel
3 cups peanut oil
2 teaspoons minced fresh garlic
2 cloves garlic, minced
2 teaspoons sesame oil
1 orange, halved and sliced for garnish (optional)

1. Remove skin from chicken thighs and cut away any fat. Using heavy cleaver or chef's knife, cut chicken thighs crosswise through bone into 1½-inch pieces.
2. Combine marinade ingredients in large bowl and add chicken pieces. Stir vigorously about 1 minute, until marinade is smooth and chicken is evenly coated. Cover and refrigerate until ready to cook.
3. Combine seasoning sauce ingredients in small bowl. Stir to dissolve water chestnut powder or cornstarch.
4. Core and seed red pepper and split in half. Slice into ¾-inch squares. Cut each square into 2 triangles.
5. Firmly grasp scallions together and slice them into ¼-inch rounds. Break orange peel into ¼-inch pieces.
6. Heat wok or Dutch oven over high heat about 1 minute. Pour in 3 cups peanut oil and turn heat to medium. Heat oil until it reaches 350 degrees on deep-fat thermometer.
7. Stir chicken once more in marinade. Raise heat to high and add half the chicken pieces and marinade to the oil, stirring occasionally to prevent chicken pieces from sticking together. Cook about 3 to 5 minutes, or until chicken is lightly browned.
8. Using Chinese mesh spoon or long-handled slotted metal spoon, remove chicken pieces from oil and place them on baking sheet lined with several layers of paper towels. Before frying remaining chicken, bring oil back to 350 degrees.
9. To finish cooking chicken (this gives it a crispy crust), heat oil to 375 degrees. Return one fourth of the chicken to the oil and fry 1 minute, or until chicken is well browned. Drain on fresh paper towels and fry remaining chicken in batches.
10. If using wok, pour off all but 1 tablespoon of the hot oil. Otherwise, heat heavy skillet 1 minute and add the tablespoon of hot oil.
11. Preheat oven to 200 degrees.
12. Turn heat to low, add scallions, ginger, and garlic, and stir fry 15 seconds.
13. Add dried or fresh grated peel and stir fry until it turns a darker brown, about 1 minute.
14. Raise heat to high, add red pepper, and stir fry 30 seconds.
15. Stir seasoning sauce and add it to pan all at once, stirring until sauce thickens slightly, about 15 seconds.
16. Return cooked chicken to pan all at once and stir fry

rapidly until chicken has been evenly glazed with the sauce. Turn off heat and add sesame oil, stirring to blend. Empty contents onto heated flat serving dish and keep warm in oven. Garnish serving dish or plates with orange slices, if desired.

Note: If desired, oil may be heated to 375 degrees in step 6 and chicken fried 5 to 6 minutes, or until golden brown. This would eliminate the second frying process in step 9.

Stir-Fried Sugar Snap Peas
¾ pound sugar snap peas or snow peas
2 tablespoons peanut oil
½ teaspoon salt
½ teaspoon sugar

1. String peas and rinse under cold running water. Drain and dry well with paper towels or in salad spinner.
2. Heat wok or skillet over high heat about 1 minute. Add peanut oil and heat until hot but not smoking. Lower heat to medium and add salt and sugar, stirring a few seconds.
3. Add sugar snaps or snow peas and stir fry continuously 1 minute. Remove peas and arrange them around chicken on serving platter like spokes of a wheel, if you wish.

Stir-Fried Spinach with Fermented Bean Curd
The seasoning sauce:
1 teaspoon water chestnut powder or cornstarch
1 tablespoon dry sherry
1 small square fermented bean curd, mashed (optional)
½ teaspoon sugar

1½ pounds fresh spinach
White distilled vinegar
2 whole scallions
1 tablespoon peanut oil
½ teaspoon salt
1 clove garlic, minced
1 teaspoon sesame oil

1. Combine seasoning sauce ingredients in small bowl. Stir to dissolve water chestnut powder or cornstarch.
2. Remove stems from spinach and wash in several changes of cold water to which several dashes of white vinegar have been added—it helps rid spinach of any grit. Dry with paper towels or in salad spinner.
3. Firmly grasp scallions together and slice them into ½-inch rounds.
4. Heat wok or heavy skillet over high heat about 1 minute. Add peanut oil and heat until it is hot but not smoking. If a piece of scallion sizzles when added, oil is hot enough. Add salt and stir until it dissolves. Add garlic and scallions, and stir fry 30 seconds.
5. Add spinach and stir fry about 2 minutes, or until leaves wilt.
6. Stir seasoning sauce and add it to pan all at once, stirring until spinach is evenly coated with sauce. Turn off heat and add sesame oil, stirring to mix. Empty contents onto serving dish. The spinach may be served warm or at room temperature.

Barbecued Lamb
Sautéed Green Beans Szechwan-style
Braised Turnips with Black Mushrooms

Precision-cut turnips and trimmed green beans add visual appeal to this menu of barbecued lamb cubes. A sprinkling of sliced scallion greens enhances the presentation.

The barbecued lamb marinated in black tea and fragrant with garlic and hot chili oil is a northern Chinese dish that is particularly good grilled on an outdoor barbecue in summer. Various cuts of beef, such as sirloin, flank, or shell steak, or filet mignon, make good substitutes for lamb. Instead of a Chinese sesame paste for the lamb's marinade, Karen Lee uses tahini, a Middle Eastern condiment, whose flavor she prefers for this recipe.

Green beans that are deep fried and then quickly stir fried are a famous Szechwan dish. Despite their double cooking, the beans retain their natural crispness. The cooks of this far western region often add ground pork to the beans for extra protein and flavor. In this version dried shrimp and Tientsin preserved vegetable also flavor the beans. The tiny dried shrimp have a salty taste and a strong odor, and are valued as a highly seasoned condiment. There is no comparable Western substitute. The preserved vegetable is shredded cabbage, which adds a distinctive crunch and saltiness to the recipe. It is sold in bulk in plastic bags, or in ceramic crocks in Chinese provision stores.

The turnips are easy to do. You steam them briefly, then stir fry, and finally braise them in a rich liquid. You can make them ahead if you wish and quickly reheat them, taking care not to overcook them. Their soft texture is an interesting contrast to the crunchy beans.

WHAT TO DRINK

The interplay of sweet and spicy in this meal makes choosing a wine a challenge. You might serve beer or, even better, a good ale. For a wine, try a French Colombard from California or perhaps a California or Washington State Semillon. Their softness will accommodate the variety of tastes in the menu.

SHOPPING LIST AND STAPLES

1½ pounds boneless leg of lamb
¼ pound ground pork
1 pound small white turnips
1 pound green beans
1 bunch scallions
5 to 6 Chinese dried black mushrooms
Fresh ginger
2 cloves garlic
15-ounce can tahini (Middle Eastern sesame seed paste)
12-ounce can Tientsin preserved vegetable
3 cups plus 1½ tablespoons peanut oil
1½ tablespoons Oriental sesame oil
1 tablespoon hot chili oil
5 tablespoons dark soy sauce
1½ tablespoons Western red wine vinegar
1 teaspoon chili paste
1 teaspoon honey
4-ounce bag dried shrimp
2½ tablespoons sugar

110

Chinese black tea
2 tablespoons dry sherry

UTENSILS

Wok
    or Dutch oven (for string beans)
    and 12-inch skillet (for completing string beans; turnips)
Large saucepan with cover
Vegetable steamer
2 large mixing bowls
3 small bowls
Metal colander
Strainer
Measuring cups and spoons
Chinese cleaver or chef's knife
Paring knife
Metal wok spatula
Chinese mesh spoon or long-handled slotted metal spoon
16-inch chopsticks or 2 long-handled wooden spoons
Deep-fat thermometer
8 skewers, preferably bamboo

START-TO-FINISH STEPS

In the morning: Bring ¾ cup water to a boil and follow lamb recipe steps 1 through 4.
1. Bring 2 cups water to a boil. Use 1 cup for shrimp in green beans recipe step 1 and the other for mushrooms in turnips recipe step 1.
2. Remove lamb from refrigerator and bring to room temperature, step 5. If using bamboo skewers, soak in water to prevent scorching.
3. Follow turnip recipe steps 2 and 3.
4. Follow lamb recipe step 6.
5. Follow green beans recipe steps 2 and 3.
6. Follow lamb recipe step 7 and turnip recipe steps 4 and 5.
7. If using double oven, preheat oven to 200 degrees. If using single-oven range, turn off heat. Follow lamb recipe step 8.
8. Complete turnip recipe steps 6 and 7, and keep warm in oven.
9. Wipe out wok. Follow green beans recipe steps 4 through 9.
10. Remove barbecued lamb and cooked turnips and mushrooms from oven. Serve with green beans.

RECIPES

Barbecued Lamb

1 tablespoon black tea leaves
½ cup tahini (sesame seed paste)
3 tablespoons dark soy sauce
1½ tablespoons sesame oil
1 tablespoon hot chili oil
1½ tablespoons sugar
1½ tablespoons Western red wine vinegar

2 whole scallions, chopped
2 cloves garlic, minced
1½ pounds boneless leg of lamb

1. Pour ¾ cup boiling water over tea leaves in large bowl and steep 5 minutes. Strain tea into measuring cup to make ½ cup. Discard leaves.
2. Return tea to large bowl and combine with remaining ingredients except lamb, and stir to mix well.
3. Using Chinese cleaver or chef's knife, cut lamb into 1¼-inch cubes.
4. Add lamb to marinade. Turn lamb to coat well and seal tightly. Refrigerate.
5. Thirty minutes before cooking, remove lamb from refrigerator.
6. Preheat broiler.
7. Place 4 or 5 cubes of lamb on each skewer, leaving ½ inch between cubes. Place skewers an inch apart on broiler rack and set rack as close as possible to heat source.
8. Broil 8 to 10 minutes, turning frequently. Keep warm in oven.

Sautéed Green Beans Szechwan-style

1 teaspoon dried shrimp
1 pound green beans
1 tablespoon dark soy sauce
1 tablespoon dry sherry
1 teaspoon chili paste
1 teaspoon honey
3 cups peanut oil
¼ pound ground pork
2 teaspoons minced fresh ginger
1 tablespoon Tientsin preserved vegetable
1 whole scallion, chopped

1. In small bowl, cover shrimp with boiling water and allow to soak 20 minutes. Drain and mince.
2. Cut off stem ends of green beans, leaving pointed ends intact. Wash beans and dry them well so they will not spatter when frying.
3. Combine soy sauce, sherry, chili paste, and honey in small bowl.
4. Heat wok or Dutch oven over high heat about 1 minute. Pour in oil and heat over medium heat until oil reaches 375 degrees on deep-fat thermometer. Or, test oil with a green bean: it should sizzle and the oil foam around it.
5. Turn heat to high and carefully add green beans all at once. Deep fry them until they wrinkle, about 3 minutes. Drain beans and hot oil in colander set over large bowl. Alternatively, you may use a Chinese mesh spoon or long-handled slotted metal spoon and quickly scoop out beans and drain them in a metal colander.
6. Return 1 tablespoon of the hot peanut oil to the wok or to a heavy skillet and turn heat to high. Add ground pork and stir about 2 minutes, or until pork turns white.
7. Add shrimp, ginger, preserved vegetable, and scallion. Cook, stirring, another minute.

8. Stir soy sauce mixture to recombine ingredients and add it to pan all at once, stirring a few seconds.
9. Add cooked, drained green beans and stir fry another minute, or until sauce is completely absorbed. Empty contents of pan onto heated flat serving dish and serve immediately.

Braised Turnips with Black Mushrooms

5 to 6 Chinese dried black mushrooms
1 pound small white turnips
1 tablespoon sugar
1 tablespoon dark soy sauce
1 tablespoon dry sherry
1½ tablespoons peanut oil

1. Cover mushrooms with 1 cup boiling water and allow to soak 20 to 30 minutes.
2. Peel turnips and cut into 1-inch cubes.
3. Bring 1 inch of water to a boil in large saucepan fitted with a vegetable steamer. Steam turnips 10 minutes.
4. Squeeze each mushroom over small bowl in which mushrooms soaked. Strain and reserve ½ cup of the liquid. Remove tough stems and rinse mushrooms under cold running water to rid of any grit trapped in gills. Cut each mushroom into quarters or eighths, depending on its size.
5. Add sugar, soy sauce, and sherry to bowl with reserved mushroom liquid.
6. Heat wok or heavy skillet over high heat about 1 minute. Add peanut oil and heat until hot but not smoking. Add mushrooms and turnips, and stir fry about 1 minute.
7. Stir soy sauce mixture before adding it to pan. Stir until turnips and mushrooms are evenly glazed. Turn into heated serving dish.

LEFTOVER SUGGESTION

The marinade for the lamb also makes a very good dip for lightly blanched or raw vegetables. Bring it to a boil before serving. The barbecued lamb is particularly good served the next day. Bring it to room temperature. Do not reheat it; the meat will dry out. The leftover green beans, if any, combined with greens, make an excellent salad.

ADDED TOUCH

Ripe, seasonal fresh fruit, served with scented or semi-fermented tea, brings any Chinese meal to a satisfying close. Pineapple and strawberries, when they are in the market, are a good combination. Slice off the top and bottom of a fresh pineapple, and save the top. Cut the body into 6 sections lengthwise. Remove the hard inner core and separate the fruit from the rind with your knife. Then cut each piece into 6 sections vertically. Place the top of the pineapple in the center of a serving platter and arrange the 6 sections around it, so that they radiate outward like wheel spokes. Scatter whole strawberries around the spokes and sprinkle with ¼ cup Grand Marnier.

FRENCH MENUS

Dennis Gilbert

Dennis Gilbert describes himself as a man who cooks for the love of it, acknowledging that his travels through northern Europe have been a major influence upon his food career, as were his experiences as a student and amateur cook at the University of Iowa. He has worked as a professional cook in a number of restaurants, and now is head chef at a restaurant in Maine. He believes that the presentation of a meal is very important, but that "dining is more than looking and smelling. People should have a substantial meal to sit down to."

For that reason, he has selected three menus from Périgord and the Auvergne, where sizable meals are commonplace. Menu 1 features *tourte à la périgourdine*, an adaptation of chicken pie that is ideal for a winter supper. *Tourte* comes from the Latin *tortus*, which means making round.

Menu 2, from the Auvergne, offers sautéed chicken breasts and *aligot*, a potato and cheese casserole. The word comes from *aligoter*, "to cut," and in a true *aligot* the melted cheese forms long ribbons that have to be cut when the dish is served.

Menu 3, also Auvergnac, consists of sautéed veal scallops with three distinctive side dishes: saffron apples, lentils with tomatoes and bacon, and a salad of celery root and sorrel. The lentil dish, according to Dennis Gilbert, orginated in the town of Le Puy.

The golden crust of the main-dish chicken pie is flecked with chopped parsley and decorated with pastry leaves. Garnish the mixed green salad with grated Parmesan and, if you wish, serve warm French bread as an accompaniment.

Tourte à la Périgourdine
Mixed Green Salad

For his version of this poultry pie, the cook uses fresh mushrooms and chicken livers in place of the truffles and *foie gras* of the traditional Périgord dish. Select chicken livers that are plump, moist, odor free, and dark red. Trim away any membrane and fat before cooking. Madeira, a fortified wine with a sediment, should be recorked after opening and stored on its side.

WHAT TO DRINK

A medium-bodied red wine would best accompany this hearty menu. Good choices include a Saint-Émilion or a California Zinfandel or Merlot.

SHOPPING LIST AND STAPLES

1 pound skinless, boneless chicken breasts
½ pound chicken livers
½ pound mushrooms
Large head Boston lettuce
Large head red leaf lettuce
Medium-size tomato
2 to 3 large shallots
2 cloves garlic
1 bunch parsley
1 lemon
1 egg
1 stick plus 6 tablespoons unsalted butter
¼ pound lard
2 ounces Parmesan cheese
1½ cups chicken stock, preferably homemade (see page 13), or canned
¼ cup plus 2 tablespoons extra-virgin olive oil
2¼ cups all-purpose flour, approximately
¾ teaspoon fennel seed
¾ teaspoon dried marjoram
Salt and freshly ground pepper
¾ cup Madeira wine

UTENSILS

Large heavy-gauge skillet or sauté pan
Small saucepan
9-inch pie pan
Salad bowl
2 large bowls
2 small bowls
Strainer
Salad spinner (optional)
Measuring cups and spoons
Chef's knife
Paring knife
Large wooden spoon
Slotted spoon
Wooden spatula
Whisk
Grater
Pastry cutter (optional)
Rolling pin
Pastry brush

START-TO-FINISH STEPS

Thirty minutes ahead: For tourte recipe, chill 5 tablespoons butter and ⅓ cup lard in freezer; clarify 1 stick plus 1 tablespoon butter and set aside.

1. Follow tourte recipe steps 1 through 9.
2. Follow salad recipe step 1.
3. Follow tourte recipe step 10.
4. While tourte is baking, follow salad recipe steps 2 and 3.
5. Follow tourte recipe step 11 and salad recipe step 4.
6. Follow tourte recipe step 12 and serve with salad.

RECIPES

Tourte à la Périgourdine

Pastry:
1 bunch parsley
2¼ cups all-purpose flour, approximately
1 teaspoon salt
⅓ cup butter, well chilled
⅓ cup lard, well chilled

Filling:
1 pound skinless, boneless chicken breasts
½ pound chicken livers
½ pound mushrooms
2 to 3 large shallots
2 cloves garlic
Medium-size tomato
1 stick plus 1 tablespoon unsalted butter, clarified
3 tablespoons all-purpose flour
1½ cups chicken stock
¾ cup Madeira wine

¾ teaspoon dried marjoram
¾ teaspoon fennel seed
Salt and freshly ground black pepper
1 egg

1. Wash parsley and pat dry with paper towels. Chop enough to measure ½ cup; set aside.
2. In large mixing bowl, combine 2 cups flour and salt. Using pastry cutter, or two knives, cut in chilled butter and lard until mixture resembles coarse cornmeal. Stir in parsley. Sprinkle dough with about ¼ cup ice water, and mix gently with fork to form ball.
3. Grease 9-inch pie plate. On lightly floured surface, roll out two thirds of pastry into a circle large enough to line pie plate. Roll pastry loosely around pin and unroll over pie plate, gently fitting the pastry into the plate. Roughly trim edges and set in freezer to chill thoroughly. Roll out remaining dough to form top crust. Place between 2 sheets of waxed paper and refrigerate.
4. Cut chicken breasts into ½-inch cubes. Wash chicken livers and pat dry with paper towels. Remove membranes and trim off any excess fat. Wipe mushrooms clean with damp paper towels and cut into ¼-inch-thick slices. Peel and mince shallots and garlic. Wash tomato and pat dry. Peel, core, halve, seed, and chop tomato. Set prepared ingredients aside.
5. Preheat oven to 450 degrees. In large skillet, heat ¼ cup clarified butter over medium-high heat. Add chicken cubes, livers, and mushrooms, and sauté, stirring constantly, 5 minutes. With slotted spoon, transfer mixture to large bowl.
6. For sauce, add remaining clarified butter to skillet. Still over medium-high heat, add shallots and garlic, and sauté, stirring constantly, 3 minutes. Sprinkle with 3 tablespoons flour and cook, stirring, about 2 minutes, or until light brown.
7. Slowly add 1½ cups stock, whisking constantly to prevent lumps. When sauce is smooth, stir in Madeira, chopped tomato, marjoram, fennel seed, and salt and pepper to taste, and bring to a boil, stirring constantly.
8. Add enough sauce (about ½ cup) to chicken mixture to moisten well; reserve remaining sauce.
9. Turn chicken mixture into chilled shell. Cover with top crust, crimping edges of pastry together to seal. Cut 5 or 6 small leaf shapes from pastry trimmings and arrange decoratively in center of pie. Bake tourte 10 minutes.
10. In small bowl, beat egg with a fork. Remove tourte from oven and reduce temperature to 350 degrees. Brush top of crust with beaten egg to glaze and bake another 15 minutes, or until top is golden.
11. Just before serving, return reserved sauce to medium heat for 5 minutes, or until heated through. Pour sauce through strainer set over small pitcher or sauceboat.
12. Remove tourte from oven and serve with sauce.

Mixed Green Salad

Large head Boston lettuce
Large head red leaf lettuce

1 lemon
¼ cup plus 2 tablespoons extra-virgin olive oil
2 ounces Parmesan cheese
Salt and freshly ground black pepper

1. Wash lettuce and dry in salad spinner or pat dry with paper towels. Tear greens into bite-size pieces, place in salad bowl, cover with plastic wrap, and refrigerate until ready to serve.
2. Squeeze enough lemon to measure about 2 tablespoons juice. In small bowl, combine olive oil and lemon juice and beat vigorously with fork until blended; set aside.
3. Grate enough Parmesan to measure ½ cup; set aside.
4. Just before serving, beat dressing to recombine and pour over salad greens. Toss greens until evenly coated, season with salt and pepper to taste, and sprinkle generously with grated Parmesan.

ADDED TOUCH

This cake has a very moist, almost pudding-like texture. Use canned, unsweetened chestnut purée to save time or, if preferred, use canned peeled chestnuts.

Chestnut Cake

15½-ounce can unsweetened chestnut purée
1 cup heavy cream, plus 1 cup (optional)
⅓ cup walnut-flavored liqueur (Nociello or eau-de-noix)
2 sticks butter, at room temperature
1½ cups sugar
8 eggs, separated
¼ teaspoon cream of tartar
1 tablespoon maple syrup (optional)

1. Preheat oven to 375 degrees.
2. Butter and flour 10-inch springform pan. In medium-size saucepan, combine 2½ cups chestnut purée, 1 cup heavy cream, and liqueur, and bring to a simmer over medium heat. Set aside and allow to cool to room temperature.
3. In bowl of electric mixer, cream butter and 1 cup sugar. One at a time, add egg yolks to butter-sugar mixture, beating after each addition until thoroughly blended.
4. In another bowl, beat egg whites and cream of tartar until frothy. Still beating, slowly add remaining ½ cup sugar and continue to beat until whites are stiff but not dry.
5. With electric mixer at lowest setting, add chestnut purée to creamed butter-egg mixture and beat just until blended.
6. With a rubber spatula, fold egg whites quickly into chestnut batter. Turn mixture into springform pan, smooth top, and bake 1 hour and 20 minutes, or until cake is set but still slightly underdone in center. Allow to cool to room temperature before unmolding.
7. Just before serving, whip heavy cream and maple syrup with chilled beaters in chilled bowl until stiff. Unmold cake and serve garnished with maple-flavored whipped cream, if desired.

Sautéed Chicken Breasts with Vegetables and Summer Savory Butter
Aligot

White china emphasizes the colors and textures of this elegant meal: chicken with vegetables and potato aligot.

118

Carrots and parsnips, two characteristic Auvergnac vegetables, are usually available year round in American supermarkets. Summer savory, an easy-to-grow annual, has a robust, peppery taste, somewhat like that of thyme. Either fresh or dried savory will do for this recipe, and herb butter can be made ahead and stored for two or three weeks in the refrigerator. Incorporating an herb butter into a reduced stock, as in this recipe, makes the sauce shimmer and produces a very flavorful result. For the potato casserole, or *aligot*, use Cantal, a firm, strong cheese that is similar to sharp Cheddar—or substitute Cheddar, if necessary.

WHAT TO DRINK

An ideal wine for this dinner is a Gewürztraminer—a dry and spicy one from Alsace or a fruitier California version. Either will nicely enrich the sauce for the chicken breasts.

SHOPPING LIST AND STAPLES

4 skinless, boneless chicken breasts (about 3 pounds total weight)
½ pound lean ham, unsliced
3 large boiling potatoes (about 1¼ pounds total weight)
½ pound parsnips
½ pound carrots
1 to 2 large shallots
2 cloves garlic
1 bunch scallions
Small bunch fresh parsley
Small bunch fresh summer savory, or 2 teaspoons dried
1 lemon
2 sticks plus 5 tablespoons unsalted butter
¼ pound Cantal or sharp Cheddar cheese
1 cup chicken stock, preferably homemade (see page 13), or canned
1 teaspoon ground coriander
Salt
Freshly ground black pepper
½ cup dry white wine

UTENSILS

Food processor (optional)
Electric mixer (if not using processor)
Large heavy-gauge skillet
Medium-size heavy-gauge skillet with cover
Medium-size saucepan with cover
Small heavy-gauge saucepan or butter warmer
Flameproof baking dish
Medium-size bowl (if not using processor)
Small bowls
Colander
Measuring cups and spoons
Chef's knife
Paring knife
Wooden spoon
Large spoon
Wooden spatula
Potato masher (if not using processor)
Tongs
Vegetable peeler
Juicer (optional)
Grater (if not using processor)
Meat pounder or rolling pin

START-TO-FINISH STEPS

One hour ahead: For summer savory butter, set out 1 stick plus 4 tablespoons butter to bring to room temperature.

Fifteen minutes ahead: Clarify 3 tablespoons of butter for chicken recipe.

1. For savory butter and aligot, wash parsley and summer savory, and pat dry. Chop enough parsley to measure 4 tablespoons and enough savory to measure 1 tablespoon. Peel and mince garlic and shallots.
2. Follow savory butter recipe step 1.
3. Follow aligot recipe steps 1 and 2.
4. Follow chicken recipe step 1.
5. Follow aligot recipe steps 3 through 5.
6. Follow chicken recipe steps 2 and 3.
7. While vegetables are cooking, follow savory butter recipe steps 2 through 4.
8. Follow chicken recipe steps 4 through 9 and aligot recipe step 6.
9. Follow chicken recipe step 10 and serve with aligot.

RECIPES

Sautéed Chicken Breasts with Vegetables and Summer Savory Butter

4 skinless, boneless chicken breasts (about 3 pounds total weight)
½ pound parsnips
½ pound carrots
3 tablespoons unsalted butter plus 3 tablespoons, clarified
Freshly ground black pepper
2 tablespoons chopped fresh parsley
½ cup dry white wine
1 cup chicken stock, preferably homemade (see page 13), or canned
⅔ cup Summer Savory Butter (see following recipe)

1. Trim chicken breasts of any excess fat and cartilage. With meat pounder or rolling pin, gently flatten breasts to about ½-inch thickness. Split breasts in half, place between two layers of paper towels, and pat dry. Set aside.
2. Peel parsnips and halve lengthwise. Lay parsnip halves flat sides down and cut on diagonal into ½-inch-thick slices. Peel and cut carrots as for parsnips. Set vegetables aside.
3. In medium-size heavy-gauge skillet, melt 3 tablespoons

butter over medium heat. When butter stops sizzling but before it browns, add parsnip and carrot slices, stirring to coat evenly with butter. Reduce heat to medium-low and cook, turning occasionally, about 5 minutes, or until vegetables are brown at the edges. Season with pepper to taste and sprinkle with 1 tablespoon chopped parsley. Cover skillet and set aside.

4. Preheat oven to 200 degrees.

5. Heat large heavy-gauge skillet over medium-high heat. Add clarified butter and, just as it begins to smoke, add chicken breasts, smooth side down. Sauté chicken about 3 minutes, or until brown on one side. With tongs, turn chicken, tilt skillet to redistribute butter evenly in pan, and sauté on second side about 2 minutes. Turn chicken and continue to cook, turning, until meat in center is still slightly pink and moist, another 2 to 5 minutes.

6. Divide chicken among individual dinner plates and keep warm in oven until ready to serve.

7. Reduce heat to medium, add ½ cup dry white wine, and deglaze pan by scraping up any browned bits clinging to bottom. Increase heat to high and cook until wine is reduced by half, about 3 minutes. Add stock to pan and reduce liquid again by half, about 3 minutes.

8. Remove skillet from heat. One tablespoon at a time, stir in ⅔ cup of prepared summer savory butter. When butter has been totally incorporated, pour just enough sauce over vegetables to coat them.

9. Remove dinner plates from oven and turn on broiler.

10. Spoon remaining sauce over chicken breast halves. Spoon carrots and parsnips around chicken, sprinkle with remaining chopped parsley, and serve.

Summer Savory Butter

1 lemon
1 tablespoon minced fresh summer savory, or 2 teaspoons dried
1 stick plus 4 tablespoons unsalted butter
1 to 2 large shallots, peeled and minced
1 clove garlic, peeled and minced
2 tablespoons chopped fresh parsley

1. Squeeze lemon and set juice aside. If using dried summer savory, combine with lemon juice in small bowl to allow herb flavor to develop.

2. Using food processor or electric mixer and bowl, cream butter until smooth.

3. Add shallots, garlic, parsley, and summer savory to butter and beat just until blended.

4. One teaspoon at a time, add lemon juice, or lemon juice with dried summer savory, if using, and beat until blended. Turn herb butter into small bowl, cover, and refrigerate until ready to use.

Aligot

3 large boiling potatoes (about 1¼ pounds total weight)
Salt
3 tablespoons unsalted butter
1 bunch scallions

120

¼ pound Cantal or sharp Cheddar cheese
½ pound lean ham
1 clove garlic, peeled and minced
1 teaspoon ground coriander

1. Peel potatoes and cut into 1½-inch cubes. In medium-size saucepan, bring potatoes, 1 teaspoon salt, and water to cover to a boil over high heat. Lower heat to medium and boil, covered, 10 to 12 minutes, or until tender.

2. Meanwhile, melt butter in small heavy-gauge saucepan or butter warmer over low heat. Wash scallions and pat dry. Trim ends and cut enough scallions into ¼-inch-thick pieces to measure 1 cup. Grate cheese in processor or on coarse side of grater. Slice ham into ½-inch-thick cubes.

3. Drain potatoes of all but 2 to 3 tablespoons of liquid. With electric mixer or potato masher, mash coarsely.

4. Add cheese, ham, garlic, coriander, and all but 2 tablespoons scallions to potatoes, and stir until combined.

5. Turn potatoes into flameproof serving dish and sprinkle with melted butter and remaining scallions. Cover with foil and keep warm.

6. Just before serving, brown under broiler for 2 minutes.

▬▬▬▬▬▬

ADDED TOUCH

Highly aromatic cardamom adds an elusive spiciness to this chocolate cake.

Chocolate Pecan Cake

1 orange
2½-ounce can pecan pieces
1 ounce (1 square) semisweet chocolate, grated
5 eggs
¼ cup plus 2 tablespoons sugar
2 tablespoons Dutch-processed unsweetened cocoa powder
½ teaspoon almond extract
1 teaspoon cardamom

1. Preheat oven to 350 degrees.

2. Grate zest of orange, being careful to avoid white pith. In food processor or with nut grinder, finely grind enough pecans to measure ¾ cup. In food processor or on coarse side of grater, grate chocolate.

3. Separate 4 eggs, placing yolks in large mixing bowl and whites in medium-size bowl. Add remaining whole egg and ¼ cup sugar to yolks, and, with electric mixer at high speed, beat until thick, about 10 minutes. Rinse and dry beaters.

4. Beat egg whites until frothy. Gradually add remaining sugar and continue beating until whites form soft peaks. Set aside.

5. To yolk mixture, add grated chocolate, cocoa, ground pecans, almond extract, orange zest, and cardamom, and stir until blended.

6. Gently fold whites into yolk mixture and turn into buttered and floured 8½ x 4¼ x 3-inch loaf pan. Bake about 40 minutes, or until a toothpick inserted in the center comes out clean. Cool in pan before turning out onto rack.

Veal Scallops with Saffron Apples
Lentils with Tomatoes and Bacon
Sorrel and Celery Root Salad

Saffron-tinted apple slices contrast handsomely with veal scallops for this Auvergnac-style meal. Serve the tossed sorrel and celery root salad and the lentils with tomatoes and bacon in separate wooden bowls.

The sautéed veal scallops cook through quickly if you gently flatten them to a uniform thickness. Ask your butcher for veal scallops, cut from the loin, that are almost white. Make sure they are trimmed of any fat or silvery membrane. Before sautéeing the scallops, pat them dry so the butter does not spatter when you place them in the pan. To seal in the juices, avoid overcrowding the pieces.

The sauce for the veal contains *crème fraîche* and saffron, the world's costliest spice. *Crème fraîche* is a thickened cultured cream product with a slightly tart nutty taste. At one time available only in France, *crème fraîche* is now found in some American supermarkets and in specialty food shops. To make your own, follow the directions on page 122. Both the green and the red lentils called for in the warm salad are imports, usually available at health food stores only. Regular supermarket lentils are acceptable, if not quite as flavorful and attractive.

Both the sorrel and celery root, or celeriac, in the salad are typically French vegetables. Sorrel, or sour grass, is a tart perennial herb that resembles spinach. If you substitute spinach, increase the amount of lemon juice and vinegar in the dressing to 1 tablespoon each. Celery root tastes a bit like nutty celery. Buy it no larger than 4 inches in diameter or the flesh will be woody. Since the skin is very thick, you will trim away almost half of the root when you peel it.

WHAT TO DRINK

A full-bodied white Burgundy would be a perfect accompaniment for this meal. A good-quality California Chardonnay would also be excellent.

SHOPPING LIST AND STAPLES

8 to 12 veal scallops (about 1½ pounds total weight)
½ pound smoked slab bacon, unsliced
2 large tomatoes (about 1¼ pounds total weight)
1 cucumber
1 celery root (about 1½ pounds)
Large red bell pepper
Small onion
¾ pound fresh sorrel or spinach
Small bunch parsley
1 to 2 large shallots
3 cloves garlic
Large lemon

4 medium-size tart apples, preferably Northern Spy, Cortland, or Granny Smith (about 2 pounds total weight)
1 cup crème fraîche or heavy cream
1 stick unsalted butter
2 ounces Parmesan cheese
½ cup veal or chicken stock, preferably homemade (see page 13), or canned
¼ cup plus 2 tablespoons olive oil
2 teaspoons tarragon vinegar
2 tablespoons Dijon mustard
1 tablespoon anchovy paste
¾ pound green or red lentils
½ cup flour for dredging
1 teaspoon dry mustard
½ teaspoon dried rosemary
½ teaspoon dried sage
1 teaspoon saffron threads
Salt
Freshly ground black pepper
⅓ cup dry white wine plus ¼ cup dry white vermouth, or about ½ cup dry white vermouth

UTENSILS

Large heavy-gauge skillet or sauté pan
Medium-size heavy-gauge skillet or saucepan
Medium-size heavy-gauge saucepan with cover
2 small saucepans
9-inch pie pan
Heatproof serving platter
Large flat plate
Wooden salad bowl
Heatproof serving bowl
Large mixing bowl
Small bowl
Colander
Large sieve
Salad spinner (optional)
Measuring cups and spoons
Chef's knife
Paring knife
Large spoon
Slotted metal spatula
Wooden spatula
Tongs
Melon baller or teaspoon
Vegetable peeler
Grater
Juicer (optional)
Wooden mallet or rolling pin
Small jar with tight-fitting lid

START-TO-FINISH STEPS

The day before: If making your own crème fraîche, combine ½ pint heavy cream and ½ pint sour cream at room temperature in small bowl and whisk until blended. Turn

into glass jar, cover tightly, and let stand at room temperature 6 to 8 hours. Refrigerate until ready to use.

One hour ahead: For lentils recipe, set out 2 tablespoons butter to reach room temperature.

Fifteen minutes ahead: Clarify 6 tablespoons butter for veal.

1. Follow salad recipe steps 1 through 5.
2. Follow lentils recipe steps 1 through 4.
3. While tomato mixture is simmering, follow veal recipe steps 1 through 3.
4. Follow lentils recipe steps 5 through 7.
5. While lentils are simmering, follow salad recipe steps 6 through 8.
6. Follow lentils recipe step 8 and veal recipe steps 4 through 7.
7. Follow salad recipe step 9, veal recipe step 8, and serve with lentils.

RECIPES

Veal Scallops with Saffron Apples

Large lemon
4 medium-size tart apples, preferably Northern Spy, Cortland, or Granny Smith (about 2 pounds total weight)
1 to 2 large shallots
2 cloves garlic
1 teaspoon saffron threads
8 to 12 veal scallops (about 1½ pounds total weight)
½ cup flour for dredging
6 tablespoons unsalted butter, clarified
⅓ cup dry white wine or dry white vermouth
½ cup veal or chicken stock, preferably homemade (see page 13), or canned
1 cup crème fraîche or heavy cream

1. Preheat oven to 200 degrees.
2. Squeeze lemon, reserving 2 teaspoons juice for salad dressing. Wash, halve, and core apples; cut into ¼-inch-thick wedges. Peel and mince enough shallots to measure ¼ cup. Peel and mince garlic. Combine apples, lemon juice, shallots, garlic, and saffron in large mixing bowl and toss to combine; set aside.
3. Trim veal of any fat or membrane. With a wooden mallet or rolling pin, flatten, but do not pound, veal scallops to a uniform thickness of about ¼ inch.
4. Place ½ cup flour in pie pan and lightly dredge veal scallops on both sides. Shake off excess flour and set aside on large flat plate.
5. In large heavy-gauge skillet, heat 3 to 4 tablespoons clarified butter over medium-high heat. Place as many scallops in skillet as will fit without overcrowding, increase heat to high, and brown veal quickly, 2 to 3 minutes on each side, adding more clarified butter as needed. With tongs, transfer scallops to heatproof serving platter and keep warm in oven. Repeat for remaining scallops.
6. For sauce, carefully pour off any fat and butter remain-

ing in skillet. Add ⅓ cup wine and deglaze pan over medium-high heat, scraping up any browned bits clinging to bottom of pan with a wooden spatula. Cook until liquid is reduced to 2 tablespoons, about 2 minutes. Add veal or chicken stock. From serving platter, pour accumulated veal juices back into skillet. Increase heat to high and cook, stirring, until sauce is reduced to ¼ cup, about 2 minutes.

7. Add crème fraîche, or heavy cream, to reduced stock, and cook at just under boiling point until sauce thickens, 3 to 5 minutes.

8. Add apple mixture to sauce and stir gently until combined. Reduce heat and simmer gently until apples are heated through, about 2 minutes. Pour sauce over veal scallops, top with apples, and serve immediately.

Lentils with Tomatoes and Bacon

¾ pound green or red lentils (about 1½ cups)
Salt
½ pound smoked slab bacon, unsliced
Small onion
2 large tomatoes
½ teaspoon dried sage
½ teaspoon dried rosemary
¼ cup dry white vermouth
Small bunch parsley
2 tablespoons unsalted butter

1. Pick over lentils to remove pebbles or other foreign matter. Place lentils in large sieve and rinse thoroughly under cold running water. Transfer to medium-size heavy-gauge saucepan. Add ½ teaspoon salt and water to cover, and bring to a boil over high heat, skimming off any scum that rises to surface.

2. While lentils are coming to a boil, slice bacon into ½-inch cubes, about 1¼ cups. Peel and chop enough onion to measure ⅓ cup. Wash tomatoes and pat dry. Peel, core, halve, seed, and chop tomatoes; set aside.

3. Boil lentils 1 minute, cover, and remove from heat.

4. In medium-size heavy-gauge skillet, fry bacon cubes over medium heat until crisp, about 5 minutes. Add onion and sauté until onion is translucent, about 3 minutes. Carefully pour off bacon fat from skillet. Add tomatoes, sage, rosemary, and vermouth, and simmer until nearly all liquid has evaporated, about 15 minutes. Set aside.

5. In large sieve, drain lentils and rinse under cold running water. Return lentils to saucepan, add fresh water to cover by 1 inch, and bring lentils to a boil over high heat.

6. While lentils are coming to a boil, wash parsley and pat dry with paper towels. Chop enough parsley to measure 2 tablespoons.

7. Lower heat under lentils to a simmer, cover, and cook gently until tender, about 10 minutes for green lentils or 4 minutes for red lentils.

8. Transfer lentils to sieve, drain thoroughly, and turn into heatproof serving bowl. Add bacon-tomato mixture, butter, and chopped parsley, and toss gently to combine. Keep warm in 200-degree oven until ready to serve.

Sorrel and Celery Root Salad

¼ cup plus 2 tablespoons olive oil
2 teaspoons tarragon vinegar
2 teaspoons lemon juice
2 teaspoons Dijon mustard
1 teaspoon dry mustard
1 tablespoon anchovy paste
1 cucumber
Large red bell pepper
1 celery root (about 1½ pounds)
¾ pound fresh sorrel or spinach
1 clove garlic
2 ounces Parmesan cheese
Salt and freshly ground black pepper

1. For dressing, combine olive oil, vinegar, lemon juice, mustards, and anchovy paste in small jar with tight-fitting lid, and shake until thoroughly blended. Set aside at room temperature.

2. Peel cucumber, halve lengthwise, and scrape out seeds with teaspoon or melon baller. Cut halves into ½-inch-thick crescents. Place in colander, sprinkle with 1 tablespoon salt, and set aside to drain.

3. Wash red pepper and pat dry. Core, seed, and cut pepper into 1-inch squares. Place pepper in small bowl, drizzle with 2 to 3 tablespoons dressing, toss gently, and set aside.

4. In small saucepan, bring 1 quart of water to a boil over high heat. While water is heating, peel celery root and cut in half. Cut halves into ¼-inch-thick slices, then into julienne strips. Plunge celery root into boiling water and blanch 10 seconds. Transfer to sieve and refresh under cold running water. Drain thoroughly, wrap in paper towels, and refrigerate until ready to assemble salad.

5. Wash sorrel, or spinach, if using, and remove any discolored leaves. Dry in salad spinner or pat dry with paper towels. Wrap in paper towels and refrigerate.

6. Peel garlic clove and rub over inside surface of wooden salad bowl. Discard garlic. Cover bowl and set aside.

7. In food processor or with grater, grate enough Parmesan to measure 2 tablespoons.

8. Rinse cucumber under cold running water to remove salt. Place in cloth napkin or kitchen towel and squeeze out any excess moisture. Add cucumbers to peppers and toss.

9. Place sorrel and celery root in salad bowl. Shake dressing to recombine, pour over sorrel and celery root, and toss. Top with peppers and cucumbers, sprinkle with Parmesan, and season with black pepper to taste.

Sorrel

123

Danièle Delpeuch

MENU 1 (Right)
Turkey with Prunes and Cream Sauce
Tomato Tart
Chicory Salad with Lardons

MENU 2
Turkey Paupiettes
Sautéed Broccoli
Lentils Vinaigrette

MENU 3
Braised Duck with Onions
Zucchini Flan
Belgian Endive and Orange Salad

A devotee of the rich, hearty cooking of Périgord, Danièle Delpeuch has dedicated a great deal of her time to learning the traditional culinary methods of that region. Primarily agricultural, Périgord offers an abundance of fresh produce and superb poultry, and cooks regularly shop the farmers' markets for the best buys. For her three menus, Danièle Delpeuch selects dishes typical of southwestern France and adapts them for the American kitchen.

The entrée of Menu 1 is based on a dish popular in the Dordogne River valley, where most well-equipped farm kitchens have a prune-drying oven. Instead of serving the usual rabbit with prunes, however, the cook substitutes boneless turkey breast, which goes equally well with the fruit. A mustardy tomato tart and a salad of chicory with *lardons* (coarsely diced bacon) are the accompaniments.

For Menu 2, she offers a Périgourdine dish traditionally served at wedding banquets and known locally as *oiseaux sans têtes*, or birds without heads. The bird here is turkey—in the form of scallops—rolled around a seasoned mixture of mushrooms, Smithfield ham, and chicken livers. In Périgord a cook would use wild *cèpes*, Bayonne ham, and *foie gras*—and add sliced truffles to the sauce just before serving.

Usually, when preparing a duck recipe at home, this cook uses her own farm-raised Barbarie ducklings. Menu 3 is her adaptation of a simple regional specialty— whole braised duckling with onions. Here the duck is quartered and its juices combine with sweet onions as the seasoning for the meat. With this hearty main dish, she serves zucchini flan and a light bittersweet salad of Belgian endive and orange sections.

An ample portion of turkey with plump prunes and cream sauce, chicory salad with lardons, and a wedge of tomato tart make a substantial meal for family or company.

Turkey with Prunes and Cream Sauce
Tomato Tart
Chicory Salad with Lardons

To make a successful tart crust by hand, use the same amounts of ingredients given for the food processor method (page 127), but make sure the butter is cool yet pliable. Gently mix the egg yolk with the butter before adding it to the flour and baking powder (to assure even distribution). Add just enough ice water to make the ingredients cohere when blended with your fingers or with a pastry blender. When rolling out the dough, handle it gently and quickly; otherwise the butter will soften and the pastry will be tough and greasy.

WHAT TO DRINK

Select an Alsatian Pinot Blanc or a Gewürztraminer for this menu. Or try the same wines from Italy or California.

SHOPPING LIST AND STAPLES

1-pound section of boneless, skinless turkey breast
¼ pound slab bacon (4 to 5 slices)
Large head chicory
Small bunch fresh parsley
1 lemon
16-ounce can Italian plum tomatoes
1 cup duck stock or chicken stock, preferably homemade (see page 13), or canned
3 large eggs
½ pint heavy cream
1 stick plus 1 tablespoon unsalted butter, approximately
2 ounces Gruyère cheese
3 tablespoons duck fat or chicken fat
1 tablespoon vegetable oil, plus 3 tablespoons (if not using duck fat or chicken fat)
2 tablespoons Dijon mustard
8-ounce package pitted whole prunes
1⅔ cups all-purpose flour
½ teaspoon baking powder
1 teaspoon saffron threads
Salt and freshly ground pepper

UTENSILS

Food processor (optional)
2 large heavy-gauge skillets
8-inch quiche or tart pan
Medium-size bowl, plus 1 additional (if not using processor)
2 small bowls
Strainer
Measuring cups and spoons
Chef's knife
Paring knife
2 wooden spoons
Whisk
Slotted spoon
Grater (if not using processor)
Rolling pin
Pastry blender (if not using processor)
Pastry brush

START-TO-FINISH STEPS

1. Wash parsley and dry with paper towels. Chop parsley to measure 2 tablespoons for turkey recipe and 1 tablespoon for salad recipe.
2. Follow turkey recipe step 1 and salad recipe step 1.
3. Follow tomato tart recipe steps 1 through 8.
4. While the tomato tart is baking, follow turkey recipe steps 2 and 3.
5. Follow turkey recipe step 4 and salad recipe steps 2 through 6.
6. Follow tomato tart recipe step 9, turkey recipe step 5, and serve with salad.

RECIPES

Turkey with Prunes and Cream Sauce

1 cup pitted whole prunes
1-pound section of boneless, skinless turkey breast
3 tablespoons duck fat, chicken fat, or vegetable oil
Salt and freshly ground pepper
1 cup duck stock or chicken stock
½ cup heavy cream
1 teaspoon saffron threads
2 tablespoons chopped fresh parsley

1. In small bowl, combine prunes with enough warm water to cover and let soak 15 minutes.
2. Rinse turkey and dry with paper towels. Cut in half horizontally, then cut into 2-inch-long, ¼-inch-thick strips.
3. In large heavy-gauge skillet, heat fat or oil over medium heat. Add turkey strips, season with salt and pepper, and sauté, stirring occasionally, about 5 minutes, or until lightly browned on all sides.
4. Add stock, reduce heat to medium, and simmer about

15 minutes, uncovered, or until reduced to about ½ cup.
5. Drain prunes and add to skillet. Stir in cream, saffron, and parsley, and simmer just until heated through. Divide among 4 dinner plates and serve immediately.

Tomato Tart

Pastry:
1 stick unsalted butter, chilled, plus 1 tablespoon for greasing pan
1⅔ cups all-purpose flour
½ teaspoon baking powder
Large egg
Pinch of salt

Filling:
16-ounce can Italian plum tomatoes
2 ounces Gruyère cheese
2 tablespoons Dijon mustard
2 large eggs
½ cup heavy cream
Salt and freshly ground pepper

1. Preheat oven to 350 degrees. Butter 8-inch quiche or tart pan and set aside.
2. For pastry: Cut 1 stick butter into pieces. Combine flour and baking powder in food processor fitted with steel blade and process briefly to blend. Separate egg, adding yolk to dry ingredients in processor and reserving white for another use. Add butter, salt, and 1 tablespoon ice water, and process, adding more ice water, 1 tablespoon at a time, just until dough gathers around blade, 10 to 15 seconds. Or see page 126 for hand method.
3. On lightly floured surface, roll out pastry into a 10-inch round and fit into prepared pan. Trim off excess pastry and flute edge. Rinse and dry processor bowl, if using.
4. For filling: Turn tomatoes into strainer set over medium-size bowl and drain; reserve juice for another use. Quarter tomatoes.
5. Grate enough Gruyère to measure ¼ cup.
6. Brush bottom of pastry shell with mustard. Arrange tomatoes in shell and press down gently with fork.
7. In small bowl, combine 2 eggs, cream, and salt and pepper to taste, and whisk until blended. Pour egg mixture over tomatoes and sprinkle with Gruyère.
8. Bake tart in center of oven 30 minutes, or until pastry is golden and tart is set in middle.
9. Cut tart into generous wedges and divide among 4 small plates.

Chicory Salad with Lardons

Large head chicory
¼ pound slab bacon (4 to 5 slices)
1 tablespoon vegetable oil
1 lemon
1 tablespoon chopped fresh parsley
Salt and freshly ground pepper

1. Wash chicory and dry with paper towels. Remove any bruised or discolored leaves and discard. Break into bite-

size pieces and place in salad bowl. Cover and refrigerate until ready to serve.
2. Line plate with paper towels.
3. In large heavy-gauge skillet, bring about 1 inch of water to a rapid boil over high heat. While water is heating, cut bacon into ¾-inch cubes. Add bacon to boiling water and blanch about 2 minutes, or until softened. With slotted spoon, transfer bacon to towel-lined plate; rinse skillet and dry.
4. Add oil to skillet and heat over medium-high heat 30 seconds. Add bacon and sauté, stirring occasionally, until browned and crisp, about 5 minutes.
5. Meanwhile, halve lemon and juice one half; reserve remaining half for another use.
6. Remove chicory from refrigerator. Add warm bacon and fat from pan to chicory, sprinkle with lemon juice and parsley, and season with salt and pepper to taste. Toss salad to combine, and divide among dinner plates.

ADDED TOUCH

Be sure to have the egg whites at room temperature before beating them, and make sure beater and bowl are grease free or the whites will not expand properly.

Walnut Mousse

1 cup walnut pieces
2 large eggs
1 cup milk
¼ cup sugar
2 tablespoons all-purpose flour
4 ounces (4 squares) semisweet chocolate
6 tablespoons unsalted butter

1. Finely grind walnuts.
2. Separate eggs, placing yolks in small bowl and whites in medium-size bowl.
3. In small saucepan, bring milk just to a boil over medium heat. Meanwhile, add sugar and flour to egg yolks and whisk until well blended. Whisk a little of the hot milk into egg yolk mixture and then add yolk mixture to milk in saucepan, whisking until blended.
4. Bring mixture to a boil over medium heat, whisking constantly.
5. Remove pan from heat and fold in walnuts.
6. In medium-size bowl, beat egg whites with electric mixer at high speed until stiff. Fold one-third of egg whites into mousse and then gently fold mousse into remaining egg white.
7. With rubber spatula, turn mousse into a deep serving dish. If serving immediately, set aside at room temperature; or cover and refrigerate until ready to serve.
8. Just before serving, combine chocolate and butter in top half of double boiler over, not in, barely simmering water, and heat, stirring occasionally with metal spoon, until chocolate is melted.
9. Divide mousse among individual bowls and top each serving with hot chocolate sauce.

Turkey Paupiettes
Sautéed Broccoli
Lentils Vinaigrette

A flavorful ham, such as Smithfield or prosciutto, is used in the stuffing for the turkey scallops. Smithfield is the name of a special type of dry-cured, smoked, and aged ham processed only in Smithfield, Virginia. The most famous of all American country hams, a Smithfield has salty, dark red meat. It can be purchased at a butcher or gourmet shop or through the mail. Prosciutto is an Italian-style dry-cured unsmoked ham; its moist deep pink meat is well seasoned but not particularly salty. Prosciutto is sold at Italian groceries and specialty food stores.

Impress your guests with a French country dinner: thin turkey scallops wrapped around a savory filling, sautéed broccoli florets, and lentils vinaigrette garnished with diced red peppers and parsley.

WHAT TO DRINK

This meal demands a balanced and subtle red wine. Try a Bordeaux from one of the less expensive classified growths, a moderately priced California Merlot, or a Cabernet from northern Italy.

SHOPPING LIST AND STAPLES

1-pound section of boneless, skinless turkey breast, cut into four ¼-inch-thick scallops
¼ pound Smithfield ham, prosciutto, or other dry-cured ham, unsliced
2 ounces chicken livers (about 2 livers)
½ pound fresh cultivated white mushrooms
1 head broccoli

Medium-size onion
Medium-size carrot
Small red bell pepper
3 cloves garlic
3 shallots
Large bunch fresh parsley
Small bunch fresh thyme, or ½ teaspoon dried
2 large eggs
½ pint crème fraîche or heavy cream
3 tablespoons vegetable oil, plus 5 tablespoons (if not using duck fat)
5 tablespoons duck fat (optional)
1½ tablespoons white wine vinegar
½ pound brown lentils (about 1 cup)
1 bay leaf
Salt
Freshly ground pepper
⅓ cup Madeira wine
⅓ cup dry white wine

UTENSILS

Food processor (optional)
2 large heavy-gauge skillets
Large saucepan
Heatproof platter
Large bowl
Medium-size heatproof bowl, plus 1 additional bowl (if not using processor)
Small bowl
Colander
Strainer
Measuring cups and spoons
Meat pounder or cleaver
Chef's knife
Paring knife
2 wooden spoons
Metal tongs
Cheesecloth
Kitchen string

START-TO-FINISH STEPS

1. Peel and finely chop shallots and 1 garlic clove for lentils recipe. Peel and coarsely chop remaining 2 cloves garlic for turkey recipe. Wash parsley, and fresh thyme if using, and dry with paper towels. Finely mince enough parsley to measure 3 tablespoons for turkey recipe and chop enough to measure 2 tablespoons for lentils recipe.
2. Follow lentils recipe steps 1 through 4.
3. While lentils simmer, follow turkey recipe steps 1 through 7.
4. While turkey is browning, follow lentils recipe steps 5 and 6.

5. Follow turkey recipe steps 8 through 10.

6. While sauce is reducing, follow broccoli recipe steps 1 through 4.

7. Follow turkey recipe steps 11 and 12, and lentils recipe steps 7 and 8.

8. Follow turkey recipe step 13 and serve with broccoli and lentils.

RECIPES

Turkey Paupiettes

1-pound section of boneless, skinless turkey breast, cut into four ¼-inch-thick scallops
Salt and freshly ground pepper
¼ pound Smithfield ham, prosciutto, or other dry-cured ham, unsliced
2 ounces chicken livers (about 2 livers)
½ pound fresh cultivated white mushrooms
2 cloves garlic, coarsely chopped
3 tablespoons finely minced parsley
2 large eggs
3 tablespoons duck fat or vegetable oil
⅓ cup Madeira wine
⅓ cup dry white wine
¾ cup crème fraîche or heavy cream

1. Place each turkey scallop between two sheets of waxed paper and gently pound with meat pounder or cleaver to about ⅛-inch thickness. Season scallops on both sides with salt and pepper.

2. Trim off excess fat from ham and discard. Rinse chicken livers under cold running water and dry with paper towels. Remove membranes and discard. Coarsely chop ham to make about ¾ cup and chop chicken livers.

3. Wipe mushrooms clean with damp paper towels and chop coarsely to measure about 2½ cups.

4. In food processor fitted with steel blade, combine ham, chicken livers, mushrooms, garlic, and 1 tablespoon parsley. Separate eggs, adding yolks to processor and reserving whites for another use, and process until mixture is well combined, about 20 seconds. Or, mince ingredients with chef's knife and combine with yolks in medium-size bowl.

5. Spread about 2 tablespoons of stuffing mixture on each flattened turkey scallop. Roll up scallops, tucking in edges, and tie securely with kitchen string. Reserve remaining stuffing mixture.

6. Preheat oven to 200 degrees.

7. In large heavy-gauge skillet, heat duck fat or oil over medium heat. Add the paupiettes and sauté, turning occasionally, about 10 minutes, or until lightly browned.

8. Transfer paupiettes to heatproof platter and keep warm in oven.

9. Add remaining stuffing to skillet and sauté, stirring, 1 minute. Stir in Madeira and white wine, and bring to a boil over medium-high heat, scraping up any brown bits clinging to bottom of pan. Return paupiettes and any accumulated juices to skillet and cook, turning occasionally, 8 to 12 minutes, or until sauce is syrupy and reduced by half.

10. Meanwhile, place 4 dinner plates in oven to warm.

11. Using tongs, transfer paupiettes to warmed dinner plates and remove strings.

12. Stir crème fraîche or heavy cream into sauce and simmer 1 to 2 minutes, or until heated through. Add salt and pepper to taste.

13. Spoon sauce over each paupiette and sprinkle with remaining parsley.

Sautéed Broccoli

1 head broccoli
2 tablespoons duck fat or vegetable oil
Salt and freshly ground pepper

1. Wash and trim broccoli; cut into large florets.

2. In large heavy-gauge skillet, heat duck fat or oil over medium heat until hot, about 1 minute.

3. Add broccoli, season to taste with salt and pepper, and sauté, shaking pan occasionally, 5 to 8 minutes, or just until crisp-tender.

4. Turn broccoli into heatproof bowl and keep warm in 200-degree oven until ready to serve.

Lentils Vinaigrette

½ pound brown lentils (about 1 cup)
Medium-size onion
Medium-size carrot
1 bay leaf
2 sprigs fresh thyme, or ½ teaspoon dried
2 sprigs parsley, plus 2 tablespoons chopped parsley
Salt
3 tablespoons vegetable oil
1½ tablespoons white wine vinegar
1 clove garlic, finely chopped
3 shallots, finely chopped
Freshly ground pepper
Small red bell pepper

1. Place lentils in colander and rinse under cold running water; pick over carefully.

2. Peel and quarter onion. Wash and peel carrot; cut crosswise into 4 pieces.

3. In a double thickness of cheesecloth, tie together bay leaf, thyme, and 2 sprigs parsley for *bouquet garni*.

4. Place lentils in large saucepan with enough cold water to cover. Add onion, carrot, and *bouquet garni*. Season to taste with salt and bring to a simmer, uncovered, over medium-low heat. Continue to simmer gently 45 minutes, checking occasionally to replenish water if necessary.

5. In small bowl, combine oil, vinegar, garlic, shallots, and salt and pepper to taste, and beat with fork until blended.

6. Wash red bell pepper and dry with paper towel. Core, halve, and seed pepper. Cut into ¼-inch dice; set aside.

7. Discard onion, carrot, and *bouquet garni*. Turn lentils into strainer, drain, and transfer to large bowl.

8. Stir vinaigrette to recombine and pour over lentils; toss to combine. Divide lentils among dinner plates and sprinkle with diced bell pepper and chopped parsley.

Braised Duck with Onions
Zucchini Flan
Belgian Endive and Orange Salad

A good red wine complements braised duck with onions, slices of zucchini flan, and a Belgian endive and orange salad.

Zucchini are at their peak during the summer months but are available at supermarkets throughout the year. For the zucchini flan, select small squash, about 4 inches long, with glossy, deep green unblemished skin (large zucchini are too coarse and seedy). If you do not plan to use the zucchini immediately, store them in a perforated plastic bag in the refrigerator, where they will keep for several days. For this recipe, the skin is left on for added color.

If you have the time, reserve the excess fat from the cavity of the duck and render it yourself.

WHAT TO DRINK

A red wine of sufficient character to balance the richness of the duck is essential here. The best choice would be a Châteauneuf-du-Pape from France's Rhône valley. The famous "black" wine of Cahors, if you can find it, would also be suitable.

SHOPPING LIST AND STAPLES

5 pound whole duck
2 pounds onions
3 medium-size zucchini (about 1 pound total weight)
3 large heads Belgian endive
Small bunch watercress for garnish (optional)
3 small oranges
1 lemon
3 large eggs
¼ pound Gruyère cheese
¼ cup duck fat (optional)
5 tablespoons vegetable oil, approximately, plus ¼ cup (if not using duck fat)
Salt and freshly ground black pepper

UTENSILS

Food processor or blender
2 large heavy-gauge skillets
Flameproof casserole or Dutch oven with cover
8-inch ovenproof ring mold or 1-quart soufflé dish
Medium-size bowl
1 small bowl, plus 1 additional (if using processor)
Salad spinner (optional)
Measuring cups and spoons
Cleaver

Chef's knife
Paring knife
2 wooden spoons
Spatula
Whisk
Metal tongs
Grater (if not using processor)
Juicer

START-TO-FINISH STEPS

1. Follow zucchini flan recipe steps 1 through 5.
2. Follow duck recipe steps 1 through 4.
3. Follow zucchini flan recipe steps 6 and 7.
4. While zucchini flan is baking, follow duck recipe step 5.
5. While duck is braising, follow salad recipe steps 1 through 3.
6. Follow zucchini flan recipe step 8, duck recipe step 6, salad recipe step 4, and serve.

RECIPES

Braised Duck with Onions

5 pound whole duck
¼ cup duck fat or vegetable oil
2 pounds onions
Small bunch watercress for garnish (optional)
Salt
Freshly ground black pepper

1. Remove any excess fat from cavity of duck. Trim off neck skin. Chop off wing tips and reserve with neck and gizzard for another use. With cleaver, quarter duck: Turn duck, skin-side up, on cutting surface and cut through the breastbone. Turn duck over, push back breast halves, and cut backbone in two. Next, place each half skin-side up and, feeling for end of rib cage, cut pieces in half just below ribs. Turn quarters skin-side down and, with sharp knife or cleaver, trim excess skin and any visible fat from each piece. Turn pieces over and prick skin lightly with a fork or skewer to help release fat during cooking.
2. In large heavy-gauge skillet, heat 2 tablespoons duck fat or oil over high heat. Add duck and sauté, turning occasionally, until golden and crisp all over, about 15 minutes.
3. Meanwhile, peel onions and cut crosswise into ¼-inch-thick slices to measure about 4 cups. Wash watercress, if

using, and dry in salad spinner or with paper towels. Reserve 4 sprigs for garnish and refrigerate remainder for another use.

4. In flameproof casserole or Dutch oven large enough to hold the duck in a single layer, heat remaining duck fat or oil over medium heat. Add onions and sauté, stirring occasionally, until softened and light golden, about 10 minutes.

5. Transfer duck to casserole and season to taste with salt and pepper. Cover and braise over medium-low heat 20 to 25 minutes, or until still somewhat rare and juice runs faintly pink.

6. Divide duck among 4 dinner plates, top with onions, and garnish with a sprig of watercress, if desired.

Zucchini Flan

3 medium-size zucchini (about 1 pound total weight)
2 tablespoons vegetable oil, approximately
¼ pound Gruyère cheese
3 large eggs
Salt and freshly ground black pepper

1. Preheat oven to 350 degrees. Line a platter with paper towels.

2. Wash zucchini and dry with paper towels. Trim off ends and discard. Cut crosswise into ½-inch-thick slices. Cut four slices in half for garnish and reserve.

3. In large heavy-gauge skillet, heat 2 tablespoons oil over medium heat. Add zucchini and sauté, stirring occasionally, 8 to 10 minutes, or until softened but not browned.

4. Meanwhile, grate enough cheese in food processor or with grater to measure 1 cup. If using processor, transfer cheese to small bowl. In another small bowl, beat eggs until blended.

5. Transfer sautéed zucchini to paper-towel-lined platter to drain.

6. When drained, place zucchini in food processor fitted with steel blade or in blender and purée. Add eggs, grated cheese, and salt and pepper to taste, and process until blended.

7. Lightly oil an 8-inch ovenproof ring mold or 1-quart soufflé dish. Fill prepared dish three-quarters full with zucchini mixture and bake about 35 minutes, or until knife inserted in center of flan comes out clean.

8. To unmold, run knife around edge of flan while still warm. Place large flat serving plate over mold or dish and invert. Cut flan into 1-inch-thick slices and divide among dinner plates. Garnish with reserved zucchini.

Belgian Endive and Orange Salad

3 large heads Belgian endive
3 small oranges
1 lemon
3 tablespoons vegetable oil
Salt and freshly ground black pepper

1. Remove and discard any bruised outer leaves from endive. Wipe endive with damp paper towels, separate leaves, and place in medium-size bowl.

2. Peel 2 oranges, removing as much white pith as possible. Using very sharp paring knife, cut along membrane on either side of each orange segment. Pull segments apart and place in bowl with endive.

3. Juice remaining orange and half of lemon; reserve remaining half for another use. Combine citrus juices in small bowl, add oil, and salt and pepper to taste, and whisk until blended; set aside.

4. Just before serving, whisk dressing to recombine and pour over endive and oranges. Toss until evenly coated and divide salad among dinner plates.

ADDED TOUCH

This pancake-like fruit pastry is usually made with black cherries, but you may use fresh or canned red cherries.

Cherry Clafouti

1 tablespoon unsalted butter, approximately
¾ cup all-purpose flour
Pinch of salt
2 to 3 tablespoons sugar
4 large eggs
1⅔ cups milk
3 drops vanilla extract
1 pound sweet red cherries, stemmed and pitted, or one
    17-ounce can sweet cherries, drained

1. Butter a 10-inch-round gratin dish or pie pan.

2. Preheat oven to 350 degrees.

3. In mixing bowl, sift together flour, salt, and sugar.

4. In medium-size bowl, combine eggs and milk, and whisk until blended. Gradually stir egg mixture into dry ingredients. Stir in vanilla.

5. Turn mixture into prepared baking dish. Distribute cherries evenly over batter and bake in center of oven about 35 minutes, or until clafouti is set in the middle.

6. Cut clafouti into wedges and serve warm or cold.

Maria and Guy Reuge

Maria and Guy Reuge work well in tandem despite their very different culinary backgrounds (she learned to cook in the American South, he in France). When they collaborate on menu planning, the resultant meals are often eclectic—and always delicious. Having traveled together frequently in the south of France, they are united in their particular fondness for the foods of that area. Here they offer some dishes that are classically French and others that are Guy Reuge's own interpretations.

The Reuges describe Menu 1 as Provençal, except for the recipe for stuffed eggs with salmon caviar and anchovies, which comes from the principality of Monaco. The entrée is a generous portion of monkfish sauced with a mixture of tomatoes and shallots (a classic Provençal touch) and served with braised fennel.

Menu 2 features two dishes popular in Languedoc: mussels stuffed with an herb-and-almond butter and pork chops with anchovy sauce. The accompanying zucchini sticks are sautéed quickly to preserve their bright green color.

The cooks' third menu, also from Provence, is extremely adaptable to what is best in the market. For example, in the herbed goat cheese salad you can use another soft-leafed lettuce in place of the *mâche* (lamb's lettuce), which is often hard to find. For the seafood stew, select the best and freshest firm-fleshed white fish available.

A Monégasque specialty—stuffed eggs garnished with caviar and anchovies—is paired with sautéed monkfish in a chunky tomato sauce and braised fennel bulbs, two dishes popular in Provence. Serve the eggs as a first course, if desired.

Eggs Monégasque
Monkfish Provençal
Braised Fennel

Because it has firm, sweet flesh resembling that of lobster, inexpensive monkfish is increasingly popular in this country. Also marketed as goosefish or anglerfish, monkfish is available on the Atlantic and Gulf coasts but is not often sold elsewhere. Suitable alternatives are scrod and halibut. Dusting the fish fillets with flour gives them a golden color when sautéed.

Fresh fennel, also known as *finocchio*, has feathery green leaves topping a bulbous base; its anise flavor, which mellows when the bulbs are braised, is a good complement for fish. Select bulbs that are pale green, firm, and have no soft or brownish spots. Fennel is sold in Italian groceries and well-stocked supermarkets during the fall and winter. If necessary, you can substitute the same amount of sliced celery plus one-half teaspoon fennel seeds, but the flavor will not be quite the same.

WHAT TO DRINK

The cooks suggest a white wine from the Côtes de Provence as an ideal accompaniment for this menu. Or, try a white Châteauneuf-du-Pape.

SHOPPING LIST AND STAPLES

4 monkfish fillets (about 2 pounds total weight)
4 small or 2 large fennel bulbs (about 2 pounds total weight)
1 large plus 4 medium-size ripe tomatoes (about 2¾ pounds total weight), or 1 large ripe tomato plus 14-ounce can plum tomatoes
Small head red leaf lettuce
3 medium-size shallots
Small clove garlic
1 bunch parsley
1½ cups chicken stock, preferably homemade (see page 13), or canned
5 large eggs
1 stick plus 1 tablespoon unsalted butter
2 tablespoons good-quality olive oil
¼ cup mayonnaise
2-ounce tin flat anchovy fillets
4-ounce jar salmon caviar
¼ cup all-purpose flour, approximately
Salt
Freshly ground pepper

UTENSILS

Large heavy-gauge nonaluminum skillet with cover
Medium-size nonaluminum skillet with cover
Large saucepan
Medium-size saucepan
1½-quart flameproof casserole with cover
9-inch pie pan (optional)
Heatproof platter
Medium-size bowl
Small bowl
Colander
Sieve
Measuring cups and spoons
Chef's knife
Paring knife
Wooden spoon
Slotted spoon
Slotted spatula
Whisk
Pastry bag fitted with medium-size fluted tip (optional)

START-TO-FINISH STEPS

One hour ahead: Set out eggs to come to room temperature.

1. Follow monkfish recipe step 1 and fennel recipe steps 1 through 4.
2. While fennel is baking, follow eggs recipe steps 1 and 2 and monkfish recipe steps 2 through 5.
3. Follow eggs recipe step 3 and monkfish recipe step 6.
4. Follow eggs recipe steps 4 through 10.
5. Follow monkfish recipe steps 7 through 9.
6. Follow fennel recipe steps 5 through 8.
7. While liquid is reducing, follow monkfish recipe steps 10 through 13.
8. Follow fennel recipe step 9 and monkfish recipe steps 14 and 15.
9. Follow fennel recipe step 10, monkfish recipe step 16, and serve with eggs.

RECIPES

Eggs Monégasque

5 large eggs
¼ cup mayonnaise

Small head red leaf lettuce
Large ripe tomato
4 anchovy fillets
4-ounce jar salmon caviar

1. Place eggs in medium-size saucepan, add enough cold water to cover, and bring to a boil over high heat. Boil eggs, stirring occasionally, 10 minutes. Stirring will keep the yolks centered.
2. Half-fill medium-size bowl with cold water; set aside.
3. Drain eggs and transfer to bowl of cold water.
4. When cool, peel eggs, halve lengthwise, and remove yolks. Force 4 yolks and 1 whole hard-boiled egg through sieve into small bowl. Reserve remaining egg white halves.
5. Add mayonnaise to sieved eggs and stir to combine.
6. If desired, transfer egg mixture to pastry bag fitted with medium-size fluted tip and pipe decoratively into reserved egg white halves. Or, spoon mixture into egg white halves. Place stuffed eggs on plate, cover with plastic wrap, and refrigerate.
7. Meanwhile, wash lettuce and dry with paper towels. Remove and discard any bruised or discolored leaves. Using 1 or 2 leaves for each, line 4 individual salad plates with lettuce; set aside. Reserve remaining lettuce for another use.
8. Wash and dry tomato. Core tomato and cut crosswise into 8 slices. Divide among lettuce-lined plates.
9. Drain anchovies and split lengthwise; set aside.
10. Divide stuffed eggs among prepared plates and top each egg half with 1 anchovy strip and some salmon caviar. Cover and refrigerate until ready to serve.

Monkfish Provençal

4 medium-size ripe tomatoes (about 2 pounds total weight), or 14-ounce can plum tomatoes
3 medium-size shallots
Small clove garlic
1 bunch parsley
¼ cup all-purpose flour, approximately
4 monkfish fillets (about 2 pounds total weight)
2 tablespoons good-quality olive oil
4 tablespoons unsalted butter
Salt and freshly ground pepper

1. If using fresh tomatoes, bring 2 quarts water to a boil in large saucepan over high heat.
2. Peel and mince enough shallots to measure 3 tablespoons.
3. Peel and mince enough garlic to measure 1 teaspoon.
4. Plunge tomatoes into boiling water and blanch 15 seconds.
5. Transfer tomatoes to colander and cool under cold running water.
6. Wash parsley and dry with paper towels. Trim stems and discard. Mince enough parsley to measure ¾ cup; set aside. Reserve remainder for another use.
7. Peel, core, halve, and seed tomatoes. Coarsely chop

enough to measure 4 cups; set aside.
8. Place flour in pie pan or on sheet of waxed paper.
9. Rinse fish under cold running water and dry with paper towels. Cut each fillet on diagonal into 1-inch-wide slices.
10. Heat oil in large heavy-gauge nonaluminum skillet over high heat until very hot but not smoking.
11. Working quickly, lightly dredge each piece of fish in flour, gently shake off excess, and add to skillet. Fry 1½ minutes per side, or until golden brown.
12. With slotted spatula, transfer monkfish to heatproof platter, cover loosely with foil, and keep warm in 200-degree oven.
13. Place 4 dinner plates in oven to warm.
14. Pour off oil from skillet, add butter, and heat over medium-high heat until butter starts to sizzle.
15. Add shallots, garlic, parsley, tomatoes, and any juices that have accumulated on platter with fish, and stir to combine. Stir in salt and pepper to taste. Cover skillet, remove from heat, and keep warm until ready to serve.
16. Divide sauce among dinner plates, top with fish, and serve.

Braised Fennel

4 small or 2 large fennel bulbs (about 2 pounds total weight)
1½ cups chicken stock
5 tablespoons unsalted butter
Salt and freshly ground pepper

1. Preheat oven to 400 degrees.
2. Rinse and dry fennel. Remove stalks and trim bottom of bulbs. Set aside 8 feathery tops for garnish and discard remaining trimmings. If using small bulbs, halve lengthwise; if using large bulbs, cut into quarters. Set aside.
3. Cut out waxed-paper disk large enough to cover 1½-quart flameproof casserole and butter 1 side; set aside.
4. Combine fennel, stock, 1 tablespoon butter, and salt and pepper to taste in flameproof casserole and bring to a boil over high heat. Top casserole with prepared waxed paper, cover, and bake 40 minutes.
5. Remove fennel from oven and reduce oven temperature to 200 degrees, leaving oven door ajar for a few minutes to reduce temperature more rapidly.
6. Meanwhile, drain cooking liquid into medium-size nonaluminum skillet. Return covered casserole with fennel to 200-degree oven and keep warm until ready to serve.
7. Cut remaining butter into bits; set aside.
8. Bring liquid in skillet to a boil over high heat. Lower heat to medium and simmer 4 to 5 minutes, or until liquid is reduced to about 1 tablespoon.
9. Add butter, a few bits at a time, to reduced cooking liquid, whisking after each addition, until butter is totally incorporated and sauce is thick and smooth. Add salt and pepper to taste. Cover pan, remove from heat, and keep sauce warm until ready to serve.
10. Divide fennel among 4 dinner plates, top with equal portions of sauce, and garnish each serving with feathery fennel tops.

Mussels Stuffed with Herbed Almond Butter
Pork Chops with Anchovy Sauce
Sautéed Zucchini Sticks

Herbed mussels arranged pinwheel-style go well with pork chops with anchovy sauce and sautéed zucchini sticks.

The thick meaty pork chops are served with a pungent anchovy sauce. Be sure to chill the butter thoroughly before adding it to the deglazed pan juices. Adding the butter bit by bit and then whisking rapidly ensures that the sauce emulsifies properly and achieves a smooth, velvety texture.

Since zucchini is often watery, you might want to salt the sticks before sautéing them, then allow them to rest for half an hour to extract excess moisture. Before cooking, blot the squash with paper towels. If you are on a salt-free diet, rinse off the salt before patting the sticks dry.

WHAT TO DRINK

A light red wine, such as a simple Côtes du Rhône or a Beaujolais, is in order here. White wine enthusiasts may prefer a well-chilled Gewürztraminer with these dishes.

SHOPPING LIST AND STAPLES

Four ¾-inch-thick loin pork chops (about 2 pounds total weight)
1¾ pounds mussels (about 2 dozen)
2 medium-size zucchini (about 1 pound total weight)
3 shallots
Small clove garlic
Small bunch fresh parsley
Small bunch fresh thyme, or ½ teaspoon dried
1 lemon, plus 2 lemons (optional)
1 orange (optional)
½ cup beef stock, preferably homemade, or canned
1 stick plus 1 tablespoon unsalted butter
1 tablespoon good-quality olive oil
2-ounce tin flat anchovy fillets
¼ cup all-purpose flour
3½-ounce can sliced blanched almonds
Salt and freshly ground pepper
1 cup dry white wine, approximately

UTENSILS

Food processor or blender
Large nonaluminum kettle or stockpot with cover
Large heavy-gauge nonaluminum skillet
Medium-size skillet or sauté pan with cover
13 x 9 x 2-inch baking dish
9-inch pie pan (optional)
Large bowl
Small bowl
Large sieve
Measuring cups and spoons
Chef's knife
Paring knife
Wooden spoon
Rubber spatula
Metal spatula
Whisk
Metal tongs
Vegetable brush
Stiff-bristled brush
Vegetable peeler

START-TO-FINISH STEPS

One hour ahead: Set out butter to come to room temperature for pork chops recipe.

1. Wash parsley and dry with paper towels. Trim stems and discard. Set aside ⅓ cup loosely packed sprigs for mussels recipe, and 4 sprigs if using for garnish for pork chops recipe. Mince enough parsley to measure 1 tablespoon for pork chops recipe. If using fresh thyme for zucchini recipe, rinse and pat dry. Mince enough thyme leaves to measure 1 teaspoon.
2. Follow mussels recipe steps 1 through 11.
3. Follow pork chops recipe steps 1 through 5.
4. While pork chops are browning, follow mussels recipe step 12.
5. Follow pork chops recipe steps 6 through 11 and zucchini recipe step 1.
6. Follow mussels recipe step 13.
7. While mussels are baking, follow pork chops recipe steps 12 and 13 and zucchini recipe steps 2 and 3.
8. Follow mussels recipe step 14, pork chops recipe step 14, and serve with zucchini.

RECIPES

Mussels Stuffed with Herbed Almond Butter

1¾ pounds mussels (about 2 dozen)
3 shallots
½ cup dry white wine
Small clove garlic
1 lemon, plus 2 lemons for garnish (optional)
⅓ cup loosely packed parsley sprigs
4 tablespoons unsalted butter
2 tablespoons sliced blanched almonds
¼ teaspoon freshly ground pepper

1. Preheat oven to 400 degrees.
2. Using stiff-bristled brush, scrub mussels under cold running water, remove beards, and rinse. Remove and discard any cracked or open mussels; set remainder aside.
3. Peel and mince enough shallots to measure ⅓ cup.
4. Combine mussels, shallots, and white wine in large nonaluminum kettle or stockpot and steam, covered, over high heat 4 minutes, shaking pan 2 or 3 times.
5. Meanwhile, crush garlic under flat blade of chef's knife. Remove peel and discard.
6. Squeeze enough lemon juice to measure 1 tablespoon.
7. Turn mussels into large sieve set over large bowl to drain. Return mussel liquor to kettle or stockpot and bring to a boil over high heat. Boil 2 to 3 minutes, or until liquid is reduced to about 1 tablespoon.
8. Meanwhile, mince garlic and parsley in food processor fitted with steel blade or in blender.

9. With machine running, add butter, 1 tablespoon at a time, and process until totally incorporated.

10. Add the reduced mussel liquor, lemon juice, almonds, and pepper, and process until herbed almond butter is well blended and smooth; set aside.

11. Remove and discard any unopened mussels. Remove and discard top shells from remaining mussels, leaving meat in bottom shells. Top each mussel with about 2 teaspoons of herbed almond butter, mounding it slightly, and arrange stuffed mussels in a single layer in 13 x 9 x 2-inch baking dish; set aside.

12. If using lemons for garnish, wash under cold running water and dry. Cut crosswise into thin slices. Divide slices among 4 salad plates; set aside.

13. When ready to serve, bake mussels 5 to 7 minutes, or until butter is just melted.

14. Divide mussels among prepared plates and serve.

Pork Chops with Anchovy Sauce

4 to 6 anchovy fillets
4 tablespoons unsalted butter, at room temperature
¼ cup all-purpose flour
1 tablespoon good-quality olive oil
Four ¾-inch-thick loin pork chops (about 2 pounds total weight)
1 orange for garnish (optional)
⅓ cup dry white wine
½ cup beef stock
Freshly ground pepper
1 tablespoon minced fresh parsley, plus 4 sprigs parsley for garnish (optional)

1. Drain anchovies, rinse under cold running water, and pat dry with paper towels.

2. Combine anchovies and butter in food processor fitted with steel blade or in blender and process until smooth. Turn mixture into small bowl, cover with plastic wrap, and refrigerate.

3. Place flour in pie pan or on sheet of waxed paper.

4. Heat oil in large heavy-gauge nonaluminum skillet over medium-high heat until hot but not smoking.

5. Dry pork chops with paper towels. Working quickly, dredge chops with flour, gently shake off excess, and add chops to skillet. Brown 4 minutes on one side.

6. Using tongs, turn chops and brown another 4 minutes.

7. Meanwhile, cut chilled anchovy butter into bits.

8. Wash and dry orange if using for garnish. Using sharp paring knife or vegetable peeler, cut four ½-inch-wide strips of peel. Reserve orange for another use.

9. Transfer chops to platter, cover loosely with foil, and keep warm on stove top.

10. Pour off fat from skillet. Add wine and bring to a boil over medium-high heat, stirring and scraping up any browned bits clinging to bottom of pan.

11. Add stock and boil mixture 3 to 4 minutes, or until reduced to about 2 tablespoons.

12. Reduce heat under skillet to low. Add anchovy butter to skillet, a few bits at a time, whisking until butter is

totally incorporated; simmer gently 1 to 2 minutes, or until sauce is thickened.

13. Add pepper to taste, remove sauce from heat, and keep warm on stove top.

14. Divide pork chops among 4 dinner plates. Top with sauce, sprinkle with minced parsley, and serve with a twist of orange rind and a sprig of parsley, if desired.

Sautéed Zucchini Sticks

2 medium-size zucchini (about 1 pound total weight)
1 tablespoon unsalted butter
1 teaspoon minced fresh thyme, or ½ teaspoon dried, crushed
Salt and freshly ground pepper

1. Using vegetable brush, scrub zucchini under cold running water, rinse, and dry with paper towels. Trim but do not peel. Cut each zucchini crosswise into 4 pieces, then halve each piece lengthwise. Cut each piece lengthwise again into ¼-inch-wide sticks; set aside.

2. Heat butter in medium-size skillet or sauté pan over medium-high heat just until it starts to sizzle. Add zucchini and sauté, stirring and tossing, 3 minutes.

3. Add thyme, and salt and pepper to taste, and toss to combine. Cover pan, remove from heat, and set aside until ready to serve.

ADDED TOUCH

For these thin apple tarts, use puff pastry, either freshly made or purchased frozen from the supermarket.

Honey-Glazed Apple Tarts

1-pound package frozen puff pastry, thawed
4 baking apples, preferably Granny Smith
4 teaspoons unsalted butter
2 tablespoons granulated sugar
¼ cup honey

1. Divide puff pastry into quarters. On lightly floured surface, roll each quarter into ⅛-inch-thick round.

2. Place a 6- to 8-inch round plate, face down, over each round and cut around plate with paring knife. Carefully transfer 4 dough circles to 2 baking sheets, cover with plastic wrap, and chill 1 hour.

3. Peel, core, and halve apples. Cut lengthwise into ⅛-inch-thick slices. You should have about 5 cups.

4. Preheat oven to 400 degrees.

5. Remove dough circles from refrigerator and prick with fork. Arrange apple slices in concentric circles on dough; dot each tart with 1 teaspoon butter and sprinkle with ½ tablespoon sugar. Bake 15 to 20 minutes, or until crust is golden.

6. While tarts are baking, heat honey in small saucepan over medium heat about 1 minute, or until warm and slightly runny.

7. Remove tarts from oven and brush with honey. Serve warm.

Herbed Goat Cheese Salad
Provençal Fish Stew

A one-pot seafood stew, fragrant with garlic, wine, and saffron, is accompanied by a mildly tart goat cheese salad.

For the fish stew, select any available variety of firm-fleshed fish: Swordfish could be substituted for the shark, and scrod for the monkfish. Shark—still a bargain—is a firm, dry, delicately flavored fish that many Americans have yet to discover. The most popular variety is the dark-fleshed mako.

Saffron, which colors and flavors the stew, is a pungent and expensive spice frequently used in Mediterranean cooking. Fortunately, a little goes a long way; a quarter of a teaspoon is ample for this recipe. Shop for saffron in specialty food stores or good supermarkets, but avoid a product call Mexican saffron—it is, in fact, safflower.

WHAT TO DRINK

A southern French rosé is a natural choice with a Provençal chowder. The very best is Tavel, but almost any rosé from Provence or the Rhône Valley would be good.

SHOPPING LIST AND STAPLES

12 littleneck clams (about 1 pound total weight)
12 mussels (about ¾ pound total weight)
8 medium-size shrimp (about ½ pound total weight)

141

¼-pound monkfish fillet
¼-pound sea bass fillet
¼-pound mako shark steak
1 head Boston lettuce
Small head red leaf lettuce
Small bunch mâche (optional)
Small head radicchio (optional)
2 medium-size ripe tomatoes, or 8¼-ounce can
    plum tomatoes
2 medium-size onions (about 1 pound total weight)
2 small cloves garlic
Small bunch parsley
1 egg
1 pint heavy cream
8-ounce log Montrachet or other soft goat cheese
5 tablespoons good-quality olive oil
1 tablespoon red wine vinegar
¼ teaspoon Dijon mustard
Hot pepper sauce
Small loaf French or Italian bread
¼ teaspoon saffron threads
Salt
Freshly ground pepper
Coarsely ground black pepper
½ cup dry white wine

UTENSILS

Large nonaluminum sauté pan or large deep non-
    aluminum skillet with cover
Small flameproof skillet or small baking sheet
Medium-size saucepan
Broiler pan with rack
Large bowl
Small nonaluminum bowl
Salad spinner (optional)
Colander
Measuring cups and spoons
Chef's knife
Serrated bread knife (optional)
Paring knife
Wooden spoon
Slotted spoon
Wide metal spatula
Whisk
Pastry brush
Stiff-bristled brush

START-TO-FINISH STEPS

1. Follow salad recipe steps 1 through 7.
2. Follow stew recipe steps 1 through 13 and salad recipe steps 8 and 9.
3. Follow stew recipe steps 14 and 15.
4. While broth reduces, follow salad recipe steps 10 through 12.
5. Follow stew recipe step 16 and salad recipe step 13.
6. Follow stew recipe step 17 and serve with salad.

RECIPES

Herbed Goat Cheese Salad

1 head Boston lettuce
Small head red leaf lettuce
Small bunch mâche (optional)
Small head radicchio (optional)
1 egg
¼ teaspoon Dijon mustard
1 tablespoon red wine vinegar
Salt
Freshly ground pepper
¼ cup good-quality olive oil
1 tablespoon heavy cream
Small clove garlic
Small loaf French or Italian bread
8-ounce log Montrachet or other soft goat cheese
½ teaspoon coarsely ground black pepper

1. Wash Boston and red leaf lettuces, and mâche and radicchio if using, in several changes of water and dry in salad spinner or with paper towels. Remove and discard any bruised or discolored leaves. Reserve half of red leaf lettuce for another use. Tear remaining salad greens and radicchio into bite-size pieces and combine in large bowl. Cover bowl with plastic wrap and refrigerate until ready to serve.

Boston lettuce

Mâche   *Radicchio*

2. Separate egg, placing yolk in small nonaluminum bowl and reserving white for another use.
3. Add mustard, vinegar, and salt and pepper to taste to yolk, and whisk until blended.
4. Whisking continuously, gradually add 3 tablespoons oil and whisk until dressing is thick and smooth. Add cream and whisk until blended. Cover bowl with plastic wrap and refrigerate until ready to serve.
5. Crush garlic under flat blade of chef's knife; remove peel and discard. Set garlic aside.
6. Cut four ½-inch-thick slices from bread; reserve remaining bread for another use.

7. Rub cut sides of bread with crushed garlic and brush with half of remaining olive oil; set aside.

8. Preheat broiler.

9. Cut cheese crosswise into four 1½-inch-thick slices. Brush cheese slices with remaining olive oil and sprinkle with coarsely ground pepper.

10. Arrange cheese slices in a single layer in small flameproof skillet or on baking sheet and broil about 2½ inches from heating element 2 to 3 minutes, or just until bubbly.

11. While cheese is broiling, place bread around it on broiler rack to toast.

12. Meanwhile, whisk dressing to recombine and pour over salad. Toss salad until evenly coated and divide among 4 salad plates.

13. Transfer toasts to salad plates. Using metal spatula, top each toast with a slice of cheese.

Provençal Fish Stew

2 medium-size ripe tomatoes, or 8¼-ounce can
  plum tomatoes
Small clove garlic
2 medium-size onions (about 1 pound total weight)
8 medium-size shrimp (about ½ pound total weight)
12 littleneck clams (about 1 pound total weight)
12 mussels (about ¾ pound total weight)
¼-pound monkfish fillet
¼-pound sea bass fillet
¼-pound mako shark steak
1 tablespoon good-quality olive oil
Small bunch parsley
¼ teaspoon saffron threads
½ cup dry white wine
Hot pepper sauce
1 cup heavy cream
Salt
Freshly ground pepper

1. If using fresh tomatoes, bring 1 quart of water to a boil in medium-size saucepan over high heat.

2. Meanwhile, peel garlic and mince enough to measure 1 teaspoon; set aside.

3. Plunge fresh tomatoes into boiling water and blanch 15 seconds. Transfer tomatoes to colander and cool under cold running water. Peel, core, halve, and seed tomatoes.

Squeeze out seeds with one hand.

Coarsely chop enough fresh tomatoes to measure 1 cup. If using canned tomatoes, drain and chop enough to measure 1 cup; set aside.

4. Halve, peel, and chop enough onion to measure 2 cups; set aside.

5. Pinch off legs of shrimp, several at a time, then bend back and snap off sharp, beaklike piece of shell just above tail. Remove shell and discard. Using sharp paring knife, make shallow incision along back of each shrimp, exposing black digestive vein. Extract black vein and discard. Rinse shrimp under cold running water, drain, and dry with paper towels; set aside.

6. Using stiff-bristled brush, scrub clams and mussels under cold running water; remove beards from mussels. Remove and discard any cracked or open shellfish. Rinse shellfish and set aside.

7. Rinse all fish under cold running water and dry thoroughly with paper towels. Cut into 1½-inch-wide strips; set aside.

8. In large nonaluminum sauté pan or deep nonaluminum skillet, heat olive oil over medium-high heat until hot but not smoking. Add onions and sauté, stirring occasionally, 5 minutes, or until lightly golden.

9. Meanwhile, wash parsley and pat dry with paper towels. Trim stem ends and discard. Mince enough parsley to measure 1 tablespoon; set aside. Reserve remaining parsley for another use. With your fingers, crumble saffron threads.

10. Add garlic, saffron, and white wine to onions, and stir, scraping up any browned bits that are clinging to bottom of pan.

11. Add clams and simmer, covered, 4 minutes.

12. Add mussels and simmer, covered, another 2 minutes.

13. Add shrimp, monkfish, bass, and shark, and simmer, uncovered, 3 minutes, or just until shrimp turn pink and fish flakes easily with a fork.

14. Remove and discard any unopened shellfish. With slotted spoon, transfer fish and remaining shellfish to serving dish, cover loosely with aluminum foil, and keep warm on stove top.

15. Add chopped tomatoes, and hot pepper sauce to taste to broth and bring to a boil over high heat. Boil 8 minutes, or until sauce is reduced slightly.

16. Reduce heat to medium, stir in cream, and continue to reduce sauce, stirring occasionally, 3 to 4 minutes, or until thick.

17. Add salt and pepper to taste. Pour sauce over fish and shellfish in serving bowl. Sprinkle with chopped parsley and serve immediately.

LEFTOVER SUGGESTION

Any leftover fish stew may be drained, put into a covered container, and chilled for a seafood salad the next day. For the salad, arrange the fish on a bed of lettuce and garnish it with halved hard-boiled eggs, tomatoes, chopped scallions, and capers; drizzle with a mild vinaigrette and serve with crusty bread.

Jill Van Cleave and William Rice

J ill Van Cleave and William Rice favor straight-
forward, no-nonsense meals that do not overtax the
cook. "We never attempt culinary feats when we prepare meals for company," he says. "Our party
food is what we would cook for ourselves, that is, food with
character." As a cooking team, they also share the shopping, the prepping, and the table setting, which they
consider as important as the meal itself.

Having traveled extensively in France, the couple selected menus that highlighted their favorite regional
dishes, which they have adapted to their own tastes. For
instance, the first course of Menu 1, a cold-weather Bur-
gundian meal, combines two of the region's specialties:
snails (*escargots*) and Burgundy wine. Rather than lavish-
ing the snails with butter, as in the traditional *escargots à
la bourguignonne*, the cooks have devised a garlic-scented
wine sauce, and they serve the snails on croutons rather
than in their shells. The entrée consists of thick pork chops
in a Dijon mustard sauce.

Menu 2, a company lunch or dinner, includes three
typical Lyonnaise dishes: a salad of tart greens and bits of
bacon, an entrée of chicken flavored with garlic and vinegar, and, for dessert, rich *pots de crème* that combine
chocolate and chestnuts.

For Menu 3, a Gascony meal, the cooks offer broiled
duck breasts garnished with prunes simmered in Armagnac, Gascony's own renowned brandy. Mashed potatoes
flavored with garlic accompany the main course.

*Offer your guests the snails in red Burgundy wine sauce either
with the main course or as an appetizer. Just before serving the
entrée, spoon some sauce over each pork chop and sprinkle
generously with chive slivers. The carrots are glazed and then
rolled in minced parsley.*

Snails in Burgundy Wine Sauce
Pork Chops Dijonnaise
Glazed Carrots

In France, snails are a gastronomic prize and snail hunting a national pastime. Canned snails, without shells or with separately packed shells, are available in specialty food shops and many supermarkets.

Dijon mustard, used in the sauce for the pork chops, is a type of mustard named for the principal city of Burgundy. It is made from ground mustard seeds, white wine, and a variety of seasonings.

WHAT TO DRINK

A good red Burgundy is the obvious partner for this meal. Try a Côte de Nuits or a Côte de Beaune-Villages.

SHOPPING LIST AND STAPLES

Four ¾- to 1-inch-thick center-cut loin pork chops (about 2 pounds total weight)
2 slices bacon
1½ pounds carrots
Small onion
Large clove garlic
Small bunch parsley
Small bunch chives
4 tablespoons unsalted butter
Two 7½-ounce cans giant snails without shells
½ cup chicken stock, preferably homemade (see page 13), or canned
16-ounce can tomato purée
1 tablespoon vegetable oil
2 tablespoons Dijon mustard
⅔ cup flour, approximately
4 slices home-style white bread
1½ teaspoons sugar
Salt and freshly ground black pepper
1 cup red Burgundy wine
½ cup dry white Burgundy wine
1 tablespoon brandy

UTENSILS

Large skillet
2 medium-size saucepans, one with cover
13 x 9 x 2-inch baking dish
13 x 9-inch cookie sheet
Small bowl
Measuring cups and spoons
Chef's knife
Paring knife
2 wooden spoons
Metal tongs
3-inch round pastry cutter (optional)
Small whisk
Vegetable peeler

START-TO-FINISH STEPS

One hour ahead: For snails recipe, set out 2 tablespoons butter to bring to room temperature.

1. Wash parsley and chives, and pat dry with paper towels. Reserve 4 parsley sprigs for snails, if using for garnish, and chop 2 tablespoons for carrots. For pork chops, chop 2 tablespoons chives and sliver 2 tablespoons, if using for garnish.
2. Follow snails recipe steps 1 through 5.
3. While bacon is browning, follow carrots recipe step 1.
4. Follow snails recipe step 6 and pork chops recipe steps 1 and 2.
5. While pork chops are browning, follow snails recipe step 7 and carrots recipe step 2.
6. While snails are simmering, follow pork chops recipe step 3.
7. Follow snails recipe step 8 and carrots recipe steps 3 and 4.
8. Follow snails recipe steps 9 and 10, and serve as a first course.
9. Follow pork chops recipe step 4 and remove carrots from heat.
10. Follow pork chops recipe step 5 and carrots recipe step 5.
11. Follow pork chops recipe steps 6 and 7, and serve with carrots.

RECIPES

Snails in Burgundy Wine Sauce

4 slices home-style white bread
Small onion
Large garlic clove
2 slices bacon
1 cup red Burgundy wine
½ cup chicken stock
1 tablespoon brandy
Salt and freshly ground black pepper
Two 7½-ounce cans giant snails without shells

2 tablespoons unsalted butter
2 tablespoons flour
4 sprigs parsley for garnish (optional)

1. Preheat oven to 350 degrees.
2. With a pastry cutter or paring knife, cut out a 3-inch-round crouton from each slice of bread. Arrange croutons in a single layer on cookie sheet and toast in oven 5 minutes, or until lightly brown.
3. Meanwhile, peel and mince onion and garlic. Dice bacon.
4. Transfer toasted croutons to 4 small soup bowls or salad plates.
5. In medium-size saucepan, cook bacon 3 to 5 minutes, or until browned.
6. Add onion and garlic, and cook another 3 to 5 minutes, or until onion is translucent.
7. Add red wine, stock, brandy, and salt and pepper to taste, and bring to a boil over medium heat. Rinse and drain snails, and add to liquid in pan. Reduce heat to low and simmer snails 5 minutes.
8. With metal tongs, transfer snails to medium-size bowl, cover with foil and keep warm.
9. In small bowl, blend butter with flour until smooth. Add butter-flour mixture to sauce all at once, whisking until blended, and cook, stirring, about 3 minutes, or until thick and smooth. Remove pan from heat.
10. Divide snails among bowls or plates containing croutons, top each with a few spoonfuls of sauce, and serve garnished with a parsley sprig, if desired.

Pork Chops Dijonnaise

Four ¾- to 1-inch-thick center-cut loin pork chops (about 2 pounds total weight)
¼ cup flour, approximately
1 tablespoon vegetable oil
Salt and freshly ground pepper
½ cup dry white Burgundy wine
2 tablespoons Dijon mustard
1 tablespoon tomato purée
2 tablespoons chopped chives plus 2 tablespoons slivered chives for garnish (optional)

1. Press pork chops between 2 layers of paper towels to absorb moisture. Place flour on sheet of waxed paper. Lightly dredge chops in flour; shake off excess.
2. In large skillet, heat oil over medium-high heat. Add chops and brown 4 to 5 minutes per side.

3. Season chops with salt and pepper to taste, and transfer to shallow baking dish. Bake in 350-degree oven 15 minutes.
4. Pour off fat from skillet. Add wine, mustard, tomato purée, and chopped chives to skillet, and stir sauce over medium heat, scraping up any browned particles clinging to bottom of pan. Reduce heat to low and simmer sauce, stirring often, 5 minutes. Turn off heat under skillet.
5. Divide baked chops among individual dinner plates and lower oven temperature to 200 degrees, leaving oven door ajar a few moments to hasten cooling. Return chops to oven and keep warm.
6. Add juices that have accumulated in baking pan to sauce in skillet. Reheat sauce over medium heat until bubbly; turn off heat and season with salt and pepper to taste.
7. Top each chop with a few spoonfuls of sauce and garnish with chive slivers, if desired.

Glazed Carrots

1½ pounds carrots
2 tablespoons unsalted butter
1½ teaspoons sugar
¼ teaspoon salt
2 tablespoons chopped parsley

1. Peel and trim carrots. Cut into 2-inch-long pieces of approximately uniform thickness.
2. In medium-size saucepan, melt butter over medium heat. Add carrots and cook, turning often, 3 to 5 minutes.
3. Sprinkle carrots with sugar and salt, and continue cooking another 3 minutes.
4. Pour ½ cup warm water over carrots, raise heat to high, and bring to a boil. Reduce heat to medium, cover, and cook at a brisk simmer, 10 to 15 minutes, or until carrots are tender but still firm when pricked with the point of a knife. Remove pan from heat.
5. About 5 minutes before serving, reheat carrots, uncovered, over high heat until liquid has reduced to a glaze. Sprinkle with chopped parsley and turn carrots until evenly coated. Remove pan from heat.

LEFTOVER SUGGESTION

Any leftover cooked carrots can be used in many ways: mash them and reheat them with crème fraîche, or purée them to thicken sauces or soups. Try stirring puréed carrots into bread dough for extra moisture.

Chicken with Garlic-Vinegar Sauce
Lyonnaise Salad
Chocolate Pots de Crème with Chestnuts

Chicken with garlic-vinegar sauce and a green salad are ideal buffet fare. Serve the chilled pots de crème *in individual ramekins.*

ost supermarket vinegars are too harsh and acidic for this chicken recipe. If you cannot find imported natural red Burgundy wine vinegar in your local gourmet shop, dilute regular vinegar by mixing it half and half with the wine suggested for this meal.

The chocolate *pots de crème* are so-called because they are traditionally served in small lidded porcelain pots.

WHAT TO DRINK

This menu can be paired with either a white or a red wine. For white, choose a crisp, dry California Sauvignon Blanc. For red, opt for a light and fruity French Beaujolais.

SHOPPING LIST AND STAPLES

2½- to 3-pound chicken, cut into 12 serving pieces
¼ to ½ pound thick-cut bacon (4 to 6 slices)
2 medium-size tomatoes (¾ to 1 pound total weight), or 16-ounce can Italian plum
1 head chicory
1 head escarole
Small bunch scallions (optional)
Small bunch parsley
4 large cloves garlic plus 1 clove (if making croutons)
5 eggs
½ pint heavy cream
4 tablespoons unsalted butter
15½-ounce can whole chestnuts, preferably water-packed
½ cup chicken stock, preferably homemade (see page 13), or canned
½ cup vegetable oil
½ cup olive oil (if making croutons)
¾ cup red wine vinegar, preferably natural red Burgundy wine vinegar
2 teaspoons Dijon mustard
1½ teaspoons vanilla extract
1 large loaf French bread or baguette (if making croutons)
1 cup croutons, ½-inch-thick (if not using homemade)
4 squares sweet chocolate (4 ounces)
2 tablespoons sugar
Salt and freshly ground pepper

UTENSILS

Electric mixer
Large deep skillet or flameproof casserole with cover
Small skillet
Small heavy-gauge saucepan
Salad bowl
Large bowl
Small bowl
Salad spinner (optional)
Measuring cups and spoons
Chef's knife
Paring knife
2 wooden spoons
Metal spoon
Slotted spatula
Whisk
Metal tongs
4 ramekins, or porcelain *pots de crème*

START-TO-FINISH STEPS

At least two hours ahead: For chocolate *pots de crème*, follow steps 1 to 4.

Ahead of time: To make homemade croutons for salad, cut four ½-inch slices from large loaf of French bread or eight ½-inch slices from baguette into ½-inch dice. In heavy-gauge skillet, heat ½ cup olive oil over medium-high heat. Add peeled and minced garlic clove (or more to taste), stir, and add bread. Fry briefly, stirring, until bread is golden, about 1 to 2 minutes. Transfer croutons to paper towels to drain.

1. Follow chicken recipe step 1 and salad recipe steps 1 through 3.
2. Follow chicken recipe steps 2 through 4.
3. Follow salad recipe steps 4 and 5.
4. Follow chicken recipe step 5 and serve with salad.
5. Follow pots de crème recipe step 5 and serve for dessert.

RECIPES

Chicken with Garlic-Vinegar Sauce

2 medium-size tomatoes (¾ to 1 pound total weight), or 16-ounce Italian plum
Small bunch parsley
4 tablespoons unsalted butter
1 tablespoon vegetable oil
4 large cloves garlic
2½- to 3-pound chicken, cut into 12 serving pieces
Salt and freshly ground pepper

¼ cup plus 1 tablespoon red wine vinegar, preferably natural red Burgundy wine vinegar
½ cup chicken stock

1. If using fresh tomatoes, peel, core, halve, and seed. If using canned tomatoes, drain. Coarsely chop tomatoes and set aside. Wash parsley, pat dry with paper towels, and chop enough to measure 3 tablespoons. Refrigerate remaining parsley in plastic bag for another use.
2. In large deep skillet or flameproof casserole that will hold chicken in a single layer, combine 2 tablespoons butter, oil, and 4 unpeeled cloves garlic over medium-high heat. When butter stops foaming, add chicken pieces, and sauté, turning once, until pieces are lightly browned, about 5 minutes. Season chicken with salt and pepper to taste.
3. Add ¼ cup vinegar to skillet and bring to a boil. Add tomatoes, stock, and 2 tablespoons of chopped parsley, and, with wooden spoon, scrape up browned bits clinging to bottom of pan. When liquid returns to a boil, cover skillet, reduce heat to low, and simmer, turning chicken pieces once, about 15 minutes.
4. Transfer chicken to serving dish and cover loosely with foil to keep warm.
5. Remove garlic cloves from skillet and push cloves out of skins. Mince cloves and return to skillet. Mash garlic with wooden spoon. Add remaining tablespoon vinegar and simmer liquid over medium heat, stirring constantly, until reduced by one third. Remove pan from heat, cover, and keep warm.
6. Add salt and pepper to taste. Return skillet to heat, add remaining 2 tablespoons butter, and whisk until sauce is smooth and heated through. Pour sauce over chicken and garnish with remaining chopped parsley.

Lyonnaise Salad

1 head escarole
1 head chicory
1 cup croutons, ½-inch thick, preferably homemade
2 teaspoons Dijon mustard
¼ cup plus 2 tablespoons red wine vinegar
¼ to ½ pound thick-cut bacon (4 to 6 slices)
¼ cup plus 2 tablespoons vegetable oil
Small bunch scallions (optional)
Salt and freshly ground pepper

1. Wash greens and dry in salad spinner or pat dry with paper towels. Tear into bite-size pieces and combine with croutons in salad bowl. If using scallions, wash and pat dry. Finely chop white part of 2 scallions and set aside; reserve remaining whole scallions and green parts for another use.
2. Combine mustard and vinegar in small bowl and whisk until blended; set aside.
3. Cut bacon strips crosswise into ½-inch pieces to make about 1 cup. In small skillet, cook bacon over medium heat until fat is rendered and pieces are brown, about 5 minutes. With slotted spatula, transfer bacon to paper towels to drain; add to salad bowl.
4. Pour off all but about 2 tablespoons drippings from skillet. Add vegetable oil and stir until blended. To avoid spattering, remove skillet from heat and carefully add mustard-vinegar mixture. Return skillet to medium heat and bring liquid just to a boil. Remove from heat, stir, and pour over salad.
5. Season salad with salt and pepper to taste, toss, and sprinkle with scallions.

Chocolate Pots de Crème with Chestnuts

15½-ounce can whole chestnuts, preferably water-packed
5 eggs
4 squares sweet chocolate (4 ounces)
1 cup heavy cream
2 tablespoons sugar
Pinch of salt
1½ teaspoons vanilla extract

1. Drain chestnuts and coarsely chop enough to measure ½ cup. Slice 2 chestnuts in half for garnish, if desired. Separate eggs, placing yolks in large bowl and reserving whites for another use.
2. In small heavy-gauge saucepan, combine chocolate and heavy cream, and bring just to a boil, stirring frequently with wooden spoon, over medium heat. Remove pan from heat immediately.
3. Add sugar and a pinch of salt to yolks, and beat with an electric mixer at high speed until eggs thicken. Slowly add scalded chocolate cream, stirring constantly to avoid cooking egg yolks or curdling cream mixture. Stir in vanilla and fold in chopped chestnuts.
4. Divide mixture among 4 small ramekins or porcelain pots de crème without lids and refrigerate until set, at least 2 hours.
5. When ready to serve, remove from refrigerator and garnish each ramekin with a chestnut half, if desired.

Broiled Duck Breast with Prunes in Armagnac
Garlic Potatoes

Slices of duck breast with prunes simmered in brandy and garlic-rich mashed potatoes make an elegant company dinner.

Broiled duck breast with prunes in Armagnac is a dramatic entrée for an informal meal. Most supermarkets sell frozen whole ducks, but you may sometimes find fresh whole ducks or packaged fresh duck breast (the meaty part of the bird) as well.

Mashed potatoes redolent of garlic accompany the duck. The recipe suggests keeping the potatoes warm in their cooking water until you are ready to mash them; this adds flavor and eliminates possible scorching if you need to reheat the potatoes before mashing.

WHAT TO DRINK

The best accompaniment for this menu would be a good claret, such as a Saint-Estèphe, Saint-Julien, Pauillac, or one from another commune.

SHOPPING LIST AND STAPLES

2 boneless duck breasts (about 2 pounds total weight), or
   2 whole ducks
4 Idaho potatoes (about 1¾ pounds total weight)
10 cloves garlic
Small bunch parsley
½ pint heavy cream (optional)
4 tablespoons unsalted butter
½ cup beef stock, preferably homemade, or canned
8-ounce box pitted prunes
1 teaspoon dried thyme
Salt and freshly ground pepper
½ cup Armagnac or Cognac

UTENSILS

Large saucepan with cover
Small saucepan with cover
Broiler pan
Medium-size bowl
Small bowl
Food mill, ricer, or potato masher
Measuring cups and spoons
Chef's knife
Boning knife
Ladle
Wooden spoon
Metal tongs
Vegetable peeler

START-TO-FINISH STEPS

1. Follow duck recipe steps 1 through 4.
2. Follow potatoes recipe steps 1 and 2.
3. While pototoes are boiling, follow prunes recipe step 1.
4. While prunes are simmering, follow duck recipe step 5.
5. Follow potatoes recipe step 3.
6. Follow prunes recipe step 2, duck recipe step 6, and serve with garlic potatoes.

RECIPES

Broiled Duck Breast with Prunes in Armagnac

2 boneless duck breasts (about 2 pounds total weight), or
   2 whole ducks
2 cloves garlic
Small bunch parsley
1 teaspoon dried thyme
Salt and freshly ground pepper
Prunes in Armagnac (see following recipe)

1. Split boneless duck breasts in half and pat dry with paper towels. If using whole ducks, with a sharp boning knife, remove wings as close to bone as possible in order to leave maximum amount of meat on breast. Remove drumsticks and reserve with wings for another use. To separate breast from carcass, locate breastbone and make incision the length of the ridge (see illustration). Holding knife against breastbone and away from flesh, cut downward to

With boning knife, separate duck breast from carcass.

Trim away excess fat.

remove each breast section in one piece. Place each section skin side down and trim away excess fat, leaving skin intact, so that you have four half-heart-shaped pieces. Make ¼-inch-deep slashes in skin side of breast pieces.

2. Set broiler rack about 4 inches from heating element and preheat broiler. Peel garlic and mince enough to measure 1 teaspoon. Wash parsley, pat dry with paper towels, and chop enough to measure 1 teaspoon.

3. In small bowl, blend together garlic, parsley, thyme, ½ teaspoon salt, and pepper to taste.

4. Rub both sides of breast pieces with seasoning mixture. If not broiling immediately, let duck stand at room temperature.

5. Place breasts, skin side up, on broiler pan and broil 5 minutes. Turn breasts and broil 2 minutes more, or until centers of breasts are pink and juicy. Remove pan from broiler, cover with foil to keep warm, and set aside.

6. With chef's knife, slice each half breast across grain into 4 slices. Transfer to dinner plates and garnish each serving with 4 prunes and cooking liquid, and serve.

Prunes in Armagnac

8-ounce box pitted prunes
½ cup Armagnac or Cognac
½ cup beef stock, preferably homemade, or canned
Salt and freshly ground pepper

1. In small saucepan, combine prunes, Armagnac and stock. Bring to a slow simmer over low heat and cook 20 minutes, or until prunes are soft. Remove pan from heat, season with salt and pepper to taste, and cover to keep warm.

2. Just before serving, reheat prunes in liquid, if necessary.

Garlic Potatoes

4 Idaho potatoes (about 1¾ pounds total weight)
8 cloves garlic
Salt
4 tablespoons unsalted butter
¼ cup heavy cream (optional)
Freshly ground pepper

1. Peel potatoes and cut enough into ½-inch cubes to measure about 4 cups. Cut unpeeled garlic cloves in half.

2. In large saucepan, combine potatoes, garlic, 1 tablespoon salt, and 6 cups water. Cover and bring to a rolling boil over high heat. Reduce heat, keeping water at a boil, and continue cooking potatoes 10 to 12 minutes, or until tender. Turn off heat; leave potatoes in water until ready to proceed. Ladle out ⅓ cup of cooking liquid and reserve.

3. Pour off remaining cooking liquid from potatoes; remove garlic, and discard peels. Transfer potatoes and garlic to a food mill or ricer, if using; or you can leave potatoes in saucepan and use a potato masher, in which case you may prefer to remove garlic cloves. Mill, rice, or mash potatoes over medium-size bowl. Add butter and ⅓ cup reserved cooking liquid, and beat potatoes with wooden spoon until fluffy. Add heavy cream, if desired, and beat until blended. Season with salt and pepper to taste.

ADDED TOUCH

These individual jelly tarts are as easy to make as cookies. For variety, you can fill the pastry shells with any type of preserves, jam, or combination of jellies and jams.

Jelly Tarts

2 cups flour
¼ cup sugar
Salt
1 stick butter
1 egg
Prune, quince, apricot, blackberry, or black raspberry preserves

1. In medium-size bowl, combine flour, sugar, and about ¼ teaspoon salt, and stir until blended.

2. With pastry blender or two knives, cut in butter until mixture resembles coarse cornmeal.

3. Separate egg, reserving white for another use. Add yolk and ⅓ cup cold water to flour mixture, and stir until dough can be gathered into a ball. Cover bowl and refrigerate for at least 1 hour.

4. Preheat oven to 375 degrees. Lightly grease baking sheet.

5. On a lightly floured board, roll out chilled pastry to ⅛-inch-thickness. With a knife, cut into 4-inch circles.

6. Turn up outside edge of each circle, forming a narrow rim around tart to contain preserves.

7. Place tarts on sheet and bake 20 minutes, or until lightly golden. Transfer to a rack to cool.

8. Just before serving, place 1 heaping teaspoon preserves in center of each small tart.

MEXICAN MENUS

Elizabeth Schneider

MENU 1 (Right)
Rock Cornish Hens in Fragrant Green Sauce
Rice with Cumin and Pimiento
Grapefruit, Kiwi, and Watercress Salad

MENU 2
Avocado Soup
Green Chili and Cheese Enchiladas
Carrot, Apple, and Walnut Salad

MENU 3
Pineapple-Tequila Cooler
Corn Pudding with Chilies and Cheese
Zucchini and Tomato Salad with Pine Nuts

When she was a novice cook, Elizabeth Schneider insisted on only authentic ingredients and recipes. However, with time and experience, she discovered that going by the book did not matter as much as making simple, high-quality meals with the freshest ingredients. So, too, she has found that American cooks tend to be unconventional, mixing and matching cuisines and adapting ingredients to suit their own tastes. In this spirit, Elizabeth Schneider enjoys experimenting with Mexican foods, particularly the dishes of New Mexico.

Menu 1, a festive year-round dinner, offers more traditional Mexican fare, Rock Cornish game hens in a green sauce resembling both *mole verde* (herbal green sauce) and *pollo en pipián* (chicken in pumpkin seed sauce), while Menus 2 and 3 are both vegetarian hybrids in the New Mexico style. The main course of Menu 2, suitable for lunch or a family supper, is green chili and cheese enchiladas filled with a combination of farmer cheese and sour cream. In Menu 3, the main course is a corn pudding—containing fresh corn kernels, cornmeal, chilies, and bits of cheese—a combination of southwestern tamale pie, southern spoonbread, and northeastern corn custard.

Casual pottery underlines the simple elegance of game hens coated with a thick green sauce, sprinkled with pumpkin seeds, and served with rice tossed with diced pimientos—a meal for family or company. A two-toned salad of lime green kiwi and red grapefruit slices, arranged on watercress, accompanies the main course.

Rock Cornish Hens in Fragrant Green Sauce
Rice with Cumin and Pimiento
Grapefruit, Kiwi, and Watercress Salad

The Rock Cornish game hen is a delicate foil for spicy sauces, such as "fragrant green." Weighing about one and one half pounds, it is ideal for two servings. For this recipe, the hens are poached in stock, a method that Mexican cooks often use. To prepare the sauce, which contains tomatillos and chilies, you can use either a food processor or a blender. For information about chilies, see pages 14 and 15.

The salad calls for kiwis—fuzzy, brown-skinned oval fruit with lime-green flesh and melon-like texture. A perfectly ripe kiwi yields slightly to the touch.

WHAT TO DRINK

A French Pouilly Fumé or Sancerre or a California Sauvignon Blanc would go well here as would a pale ale.

SHOPPING LIST AND STAPLES

2 large Rock Cornish hens, quartered (about 3 pounds total weight)
Large bunch watercress
Small bunch scallions
Large bunch coriander
Medium-size bunch mint
Large clove garlic
3 large, medium-hot, fresh green chilies, or 4-ounce can
2 medium-size ruby red or pink grapefruit (about 2 pounds total weight)
3 kiwis
1 lemon
1⅔ cups chicken stock, preferably homemade (see page 13), or canned
13-ounce can tomatillos, or 14 to 18 fresh tomates verdes
4-ounce jar whole pimiento
2 tablespoons olive oil
2 tablespoons vegetable oil, plus 1 tablespoon (if not using walnut oil)
1 tablespoon walnut oil (optional)
1 tablespoon cider vinegar
2 teaspoons honey
1½ cups long-grain white rice
4-ounce bag pepitas (hulled pumpkin or squash seeds)
2 slices white bread
1½ teaspoons paprika
1 teaspoon ground cumin
Ground cinnamon
Salt and freshly ground pepper

UTENSILS

Food processor or blender
Large skillet with cover
Small skillet
Large, heavy-gauge saucepan with cover
Medium-size saucepan
Platter
Small bowl
Salad spinner (optional)
Measuring cups and spoons
Chef's knife
Paring knife
Wooden spoon
Long, double-pronged fork
Rubber spatula
Juicer (optional)
Tongs
Vegetable peeler

START-TO-FINISH STEPS

1. Wash coriander and mint for Cornish hens recipe and watercress for salad. Dry in salad spinner or pat dry with paper towels. Coarsely chop coriander and mint, and set aside. Wrap watercress in paper towels and refrigerate until needed. Juice lemon for salad dressing; reserve.
2. Follow rice recipe steps 1 through 5.
3. Follow Cornish hens recipe steps 1 through 8.
4. Follow salad recipe steps 1 through 4.
5. Follow rice recipe step 6, Cornish hens recipe step 9, and salad recipe step 5.

RECIPES

Rock Cornish Hens in Fragrant Green Sauce

1⅔ cups chicken stock
6 tablespoons pepitas (hulled pumpkin or squash seeds), plus 2 tablespoons for garnish
2 large Rock Cornish hens, quartered (about 3 pounds total weight)
13-ounce can tomatillos, or 14 to 18 fresh tomates verdes
3 large, medium-hot, green chilies, roasted, peeled, and seeded, or 3 canned chilies, rinsed, drained, and patted dry
2 slices white bread
4 scallions

1 cup coarsely chopped fresh coriander, packed
1 cup coarsely chopped fresh mint, packed

1. In large skillet, bring stock to a simmer over medium heat.
2. While stock is heating, toast pepitas in small skillet over medium heat, stirring frequently, about 2 to 3 minutes, or until they puff up. (Some pepitas "explode.") Set aside.
3. Add hens to stock, reduce heat to low, cover and simmer, turning once, 16 minutes, or until firm and juices run clear when hens are pierced with fork.
4. Meanwhile, if using canned tomatillos, rinse, drain, and pat dry or, if using tomates verdes, remove rough outer layer, rinse, and pat dry. In medium-size saucepan, simmer tomatillos in water to cover, over low heat 8 to 10 minutes, or until almost soft.
5. Prepare chilies (see pages 14, 15). Cut white bread into cubes. Trim scallions, cut off white portion, and reserve for another use. Wash green portion, pat dry with paper towels, and coarsely chop.
6. In food processor fitted with metal blade or in blender, chop cubed bread. Add 6 tablespoons toasted pepitas and process mixture until finely chopped. Drain tomatillos, add to bread crumb-pepita mixture, and chop. In succession, add chilies, scallions, coriander, and mint, chopping after each addition.
7. Remove hens from stock and set aside. For sauce, add stock to mixture in processor or blender and purée.
8. Return hens to skillet and combine with sauce. Simmer 10 minutes, turning once.
9. Arrange 2 hen quarters on each of 4 plates, spooning some sauce over each quarter. Garnish with remaining pepitas and serve remaining sauce separately.

Rice with Cumin and Pimiento

Large clove garlic
4-ounce jar whole pimiento
1½ cups long-grain white rice
2 tablespoons olive oil
1½ teaspoons paprika
1 teaspoon ground cumin
1 teaspoon salt

1. Peel and mince garlic. Drain pimiento and cut into ½-inch dice.
2. In heavy-gauge saucepan, heat oil over medium-high heat. Add rice and garlic, and cook 2 to 3 minutes, or until lightly browned.
3. Add paprika and cumin and cook, stirring, 1 minute.
4. Add salt and 2½ cups water and, stirring, bring to a rolling boil, over high heat. Add pimiento.
5. Reduce heat to low, cover, and cook 20 minutes. Without uncovering, remove pan from heat and let stand until serving time (up to 40 minutes, or until water is absorbed).
6. Fluff rice with fork and divide among 4 plates.

Grapefruit, Kiwi, and Watercress Salad

2 medium-size ruby red or pink grapefruit (about 2 pounds total weight)
3 kiwis
2 tablespoons lemon juice
1 tablespoon cider vinegar
¼ teaspoon salt
1 tablespoon walnut oil, preferably, or vegetable oil
2 tablespoons vegetable oil
2 teaspoons honey
Large bunch watercress
Ground cinnamon
Freshly ground pepper

1. Peel grapefruit and remove pith. Cut each in half lengthwise and then slice crosswise into ½-inch-thick semicircles. Set aside.
2. Peel kiwi fruit and slice into ⅛- to ¼-inch-thick rounds. Set aside.
3. Prepare dressing: In small bowl, combine lemon juice, vinegar, and salt. Drain any accumulated grapefruit juice into dressing. Stir with fork until salt dissolves. Add walnut oil, vegetable oil, and honey, and beat until blended. Set aside.
4. Arrange watercress around edge of decorative platter. Overlap grapefruit slices in ring within watercress and arrange kiwi slices in center.
5. Just before serving, beat dressing to recombine and pour over salad. Sprinkle with cinnamon and pepper to taste.

Kiwi fruit

Avocado Soup
Green Chili and Cheese Enchiladas
Carrot, Apple, and Walnut Salad

I n New Mexico, green chili and cheese enchiladas often are made with fragile blue-corn tortillas, which break easily when rolled. These are difficult to find in some areas of the country, so this recipe calls for standard corn tortillas, preferably fresh, or, if they are unavailable, frozen ones.

If you can find blue tortillas, bake them flat: Spread one third of the sauce in the bottoms of two 13 x 9 x 2-inch baking dishes. Add another third of the sauce to the farmer-cheese filling. Place two blue-corn tortillas, edges

Vivid textile patterns and informal tableware set off this New Mexico-style meal of carrot, apple, and walnut salad, smooth and rich avocado soup, and enchiladas garnished with radishes and Romaine lettuce.

not touching, on the sauce in each baking dish. Using half of the cheese filling, spread a layer on each tortilla. Top with another layer of tortillas and the rest of the cheese mixture, spreading it to the edges of the tortillas. Add a final layer of tortillas and spread the remaining green chili sauce on top. Sprinkle the grated cheese over all, and bake in a 350-degree oven about 15 minutes, or until the cheese melts and the sauce bubbles.

WHAT TO DRINK

If you want to depart from beer, serve a dry sparkling wine. Your options are many, ranging from nonvintage Champagne through Spanish, Italian, California, and New York sparkling wines.

SHOPPING LIST AND STAPLES

2 medium-size avocados
1 pound carrots
Small head Romaine lettuce (about ¾ pound)
Small bunch radishes
6 large, medium-hot, fresh green chilies,
    or two 4-ounce cans
Small bunch coriander
Small bunch scallions
Small clove garlic
2 medium-size crisp red apples, such as Winesap or
    Cortland (about ¾ pound total weight)
1 to 2 limes
2 cups buttermilk
½ pint sour cream
½ pound farmer cheese
¼ pound sharp Cheddar cheese
5 tablespoons corn oil
¼ cup cider vinegar
2 teaspoons sugar
12 fresh corn tortillas, or 1 package frozen
3-ounce can walnut pieces
1 teaspoon ground cumin
1 teaspoon freshly ground coriander seeds, or
    1 to 2 teaspoons packaged ground coriander

Salt
Freshly ground white pepper

UTENSILS

Food processor or blender
Small saucepan
13 x 9 x 2-inch baking/serving dish
Baking sheet or tray
Large bowl
3 small bowls
Salad spinner (optional)
Measuring cups and spoons
Chef's knife
Paring knife
Metal spoon
Metal spatula
Grater (if not using food processor)
Juicer (optional)
Pastry brush
Vegetable peeler

START-TO-FINISH STEPS

One hour ahead: Refrigerate avocados for soup recipe. If using frozen tortillas for enchiladas recipe, set out to thaw.

1. Juice lime for soup recipe and follow steps 1 through 4.
2. Follow salad recipe steps 1 through 3.
3. Preheat oven to 400 degrees for enchiladas recipe and follow steps 1 through 11.
4. Follow soup recipe step 5 and serve.
5. Follow enchiladas recipe step 12 and salad recipe step 4.

RECIPES

Avocado Soup

2 medium-size avocados, chilled
2 tablespoons lime juice
1 teaspoon sugar
1 teaspoon salt
1 teaspoon ground cumin
2 cups buttermilk
Salt
Freshly ground white pepper

1. Halve avocados lengthwise. Remove and discard pits. Cut 1 avocado half crosswise into 2 quarters. Cover one quarter with plastic wrap and refrigerate until needed. With metal spoon, scoop remaining avocado into processor fitted with metal blade or into blender.
2. Add lime juice, sugar, salt, and cumin to avocado and purée.
3. With motor still running, gradually add buttermilk. When buttermilk is totally incorporated, slowly add about 1 cup ice water. Soup should be of pourable consistency; it will thicken slightly when chilled. (Do this step in two batches if necessary.) Season with salt and pepper to taste.
4. Pour soup into 4 bowls set on baking sheet or tray, cover, and freeze until serving time, up to one-half hour. (If holding longer, refrigerate first, then freeze for one-half hour.)
5. Just before serving, peel reserved avocado quarter and slice into 8 crescents. Remove soup from freezer and float 2 crescents in each bowl.

Green Chili and Cheese Enchiladas

6 large, medium-hot, fresh green chilies, roasted, peeled, and seeded, or 6 canned chilies, rinsed, drained, and patted dry
Small head Romaine lettuce
⅓ cup coriander leaves
Small clove garlic
3 tablespoons corn oil, approximately
4 scallions
1 cup farmer cheese
1 cup sour cream
12 fresh corn tortillas, or 12 frozen tortillas, thawed
¼ pound sharp Cheddar cheese
Radishes for garnish

1. Prepare chilies (see pages 14, 15).
2. Wash lettuce and dry in salad spinner or pat dry with paper towels. Tear 4 leaves into pieces; set aside re-mainder. Wash coriander leaves and dry in salad spinner or pat dry with paper towels. Chop coarsely. Peel garlic and chop coarsely.
3. For sauce, combine chilies, torn Romaine leaves, coriander, garlic, and 1 tablespoon oil in processor fitted with metal blade or in blender and process until coarsely textured.
4. Pour one third of chili sauce into baking dish. Distribute evenly over bottom of dish.
5. Trim scallion greens and reserve whites for another use. Wash greens, pat dry with paper towels, and cut into ⅛-inch-thick rounds.
6. In small bowl, crumble farmer cheese. Stir in scallions, sour cream, and half of remaining chili sauce.
7. Fill and roll tortillas: Divide farmer cheese mixture among tortillas, spooning it into long strips laid slightly off center. From the "short" sides, roll neatly into enchiladas and place them seam-side-down in baking dish.
8. Measure remaining corn oil into small bowl. With pastry brush, baste enchiladas, being sure to coat edges as well as tops and sides. Cover dish with aluminum foil, set in upper level of 400-degree oven, and bake about 10 minutes, or until enchiladas are heated through.
9. Heat remaining chili sauce in saucepan over low heat.
10. In processor fitted with shredding blade or with grater, shred enough Cheddar cheese to measure 1½ cups, loosely packed. With chef's knife, chop reserved Romaine leaves into ⅛-inch-thick shreds. Wash and trim radishes; cut decoratively, if desired.
11. Remove baking dish from oven, uncover, and spread warmed chili sauce evenly over enchiladas. Sprinkle with grated cheese, return to oven, and bake, uncovered, 5 minutes, or until cheese has melted and sauce is bubbly.
12. With spatula, transfer 3 enchiladas to each of 4 plates. Garnish with shredded lettuce and radishes.

Carrot, Apple, and Walnut Salad

1 pound carrots
2 medium-size crisp red apples, such as Winesap or Cortland (about ¾ pound total weight)
1 teaspoon granulated sugar
1 teaspoon freshly ground coriander seeds, or 1 to 2 teaspoons packaged ground coriander
¾ teaspoon salt
¼ cup cider vinegar
2 tablespoons corn oil
¼ cup walnut pieces, coarsely chopped

1. Trim and peel carrots. Shred in food processor fitted with shredding blade or with grater. Transfer to large bowl.
2. Wash and core apples; cut into quarters. Slice into thin crescents and add to carrots.
3. For dressing, blend sugar, coriander, salt, vinegar, and oil in small bowl. Pour over carrots and apples, and toss until evenly coated. Cover and chill until serving time.
4. Just before serving, add walnuts and toss. Divide among 4 bowls and serve with enchiladas.

Pineapple-Tequila Cooler
Corn Pudding with Chilies and Cheese
Zucchini and Tomato Salad with Pine Nuts

This menu works well as a buffet brunch or luncheon: Start with the iced pineapple-tequila drink, then, when the corn pudding is bubbly and brown, serve it in its baking dish with zucchini-tomato salad on the side.

Stone-ground cornmeal, which the cook prefers for the main-course pudding, is a coarse meal in which more of the nutrients of the corn kernel have been preserved. You can readily find this type of meal in health food stores and specialty food shops. Refrigerate stone-ground cornmeal in an airtight container for up to three months.

WHAT TO DRINK

Precede this meal with the cook's Pineapple-Tequila Cooler. You might then switch to the delicate fruitiness and slight sweetness of a German or a New York State Riesling.

SHOPPING LIST AND STAPLES

4 small zucchini (about 1 to 1¼ pounds total weight)
4 medium-size tomatoes (about 1½ pounds total weight)
4 medium-size ears fresh corn, or two 10-ounce packages
    frozen kernels
3 medium-large, medium-hot fresh green chilies, or
    4-ounce can
Small bunch scallions
Small clove garlic
Small bunch basil
Small bunch parsley
Small bunch mint (optional)
3 grapefruit (about 3½ pounds total weight)
20-ounce can plus 8-ounce can pineapple chunks, in
    unsweetened juice
2 eggs
2¼ cups buttermilk
2 tablespoons unsalted butter
¾ pound Monterey Jack cheese or Danish Havarti
⅓ cup olive oil
2 tablespoons red wine vinegar
3 tablespoons Grenadine syrup, approximately
1 cup yellow cornmeal, preferably stone-ground
½ teaspoon sugar
2-ounce jar pine nuts
¾ teaspoon baking soda
½ teaspoon baking powder
Salt and freshly ground pepper
1¼ cups tequila, preferably gold

UTENSILS

Food processor or blender
Small skillet
Large saucepan
8 x 8 x 2-inch baking dish
Salad bowl or platter
2-quart pitcher
Large bowl
2 medium-size bowls
Colander
Medium-fine sieve
Measuring cups and spoons
Chef's knife

Paring knife
Long-handled spoon
Wooden spoon
Long, double-pronged fork
Rubber spatula
Grater
Juicer (optional)
Tongs

START-TO-FINISH STEPS

Two hours ahead: If using frozen corn for pudding recipe, set out to thaw. Refrigerate pineapple for tequila drink; squeeze grapefruit juice and refrigerate.

Thirty minutes ahead: Prepare chilies (see pages 14, 15) for corn pudding recipe.

1. Follow tequila recipe steps 1 through 4.
2. Follow salad recipe steps 1 through 5 and tequila recipe step 5.
3. Follow salad recipe steps 6 and 7.
4. Follow corn pudding recipe steps 1 through 10.
5. While corn pudding is baking, follow salad recipe steps 8 and 9, and tequila recipe step 6.
6. Follow corn pudding recipe step 11, salad recipe step 10, and serve.

RECIPES

Pineapple-Tequila Cooler

20-ounce can plus 8-ounce can pineapple chunks, in
    unsweetened juice
2 cups freshly squeezed grapefruit juice, chilled
1 cup tequila, preferably gold
3 tablespoons Grenadine syrup, approximately
Mint sprigs for garnish

1. In food processor fitted with metal blade or in blender, purée pineapple chunks and juice until smooth (in two batches, if necessary).
2. Transfer purée to large bowl. Stir in grapefruit juice and tequila.
3. Press mixture through sieve set over pitcher. Discard pulp.
4. Add Grenadine syrup to taste. Stir, cover, and refrigerate.
5. Wash mint sprigs, if using. Pat dry, wrap in paper towels, and refrigerate until ready to serve.
6. Pour cooler into 4 tall glasses filled with ice and serve garnished with mint sprigs.

Corn Pudding with Chilies and Cheese

4 medium-size ears fresh corn, or two 10-ounce packages
    frozen kernels, thawed
4 scallions
3 medium-large, medium-hot, fresh green chilies,
    roasted, peeled, and seeded, or 3 canned chilies,
    rinsed, drained, and patted dry

¾ pound Monterey Jack or Danish Havarti
1 cup yellow cornmeal, preferably stone-ground
½ teaspoon baking powder
¾ teaspoon baking soda
½ teaspoon salt
2 eggs
2¼ cups buttermilk
2 tablespoons unsalted butter

1. Place baking dish in cold oven and set oven temperature at 425 degrees.
2. While oven is heating, shuck fresh corn, if using, and trim stub of cob so that thick end will rest flat against cutting surface. To hull corn, grip corn with one hand and slice downward, following contours of cob. Rotate corn and repeat process. (You should have 1¾ to 2¼ cups kernels.)
3. Trim scallions, wash, and pat dry. Slice into ⅛-inch-thick pieces. Dice chilies.
4. Dice enough cheese to measure 1 cup and grate remainder. Set aside.
5. In large bowl, combine cornmeal, baking powder, baking soda, and salt.
6. In medium-size bowl, combine slightly beaten eggs, corn, chilies, scallions, diced cheese, and buttermilk.
7. Remove heated baking dish from oven. Melt butter in dish, rotating dish until evenly coated.
8. Immediately, pour the egg mixture into the cornmeal mixture, stirring just until combined. (Do not beat.)
9. With rubber spatula, scrape pudding into hot baking dish, top with cheese, and place in upper third of oven.
10. Bake about 25 minutes, or until golden and firm, but slightly soft in center.
11. Remove pudding from oven and serve.

Zucchini and Tomato Salad with Pine Nuts

2½ teaspoons salt
¼ cup coarsely chopped basil
2 tablespoons minced parsley plus additional sprigs for garnish (optional)
Small clove garlic
4 small zucchini (about 1 to 1¼ pounds total weight)
4 medium-size tomatoes (about 1½ pounds total weight)
¼ cup pine nuts
½ teaspoon sugar
Freshly ground pepper
2 tablespoons red wine vinegar
⅓ cup olive oil

1. Bring 2 quarts water and 2 teaspoons salt to a boil over high heat.
2. While water is heating, wash basil and parsley and pat dry with paper towels. If using parsley sprigs for garnish, wrap in paper towels and refrigerate. Coarsely chop basil and mince parsley. Peel garlic and chop coarsely.
3. Wash zucchini. Blanch in boiling water 3 to 4 minutes, or until slightly soft. Meanwhile, fill medium-size bowl with ice water.

4. Transfer zucchini to colander with tongs. Refresh under cold running water, then plunge into ice water.
5. Immerse tomatoes in pot of still boiling water. In about 1 minute, or as soon as water returns to a boil, transfer tomatoes to colander. Refresh under cold running water, then plunge into ice water with zucchini. Leave 5 minutes.
6. Drain zucchini and tomatoes and pat dry with paper towels. Slice zucchini into ⅛-inch-thick rounds. Peel and core tomatoes. Slice in half crosswise and gently squeeze out seeds. Reserve 2 halves and cut remaining tomatoes into ¼- to ½-inch-thick slices.
7. Combine tomato and zucchini slices in salad bowl or arrange on platter, cover, and refrigerate.
8. In small dry skillet, toast pine nuts over medium heat 3 to 4 minutes, or until fragrant and lightly browned. Set aside.
9. In food processor fitted with metal blade or in blender, purée reserved tomato halves, remaining ½ teaspoon salt, sugar, pepper, basil, parsley, garlic, and vinegar. With motor running, add olive oil in a slow, steady stream and process, until mixture is thick and smooth. Set aside.
10. Just before serving, beat dressing to recombine, pour over salad, sprinkle with pine nuts, and garnish with parsley sprigs, if desired.

ADDED TOUCH

This refreshingly light gelatin dessert is made with fresh fruit juices.

Citrus Gelatin

½ cup granulated sugar
2 envelopes unflavored gelatin
2 small grapefruit
2 medium-size juice oranges
1 lemon
Few drops red and yellow food coloring (optional)
Four orange slices, decoratively cut, for garnish (optional)

1. Combine sugar, gelatin, and 1½ cups cold water in medium-size saucepan. Do not stir.
2. Wash 1 grapefruit and 1 orange, and pat dry with paper towels. Cut thin strips of rind, avoiding white pith. Add strips of rind to saucepan with gelatin.
3. Halve oranges and grapefruit, and squeeze enough juice to measure 1½ cups combined. Halve lemon and squeeze ¼ cup juice. Add juices to saucepan.
4. Simmer mixture, stirring constantly, about 5 minutes, or until mixture becomes clear.
5. Strain mixture through fine sieve set over bowl. Discard solids and rinse sieve. If desired, add very small amount of food coloring to mixture. Set sieve over serving bowl and strain mixture again.
6. Cover and refrigerate at least 3 hours, or until completely set.
7. Spoon into individual goblets or bowls and serve garnished with orange slices, if desired.

Jane Butel

L ike most smart cooks, Jane Butel knows that there are no substitutes for fresh, wholesome ingredients. Her insistence on using only "the freshest and purest" underlines her approach to Southwestern-style Mexican cooking. For these dishes to retain their authentic Mexican flavors, she suggests using only top-quality pure spices, seasonings, and other ingredients.

Although she has roamed the Southwest to discover traditional recipes and has worked with Pueblo Indian cooks in New Mexico, Jane Butel believes that Mexican meals should be interpretive. No cook need feel bound to follow her recipes and techniques exactly.

Just right for an informal brunch or light supper, Menu 1 features marinated scallops and open enchiladas with fried eggs. Sweet peppers and cumin rice in Menu 2 accompany chicken tacos, a popular dish in Mexico as well as in the United States. For dessert, serve rich chocolate sundaes with Kahlúa, a Mexican coffee-flavored liqueur, which is spooned into the bottom of each bowl.

Texans are credited with inventing *chili con carne*—a stew-like dish of cubed beef simmered in a spicy sauce— but there are probably as many versions of chili as there are cooks. Jane Butel's chili recipe in Menu 3 is a perfect example of her individualistic approach to cooking. You can personalize her chili by varying the suggested garnishes to suit your taste. New Mexican refried beans and a substantial salad complete this meal.

Fresh flowers and colorful pottery dishes set the tone for this cheery brunch. Top each of the easily assembled open enchiladas with a fried egg and garnish the plates with lettuce and a halved cherry tomato. The marinated scallops, with their dressing of onions and peppers, sit on a bed of lettuce.

167

Marinated Scallops
Santa Fe-style Open Enchiladas with Fried Eggs

For an impressive meal that looks complicated but isn't, prepare marinated scallops as a first course or as a salad to go with the enchiladas.

The Santa Fe-style open enchiladas consist of lightly fried tortillas layered with grated cheese, chopped onion, and spicy red chili sauce and topped with a fried egg. Jane Butel prefers to use blue-corn tortillas but regular corn tortillas work just as well.

WHAT TO DRINK

Serve cold beer or ale, a well-chilled white wine, such as a crisp, acidic Verdicchio or Muscadet, or even fresh lemonade with this menu.

SHOPPING LIST AND STAPLES

1 pound bay scallops
Small head Romaine lettuce
Small head leaf lettuce
4 cherry tomatoes
Large green bell pepper
Large Spanish onion
Medium-size purple onion
4 cloves garlic
1 fresh jalapeño or 4-ounce can
2 limes
4 eggs
4 tablespoons unsalted butter
¼ pound Muenster cheese
¼ pound Cheddar cheese
1 quart beef stock, preferably homemade, or canned
¼ cup olive oil
½ cup vegetable oil
2 tablespoons wine vinegar, preferably white
1 dozen 6-inch corn tortillas, preferably blue-corn
¼ cup flour
½ cup California (mild), New Mexican (hot), or other pure chili powder
Ground oregano, preferably Mexican
Ground cumin
Crushed red pepper flakes (optional)
Salt and freshly ground pepper

UTENSILS

Large skillet
Small skillet
2 medium-size saucepans, one heavy-gauge
Platter
4 ovenproof dinner plates
Medium-size bowl
Salad spinner (optional)
Measuring cups and spoons
Chef's knife
Paring knife
Wooden spoon
Metal spatula
Rubber spatula
Grater
Whisk
Tongs

START-TO-FINISH STEPS

1. Peel and mince garlic for scallops and chili sauce.
2. Follow scallops recipe steps 1 through 5.
3. For scallops and enchiladas recipes, rinse lettuce and dry in salad spinner or pat dry with paper towels. Reserve 8 leaves of leaf lettuce for scallops. Tear remaining lettuce into 2-inch square pieces. Wrap all in paper towels and refrigerate.
4. Follow chili sauce recipe steps 1 through 3.
5. Follow enchiladas recipe steps 1 through 5, and sauce recipe step 4.
6. Follow scallops recipe step 6 and serve.
7. Follow enchiladas recipe steps 6 through 10 and serve.

RECIPES

Marinated Scallops

2 limes
1 fresh jalapeño, washed and patted dry, or 1 canned, rinsed and drained
Medium-size purple onion
Large green bell pepper
¼ cup olive oil
1 tablespoon jalapeño juice, if using canned jalapeño
2 cloves garlic, peeled and minced
Pinch of ground oregano, preferably Mexican
Pinch of ground cumin
1 pound bay scallops
2 tablespoons wine vinegar, preferably white
Salt and freshly ground pepper
8 leaves leaf lettuce
Crushed red pepper flakes (optional)

1. Squeeze enough lime to measure 3 tablespoons juice. Prepare jalapeño (see pages 14, 15) and cut into ⅛-inch-thick slices. Peel onion and slice thinly. Rinse green pepper and pat dry. Halve, core, and seed pepper. Cut pepper into ⅛-inch julienne.

2. In large skillet, combine lime juice, 2 tablespoons olive oil, jalapeño slices to taste, jalapeño juice, if using, garlic, oregano, and cumin and bring to a boil over medium heat.

3. Add scallops, stirring continuously. Reduce heat and simmer 3 to 5 minutes, or until scallops have whitened and become firm. Remove skillet from heat and transfer mixture to medium-size bowl.

4. Return skillet to medium heat and add remaining olive oil. Add onion and green pepper, and sauté, stirring frequently, about 5 minutes, or just until crisp-tender.

5. Remove skillet from heat, add vinegar and salt and pepper to taste, and stir to blend. Set mixture aside, stirring occasionally.

6. Line 4 plates with lettuce and top with scallops. Stir sauce and pour over scallops. Sprinkle with red pepper flakes if desired.

Santa Fe-style Open Enchiladas with Fried Eggs

¼ pound Muenster cheese
¼ pound Cheddar cheese
Large Spanish onion
½ cup vegetable oil, approximately
1 dozen 6-inch corn tortillas, preferably blue-corn
Red Chili Sauce (see following recipe)
4 eggs
4 cherry tomatoes
2 cups Romaine and leaf lettuce, torn into 2-inch pieces

1. Shred enough Muenster and Cheddar cheese to measure 1 cup each. Peel onion and chop finely. Halve tomatoes.

2. Preheat oven to 250 degrees.

3. In small skillet, heat oil over medium-high heat.

4. Line platter with paper towels and place 4 heatproof dinner plates in oven.

5. When oil is almost smoking, lightly fry tortillas, one at a time, about 10 seconds, or just until soft. Do not let tortillas become crisp. As they are done, transfer tortillas to paper-towel-lined platter, layering tortillas between towels. When all are done, if not preparing enchiladas immediately, cover platter loosely with foil and place in oven. Reserve oil in skillet.

6. Remove dinner plates and tortillas from oven and raise oven temperature to 350 degrees.

7. To assemble enchiladas, place a dollop of sauce on each plate and top with a tortilla. Top each tortilla with sauce, a spoonful or two of mixed cheeses, and a sprinkling of onion. Cover with another tortilla and then repeat with remaining tortillas and toppings. Place plates in oven until cheese has melted, about 5 minutes.

8. Meanwhile, wash, pat dry, and halve cherry tomatoes.

9. Using skillet in which tortillas were cooked, fry eggs 1 at a time. Top each enchilada with a fried egg.

10. Garnish each plate with lettuce and 2 cherry tomato halves. Serve additional sauce separately, if desired.

Red Chili Sauce

1 quart beef stock
4 tablespoons unsalted butter
¼ cup flour
½ cup pure chili powder
2 cloves garlic, peeled and minced
Pinch of ground cumin
Pinch of ground oregano, preferably Mexican
Salt

1. In medium-size saucepan, bring beef stock to a boil over medium heat.

2. In another medium-size heavy-gauge saucepan, melt butter over medium heat. When butter foams, add flour and cook, stirring, until mixture turns a light gold, about 3 minutes. Remove pan from heat.

3. Stir in chili powder and gradually add beef stock, whisking until smooth. Add garlic, cumin, and oregano.

4. Stirring constantly, bring sauce to a simmer over medium-high heat. Adjust heat to maintain a gentle simmer and cook ten minutes. Add salt to taste and set aside.

ADDED TOUCH

This New Mexico-style dish, based on an old Indian recipe, is best in summer when all the vegetables are at the peak of their flavor.

Squash with Tomatoes and Corn

3 to 4 fresh green chilies, roasted, peeled, and seeded, or 4-ounce can, rinsed, drained, and patted dry
3 small zucchini (about 1 pound total weight)
2 small yellow crookneck summer squash (about ¾ pound total weight)
2 large ripe tomatoes (about 1 pound total weight), or 16-ounce can, drained
2 ears fresh corn, or 10-ounce package frozen, thawed
Salt
2 tablespoons unsalted butter
1 teaspoon minced fresh coriander, approximately

1. Prepare chilies (see pages 14, 15).

2. Wash squash, pat dry, and slice thinly.

3. Core, halve, and seed fresh tomatoes, if using, and cut each half into quarters. If using canned tomatoes, drain. Hull fresh corn or measure 1 cup frozen. Chop chilies.

4. Heat ¼-inch water in medium-size saucepan over medium-high heat. Add squash and steam until barely tender, 3 to 4 minutes.

5. Add tomatoes, corn and chilies to squash, stir to combine, and cook until crisp tender, about 3 to 5 minutes. Add salt to taste.

6. Wash coriander and pat dry. Mince enough to measure 1 teaspoon.

7. Top vegetables with butter and coriander to taste. Toss to combine, cover, and keep warm until ready to serve.

Chicken Tacos
Sweet Peppers and Cumin Rice
New Mexican Chocolate Sundaes

Three chicken tacos and a portion of sweet peppers and cumin rice make a filling lunch or dinner.

Taco shells are sold ready-made in supermarkets but are easy to make at home: Pour half an inch of vegetable oil into a skillet. Heat the oil until a cube of fresh bread sizzles and floats to the surface of the oil. Lightly fry each tortilla on one side and, while it is still pliable, turn the tortilla over and fold it in half. Fry each folded tortilla, turning it until it is crisp on both sides.

WHAT TO DRINK

A light pilsner beer or a spicy wine, such as a Gewürztraminer, would interact very nicely with these dishes.

SHOPPING LIST AND STAPLES

1 pound boned and skinned chicken breasts
Medium-size tomato
Small head Iceberg lettuce
Medium-size red bell pepper
Medium-size green bell pepper
3 bunches scallions
Medium-size Spanish onion
3 cloves garlic
3 fresh jalapeños, or 4-ounce can
½ pint heavy cream

1 quart good-quality vanilla ice cream
2 tablespoons unsalted butter
¼ pound Monterey Jack cheese
¼ pound Cheddar cheese
2 cups chicken stock, preferably homemade (see page 13), or canned
4½-ounce package taco shells
1½ cups long grain rice
4 ounces sweet chocolate
3-ounce can pecan halves
1½ teaspoons cumin
½ teaspoon ground oregano, preferably Mexican
1 teaspoon cinnamon
½ teaspoon ground cloves
Salt and freshly ground pepper
¼ cup Kahlúa, preferably, or other coffee liqueur

UTENSILS

2 medium-size heavy-gauge saucepans with covers
2 small heavy-gauge saucepans
11 × 17-inch cookie sheet
1 large bowl
2 medium-size bowls
2 small bowls
Measuring cups and spoons
Chef's knife
Paring knife
Slotted spoon
Wooden spoon
Grater

START-TO-FINISH STEPS

1. Follow tacos recipe step 1.
2. Follow rice recipe steps 1 through 5.
3. Follow sundaes recipe step 1.
4. Follow tacos recipe steps 2 through 6.
5. Follow sundaes recipe steps 2 and 3.
6. Follow rice recipe step 6.
7. Follow tacos recipe steps 7 and 8, and serve with rice.
8. Follow sundaes recipe step 4 and serve.

RECIPES

Chicken Tacos

1 pound boned and skinned chicken breasts
2 cups chicken stock
12 taco shells
Medium-size Spanish onion, peeled and minced
1 clove garlic, peeled and minced
Medium-size tomato, diced
2 cups shredded Iceberg lettuce
1 cup shredded Monterey Jack and Cheddar cheese combined
3 jalapeños, finely minced

1. Preheat oven to 250 degrees.
2. Combine chicken and stock in medium-size saucepan

and bring to a simmer over medium-high heat. Cover and simmer 15 to 20 minutes, or until chicken is tender.
3. Transfer chicken and stock to a medium-size bowl and set bowl, uncovered, in larger bowl filled with cold water.
4. Arrange taco shells on cookie sheet and place in oven with 4 dinner plates.
5. Combine onion, garlic, and tomato in small bowl.
6. Drain chicken, reserving stock for rice recipe. Cut chicken into ⅛-inch julienne strips. Place strips in another bowl, barely moisten with stock, cover, and set aside.
7. Remove taco shells and plates from oven and raise oven temperature to 400 degrees. Divide chicken, lettuce, and tomato mixture among taco shells and top with cheese.
8. Return tacos to oven for 1 minute, or just until cheese melts. Transfer to dinner plates and top with jalapeños.

Sweet Peppers and Cumin Rice

3 bunches scallions
Medium-size red bell pepper
Medium-size green bell pepper
1½ cups chicken stock (reserved from taco recipe)
2 tablespoons unsalted butter
2 cloves garlic, peeled and minced
1½ teaspoons cumin
½ teaspoon ground oregano, preferably Mexican
1½ cups long grain rice

1. Wash scallions, pat dry, and chop enough of white portion to measure 1½ cups. Reserve greens for other use. Halve, core, seed, and dice bell peppers.
2. In small saucepan, bring chicken stock to a boil over medium heat.
3. In large heavy-gauge saucepan, melt butter over medium heat. Add scallions and peppers, and cook, stirring frequently, until soft.
4. Stir in garlic, cumin, oregano, and rice.
5. Stir in stock. Lower heat, cover, and simmer 15 minutes without uncovering.
6. Taste rice, adjust seasoning, and return to heat, if necessary. Keep covered until ready to serve.

New Mexican Chocolate Sundaes

½ cup Kahlúa, preferably, or other coffee liqueur
1 quart good-quality vanilla ice cream
4 ounces sweet chocolate
1 cup heavy cream
1 teaspoon cinnamon
½ teaspoon ground cloves
12 pecan halves

1. Place 1 tablespoon Kahlúa in each dessert dish, top with scoops of ice cream, and place in freezer.
2. Break chocolate into pieces and place in small heavy-gauge pan over medium-low heat.
3. As chocolate melts, gradually add cream, stirring to combine after each addition. Add cinnamon and cloves, and stir until blended. Cover pan and remove from heat.
4. Spoon sauce over ice cream and garnish with pecans.

Chili with No Beans
New Mexican Refried Beans
Western Salad with Avocado Dressing

Casual serving bowls are ideal for the beef chili, refried beans, and the Western salad—a meal best served buffet style. For an authentic touch, garnish the salad with tostaditas. Pass warmed French bread, if you wish.

172

Bowls of piping hot chili are ideal for a cold-weather meal. This quick version calls for sirloin steak, but you can use chuck, a less tender but more flavorful cut of beef, and simmer the cubes in the spicy liquid for two hours or longer. Garnish the chili with any, or all, of these toppings: chopped onions, chopped jalapeños, crushed pequín chilies, sour cream, and lime wedges.

The substantial Western salad is served with a creamy avocado-based dressing; the acid in the lime juice helps to retain the avocado's bright color.

WHAT TO DRINK

Start with margaritas (see page 14) and continue with sangria or switch to beer.

SHOPPING LIST AND STAPLES

3 pounds top sirloin, cut into ½-inch cubes
¼ pound thick-cut homestyle bacon
Large head Romaine lettuce
Medium-size bunch watercress
1 pint cherry tomatoes
Medium-size avocado
Medium-size bunch scallions
Large yellow onion
5 large cloves garlic
1 fresh jalapeño, or 4-ounce can
1 lime
16-ounce can pinto beans
3½-ounce can pitted black olives
2 tablespoons unsalted butter
¼ pound Monterey Jack cheese
¼ pound Cheddar cheese
¼ cup olive oil, approximately
¼ cup red or white wine vinegar, approximately
6-ounce bag tostaditas (tortilla chips)
1 ounce pure California (mild) chili powder
1 ounce pure New Mexican (hot) chili powder
2 teaspoons ground cumin
2 teaspoons oregano, preferably Mexican
Salt and freshly ground pepper
Two 12-ounce bottles beer or 2 cups red wine

UTENSILS

Large heavy-gauge skillet
Large heavy-gauge saucepan

Small saucepan
Salad bowl
Large bowl
Medium-size bowl
Small bowl
Platter
Plate
Measuring cups and spoons
Chef's knife
Paring knife
Slotted spoon
Wooden spoon
Potato masher (optional)
Grater

START-TO-FINISH STEPS

1. For chili recipe and beans recipe, peel and mince garlic. Grate cheeses and combine in small bowl.
2. Follow salad recipe steps 1 through 3.
3. Follow chili recipe steps 1 through 5.
4. While beef is cooking, follow beans recipe steps 1 through 4.
5. Follow chili recipe steps 6 and 7, beans recipe step 5, salad recipe steps 4 and 5, and serve.

RECIPES

Chili with No Beans

Large yellow onion
2 tablespoons unsalted butter
3 pounds top sirloin, cut into ½-inch cubes
1½ tablespoons minced garlic
¼ cup pure California (mild) chili powder
¼ cup pure New Mexican (hot) chili powder
2 teaspoons ground cumin
2 teaspoons oregano, preferably Mexican, crushed
1½ teaspoons salt
2 cups beer or red wine
1 cup grated Monterey Jack and Cheddar cheese
  combined

1. Peel and chop onion.
2. In large heavy-gauge saucepan, melt butter over medium heat. Add onions and cook, stirring frequently, about 5 minutes, or until transparent.
3. While onions are cooking, combine meat with garlic, chili powder, cumin, oregano, and salt in large bowl.
4. Bring 2 cups beer or red wine and 2 cups water to a boil in small saucepan over medium-high heat.
5. Add one quarter of meat to saucepan with onions, raise heat to medium-high, and cook, stirring, about 2 to 3 minutes, until meat has browned lightly and is encrusted with spices. Transfer to platter and repeat with remaining meat.
6. Return all meat to saucepan, add hot liquid, and stir to combine. Adjust heat to a simmer and cook, uncovered, 10 to 15 minutes, or until meat is tender.

7. If cooking liquid has not reduced to form a thick sauce, remove meat from pan with slotted spoon and, stirring constantly, reduce sauce over medium-high heat. Return meat to saucepan and stir. Turn chili into large serving bowl and top with grated cheese.

New Mexican Refried Beans

3 strips thick-cut homestyle bacon
Medium-size bunch scallions
2 tablespoons minced garlic
2 cups pinto beans, with liquid
Salt and freshly ground pepper
½ cup grated Monterey Jack and Cheddar cheese
  combined

1. Cut bacon into ½-inch squares. Wash scallions, pat dry, and chop enough to measure ¼ cup plus 2 tablespoons. Line plate with paper towels.
2. Cook bacon in large heavy-gauge skillet over medium heat, stirring, until it is crisp, about 5 minutes. With slotted spoon, transfer bacon to plate.
3. Add ¼ cup scallions and garlic to skillet and sauté over medium heat until they start to turn golden.
4. Add beans with their liquid and stir to combine. Toss and mash beans with potato masher or back of spoon until all liquid has been absorbed and beans are of uniform consistency. Add bacon and salt and pepper to taste.
5. Transfer beans to medium-size serving bowl and top with grated cheese and remaining scallions.

Western Salad with Avocado Dressing

Large head Romaine lettuce
Medium-size bunch watercress
16 cherry tomatoes
½ cup pitted black olives
Medium-size avocado
1 lime
½ jalapeño, approximately, finely minced
Salt and freshly ground pepper
¼ cup olive oil
¼ cup red or white wine vinegar
Tostaditas (tortilla chips), optional

1. Wash lettuce, watercress, and tomatoes, and pat dry. Tear lettuce and watercress into bite-size pieces. Halve olives crosswise. Combine lettuce, watercress, tomatoes, and olives in salad bowl. Cover and refrigerate.
2. Squeeze enough lime to measure ½ teaspoon juice. Prepare jalapeño (see pages 14, 15).
3. Halve avocado lengthwise, remove pit, and discard. Scoop flesh into medium-size bowl and mash roughly with fork. Add lime juice and jalapeño, and stir to combine. Adjust seasoning, adding salt, pepper, lime juice, and jalapeño as desired, cover, and refrigerate.
4. Pour oil over salad and toss until well coated. Add vinegar, toss again, and add salt and pepper to taste.
5. Spoon avocado mixture into center of salad and serve surrounded by tostaditas, if desired.

Sue B. Huffman

For Sue Huffman, cooking has been a lifelong avocation; she learned to cook when she was five. Now a magazine food editor, she describes herself as a home-style cook who prefers unadorned one-course or one-pot meals without any heavy sauces and frills. Her interest in Tex-Mex and Mexican foods stems from her Oklahoma childhood ("I grew up eating Tex-Mex," she says) and from her stay in southern California, where she became acquainted with both Cal-Mex and genuine Mexican cuisines. She also learned to value fresh herbs, particularly coriander, a featured ingredient in several of her recipes.

In Menu 1, chopped coriander flavors the sour-cream-based spread for the chicken breasts and colors the accompanying rice. She uses chopped coriander again for both color and flavor in the chicken soup of Menu 2.

The tamale pie in Menu 3 has an unusual crust made of *masa harina*—Mexican corn flour—rather than the standard yellow cornmeal. Perfect for an informal supper, the tamale pie is accompanied by a lettuce and papaya salad.

Chicken "cutlets"—topped with a mixture of sour cream, grated cheese, and chopped chilies—comprise the main course which is complemented by "green" rice with chopped coriander and parsley and a side salad of orange, onion, and Jerusalem artichoke slices arranged on lettuce leaves.

175

Chicken Breasts with Sour Cream and Jalapeños
Green Rice
Jerusalem Artichoke and Orange Salad

Boned, skinned turkey breasts, or scallops, are good substitutes for chicken. Most supermarkets package fresh turkey scallops, but, if your market stocks only whole breasts, ask the butcher to prepare them for you. If you cannot find fresh coriander for the sour-cream topping, omit it; seeds or dried flakes are not a suitable substitute here.

Despite their name, Jerusalem artichokes, or sunchokes, are not related to green-globe artichokes. They are the knobby root of a type of sunflower. Eaten raw, they have the texture of water chestnuts and a slightly sweet, nutty flavor. Many supermarkets and health-food stores stock them. Refrigerated in a tightly closed plastic bag, they will keep for a week or two. If available, jícama is a worthy substitute.

WHAT TO DRINK

A crisp, dry white wine, like a French Muscadet, an Italian Verdicchio, or a California Sauvignon Blanc, works very well with the bright flavors of this menu. A full-bodied amber ale also would be satisfactory.

SHOPPING LIST AND STAPLES

4 whole chicken breasts, boned, skinned, and pounded to ¼- to ½-inch thickness (about 1½ pounds total weight)
2 Jerusalem artichokes (about ½ pound total weight)
Small head Romaine lettuce
1 to 2 fresh jalapeños, or 4-ounce can
Medium-size red onion
Small white onion
2 cloves garlic
Large bunch parsley
Large bunch coriander
2 navel oranges
2 limes
½ pint sour cream
1 tablespoon unsalted butter
¼ pound Monterey Jack cheese
2½ cups chicken stock, preferably homemade (see page 13) or canned
3 tablespoons vegetable oil
1 tablespoon honey
1½ cups long-grain rice
Dash of ground coriander seed
Salt and freshly ground pepper

UTENSILS

Food processor or blender
Electric mixer
Large heavy-gauge skillet
Medium-size saucepan with cover
Broiler tray
Medium-size bowl
2 small bowls
Colander
Salad spinner (optional)
Measuring cups and spoons
Chef's knife
Paring knife
Wooden spoon
Metal spatula
Rubber spatula (optional)
Grater
Juicer (optional)

START-TO-FINISH STEPS

1. Follow rice recipe step 1.
2. While water is heating, wash coriander and parsley for chicken and rice recipes; pat dry, trim stems, and chop 2 tablespoons coriander for chicken recipe. Peel onions; quarter white onion for rice recipe and thinly slice red onion for salad recipe. Peel garlic for rice recipe.
3. Follow rice recipe steps 2 and 3.
4. While rice is soaking, follow salad recipe steps 1 through 6.
5. Follow rice recipe steps 4 through 6.
6. While rice is cooking, follow chicken recipe steps 1 through 3.
7. Follow rice recipe step 7.
8. Follow chicken recipe steps 4 through 6.
9. Follow chicken recipe step 7, rice recipe step 8, and serve with salad.

RECIPES

Chicken Breasts with Sour Cream and Jalapeños

1 to 2 fresh jalapeños, or 4-ounce can
¼ pound Monterey Jack cheese
2 tablespoons chopped coriander
½ cup sour cream

4 whole chicken breasts, boned, skinned, and pounded to ¼- to ½-inch thickness (about 1½ pounds total weight)
Salt
Freshly ground pepper
1 tablespoon unsalted butter
1 tablespoon vegetable oil

1. If using fresh jalapeños, wash and pat dry; seed and derib, if desired. If using canned, rinse, drain, and pat dry. Chop chilies.
2. Shred enough cheese to measure ¼ cup. In small bowl, combine cheese with chilies, chopped coriander, and sour cream. Set aside.
3. Preheat broiler. Line broiler tray with aluminum foil and set aside.
4. Sprinkle both sides of chicken breasts with salt and pepper to taste.
5. Combine butter and oil in large heavy-gauge skillet over medium-high heat. Sauté chicken breasts, 2 at a time, about 5 minutes per side, or until brown. Transfer to broiler tray.
6. Top each chicken breast with a generous spoonful of sour-cream mixture. Broil 4 to 5 inches from heating element about 5 minutes, or until topping bubbles.
7. Transfer to platter and serve immediately.

Green Rice

1½ cups long-grain rice
¼ cup plus 2 tablespoons coriander leaves, tightly packed
½ cup parsley leaves, tightly packed
Small white onion, quartered
2 cloves garlic, peeled
2½ cups chicken stock
2 tablespoons vegetable oil
Salt
Freshly ground pepper

1. Bring 1 quart water to a boil over high heat.
2. Combine rice with boiling water to cover in medium-size bowl. Stir once and set aside to soak 15 minutes.
3. In food processor fitted with steel blade, chop coriander, parsley, onion, and garlic. Add ¼ cup chicken stock and purée. Or, with chef's knife, finely chop coriander, parsley, onion, and garlic; then place in blender, add stock, and purée. Set aside.
4. Transfer soaked rice to colander. Rinse under cold running water and drain.
5. Heat oil in medium-size saucepan over high heat. Add rice and sauté, stirring, about 5 minutes, or until translucent.
6. Reduce heat to medium. Stir in coriander-parsley mixture and cook, stirring frequently, about 10 minutes, or until fairly dry.
7. Add the remaining stock and salt and pepper to taste. Bring to a boil over high heat, stir once, reduce to a simmer, and cover. Cook 15 minutes, or until rice is just tender and stock is absorbed.
8. Turn rice into serving bowl.

Jerusalem Artichoke and Orange Salad

8 leaves Romaine lettuce
2 navel oranges
2 Jerusalem artichokes
1 cup sliced red onion, approximately
2 limes
1 tablespoon honey
Dash of ground coriander seed

1. Wash lettuce leaves; dry in salad spinner or pat dry with paper towels.
2. Peel oranges and cut into ¼-inch-thick rounds.
3. Peel artichokes and cut into ¼-inch-thick pieces.
4. Arrange lettuce leaves on individual serving plates. Top with alternating slices of orange and artichoke.
5. Separate onion slices into rings and scatter over salads.
6. Squeeze enough lime to measure ¼ cup juice. Combine with honey and ground coriander in small bowl; beat until blended. Spoon dressing over salad, cover, and refrigerate until ready to serve.

ADDED TOUCH

If you wish, you can prepare this rich mousse a day ahead. Coffee-flavored liqueur and brewed coffee intensify the flavor.

Chocolate Kahlúa Mousse

4 ounces semisweet chocolate
2 tablespoons strong coffee
3 large eggs
3 tablespoons Kahlúa
1 teaspoon vanilla extract
1 cup heavy cream

1. In freezer, chill medium-size bowl and beaters for whipping cream.
2. Meanwhile, break chocolate into pieces, combine with coffee in small, heavy-gauge saucepan, and melt, stirring, over very low heat.
3. Separate eggs, yolks into small bowl and whites into medium-size bowl.
4. With wire whisk, beat yolks. Gradually whisk a small amount of chocolate mixture into yolks; then, over very low heat, whisk yolk mixture back into remaining chocolate mixture. Stir just until combined. Remove from heat and stir in Kahlúa and vanilla. Set aside to cool.
5. In chilled bowl, whip cream with electric mixer until stiff but not buttery. Wash and dry beaters.
6. Beat whites at low speed until foamy. Increase speed to medium and beat until stiff peaks form.
7. With rubber spatula, fold about one third of whites into cooled chocolate mixture. Add remaining whites, folding in gently but thoroughly.
8. Add whipped cream to egg white-chocolate mixture, folding gently but thoroughly.
9. Turn mixture into 1-quart serving dish. Cover and refrigerate at least 4 hours or overnight.
10. Spoon into individual bowls or goblets and serve.

Chicken Soup with Tortilla Strips
Mexican Corn Bread
Chorizo with Zucchini

A wedge of corn bread baked with jalapeño chilies accompanies the main-course chicken soup garnished with avocado slices. Stir-fried chorizo sausage with zucchini completes this festive meal.

This filling meal can be as mild or as spicy as you like, depending on the kind and quantity of chilies you use and the sausage you select. The chicken soup, a flavorful blend of spices, gains richness from the chicken breast-bones, which you simmer in stock until the meat is tender.

WHAT TO DRINK

Almost any kind of beer is right with this menu, but, when fresh peaches are in season, consider a pitcher of sangria.

SHOPPING LIST AND STAPLES

1 whole chicken breast (about 1½ pounds), skinned and split
3 mild or hot chorizo or Italian sausages (½ to ¾ pound total weight)
3 medium-size zucchini (about 1 pound total weight)
Small bunch carrots (with tops, optional)
Small bunch celery (if not using carrot tops)
1 to 2 fresh jalapeños, plus one additional (optional), or 4-ounce can
Small onion
3 cloves garlic
Medium-size bunch coriander
Small avocado
2 to 3 limes
1 egg
½ pint sour cream
¼ pound sharp Cheddar cheese
6 fresh corn tortillas, or 1 package frozen
8 cups chicken stock, preferably homemade (see page 13) or five 13¾-ounce cans
8-ounce can creamed corn
8-ounce can tomato sauce
4-ounce can mild green chilies
6 tablespoons vegetable oil
½ cup yellow cornmeal
2 teaspoons baking powder
Salt and freshly ground pepper

UTENSILS

Large skillet
Medium-size skillet
Large saucepan with cover
8 x 8 x 2-inch baking dish
Plate

Large bowl
2 medium-size bowls
Colander
Measuring cups and spoons
Chef's knife
Paring knife
Wooden spoon
Fork
Metal wok spatula or slotted spoon
Whisk
Vegetable peeler (optional)
Ladle
Grater
Juicer (optional)

START-TO-FINISH STEPS

One hour ahead: If using frozen tortillas for chicken soup recipe, set out to thaw.

1. Follow corn bread recipe step 1.
2. Follow chicken soup recipe step 1.
3. While soup is simmering, follow corn bread recipe steps 2 through 6.
4. While corn bread is baking, follow soup recipe steps 2 and 3, and chorizo recipe step 1.
5. Follow corn bread recipe step 7 and soup recipe steps 4 and 5.
6. Follow chorizo recipe step 2.
7. While chorizo is browning, follow soup recipe step 6.
8. While soup is simmering, follow chorizo recipe step 3.
9. Follow soup recipe step 7, chorizo recipe step 4, and serve with corn bread.

RECIPES

Chicken Soup with Tortilla Strips

Medium-size carrot, peeled and halved crosswise
Small bunch carrot or celery tops
9 sprigs coriander
Small onion, peeled and quartered
1 whole chicken breast (about 1¼ pounds), skinned and split
Medium-size clove garlic, peeled and crushed
Freshly ground pepper
8 cups chicken stock
6 fresh or frozen corn tortillas
3 tablespoons vegetable oil
Small avocado
½ cup tomato sauce
2 tablespoons freshly squeezed lime juice
1 to 2 jalapeño chilies, seeded and quartered
Salt

1. Combine carrot, celery or carrot tops, 6 sprigs of coriander, onion, chicken breast, garlic, pepper to taste, and stock in large saucepan and bring to a boil over medium-high heat. Reduce heat and simmer, covered, about 25 minutes, or until chicken is tender.

2. Line plate with paper towels. Cut tortillas into ½-inch-wide strips. Heat oil in medium-size skillet over medium-high heat until it shimmers. Add tortilla strips and fry, stirring constantly, about 2 minutes, or until golden. Transfer to paper-towel-lined plate.
3. Strain soup into large bowl. Refrigerate chicken, uncovered. Return strained broth to saucepan; set aside.
4. Ten minutes before serving, bring soup to a simmer over medium-high heat.
5. Peel, halve, and pit avocado. Cut crosswise into ½- to ¾-inch-thick slices. Set aside.
6. Bone cooled chicken breast and shred meat. Add shredded meat, tortilla strips, tomato sauce, lime juice, remaining coriander sprigs, and jalapeño quarters to soup and stir. Simmer 5 minutes.
7. Add salt and freshly ground pepper to taste, ladle into individual bowls, and serve garnished with avocado slices.

Mexican Corn Bread

½ cup yellow cornmeal
2 teaspoons baking powder
¼ teaspoon salt
1 egg
3 tablespoons vegetable oil
½ cup sour cream
1 cup creamed corn
1 cup shredded sharp Cheddar cheese
¼ cup canned chopped mild green chilies
½ fresh jalapeño, seeded and chopped (optional)

1. Preheat oven to 400 degrees.
2. Lightly grease baking dish.
3. Combine dry ingredients in medium-size bowl.
4. In another medium-size bowl, lightly beat egg. Beat in oil, then sour cream. Stir in creamed corn and shredded cheese.
5. Pour corn mixture into cornmeal mixture. Add chilies, and jalapeño, if using. Stir just until combined.
6. Turn into greased baking dish and bake 25 minutes, or until corn bread is puffed and golden brown.
7. Remove corn bread from oven. Cut into squares, cover loosely with foil, and keep warm until serving time.

Chorizo with Zucchini

3 mild or hot chorizo or Italian sausages
3 medium-size zucchini (about 1 pound total weight)
2 cloves garlic, peeled and crushed
1 to 2 teaspoons freshly squeezed lime juice
Salt

1. Cut chorizo or Italian sausages crosswise into ¼- to ½-inch-thick slices. Rinse zucchini, pat dry, and cut crosswise into ¼-inch-thick slices.
2. Sauté chorizo in large skillet over medium-high heat about 5 minutes, or until browned.
3. Add zucchini and garlic, and stir fry about 5 minutes, or until zucchini is barely tender.
4. Stir in lime juice, add salt to taste, and turn into serving bowl.

Tamale Pie with Green Sauce
Tossed Green Salad with Papaya

Tomatoes and scallions decorate the tamale pie, which is accompanied by a salad of lettuce and papaya with lime-juice dressing.

Tamales are corn flour (*masa harina*) dough, with or without filling, baked in cornhusks. Here, the main-dish tamale pie is a simple variation on the original tamale. The dough, in this instance a pie crust, is covered with seasoned ground beef and melted cheese and topped with scallions and tomatoes. The green sauce served with the pie contains tomatillos and fresh coriander.

WHAT TO DRINK

Try a robust red wine here: either a California Zinfandel or an Italian Dolcetto.

SHOPPING LIST AND STAPLES

1 pound ground beef
Medium-size head Romaine lettuce
2 medium-size tomatoes (about 1 pound total weight)
Medium-size bunch scallions
Medium-size onion, plus 1 small
1 large and 2 medium-size cloves garlic
Small bunch coriander
1 to 2 fresh jalapeños, or 4-ounce can
Small papaya
1 to 2 limes

180

½ pound Cheddar cheese, approximately
½ pint sour cream
13-ounce can tomatillos
¼ cup plus 2 tablespoons vegetable oil
1¼ cups masa harina
2 tablespoons chili powder
1 tablespoon plus a dash of ground cumin
Dash of oregano
Salt and freshly ground pepper

UTENSILS

Food processor or blender
Large skillet
9-inch pie plate
3 small bowls
Measuring cups and spoons
Chef's knife
Paring knife
Wooden spoon
Fork
Metal spatula or pie server
Rubber spatula
Grater
Juicer
Garlic press

START-TO-FINISH STEPS

1. Follow tamale pie recipe steps 1 through 4.
2. Follow sauce recipe steps 1 and 2.
3. Follow salad recipe step 1.
4. Follow tamale pie recipe steps 5 and 6.
5. Follow salad recipe step 2.
6. Follow tamale recipe step 7, sauce recipe step 3, salad recipe step 3, and serve.

RECIPES

Tamale Pie with Green Sauce

Crust:
1¼ cups masa harina
2 tablespoons vegetable oil
¾ teaspoon salt

Filling:
1 pound ground beef
1 cup chopped onion
Large clove garlic, peeled and pressed
2 tablespoons chili powder
1 tablespoon ground cumin
Dash of oregano
Salt and freshly ground pepper
1½ cups shredded sharp Cheddar cheese

Topping:
1 bunch scallions
2 medium-size tomatoes
Green Sauce (see following recipe)

1. Preheat oven to 400 degrees.
2. Combine masa harina, ⅔ cup water, oil, and salt in 9-inch pie plate, and stir with fork until blended. With your fingers, pat crust evenly onto bottom and sides of pie plate. Bake 10 minutes or until crust is lightly golden.
3. For filling, sauté beef in large skillet over medium heat, stirring with fork to break up lumps, about 5 minutes, or until fat is rendered. Add onion and garlic, and sauté, stirring, about 5 minutes, or until soft. Remove crust from oven and set aside.
4. Drain fat, return pan to heat, and stir in chili powder, cumin, oregano, and salt and pepper to taste. Sauté, stirring, 7 to 8 minutes, or until beef is brown. Set aside.
5. Turn beef mixture into crust, sprinkle with cheese, and bake about 5 minutes, or just until cheese melts.
6. While pie is baking, prepare topping: Wash scallions, pat dry, trim, and chop. Wash tomatoes and pat dry. Core, halve, seed, and dice.
7. Remove pie from oven, heap scallions in center and surround with tomatoes. Serve with Green Sauce.

Green Sauce

1 to 2 fresh or canned jalapeños
13-ounce can tomatillos with liquid
Small onion, peeled and halved
Medium-size clove garlic, peeled and crushed
2 tablespoons chopped coriander
Salt
¾ cup sour cream

1. If using fresh jalapeños, wash and pat dry; seed and derib, if desired. If using canned, rinse, drain, and pat dry. Chop chilies.
2. In food processor fitted with steel blade or in blender, purée tomatillos, onion, garlic, chilies, coriander, and salt to taste. Turn into small bowl, cover, and refrigerate.
3. Just before serving, blend sour cream into sauce and taste for seasoning.

Tossed Green Salad with Papaya

4 teaspoons freshly squeezed lime juice
Dash of ground cumin
Medium-size clove garlic, peeled and crushed
¼ cup vegetable oil
Salt and freshly ground pepper
8 to 10 leaves Romaine lettuce
Small papaya

1. Combine lime juice, cumin, and garlic in small bowl. Beat in vegetable oil and add salt and pepper to taste.
2. Wash Romaine and dry in salad spinner or pat dry with paper towels. Tear into bite-sized pieces. Peel papaya, halve lengthwise, scoop out seeds, and discard. Cut into ½-inch cubes. Combine Romaine and papaya in salad bowl.
3. Just before serving, stir dressing to recombine and remove garlic. Add dressing to salad and toss.

Rick Bayless

A linguist and anthropologist, as well as a cook, Rick Bayless is especially interested in Mexico and its diverse regional foods. He has discovered that each little Mexican town has its own unique recipes, and he goes directly to the street vendors and food stalls to watch and sample. His own recipes adapt this traditional Mexican fare for the American kitchen, using easily obtainable ingredients.

Menu 1, an informal meal for a fall or winter evening, starts with a chicken soup named for Tlalpán, a suburb of Mexico City. The main course, cheese *empanadas*, is a variation on Mexican turnovers, which are frequently filled with savory pork, chicken, or fish mixtures. Rather than using a conventional pastry, he has developed a quick biscuit-like dough of cornmeal and chili powder. He prepares the green bean salad the same way he would a Mexican cactus (*nopal*) salad, here substituting the beans for the hard-to-find cactus. For Menu 2, he offers a tortilla casserole, a popular Mexican breakfast dish that often contains shredded chicken or chorizo sausage. His version, however, calls for eggs and bacon. The pickled cauliflower, a recipe he learned from a Mexico City cook, is a variation on the pickled peppers often served at Mexican restaurants.

Yucatecan foods are the basis for Menu 3: black bean *tostadas* and chicken in *escabeche*, a spicy "pickling" sauce, both variations of traditional dishes of the southeastern peninsula.

Bowls of chili-spiced chicken soup, garnished with refreshing avocado slices, introduce this family-style meal. Serve the festive salad and the cheese-filled empanadas on separate dishes.

Chicken Soup Tlalpeño
Cheese Empanadas
Green Bean Salad

Salsas are staple condiments at the Mexican table. Whether hot or mild, they are tomato- or chili-based and have a relish-like consistency. The cook suggests serving a medium-hot salsa with the empanadas, but you can vary its piquancy to suit your tastes. Use a fresh salsa as soon as possible, preferably the same day you make it; it loses its flavor as it ages.

If you cannot find *chipotle* chilies, which give the chicken soup its smoky piquancy, use a pure chili powder instead (for information, see page 15). The avocado provides a cooling contrast to the fiery *chipotles*.

WHAT TO DRINK

A chilled, crisp white Muscadet from France or a young and fruity California Zinfandel would go well with this lively menu, but a good dark Mexican beer would be even better.

SHOPPING LIST AND STAPLES

2 chicken breasts, skinned and boned (about 1 pound total weight)
Small avocado
Medium-size ripe tomato (about ½ pound)
Small head Romaine lettuce
Small bunch radishes
Large carrot
Large onion (about ¾ pound)
Large clove garlic
Small bunch coriander
Small bunch parsley (optional)
Large lime (optional)
6 cups chicken stock, preferably homemade (see page 13), or canned
15-ounce can chickpeas (garbanzos)
4-ounce can whole chipotle chilies, or 1 teaspoon pure chili powder
4-ounce can diced mild green chilies
½ cup milk
¼ pound Monterey Jack cheese
¼ pound Mexican white cheese, farmer, or feta cheese
⅓ cup olive oil
1 tablespoon vegetable oil
⅓ cup vegetable shortening
2 tablespoons cider vinegar
1⅓ cups flour
2 tablespoons cornmeal

1 teaspoon sugar
1 teaspoon baking powder
1½ teaspoons New Mexico (hot), California (mild), or other pure chili powder
¾ teaspoon *fines herbes* (marjoram, thyme, etc.)
½ teaspoon dried oregano
Small bay leaf
Salt
Freshly ground black pepper

UTENSILS

Food processor (optional)
2 large saucepans, one with cover
11 × 17-inch baking sheet
Large bowl (if not using processor)
2 medium-size bowls
Small bowl
Small jar with tight-fitting lid
Colander
Measuring cups and spoons
Chef's knife
Paring knife
Wooden spoon
Slotted spoon
Ladle
Fork
Metal spatula
Grater (if not using processor)
Vegetable peeler (optional)

START-TO-FINISH STEPS

1. Peel and dice onion for soup and salad. Rinse and drain chilies for empanadas and for soup. Wash and pat dry coriander, Romaine, and parsley, if using. Chop coriander and parsley. Wrap lettuce in paper towels and refrigerate until ready to compose salad. Trim green beans.
2. Follow soup recipe steps 1 through 6.
3. While soup base is simmering, follow salad recipe step 1.
4. Follow empanadas recipe steps 1 through 3.
5. Follow salad recipe steps 2 through 5.
6. Follow empanadas recipe steps 4 through 7.
7. Follow soup recipe steps 7 and 8.
8. Follow salad recipe steps 6 and 7.
9. Follow empanadas recipe step 8, soup recipe steps 9 and 10, and serve with salad.

Chicken Soup Tlalpeño

15-ounce can chickpeas (garbanzos)
1 to 2 canned whole chipotle chilies, rinsed, drained, and
    seeded, or 1 teaspoon pure chili powder
½ cup diced carrot
1 tablespoon vegetable oil
1¼ cups diced onion
1 large clove garlic
6 cups chicken stock
¾ teaspoon *fines herbes* (marjoram, thyme, etc.)
Small bay leaf
2 chicken breasts, skinned and boned
Salt
Small avocado
Large lime for garnish (optional)

1. Rinse chickpeas under cold running water and drain.
2. Cut chilies, if using, into ⅟₁₆- to ¼-inch julienne.
3. Peel carrot and cut into ¼-inch dice.
4. In large saucepan, heat oil over medium heat. Add carrot and onion and cook, stirring occasionally, 5 minutes, or until onion is translucent.
5. Place garlic clove under flat of knife blade and lean down on blade with heel of your hand to crush garlic. Add garlic to pan and cook, stirring, another 2 minutes.
6. Stir in chickpeas, stock, and herbs. Raise heat to medium-high and bring soup to a simmer. Reduce heat to medium-low, partially cover saucepan, and simmer soup 30 to 40 minutes.
7. Cut chicken breast into ½-inch-wide strips and then cut strips into ½-inch dice.
8. With slotted spoon, remove garlic clove and bay leaf from soup; discard. Stir in diced chicken and chilies or chili powder. Simmer soup another 5 minutes, or just long enough to cook chicken through. Add salt to taste.
9. Peel, halve, and pit avocado. Cut each half lengthwise into 4 wedges. Quarter lime, if using.
10. Ladle soup into individual bowls and float 2 slices of avocado in each bowl. Serve with lime wedges, if desired.

Cheese Empanadas

¼ pound Monterey Jack cheese
2 tablespoons canned diced mild green chilies, rinsed
    and drained
1⅓ cups flour, approximately
2 tablespoons cornmeal
1½ teaspoons New Mexico (hot), California (mild), or
    other pure chili powder
1 teaspoon baking powder
1 teaspoon sugar
¼ teaspoon salt
⅓ cup vegetable shortening
½ cup milk
1 tablespoon chopped parsley for garnish (optional)

1. Preheat oven to 400 degrees.
2. In food processor or with grater, grate cheese.

3. In medium-size bowl, combine cheese and chilies. Divide mixture into 4 portions and press each into a flat oval about 2½ inches long and 1 inch wide; set aside.
4. Blend 1 cup flour, cornmeal, chili powder, baking powder, sugar, salt, and vegetable shortening in food processor fitted with steel blade. With machine running, add milk in a steady stream and process until dough forms a ball. If not using processor, combine dry ingredients in large bowl. With fork or your fingers, work in shortening until blended. Add milk and work mixture until dough forms a ball. Dough will be sticky.
5. Generously flour work surface. Place dough on work surface and dust well with flour. Pat into a ¼-inch-thick square and cut into quarters, forming 4 small squares. Turn each square so that one point is facing toward you.
6. Place one of the reserved cheese ovals on right half of each of the 4 squares. Bring the left half of square over the right so points meet and filling is enclosed. Crimp edges.
7. Transfer empanadas to ungreased baking sheet and bake about 12 minutes, or until golden brown.
8. Transfer empanadas to platter and sprinkle with parsley, if desired.

Green Bean Salad

1 tablespoon plus ⅛ teaspoon salt
¾ pound fresh green beans, trimmed
1 medium-size ripe tomato (about ½ pound)
¼ cup diced onion
1 tablespoon chopped coriander
2 radishes, cut into ⅛-inch-thick slices
2 tablespoons cider vinegar
½ teaspoon dried oregano
Freshly ground black pepper
⅓ cup olive oil
Several leaves Romaine lettuce
3 tablespoons crumbled Mexican white cheese, farmer,
    or feta cheese

1. In large saucepan, bring 3 quarts water and 1 tablespoon salt to a boil, covered, over medium-high heat.
2. Add green beans to boiling water and cook, uncovered, 5 to 7 minutes, or just until beans are crisp tender.
3. While beans are cooking, add tomato to same pan and cook 30 seconds. With slotted spoon, transfer tomato to colander, refresh under cold running water, and remove peel. Halve, core, and seed tomato; cut into ½-inch dice and place in small bowl. Add onion and coriander, and toss to combine.
4. When beans are done, transfer them to colander, refresh under cold running water, drain, and allow to cool.
5. In small jar with lid, combine vinegar, oregano, ⅛ teaspoon salt, and pepper to taste. Cover jar and shake well to blend. Add olive oil and shake until blended.
6. Combine green beans and diced tomato in medium-size bowl. Toss with dressing until evenly coated.
7. Line a small, deep serving platter with Romaine lettuce leaves. Mound green bean salad in center and sprinkle with radish slices and crumbled cheese.

Tortilla Casserole
Pickled Cauliflower

Offer individual servings of the layered tortilla casserole—garnished with crumbled cheese, cream, parsley, and radish slices—with a helping of cauliflower and carrots on the side.

This tortilla casserole, also known as *chilaquiles*, is an ideal way to use up leftover tortillas. Quick-frying softens tortillas. Cook them for a few seconds on each side until limp but not crisp. If you use frozen tortillas that have been defrosted, spread them out for a few minutes in a single layer to dry; any moisture will cause spattering when you fry them.

You can vary the pickled cauliflower by adding any crisp, fresh vegetables you have on hand. The flavors of this dish improve if you make it a day ahead.

WHAT TO DRINK

Beer or ale, iced tea, or iced coffee are preferable to wine here because of the variety of sweet and sour flavors.

SHOPPING LIST AND STAPLES

8 slices bacon (about ½ pound)
Small head cauliflower (about 1½ pounds)
2 large carrots (about ½ pound total weight)
Large onion
9 large cloves garlic
4 fresh jalapeño or serrano chilies, or 4-ounce can, whole
Small bunch fresh parsley (optional)
8 eggs
½ pint heavy cream
½ pint sour cream
2 ounces Mexican white cheese, farmer, or feta cheese
12 fresh corn tortillas, or 1 package frozen
⅔ cup chicken stock, preferably homemade (see page 13), or canned
28-ounce can tomatoes, packed in juice
¾ cup vegetable oil
⅓ cup cider vinegar
1½ tablespoons New Mexico (hot), California (mild), or other pure chili powder
½ teaspoon dried marjoram
½ teaspoon dried thyme
2 bay leaves
Salt and freshly ground black pepper

UTENSILS

Food processor or blender
2 large skillets, one with cover
Small skillet
Medium-size saucepan
11 x 17-inch cookie sheet
8 x 8 x 2-inch baking dish
2 small bowls
Colander
Strainer
Measuring cups and spoons
Chef's knife
Paring knife
Wooden spoon
Tongs
Fork

START-TO-FINISH STEPS

One hour ahead: If using frozen tortillas for casserole, set out to thaw.

1. Peel onion and halve crosswise. Coarsely chop one half for casserole recipe and slice remaining half for cauliflower recipe. Peel garlic. Coarsely chop 5 cloves for casserole and halve 4 cloves lengthwise for cauliflower.
2. Follow casserole recipe steps 1 and 2.
3. Follow cauliflower recipe steps 1 through 4.
4. Follow casserole recipe steps 3 through 6.
5. Follow cauliflower recipe step 5.
6. Follow casserole recipe steps 7 through 13 and serve with cauliflower.

RECIPES

Tortilla Casserole

28-ounce can tomatoes, packed in juice
½ cup chopped onion
5 large cloves garlic, coarsely chopped
1½ tablespoons New Mexico (hot), California (mild), or other pure chili powder
⅔ cup chicken stock
Salt
8 slices of bacon (about ½ pound)
½ cup vegetable oil
12 fresh corn tortillas, or 1 package frozen
2 ounces Mexican white cheese, farmer, or feta cheese
8 eggs
Freshly ground black pepper
¾ cup sour cream
¼ cup heavy cream
1 tablespoon chopped fresh parsley for garnish (optional)

1. Drain tomatoes and place in food processor fitted with metal blade or in blender. Reserve juice for another purpose. Add onion, garlic, and chili powder to tomatoes and process until smooth.

2. Transfer mixture to medium-size saucepan. Add stock and ½ teaspoon salt and bring to a simmer over medium-high heat. Reduce heat to medium-low and simmer tomato sauce, uncovered, about 15 minutes.

3. Cut bacon into 1-inch pieces. In large skillet, cook bacon, stirring frequently, over medium heat until golden brown and crisp, about 5 minutes.

4. Preheat oven to 375 degrees and line cookie sheet with paper towels.

5. In small skillet, heat vegetable oil over medium-high heat. When oil is almost smoking, quickly fry tortillas, one at a time, about 3 seconds per side, or just until soft and pliable. With tongs, transfer tortillas as they are done to paper-towel-lined cookie sheet.

6. When bacon is done, remove skillet from heat and carefully drain off all but 1 tablespoon fat.

7. Crumble enough cheese to measure ½ cup; set aside.

8. Return skillet with bacon to heat and reduce to medium-low. Crack eggs into skillet, break yolks, and scramble eggs with bacon until eggs are firm but still soft. Stir in two thirds of the crumbled cheese and remove pan from heat. Sprinkle with salt and pepper to taste.

9. Line bottom of 8 x 8 x 2-inch baking dish with 4 tortillas, overlapping where necessary. Spread half of bacon and egg mixture over tortillas and top with one third of tomato sauce (about ¾ cup). Repeat with 4 more tortillas, remaining half of bacon and egg mixture, and half of remaining sauce. Top with remaining 4 tortillas and completely cover with tomato sauce.

10. Bake, uncovered, until heated through and bubbling around edges, about 10 minutes.

11. While casserole is baking, combine sour cream and heavy cream in small bowl and stir until blended.

12. If using parsley, wash and pat dry. Chop enough parsley to measure 1 tablespoon.

13. Remove baking dish from oven and top with remaining crumbled cheese. Sprinkle with chopped parsley, if desired. Cut into squares and divide among individual plates. Serve remaining cream sauce separately.

Pickled Cauliflower

4 fresh jalapeño or serrano chilies, or 4 canned, rinsed, drained, and patted dry
1½ cups sliced carrots
¼ cup vegetable oil
4 large cloves garlic
½ cup sliced onion
Small head cauliflower (about 1½ pounds)
⅓ cup cider vinegar
½ teaspoon dried marjoram
½ teaspoon thyme
¾ teaspoon salt
¼ teaspoon freshly ground black pepper
2 bay leaves

1. If using fresh chilies, wash and pat dry. If using canned, prepare and set aside. Peel carrots and cut into ¼-inch-thick slices.

2. Heat oil in large, deep skillet over medium heat. Add sliced garlic, onion, carrots, and fresh chilies, if using. Toss to combine and cook, stirring frequently, about 5 minutes, until onion is soft.

3. Peel leaves from cauliflower. Turn cauliflower stem end up and, with sharp paring knife, remove core. Break head into large pieces and cut pieces in large florets. Place florets in colander and wash thoroughly under cold running water; drain.

4. In small bowl, combine vinegar, ¼ cup water, marjoram, thyme, salt, and pepper. Stir until blended and add to sautéed vegetables along with bay leaves. Add cauliflower, toss to combine, cover, and cook 8 to 10 minutes, or until cauliflower is just tender.

5. If using canned chilies, add to vegetables and adjust seasoning if necessary. Turn vegetables and cooking liquid out onto serving platter and let cool to room temperature, basting frequently with cooking liquid as they cool.

ADDED TOUCH

The easiest way to form these fritters (*churros*) is to use a cookie press. They are most delicious served hot.

Cinnamon Fritter Sticks

2 tablespoons vegetable oil
1 tablespoon sugar
½ teaspoon cinnamon
2 teaspoons salt
1 cup flour
Oil for deep frying
⅔ cup cinnamon sugar

1. In medium-size saucepan, bring oil, 1 cup water, sugar, cinnamon, and salt to a boil.

2. As soon as mixture boils, remove pan from heat and add flour, beating vigorously until smooth. Batter will be very thick and form a smooth-textured ball. Let dough cool until it can be handled.

3. Fill medium-size skillet ½-inch full of oil and heat over medium-high heat until oil registers 375 degrees on deep-fat thermometer. (Measure temperature by very carefully tilting skillet to one side.)

4. Line a platter with paper towels.

5. Spoon batter into cookie press or pastry bag fitted with ⅜-inch fluted tip. Pipe out several 5-inch lengths at a time and drop into hot oil at least an inch apart. Cook 3 to 4 minutes, turning to brown evenly.

6. When browned, transfer fritters with tongs or slotted spoon to paper-towel-lined platter. Taste one. If it is doughy inside, let oil cool slightly and then return fritters to pan and fry another minute. Repeat process until batter is used up, increasing cooking time if necessary.

7. In brown paper bag, dredge warm fritters with cinnamon sugar. Serve immediately.

Black Bean Tostadas
Chicken in Escabeche

Pieces of chicken in escabeche, *served in an earthenware bowl, are garnished with sprigs of coriander and red onion slices. Arrange the tostadas, layered with black beans, cream, and vegetable garnishes, on a platter.*

Chicken pieces crowded into a skillet will steam rather than brown, so be sure to use a skillet roomy enough for these chicken quarters, or brown them in two medium-size skillets and then consolidate them. If you have time, prepare the chicken in *escabeche* a day ahead to allow the flavor to develop; reheat before serving. Served cold, this dish is also ideal for picnics.

Tostadas are open-face "sandwiches" on a crisp fried tortilla base. The black beans for the filling are sold in cans in most supermarkets or specialty food shops. You can use dried beans instead, but you must start the recipe the night before. Soak one half pound of dried beans overnight, then drain them the next morning. Cover them with fresh water and simmer them about two hours, or until tender. Pinto or kidney beans are acceptable substitutes, but are not typical of Yucatecan cooking.

To fry crisp, the corn tortillas must be thin and thoroughly dry. The oil should be hot (375 degrees, or hot enough to brown a bread cube within 60 seconds) but *not* smoking.

WHAT TO DRINK

A firm, dry white wine would be a sprightly partner for this flavorful menu. Try a good Mâcon or St. Véran from Burgundy or a California Chardonnay.

SHOPPING LIST AND STAPLES

1 chicken (about 3½ pounds), quartered
Small head Romaine lettuce
Small bunch radishes
Medium-size yellow onion
Large red onion
5 large cloves garlic
Small bunch coriander
Two 16-ounce cans black, pinto, or kidney beans
½ pint sour cream
½ pint heavy cream
¼ pound Mexican white cheese, farmer, or feta cheese
8 fresh corn tortillas, or 1 package frozen
⅔ cup vegetable oil, approximately
¼ cup olive oil
2 tablespoons bacon drippings, preferably, or lard or vegetable oil
⅔ cup cider vinegar
½ cup flour

½ teaspoon oregano
½ teaspoon ground allspice
¼ teaspoon thyme
¼ teaspoon marjoram
¼ teaspoon ground cloves
4 bay leaves
Salt
Freshly ground black pepper

UTENSILS

2 large skillets with covers
Small skillet
11 × 17-inch cookie sheet
Heatproof serving platter
Medium-size nonaluminum bowl
2 small bowls
Colander
Salad spinner (optional)
Measuring cups and spoons
Chef's knife
Paring knife
Wooden spoon
Potato masher (optional)
Tongs
Deep-fat thermometer (optional)
Brown paper bag

START-TO-FINISH STEPS

One hour ahead: If using frozen tortillas for tostadas, set out to thaw.

1. Peel and mince garlic for tostadas and chicken recipes. Peel onions, dice yellow onion for tostadas recipe; slice red onion for chicken recipe. Set aside.
2. Follow tostadas recipe steps 1 through 4.
3. Follow chicken recipe steps 1 and 2.
4. Follow tostadas recipe steps 5 and 6.
5. While beans are cooking, follow chicken recipe steps 3 through 5.
6. Check beans. If done, replace cover, remove pan from heat, and while chicken is cooking, follow tostadas recipe steps 7 and 8.
7. Follow chicken recipe steps 6 through 8.
8. While chicken continues cooking, follow tostadas recipe step 9.
9. Follow chicken recipe steps 9 through 11, and serve with tostadas.

RECIPES

Black Bean Tostadas

⅔ cup vegetable oil, approximately
8 fresh corn tortillas, or 8 frozen tortillas, thawed
2 tablespoons bacon drippings, preferably, or lard or vegetable oil
1¼ cups diced yellow onion

Two 16-ounce cans black, pinto, or kidney beans
1 tablespoon minced garlic
½ teaspoon salt, approximately
8 leaves Romaine lettuce
3 radishes
½ cup sour cream
3 tablespoons heavy cream
½ cup crumbled Mexican white cheese, farmer, or feta cheese

1. Line cookie sheet with paper towels.
2. Heat ⅓ cup vegetable oil in small skillet over medium-high heat. When oil reaches 375 degrees, add a tortilla and fry about 30 seconds. With tongs, turn tortilla and fry another 30 seconds, or until crisp. Transfer tortilla to cookie sheet. Repeat with remaining tortillas until all are fried, adding more oil and adjusting temperature as needed.
3. In large skillet, heat bacon drippings over medium heat. Add onion and cook, stirring frequently, 5 to 6 minutes, or until soft.
4. In colander, rinse beans gently under cold running water and drain.
5. Add garlic to onions and cook, stirring, another 2 minutes.
6. Add beans and, using back of wooden spoon or potato masher, mash into coarse purée, adding up to ¼ cup water if beans seem dry. Add salt to taste. Cover skillet, reduce heat to low, and cook 5 to 10 minutes, until beans are heated through.
7. Wash Romaine leaves and dry in salad spinner or pat dry with paper towels. Wash, pat dry, and trim radishes. Stack lettuce leaves end to end and cut into ¼- to ½-inch-wide strips. Cut radishes crosswise into ¼-inch-thick slices.
8. In small bowl, combine sour cream with heavy cream.
9. To assemble tostadas, carefully spread each tortilla with about 3 tablespoons beans. Top each with a dollop of cream mixture, equal portions of shredded lettuce and radish slices, and 1 tablespoon crumbled cheese.

Chicken in Escabeche

1½ cups thinly sliced red onion, approximately
2 teaspoons minced garlic
⅔ cup cider vinegar
½ teaspoon oregano, plus additional ½ teaspoon
½ teaspoon ground allspice, plus additional ¼ teaspoon
4 bay leaves
½ cup flour
1 chicken (about 3½ pounds), quartered
¼ cup olive oil
¾ teaspoon salt
½ teaspoon freshly ground black pepper
¼ teaspoon thyme
¼ teaspoon marjoram
¼ teaspoon ground cloves
Coriander sprigs for garnish

1. Separate onion into rings and combine with garlic in nonaluminum bowl. Add vinegar, ½ cup water, ½ teaspoon oregano, ½ teaspoon allspice, and bay leaves. Stir to combine and set aside.

2. Preheat oven to 200 degrees.

3. Place flour in brown paper bag. Add chicken quarters, 2 at a time, and shake until coated. Remove chicken from bag and set aside.

4. In large skillet, heat olive oil over medium heat.

5. When oil is hot, add dark-meat quarters of chicken skin-side down and fry 8 minutes, or until golden.

6. Turn chicken and add white-meat quarters skin-side down. Fry 4 minutes.

7. Combine salt, pepper, thyme, marjoram, cloves, and remaining oregano and allspice in small bowl.

8. Turn white-meat quarters and, reserving onion, add vinegar-spice marinade from the onion to skillet. Sprinkle with herb-and-spice mixture, reduce heat to medium-low, partially cover, and simmer about 12 minutes, or until chicken is tender.

9. Transfer chicken to heatproof platter and place in oven to keep warm. Add reserved onions to skillet, increase heat to medium-high, and cook 2 to 3 minutes, just to eliminate raw taste but not crunchiness.

10. Wash coriander sprigs and pat dry.

11. To serve, pour onion and cooking liquid over chicken and garnish with coriander sprigs.

ADDED TOUCH

This old-fashioned dessert, often served in Mexico with assorted exotic fruits, is flavored with Jamaican rum.

Floating Island

1⅓ cups plus 1 tablespoon sugar
1 teaspoon freshly squeezed lemon juice
6 eggs, at room temperature, separated
⅛ teaspoon salt
Pinch of cream of tartar
1 teaspoon vanilla extract
1½ cups milk
1½ tablespoons dark Jamaican rum
1 large, ripe mango
1 pint strawberries

1. Lightly grease an 11 × 17-inch baking sheet.

2. Place ½ cup sugar in small heavy-gauge nonaluminum saucepan. Sprinkle sugar with lemon juice and 3 tablespoons water. Do not stir. Bring mixture to a boil over high heat.

3. When mixture has come to a boil, swirl pan carefully to dissolve sugar and brush down sides of pan with pastry brush dipped in cold water.

4. Let mixture boil undisturbed about 3 to 5 minutes, or until it turns a light amber color.

5. Swirl pan to distribute color, and immediately pour mixture onto greased baking sheet, and let cool. (Caramelized sugar will harden as it cools.) Rinse and dry pan.

6. When cool, pry sugar away from baking sheet, break

into small pieces, and pulverize in blender or food processor until powdery. Scrape into small bowl.

7. Preheat oven to 250 degrees.

8. Butter a 1½- to 2-quart straight-sided soufflé or baking dish. Place a tablespoon of sugar in dish and rotate dish, tilting it to coat sides; set aside.

9. Bring 2 quarts of water to a boil in medium-size nonaluminum saucepan.

10. For meringue, beat egg whites with electric mixer at medium speed until foamy. Add salt and cream of tartar, and continue to beat until whites hold stiff peaks.

11. Add ½ cup sugar, 1 tablespoon at a time, beating 30 seconds after each addition. Continue to beat meringue 3 to 4 minutes, or until very stiff, glossy, and smooth. Beat in ½ teaspoon vanilla and 2 tablespoons of the powdered caramelized sugar. Turn mixture into prepared soufflé or baking dish.

12. Place soufflé dish in another slightly larger oven-proof dish. Pour the boiling water into larger dish until water reaches a depth of 2 inches. Empty remaining water from saucepan and dry.

13. Bake meringue 40 to 50 minutes, or until light brown and firm and a toothpick inserted in center comes out clean.

14. Meanwhile, for custard sauce, heat milk in nonaluminum saucepan used for sugar until it steams.

15. With electric mixer at high speed, beat egg yolks and remaining ⅓ cup sugar in large bowl 3 to 4 minutes, until thick and lemon-colored. Add steaming hot milk and 2 tablespoons powdered caramelized sugar, beating steadily until incorporated.

16. Return egg-milk mixture to the medium-size nonaluminum saucepan and cook, stirring, over medium-low heat until mixture thickens slightly and coats back of wooden spoon. Do not permit mixture to boil. Rinse and dry the large bowl.

17. Using a fine mesh sieve, strain custard back into the large bowl and stir in rum and remaining ½ teaspoon vanilla extract. Let cool to room temperature.

18. Meanwhile, when done, remove meringue from oven and let cool in its water bath.

19. Just before serving, peel mango and cut flesh away from pit in chunks. Place in small serving bowl.

20. In colander, rinse strawberries under cold, running water, drain, and gently pat dry. Reserve 8 whole berries for garnish. Hull and slice remainder and place in another small serving bowl.

21. Place a deep, wide serving platter over soufflé dish containing cooled meringue mixture. Holding the 2 dishes firmly together, invert, so that meringue unmolds onto center of platter.

22. Pour cooled custard around outside of meringue "island," stirring in any caramel liquid that may have extruded from the meringue.

23. Garnish platter with the reserved whole strawberries and sprinkle top of meringue with remaining powdered caramelized sugar. Serve slices of meringue with custard sauce spooned over top. Pass fruit separately.

Lucinda Hutson

MENU 1 (Right)
Marinated Red Snapper
Citrus Salad with Pomegranate Seeds

MENU 2
Green Chili Casserole with Sweet-and-Spicy
Tomato Sauce
Orange and Melon Salad with Mint Marinade
Mexican Corn Muffins

MENU 3
Spicy Shrimp and Spinach Soup
Stuffed Tomato Salad

Lucinda Hutson was raised in the border town of El Paso, Texas, where she developed a love for fine Mexican food that was later heightened by her travels through the country. Today she uses her knowledge of Mexican cooking as a foundation for her own interpretive Mexican dishes, in which she eliminates frying when possible, utilizes fresh produce, and creates lively sauces. "I do not merely translate traditional recipes," she says. "Instead, I try to use traditional ingredients in an imaginative way." In Menu 1, for example, the main course of red snapper, or *huachinango*, is flavored with fresh ginger, an Asian rather than a Mexican seasoning, yet the dish is still traditionally *al mojo de ajo*—smothered with garlic.

Fresh produce, unusual combinations of herbs and spices (she urges serious Mexican cooks to grow their own herbs), as well as unique garnishes are essential to her cooking. In Menu 2, her green chili casserole, a variation on the standard *chiles rellenos* (stuffed chilies), calls for fresh Anaheim or *poblano* chilies garnished with sliced avocado and onion rings.

The spicy shrimp and spinach soup of Menu 3, a recipe the cook learned from a fisherman from the Gulf Coast state of Veracruz, is filled with herbs. When served with a crusty garlic bread, this soup-and-salad meal is perfect for lunch.

Broiled red snapper, flavored with ginger, garlic, coriander and crushed red pepper, is a light main course for a company dinner. A colorful salad of citrus sections with pomegranate seeds, avocado slices, and red onion rings on red leaf lettuce may be served with the fish or after.

192

Marinated Red Snapper
Citrus Salad with Pomegranate Seeds

The marinade for the main-course fish calls for a dash of gold tequila, which has a richer flavor than white tequila. You can substitute white tequila, however, or omit the liquor altogether, adding more lime juice if you do so.

Pomegranates come to market in the fall or early winter. If unavailable, fresh raspberries make an excellent substitute.

This is a light, refreshing meal, but to provide for larger appetites, you may want to extend it by adding rice or a basket of warm tortillas with butter on the side.

WHAT TO DRINK

Tequila gimlets (3 ounces tequila, plus 2 ounces freshly squeezed lime juice, over ice) would be a perfect drink to precede the citrus flavors of this menu; serve beer or ale with the meal itself.

SHOPPING LIST AND STAPLES

4 fillets of fresh red snapper, flounder, or any
   light white fish (about ½ pound each)
Medium-size avocado
1 head red leaf lettuce
Small bunch radishes (optional)
Medium-size red onion
Small bunch coriander
3 to 4 large cloves garlic
2-inch piece fresh ginger
Large pink or ruby red grapefruit (about 1½ pounds)
2 navel oranges
4 limes, plus 1 lime (optional)
1 fresh pomegranate, or 1 cup fresh raspberries
1 cup vegetable oil
3 tablespoons olive oil
5 tablespoons red wine vinegar
¼ cup granulated sugar
1 teaspoon dry mustard
½ teaspoon pure chili powder or paprika
¼ teaspoon crushed red pepper flakes
Salt and freshly ground pepper
1 tablespoon gold tequila (optional)

UTENSILS

Food processor or blender
Broiler pan

194

13 × 9 × 2-inch glass baking dish
Medium-size bowl
Small bowl
Salad spinner (optional)
Measuring cups and spoons
Chef's knife
Paring knife
Wide metal spatula
Fork
Vegetable peeler
Grater

START-TO-FINISH STEPS

1. Juice limes for salad and for snapper recipes.
2. Follow snapper recipe steps 1 through 4.
3. Follow salad recipe steps 1 through 8.
4. Follow snapper recipe steps 5 through 7.
5. While fish is broiling, follow salad recipe steps 9 through 12.
6. Follow snapper recipe step 8 and serve with salad.

RECIPES

Marinated Red Snapper

2-inch piece fresh ginger
3 to 4 cloves garlic
Small bunch coriander
¼ cup freshly squeezed lime juice
¼ teaspoon crushed red pepper flakes
1 tablespoon gold tequila (optional)
3 tablespoons olive oil
4 fillets of fresh red snapper, flounder, or any light
   white fish (about ½ pound each)
1 lime for garnish (optional)
4 to 6 radishes for garnish (optional)
Salt and freshly ground pepper
½ teaspoon pure chili powder or paprika

1. Peel and grate ginger. Peel and mince garlic.
2. Wash coriander and pat dry with paper towels. Chop enough to measure ¼ cup.
3. In glass baking dish, combine ginger, garlic, coriander, lime juice, red pepper, and tequila, if using, and beat with fork until blended. Add oil and beat again.
4. Place fillets in dish, turning once to coat with marinade.

Cover with plastic wrap and marinate at room temperature 30 to 40 minutes, turning occasionally.

5. Preheat broiler. Line broiler pan with foil.

6. Slice lime into 8 thin wedges, if using. Wash radishes, if using, and cut into ⅛-inch-thick slices.

7. Arrange fillets in single layer on foil-lined broiler pan set 4 to 6 inches from heating element. Cook 3 to 6 minutes per side, or until fish can be flaked easily with fork. Watch fish carefully to prevent overcooking—the longer fish has marinated, the more rapidly it will cook.

8. Transfer fish fillets to individual dinner plates and sprinkle with salt, pepper, and chili powder or paprika to taste. Serve garnished with lime wedges and radish slices, if desired.

Citrus Salad with Pomegranate Seeds

Medium-size red onion
1 lime
2 navel oranges
¼ cup granulated sugar
1 teaspoon dry mustard
5 tablespoons red wine vinegar
2 tablespoons freshly squeezed lime juice
¼ teaspoon salt
1 cup vegetable oil
Large pink or ruby red grapefruit (about 1½ pounds)
1 fresh pomegranate, or 1 cup fresh raspberries
1 head red leaf lettuce
Medium-size avocado

1. Peel onion, halve, and coarsely chop one half. Slice remaining half into ¼-inch-thick slices. Separate slices into rings, wrap in plastic, and refrigerate.

2. Using coarse side of grater, grate citrus rind.

3. In bowl of food processor or blender, combine chopped onion, grated rind, sugar, mustard, vinegar, 1 tablespoon lime juice, and salt, and process until puréed. (If using blender, citrus peel may not entirely dissolve into purée. If it does not, simply blend until it is as finely chopped as possible.)

4. With processor or blender running, drizzle in oil until dressing begins to thicken. Then gradually add remaining oil in a slow, steady stream. When oil has been completely incorporated, taste dressing and adjust seasoning, if necessary. Cover bowl or blender jar and refrigerate. Dressing will continue to thicken as it chills.

5. Peel grapefruit and oranges, removing as much white pith as possible. Section fruit by cutting between membranes; discard membranes. Place fruit in medium-size bowl and set aside.

6. If using pomegranate, cut gash in rind and, using thumbs, pry fruit open. Break into smaller sections to facilitate removal of seeds. Using your fingers, gently separate seeds with the juicy red pulp surrounding them from the hard rind; discard rind. Separate seeds from one another. If using raspberries, rinse in cool water and gently pat dry with paper towels. Add pomegranate seeds

or raspberries to bowl with citrus fruit. Cover with plastic wrap and refrigerate until needed.

7. Wash lettuce and dry in salad spinner or pat dry with paper towels. Roll lettuce in paper towels or place in plastic bag and refrigerate until needed.

8. Place individual serving plates in refrigerator to chill.

9. Just before serving, peel avocado and cut in half lengthwise. Twist to separate halves; remove and discard pit. Slice avocado into ½-inch-thick crescents. Place in small bowl and toss with remaining tablespoon lime juice.

10. Remove plates and salad ingredients from refrigerator. Line plates with lettuce leaves.

11. Gently toss citrus sections and pomegranate seeds or raspberries until combined. Add avocado and toss.

12. Divide salad among lettuce-lined plates. Top each portion with onion rings and dressing.

ADDED TOUCH

If you can't find Mexican chocolate, make your own: Melt 3 ounces dark sweet chocolate with ½ teaspoon ground cinnamon and dashes of almond and vanilla extracts.

Mexican Chocolate Ice Cream

2 squares unsweetened chocolate
3 squares Mexican chocolate
3 egg yolks
Pinch salt
1 cup granulated sugar
1 cup milk
2 cups heavy cream
Cinnamon
½ teaspoon vanilla extract
¼ teaspoon pure almond extract
½ cup toasted, slivered almonds for garnish (optional)

1. Grate both chocolates over waxed paper and set aside.

2. In medium-size bowl, beat egg yolks and salt with electric mixer at high speed 1 or 2 minutes, or until thickened. Reduce speed to medium, and gradually add sugar. Increase speed to high and continue to beat 2 to 3 minutes, or until yolks are pale yellow and fluffy.

3. Combine milk and cream in medium-size saucepan and heat over medium heat just until bubbles form at the edge and mixture starts to simmer. Immediately remove pan from heat.

4. Gradually add scalded milk-cream mixture to yolk mixture, stirring constantly until completely incorporated.

5. Return mixture to saucepan and cook, stirring constantly with whisk, over low heat 3 to 5 minutes, or until thick enough to coat the back of a spoon. (Watch mixture very carefully. Do not permit to boil or eggs will curdle.)

6. Remove custard from heat and stir in grated chocolate, ¼ teaspoon cinnamon, and vanilla and almond extracts. Continue to stir until chocolate has completely melted.

7. Place mixture in canister of ice-cream maker and proceed according to manufacturer's directions.

8. To serve, sprinkle each portion of ice cream with cinnamon or toasted slivered almonds, if desired.

Green Chili Casserole with Sweet-and-Spicy Tomato Sauce
Orange and Melon Salad with Mint Marinade
Mexican Corn Muffins

For this buffet-style brunch, serve the green chili casserole from its baking dish and offer the tomato sauce in a separate pitcher. An orange and melon salad and corn muffins with raisins and pine nuts round out the meal.

The green chili casserole is a variation on the classic Mexican dish, *chiles rellenos*, or cheese-filled batter-dipped green chilies that are fried. The accompanying tomato sauce for the casserole contains cinnamon, a southern Mexico influence. If you do not use fresh chilies for the casserole, combine the optional fresh jalapeños with the canned mild chilies for a more piquant flavor.

WHAT TO DRINK

For an unusual combination of flavors, serve a German Riesling with this menu. A Mosel, with its delicacy, fruitiness, and touch of sweetness, is another good choice.

SHOPPING LIST AND STAPLES

Small avocado (optional)
Small head red leaf lettuce
Medium-size red onion (optional)
2 bunches scallions
Small bunch fresh mint, or small bunch parsley plus
    3 tablespoons dried mint
4 large cloves garlic, plus 1 clove (optional)
6 fresh poblano or Anaheim chilies, or two 4-ounce cans
    whole green chilies
1 or 2 fresh jalapeños (optional)
Medium-size cantaloupe or honeydew, or large papaya or
    mango
3 medium-size navel oranges
4 limes
15-ounce can tomato sauce
6 eggs
½ pint half-and-half or milk
1 stick plus 2 tablespoons unsalted butter
¼ pound Monterey Jack cheese
¼ pound sharp yellow Cheddar cheese
¼ cup safflower oil
¼ teaspoon vanilla extract
½ cup plus ½ tablespoon flour
⅔ cup yellow cornmeal
1½ teaspoons baking powder
¼ teaspoon baking soda
¾ cup plus 2 teaspoons dark brown sugar, approximately,
    or ½ cup honey plus 2 teaspoons dark brown sugar
9-ounce package dark raisins
3-ounce jar pine nuts, or 4-ounce can blanched, slivered
    almonds
1 teaspoon pure chili powder
1 teaspoon ground cinnamon
1 teaspoon ground coriander seed
1 teaspoon dry mustard
Salt and freshly ground pepper
¼ cup dry sherry

UTENSILS

Medium-size saucepan
9½ × 9½-inch baking/serving dish
12-cup muffin tin
Large bowl
4 medium-size bowls
Small bowl
Platter
Salad spinner (optional)
Measuring cups and spoons
Chef's knife
Paring knife
Long-handled wooden spoon
Slotted spoon
Rubber spatula
Fork
Electric mixer
Grater
Melon baller (optional)
Cake tester or toothpick

START-TO-FINISH STEPS

One hour ahead: Remove butter for muffins from refrigerator and prepare chilies (see pages 14, 15) for casserole recipe.

1. Preheat oven to 350 degrees.
2. Peel and mince garlic and prepare scallions for chili casserole, tomato sauce, and salad, if using.
3. Follow salad recipe steps 1 through 5.
4. Follow muffins recipe steps 1 through 9.
5. Follow casserole recipe steps 1 through 8.
6. Follow salad recipe step 6.
7. Follow sauce recipe steps 1 through 3.
8. While sauce simmers, follow casserole recipe step 8.
9. Follow muffins recipe step 10.
10. Follow salad recipe step 7, sauce recipe step 4, casserole recipe step 9, and serve with warm muffins.

RECIPES

Green Chili Casserole with Sweet-and-Spicy Tomato Sauce

6 fresh poblano or Anaheim chilies, roasted, peeled, and
    seeded, or two 4-ounce cans whole green chilies, rinsed
    drained, and patted dry
1 or 2 fresh jalapeños (optional), washed and patted dry
1½ tablespoons minced garlic
½ cup minced scallions, plus ¼ cup for garnish (optional)
¼ pound Monterey Jack cheese
¼ pound sharp yellow Cheddar cheese
½ tablespoon flour
4 eggs, separated
⅓ cup half-and-half or milk
Salt and freshly ground pepper
Small avocado for garnish (optional)
Medium-size red onion for garnish (optional)
½ teaspoon pure chili powder for garnish (optional)
Sweet-and-Spicy Tomato Sauce (see following recipe)

1. Cut prepared chilies into 2-inch-long strips.
2. Butter baking dish. Place chilies in dish, add minced

garlic and scallions, and toss to combine.

3. Grate cheeses and sprinkle over chili mixture.

4. Sprinkle flour over egg yolks and beat until blended. Add half-and-half and salt and pepper to taste, and beat until incorporated. Wash and dry beaters.

5. Starting at slow and increasing speed to medium as egg whites begin to foam, beat whites until peaks form and whites are stiff but not dry.

6. Using rubber spatula, fold whites into yolks and gently turn into baking dish. With fork, gently swirl through egg layer to combine eggs with chili mixture.

7. Bake, uncovered, in 350-degree oven 25 to 30 minutes, or until crust is deeply golden.

8. Prepare remaining garnishes, if using: Peel and halve avocado lengthwise. Remove and discard pit. Cut into ½-inch-thick crescents. Peel onion and cut into ⅛-inch-thick slices. Separate into rings.

9. Remove casserole from oven and garnish with chili powder, avocado slices, red onion rings, and chopped scallions, if desired. Serve with Sweet-and-Spicy Tomato Sauce on the side.

Sweet-and-Spicy Tomato Sauce

2 tablespoons unsalted butter
¾ cup chopped scallions
1½ tablespoons minced garlic
15-ounce can tomato sauce
1½ teaspoons dark brown sugar
½ teaspoon ground cinnamon
¼ cup dry sherry

1. In medium-size saucepan, melt butter over medium heat. Add scallions and garlic, and sauté, stirring, 2 minutes, or until scallions are translucent.

2. Stir in tomato sauce, brown sugar, cinnamon, and ¼ cup water. Bring mixture to a boil and cook over high heat, stirring constantly, 2 minutes. Reduce heat to medium-high and simmer, stirring occasionally, 3 minutes.

3. Stir in sherry and simmer another 5 minutes.

4. Transfer sauce to small pitcher or bowl, sprinkle with cinnamon, and serve with green chili casserole.

Orange and Melon Salad with Mint Marinade

3 medium-size navel oranges
1 clove garlic (optional)
½ cup fresh mint leaves, or 3 tablespoons crushed dried
    mint and 3 tablespoons chopped parsley
3 tablespoons freshly squeezed lime juice
Medium-size cantaloupe or honeydew, or large papaya or
    mango, scooped into balls or cut into 1-inch chunks
1 teaspoon ground coriander seed
1 teaspoon dry mustard
1 teaspoon pure chili powder
½ teaspoon dark brown sugar, approximately
¼ cup safflower oil
Small head red leaf lettuce
¼ cup chopped scallion greens for garnish (optional)
Mint sprigs for garnish (optional)

198

1. Wash oranges and pat dry. On fine side of grater, grate rind of 2 oranges, avoiding white pith. Remove as much of remaining white pith as possible and separate oranges into sections.

2. If using garlic, peel and bruise clove by placing under flat of knife and leaning on blade with the heel of your hand. Prepare mint or parsley.

3. Scoop out melon or cut fruit into 1-inch chunks.

4. For marinade, combine orange rind, orange slices, lime juice, garlic, if using, coriander, dry mustard, chili powder, mint, and ½ teaspoon brown sugar (or to taste) in medium-size bowl. Add oil and stir with fork until blended. With back of spoon, mash mint.

5. Add melon to bowl and toss until evenly coated. Cover with plastic wrap and refrigerate, stirring occasionally, until ready to serve.

6. Wash lettuce and dry in salad spinner or pat dry with paper towels. Line platter with lettuce leaves. Cover with plastic wrap and refrigerate until ready to serve.

7. Remove garlic clove from fruit mixture and discard. Toss fruit with marinade and, with slotted spoon, transfer to lettuce-lined platter. Serve garnished with scallion greens and mint sprigs, if desired.

Mexican Corn Muffins

1 stick unsalted butter, at room temperature
2 medium-size limes
¾ cup dark brown sugar, or ½ cup honey
½ teaspoon ground cinnamon
¼ teaspoon vanilla extract
½ cup flour
⅔ cup yellow cornmeal
1½ teaspoons baking powder
¼ teaspoon baking soda
2 eggs
½ cup half-and-half or milk
⅓ cup dark raisins
½ cup pine nuts or blanched slivered almonds

1. Butter 12-cup muffin tin.

2. Grate rind of both limes, avoiding white pith.

3. In large bowl, cream butter. Add sugar or honey and beat until mixture is light and fluffy. Beat in grated rind, cinnamon, and vanilla extract.

4. Combine flour, cornmeal, baking powder, and baking soda in medium-size bowl, and stir with fork until blended.

5. In small bowl, beat eggs just until combined. Add half-and-half or milk and stir until blended.

6. To butter mixture, gradually add egg mixture, alternating additions with small amounts of flour mixture and beating after each addition until thoroughly combined.

7. When eggs and flour have been completely incorporated, beat in raisins and nuts.

8. Divide batter evenly among cups of muffin tin, filling each about two-thirds full.

9. Bake muffins in 350-degree oven about 30 to 35 minutes, or until golden and crusty around edges and cake tester or toothpick inserted in center comes out clean.

10. Transfer muffins to napkin-lined basket.

Spicy Shrimp and Spinach Soup
Stuffed Tomato Salad

The zesty shrimp and spinach soup is accompanied by tomato halves stuffed with corn, zucchini, and peppers.

The key to this soup is homemade chicken stock. Canned stock will work, but the soup will be less savory. If using canned stock, try using half chicken stock and half bottled clam juice for more flavor. You can add the sautéed onions, garlic, spices, and jalapeños to the stock early in the day, then boil the shrimp and spinach at the last minute. Use fresh, unpeeled shrimp; their shells enhance the soup's flavor. Peel the shrimp with your fingers as you eat the soup; have extra plates on the table for the shells. Serve the soup garnished with several, or all, of the suggested condiments, or subsitute some of your own choosing.

WHAT TO DRINK

A good dark Mexican beer would be refreshing with the spicy shrimp soup.

SHOPPING LIST AND STAPLES

16 to 20 medium-size fresh shrimp (¾ to 1 pound total weight), unpeeled
½ pound fresh spinach
Medium-size head Bibb lettuce
Small avocado

199

8 small or 4 medium-size firm tomatoes (about 1 pound
    total weight)
Small zucchini
Medium-size red or green bell pepper
2 medium-size white onions (about 1 pound total weight)
Large bunch scallions
1 to 2 fresh jalapeños, or 4-ounce can, whole
5 large cloves garlic
Large bunch coriander
Small bunch fresh mint
7 small limes
5 cups chicken stock, preferably homemade (see page 13),
    or 2½ cups canned chicken stock and three 8-ounce
    bottles clam juice
3 tablespoons unsalted butter
¼ pound Parmesan cheese
10-ounce package frozen corn
¼ cup olive oil
2 tablespoons red wine vinegar
1 teaspoon brown sugar
1 teaspoon dried oregano
½ teaspoon dried thyme
½ teaspoon ground cumin
¼ teaspoon crushed red pepper flakes
1 bay leaf
Salt and freshly ground pepper
¼ teaspoon freshly ground white pepper

UTENSILS

Medium-size skillet
2 medium-size saucepans, one with cover
Medium-size bowl
3 small bowls
2 plates
Salad spinner (optional)
Colander
Measuring cups and spoons
Chef's knife
Paring knife
Wooden spoon
Tablespoon
Teaspoon or melon baller
Grater

START-TO-FINISH STEPS

Thirty minutes ahead: Prepare chilies (see pages 14, 15)
for soup recipe. Set out frozen corn to thaw for salad recipe.

1. Peel and mince garlic for soup and for salad. Wash
scallions, coriander, and mint, and pat dry. Chop scallions
and coriander for soup and for salad. Chop mint for salad.
Squeeze lime juice for soup and for salad.
2. Follow soup recipe steps 1 through 4.
3. Follow salad recipe steps 1 through 8.
4. Follow soup recipe steps 5 through 10.
5. Follow salad recipe step 9, soup recipe step 11, and
serve.

200

RECIPES

Spicy Shrimp and Spinach Soup

1 to 2 fresh jalapeños, washed, patted dry, and seeded, or
    1 to 2 whole canned jalapeños, rinsed, drained, and
    seeded
2 medium-size white onions
3 tablespoons unsalted butter
3 large cloves garlic, minced
¾ teaspoon crushed dried oregano
½ teaspoon dried thyme
1 bay leaf
5 cups chicken stock, or 2½ cups canned chicken stock
    and 2½ cups bottled clam juice
Small avocado
2 tablespoons fresh lime juice
½ cup freshly grated Parmesan cheese
4 cups fresh spinach, packed
16 to 20 medium-size shrimp (¾ to 1 pound total weight),
    unpeeled
2 small limes
¼ teaspoon freshly ground white pepper
Salt
1 cup chopped coriander
½ cup chopped scallions

1. Chop prepared jalapeños finely. Peel and chop onion.
2. Melt butter in skillet over medium heat. Add jalapeños,
onions, and garlic, and cook, stirring, until onions are
translucent, about 3 minutes. Remove pan from heat.
3. Stir in oregano, thyme, and bay leaf.
4. In medium-size saucepan, bring stock to a boil over high
heat. Reduce to a simmer, add sautéed vegetables, and
return to a boil. Reduce heat and simmer 30 minutes.
5. Peel and halve avocado lengthwise. Remove and discard
pit. Cut into ½-inch dice. Place in small bowl and toss with
1 tablespoon lime juice. Grate Parmesan; set aside.
6. Wash spinach thoroughly in several changes of cold
water and drain in colander. Remove tough stems and
discard. Tear spinach into bite-size pieces.
7. Rinse shrimp under cold running water and drain. Remove legs and discard.
8. Increase heat under stock to high and return to a boil.
Add shrimp and cook about 3 minutes, just until they turn
bright pink and become firm.
9. While shrimp are cooking, quarter limes.
10. Turn off heat under shrimp. Stir in spinach and lime
juice, cover, and allow to steam 2 minutes. Season with
white pepper and salt to taste.
11. Serve soup in individual bowls garnished with avocado, coriander, scallions, Parmesan, and lime wedges.

Stuffed Tomato Salad

8 small or 4 firm medium-size tomatoes (about 1 pound
    total weight)
Salt
2 large cloves garlic, minced

3 tablespoons fresh lime juice
2 tablespoons red wine vinegar
1 teaspoon brown sugar
¼ teaspoon crushed red pepper flakes
¼ teaspoon oregano
½ teaspoon ground cumin
¼ cup olive oil
3 to 4 tablespoons chopped mint
1 tablespoon chopped coriander
Freshly ground black pepper
Medium-size red or green bell pepper
Medium-size head Bibb lettuce
Small zucchini
½ cup chopped scallions
1½ cups corn kernels, thawed and drained but still chilled

1. Tomatoes may be used peeled or unpeeled. If peeling, bring 2 quarts salted water to a boil in medium-size saucepan. Plunge tomatoes into boiling water and blanch 30 seconds. Transfer tomatoes to colander, refresh under cold running water, and remove peel with your fingers. If using tomatoes unpeeled, wash and pat dry.
2. Cut off tomato tops about ½ to ¾ inch from top. With teaspoon or melon baller, hollow out tomatoes, leaving a ¼-inch-thick shell. Discard seeds and pulp. Reserve firm flesh and chop. Lightly salt tomato shells. Cover plate with a layer of paper towels and invert shells on toweling. Leave 5 minutes.
3. For dressing, combine garlic, lime juice, vinegar, sugar, red pepper flakes, oregano, and cumin in small bowl. Beating with fork until blended, drizzle in oil. Place mint and coriander in small bowl and mash with back of tablespoon to release flavor. Add to vinaigrette along with salt and pepper to taste and beat to combine.
4. Turn tomato shells upright and add about 1½ teaspoons vinaigrette to each if using 4 medium-size tomatoes, or ¾ teaspoon if using small ones. Roll dressing around inside and outside of tomato to coat. Place tomatoes on plate, cover with plastic wrap, and refrigerate.
5. Core, halve, and seed bell pepper. Chop and set aside.
6. Wash lettuce and dry in salad spinner or pat dry with paper towels. Wrap in paper towels and refrigerate.
7. Scrub zucchini, rinse, and pat dry. Cut into ¼-inch dice.
8. In medium-size bowl, combine reserved tomato flesh, zucchini, scallions, bell pepper, corn, and salt and pepper to taste. Add remaining vinaigrette and toss to combine. Cover with plastic wrap and refrigerate.
9. Just before serving, line 4 plates with lettuce. Remove tomatoes and corn mixture from refrigerator. Pour any vinaigrette that has accumulated around tomatoes into corn mixture. Fill tomato shells generously with the corn mixture. Divide among plates and serve.

ADDED TOUCH

By serving these chicken breasts on a bed of rice, you can **transform** this soup and salad lunch into a substantial dinner.

Chicken Breasts in Lemon-Wine Sauce

4 chicken breast halves (about 1¾ pounds, total weight)
3 medium-size lemons
Medium-size yellow onion
4 large cloves garlic
1 to 2 fresh or canned jalapeño peppers, chopped
2 tablespoons unsalted butter
2 tablespoons olive oil
Salt and freshly ground white pepper
¾ cup dry white wine
¼ teaspoon ground coriander
½ teaspoon dried oregano, crumbled
½ teaspoon ground allspice
½ cup chopped scallions
½ cup chopped coriander or parsley
4-ounce jar water-packed whole red pimientos, rinsed, drained, and cut into ¼-inch-thick strips.

1. Wash chicken breasts and pat dry with paper towels. Trim excess fat from chicken and discard.
2. Grate rind of 2 lemons. Cut lemons in half and juice. Set aside. Cut remaining lemon into thin slices for garnish. Wrap in plastic and refrigerate.
3. Peel and chop onion. Peel garlic and mince 2 cloves. Bruise remaining cloves by placing them under flat of knife and leaning down on knife with heel of your hand.
4. Prepare jalapeños (see page 15). If a less fiery flavor is desired, first cut in half lengthwise and remove seeds.
5. In medium-size sauté pan, heat butter and oil over medium heat. Add the 2 bruised garlic cloves and sauté about 3 minutes, stirring frequently, until garlic is golden brown. Remove garlic from pan and discard.
6. Place chicken breasts, skin side up, in pan, raise heat to medium-high, and cook about 5 minutes, or until golden brown. Turn pieces skin side down and cook another 4 minutes, or until golden brown. Remove pan from heat.
7. Season chicken with salt and white pepper to taste, and transfer to large, covered casserole.
8. Heat fat remaining in skillet over medium-high heat. Add onion, minced garlic, and jalapeños, and cook 3 to 4 minutes, stirring frequently, just until onion is translucent. Stir in half of grated rind and cook 30 seconds. Pour mixture over chicken in casserole.
9. Add wine, ¼ cup water, 2 tablespoons lemon juice, coriander, oregano, and allspice, and bring to a boil over medium-high heat. Reduce heat to a simmer, cover, and cook about 20 minutes until chicken is tender and juices run clear when flesh is pierced with a fork.
10. While chicken is simmering, prepare scallions, coriander, and pimientos.
11. Transfer chicken to platter and cover loosely with foil. For sauce, add remaining lemon juice and rind to liquid in casserole and stir to combine. Bring to a boil over high heat, and reduce liquid by half, 5 to 8 minutes. Season with salt and pepper to taste.
12. Transfer chicken to individual plates and top each serving with sauce. Sprinkle with scallions, coriander, and pimiento strips and serve garnished with lemon slices.

MORE
INTERNATIONAL
MENUS

INDIAN · MIDDLE EASTERN
MOROCCAN · PORTUGUESE · TURKISH
GREEK · SCANDINAVIAN
HUNGARIAN · AMERICAN CREOLE

Julie Sahni

J ulie Sahni feels that eating meatless meals—at least some of the time—"improves your palate and prolongs your life." Like all good Indian cooks, she knows how to combine seasonings artfully to give each dish a distinctive character: She uses some herbs and spices for aroma, some for color, some for piquancy, and others as binders and thickeners. Her aim, whether she is teaching a class or cooking for family and friends, is to erase the Western idea that all Indian dishes are curries.

As you will discover in this collection of recipes, Indian spices can transform what might otherwise have been mundane dishes of vegetables or grains. In Menu 1, the vegetables for the stew cook in a yogurt sauce flavored with ginger, chilies, curry powder, cumin, mustard seeds, and coriander. As a foil for this spicy dish, Julie Sahni offers a platter of aromatic *basmati* rice garnished with tomatoes and cashews. Dessert is a slightly sweetened confection of sour cream, yogurt, and cream cheese.

In her second menu, the cook uses nine different spices to produce a fragrant and colorful vegetable pilaf. As side dishes, she offers braised tomatoes with chilies in a garlic sauce, and a cooling herbed yogurt salad.

Menu 3 proves that even a few spices judiciously used can make a dish savory. The meal features fresh homemade Indian cheese flavored with scallions, coriander, and black pepper, and fried eggplant slices sprinkled with cumin and Cayenne. A simple rice pilaf with raisins and sunflower seeds completes the meal.

For a dramatic presentation, serve the curried vegetable stew from a Dutch oven and encircle the basmati *rice with tomatoes and cashews. Cream pudding garnished with pistachio slices is the dessert.*

Madras Vegetable Stew
Basmati Rice
Indian Cream Pudding

In preparing the vegetable stew, you will learn a typical Indian cooking technique: frying spices in hot fat to release their flavor before combining them with other ingredients. Here, the spices are curry powder and whole cumin and mustard seeds. The trick is to shake the pan constantly during frying to prevent burning and to watch carefully because the spices brown very quickly.

Rice is an integral part of most Indian meals, and *basmati*, grown in the foothills of the Himalayas, is particularly aromatic and delicious. *Basmati* has a long slender grain and a characteristic nutty fragrance. It can be purchased in Indian groceries and specialty food shops.

Although cooking *basmati* is not particularly difficult, remember that the rice should be picked over for tiny sticks or pebbles, and that it must be washed several times and soaked for 30 minutes in cold water before cooking. Washing removes any bran, husks, or other light debris as well as excess starch; soaking softens the grains so they do not crack during cooking.

WHAT TO DRINK

Cold beer or ale would suit this meal, as would a well-chilled, crisp white wine such as a French Muscadet or an Italian Verdicchio.

SHOPPING LIST AND STAPLES

Medium-size bunch broccoli (about 1 pound)
¾ pound yellow summer squash, butternut squash, or pumpkin
2 ripe plum tomatoes (about ½ pound total weight)
4 fresh hot green chilies
Medium-size red onion
1-inch piece fresh ginger
Small bunch coriander
½ pint sour cream
1 pint plain yogurt
8-ounce package cream cheese
¼ cup plus 1 tablespoon light vegetable oil
1-pound package basmati rice
½ cup confectioners' sugar
1½ teaspoons cornstarch
⅓ cup whole roasted cashews
1 tablespoon unsalted raw pistachios
2 teaspoons curry powder
1½ teaspoons ground cumin

1 teaspoon mustard seeds
½ teaspoon cumin seeds
¼ teaspoon freshly grated nutmeg
¼ teaspoon saffron threads
Salt
Freshly ground pepper

UTENSILS

Food processor or blender
Medium-size skillet with cover
Dutch oven or large heavy-gauge saucepan, with cover
3-quart saucepan
Large bowl
Small bowl
Fine strainer or colander
Measuring cups and spoons
Chef's knife
Paring knife
Wooden spoon
Thin rubber gloves

START-TO-FINISH STEPS

Thirty minutes ahead: Set out cream cheese to come to room temperature for pudding recipe.

1. Follow rice recipe step 1 and pudding recipe steps 1 through 3.
2. Follow stew recipe steps 1 through 3 and rice recipe step 2.
3. Follow stew recipe steps 4 and 5 and rice recipe step 3.
4. Follow stew recipe step 6 and rice recipe step 4.
5. While rice is cooking, follow stew recipe step 7.
6. Follow rice recipe steps 5 and 6, stew recipe step 8, and serve.
7. Serve pudding for dessert.

RECIPES

Madras Vegetable Stew

Medium-size red onion
Medium-size bunch broccoli (about 1 pound)
¾ pound yellow summer squash, butternut squash, or pumpkin
1-inch piece fresh ginger
Small bunch coriander

4 fresh hot green chilies
1 cup plain yogurt
1½ teaspoons ground cumin
1½ teaspoons cornstarch
5 tablespoons light vegetable oil
2 teaspoons curry powder
Salt
½ teaspoon cumin seeds
1 teaspoon mustard seeds

1. Peel and halve onion. Cut each half into ¼-inch-thick slices. Set aside.
2. Wash broccoli and dry with paper towels. Trim stems and cut broccoli into 2-inch florets. Wash and trim summer squash, if using, and cut enough into ½-inch-thick slices to measure about 4 cups. If using butternut squash or pumpkin, halve, peel, seed, and cut enough into ¼-inch-thick slices to measure about 4 cups. Peel ginger and chop roughly. Wash coriander and pat dry. Remove enough coriander leaves and tender stems to measure ¼ cup loosely packed. Wearing rubber gloves, wash, stem, and split chilies.
3. Place ginger, coriander, chilies, yogurt, ground cumin, and cornstarch in blender or food processor and process until combined; set aside.
4. Heat 2 tablespoons oil in Dutch oven or large heavy-gauge saucepan over medium-high heat. When oil is hot, add curry powder and let sizzle, shaking pan constantly, about 10 seconds, or until fragrant. Add broccoli and squash and toss to coat with spices. Cook 1 minute. Add yogurt sauce, stir to combine, and season with salt to taste. Pour 1 cup water into blender or food processor container, shake to rinse, and pour water over vegetables; stir to combine.
5. Increase heat to high and bring mixture to a boil. Reduce heat to medium-low and cook, covered, 5 minutes.
6. Uncover pan, increase heat to high, and boil rapidly 1 minute; turn off heat.
7. Heat remaining 3 tablespoons oil in medium-size skillet over high heat. When oil is hot, add cumin seeds and mustard seeds. Keep cover of pan handy as seeds will sputter and pop. Shaking pan, cook seeds 1 to 2 minutes, or until cumin turns dark and sputtering subsides. Add onion, and toss and stir quickly about 2 minutes, or until onion begins to color. Turn off heat.
8. To serve, transfer stew to large serving dish and top with onion mixture.

Basmati Rice

1 cup basmati rice
2 ripe plum tomatoes (about ½ pound total weight)
⅓ cup whole roasted cashews
Salt
Freshly ground pepper

1. Place rice in large bowl and wash in several changes of cold water until water runs clear. Add enough water to cover rice by at least 1 inch and let soak 30 minutes.

2. Bring 2 quarts water to a boil in 3-quart saucepan over high heat.
3. Wash and core tomatoes; thinly slice tomatoes and set aside.
4. Drain rice and add to boiling water. Gently stir to prevent rice from settling to bottom of pan. When water returns to a boil, cook rice, uncovered, 4½ to 5 minutes, or until tender.
5. Immediately pour cooked rice into fine strainer or colander and drain.
6. Spoon rice onto serving platter and surround with tomato slices and cashews. Sprinkle tomatoes with salt and pepper to taste and serve.

Indian Cream Pudding

1 cup sour cream
⅓ cup plain yogurt
½ cup cream cheese, at room temperature
½ cup confectioners' sugar
¼ teaspoon saffron threads
¼ teaspoon freshly grated nutmeg
1 tablespoon unsalted raw pistachios

1. Combine sour cream, yogurt, cream cheese, and sugar in small bowl.
2. Lightly crush saffron with fingers and add to mixture in bowl. Add nutmeg and stir until mixture is thoroughly blended and smooth. Spoon pudding into 4 stemmed glasses or dessert bowls.
3. Slice pistachios lengthwise and sprinkle equally over puddings. Cover glasses or bowls and refrigerate until ready to serve.

ADDED TOUCH

A vegetable-fruit relish is a frequent part of Indian meals. This one is simple and quick to make and can be prepared just before mealtime. Serve it in place of a salad. Leftovers can be refrigerated in a tightly covered container for up to four days.

Carrot and Mango Relish

Medium-size carrot
Small unripe mango (about ¼ pound)
½ teaspoon Cayenne pepper
1¼ teaspoons salt
½ teaspoon dry mustard
2 tablespoons light vegetable oil

1. Peel and trim carrot and halve lengthwise. Cut each half crosswise into ⅛-inch-thick slices and place in small bowl. Peel and pit mango and cut flesh into ⅛-inch-thick slices; add to carrots. Add Cayenne, salt, and mustard and toss to mix well.
2. Heat oil in small skillet until smoking. Pour hot oil over vegetables and immediately stir to combine. Set relish aside, uncovered, at room temperature until ready to serve.

Fragrant Vegetable Pilaf
Braised Tomatoes with Chilies in Garlic Sauce
Zucchini Raita

The highly seasoned vegetable pilaf garnished with nuts and black grapes is delicious with braised tomatoes and refreshing raita.

Rice pilaf in its most basic form is simply rice that has been sautéed in fat, then simmered in liquid. The fat keeps the grains separated, and the gentle simmering makes them tender. An Indian pilaf often includes a number of ingredients besides rice: This recipe has vegetables, yogurt, and spices. Traditionally, the whole cinnamon stick and bay leaves are left in when the rice is served on a platter, but only for their decorative appearance. They are not meant to be eaten. The optional garnish of black grapes and almonds also provides a visual highlight—and an unusual flavor contrast as well.

This version of the yogurt salad called *raita* in India is made by stirring spices and barely cooked zucchini into a yogurt-sour cream mixture. Indian cooks would use a rich homemade buffalo-milk yogurt, but a good-quality commercial whole-milk yogurt makes a satisfactory substitute here.

WHAT TO DRINK

The assertive flavors and aromas of these dishes require a medium-bodied dry white wine. A California Sauvignon Blanc or a California or Alsatian Gewürztraminer would be a good choice.

1½ pounds ripe tomatoes, preferably
    Italian plum
Small head cauliflower (about 1 pound)
½ pound fresh peas, or 10 ounce-package frozen
Medium-size carrot
Small zucchini
4 fresh hot green chilies
Small bunch scallions
Large onion
8 large cloves garlic
1-inch piece fresh ginger
Small bunch mint
Small bunch coriander
Small bunch black Emperor grapes (optional)
½ pint sour cream
1 pint plain yogurt
¾ cup light vegetable oil, approximately
1 cup long-grain white rice
1½ teaspoons sugar
⅓ cup toasted slivered almonds (optional)
2 whole dried red pepper pods
1¾ teaspoons ground cumin
1 teaspoon mustard seeds
1 teaspoon cumin seeds
1 teaspoon ground coriander
½ teaspoon turmeric
½ teaspoon Cayenne pepper or red pepper
    flakes, approximately
3-inch stick cinnamon
9 whole cloves
2 bay leaves
Salt

UTENSILS

Large heavy-gauge sauté pan with cover
Medium-size heavy-gauge sauté pan
    with cover
Small skillet
Medium-size bowl
Small bowl
Colander
Measuring cups and spoons
Chef's knife
Paring knife

2 wooden spoons
Metal spatula
Grater
Vegetable peeler (optional)
Thin rubber gloves

START-TO-FINISH STEPS

1. Peel ginger. Cut two ⅛-inch-thick slices for raita recipe. Finely chop enough remaining ginger to measure 1 tablespoon for pilaf recipe.
2. Follow pilaf recipe steps 1 through 6.
3. While pilaf is cooking, follow tomatoes recipe steps 1 and 2.
4. While tomatoes are cooking, follow raita recipe steps 1 and 2 and pilaf recipe step 7.
5. While pilaf continues to cook, follow raita recipe steps 3 and 4 and tomatoes recipe step 3.
6. Follow pilaf recipe steps 8 and 9.
7. Follow raita recipe step 5, tomatoes recipe step 4, pilaf recipe step 10, and serve.

RECIPES

Fragrant Vegetable Pilaf

Small head cauliflower (about 1 pound)
Medium-size carrot
Large onion
½ pound fresh peas, or ½ cup frozen
¼ cup plus 2 tablespoons light vegetable oil
1 teaspoon cumin seeds
3-inch stick cinnamon
9 whole cloves
2 bay leaves
1 tablespoon finely chopped fresh ginger
1 teaspoon ground cumin
1 teaspoon ground coriander
½ teaspoon turmeric
¼ to ½ teaspoon Cayenne pepper or red pepper flakes
1½ teaspoons salt
½ cup plain yogurt
1 cup long-grain white rice
Small bunch black Emperor grapes (optional)
⅓ cup toasted slivered almonds (optional)

1. Wash cauliflower and dry with paper towels. Trim cauliflower and cut enough into 2- to 2½-inch florets to measure about 4 cups. Peel and trim carrot and cut cross-wise into ¼-inch-thick slices. Peel onion and finely chop enough to measure ½ cup. If using fresh peas, shell enough to measure ½ cup.

2. Heat oil in large heavy-gauge sauté pan over high heat 2 minutes.

3. Meanwhile, combine cumin seeds, cinnamon stick, cloves, and bay leaves in small bowl. When oil is hot, add spices and, shaking pan constantly, let spices sizzle about 30 seconds, or until fragrant. Add onion and ginger and cook, stirring, about 4 minutes, or until onion is lightly colored.

4. Reduce heat to medium. Add ground cumin, coriander, turmeric, Cayenne, and salt to pan and continue to cook, stirring, 1 minute. Add cauliflower and carrot and toss to coat well with spices.

5. Increase heat to high. Add yogurt, stir until well combined, and cook 2 minutes. Add rice, stir, and cook 30 seconds. Add 2 cups water, and allow mixture to come to a boil.

6. When mixture boils, reduce heat to medium and cook, partially covered, 10 minutes.

7. Add peas and stir gently. Cover pan tightly, reduce heat to very low, and cook 8 to 10 minutes, or until rice is soft and vegetables are tender.

8. Turn off heat and let pilaf rest, covered, 10 minutes.

9. Meanwhile, wash and dry grapes, if using, and remove from stems.

10. Fluff pilaf with fork, remove bay leaves and cinnamon stick, and divide pilaf among 4 dinner plates. Garnish with grapes and toasted almonds, if desired.

Braised Tomatoes with Chilies in Garlic Sauce

1½ pounds ripe tomatoes, preferably Italian plum
8 large cloves garlic
4 fresh hot green chilies
3 tablespoons light vegetable oil
1 teaspoon mustard seeds
2 whole dried red pepper pods
1 teaspoon salt

1. Wash, dry, and core tomatoes. If using plum tomatoes, quarter lengthwise; if using round tomatoes, cut into 1-inch wedges. Peel garlic and cut each clove lengthwise into 2 or 3 slices. Wearing rubber gloves, slit chilies lengthwise; remove seeds and trim stem ends.

2. Heat oil in medium-size heavy-gauge sauté pan over high heat. When oil is hot, add mustard seeds and dried pepper pods. Keep cover of pan handy as pepper seeds will sputter and pop. Shaking pan, cook seeds and pods until sputtering stops and pods turn dark. Add garlic, chilies, and salt, and sauté 1 minute. Add tomatoes and stir carefully to coat evenly with spices (tomato pieces should remain as intact as possible). Bring mixture to a simmer, reduce heat to medium-low, and cook, partially covered, 20 minutes, without stirring.

3. Remove pan from heat and let tomatoes stand, covered, until ready to serve.

4. To serve, using metal spatula divide tomatoes and sauce among 4 dinner plates.

Zucchini Raita

Small zucchini
2 large scallions
Two ⅛-inch-thick slices fresh ginger
Small bunch mint
Small bunch coriander
1⅓ cups plain yogurt
⅓ cup sour cream
1½ teaspoons sugar
¾ teaspoon salt
2 tablespoons light vegetable oil
¾ teaspoon ground cumin

1. Wash zucchini and dry with paper towels; trim ends. Using coarse side of grater, grate zucchini into colander. Press and squeeze zucchini firmly to remove excess moisture. Blot with paper towels and set aside in colander.

2. Wash, dry, and trim scallions, discarding dark green tops. Cut white parts of scallions crosswise into ⅛-inch-thick slices. You should have about ¼ cup. Finely dice ginger. Wash and dry mint and coriander. Reserve 4 sprigs mint for garnish and finely chop enough remaining mint and coriander leaves to measure ⅓ cup each.

3. In medium-size bowl, combine yogurt, sour cream, sugar, and salt. Add scallions, ginger, and chopped mint and coriander, and mix well.

4. Heat oil in small skillet over high heat until very hot. Turn off heat, sprinkle oil with ground cumin, and immediately add zucchini. Toss zucchini in hot oil until barely cooked. Add zucchini to yogurt mixture and blend well. Set aside until ready to serve.

5. To serve, divide raita among 4 dinner plates and garnish with reserved mint sprigs.

Fresh Indian Cheese with Bell Peppers
Spiced Eggplant with Mango Chutney
Pilaf

Molded homemade Indian cheese with coriander and peppers can be served with or before the fried eggplant and pilaf.

Fresh homemade cheese, a principal source of protein for Indian vegetarians, resembles a dry ricotta or pot cheese. To make the cheese successfully, be sure the milk is at a rolling boil before you add the lemon juice. The curds should begin to surface within seconds. Sometimes the curds form before all the lemon juice is added. If this happens, do not add the remaining lemon juice. If, on the other hand, the curds do not form after all the juice has been added, add a bit more juice until the white solids separate from the whey. Indian cheese can be made using vinegar or yogurt as a starter, but the cook prefers lemon juice because it creates a more delicate cheese. You can prepare the cheese up to five days in advance and refrigerate it in a covered container.

WHAT TO DRINK

Either a light red wine or a fairly full-bodied white would be enjoyable with this menu. For red, try a French Beaujolais or a California Gamay Beaujolais. For white, choose a California Chardonnay or a French white Burgundy such as a Mâcon or a Saint-Véran.

SHOPPING LIST AND STAPLES

Medium-size eggplant (1 to 1¼ pounds)
Small bunch red radishes with leaves attached (optional)
Medium-size green bell pepper
Medium-size red bell pepper
Medium-size yellow bell pepper
4 fresh hot green chilies (optional)
Small bunch scallions
Small bunch coriander
4 large lemons
3 quarts milk
2 tablespoons unsalted butter
4-ounce jar mango chutney
½ cup plus 1 tablespoon light vegetable oil, approximately
2 tablespoons all-purpose flour, approximately
¾ cup long-grain white rice
2 tablespoons roasted sunflower seeds
¼ cup dark raisins
1½ teaspoons ground cumin
1 teaspoon ground coriander
½ teaspoon Cayenne pepper
½ teaspoon fennel seeds
Salt
Freshly ground black pepper

UTENSILS

2 large heavy-gauge skillets
Medium-size skillet
Large deep heavy-gauge nonaluminum saucepan
Medium-size saucepan with cover
Four 4-ounce custard cups, or teacups
Large bowl

Medium-size bowl
Small bowl
Colander
Measuring cups and spoons
Chef's knife
Paring knife
2 wooden spoons
Metal spatula
Citrus juicer (optional)
Cheesecloth
Thin rubber gloves (optional)

START-TO-FINISH STEPS

1. Follow cheese recipe steps 1 through 6.
2. While cheese is draining, follow eggplant recipe step 1.
3. Follow cheese recipe steps 7 and 8 and pilaf recipe steps 1 and 2.
4. While rice is cooking, follow cheese recipe step 9.
5. Follow pilaf recipe step 3.
6. While rice continues to cook, follow eggplant recipe steps 2 through 4.
7. Follow pilaf recipe step 4.
8. While pilaf rests, follow cheese recipe steps 10 and 11 and eggplant recipe step 5.
9. Follow pilaf recipe step 5, eggplant recipe step 6, and serve with cheese.

RECIPES

Fresh Indian Cheese with Bell Peppers

4 large lemons
3 quarts milk
1 teaspoon salt, approximately
Medium-size green bell pepper
Medium-size red bell pepper
Medium-size yellow bell pepper
2 scallions
Small bunch coriander
1 tablespoon light vegetable oil
1 teaspoon ground coriander
¼ teaspoon freshly ground black pepper
4 fresh hot green chilies for garnish (optional)

1. Halve 3 lemons and squeeze enough juice into small bowl to measure ¾ cup; set aside. Reserve remaining lemon for garnish.
2. Place milk and 1 teaspoon salt in large deep heavy-gauge nonaluminum saucepan over high heat. Cook, stirring occasionally to prevent sticking, 12 to 15 minutes, or until milk is just below the boiling point.
3. Meanwhile, wash and dry bell peppers. Core and halve peppers and cut lengthwise into ½-inch-wide strips; set aside. (See illustration.)
4. Wash and trim scallions; discard dark green tops. Cut white parts of scallions crosswise into ⅛-inch-thick slices and place in medium-size bowl. Wash and dry coriander; set aside 4 large sprigs for garnish. Remove enough re-

maining coriander leaves from tough stems to measure ¼ cup loosely packed. Coarsely chop coriander leaves and add to scallions.

Coriander

5. Line colander with double thickness of dampened cheesecloth.

6. When milk comes to a rolling boil, add lemon juice and stir gently. Almost immediately, milk will curdle and milky white curd will float to surface; liquid whey will turn greenish yellow. Turn mixture into colander to drain 5 minutes.

7. When whey has drained off, pour 2 cups cold water over cheese and drain about 30 seconds. Gather together corners of cheesecloth and squeeze cheese gently to remove as much water as possible. Return cheese, still wrapped in cheesecloth, to colander and place in sink. Weight cheese with 1-pound can and let drain 10 to 15 minutes.

8. Meanwhile, heat dry medium-size skillet over high heat 2 minutes. Add vegetable oil and ground coriander; immediately add bell pepper strips. Sprinkle with salt to taste and toss peppers quickly to coat evenly with spices. Let peppers cook undisturbed 1 minute. Toss peppers again, reduce heat to very low, and cook another 2 minutes. Remove pan from heat and set aside.

9. Remove cheese from cheesecloth and add to bowl with scallions and coriander. Add black pepper and mix thoroughly with hands; cheese should be silky-soft without being pasty. Lightly oil four 4-ounce custard cups, or teacups. Pack cheese into cups and set aside until ready to serve.

10. If using chilies for garnish, wearing rubber gloves, wash, dry, stem, and seed chilies. Finely chop chilies; set aside. Wash and dry reserved lemon and cut into 8 slices for garnish.

11. To serve, run knife around edges of cups to loosen cheese and unmold onto 4 salad plates. Divide pepper slices among plates. Garnish each serving with a coriander sprig, 2 lemon slices, and finely chopped chilies if desired.

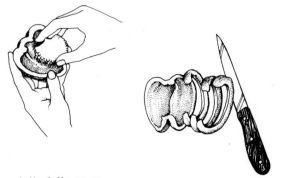
Core and slice bell peppers.

Spiced Eggplant with Mango Chutney

Medium-size eggplant (1 to 1¼ pounds)
1½ teaspoons ground cumin
½ teaspoon Cayenne pepper
¼ teaspoon freshly ground black pepper
2 tablespoons all-purpose flour, approximately
½ cup light vegetable oil, approximately
8 red radishes with leaves attached, for garnish
   (optional)
4-ounce jar mango chutney

1. Wash eggplant and dry with paper towels. Trim ends and cut eggplant crosswise into approximately ½-inch-thick slices, allowing 2 to 3 slices per person. Place eggplant in large bowl and sprinkle with cumin, Cayenne, and black pepper. Toss eggplant to coat evenly with spices; set aside.

2. Place 2 large heavy-gauge skillets over high heat.

3. While pans are heating, sprinkle about 2 tablespoons flour over eggplant slices and toss to coat evenly. If necessary, add more flour.

4. Pour about ¼ cup oil into each skillet, using just enough oil to form thin layer on bottom of pan. Divide eggplant slices between skillets, arranging them in a single layer in each. Fry slices about 4 minutes on each side, or until nicely browned on both sides, adding a bit more oil if necessary.

5. Wash radishes, if using, leaving leaves and root ends intact; set aside.

6. To serve, arrange eggplant slices on 4 dinner plates and spoon some chutney over each portion. Garnish each plate with 2 radishes, if desired.

Pilaf

2 tablespoons unsalted butter
½ teaspoon fennel seeds
¼ cup dark raisins
¾ cup long-grain white rice
Salt (optional)
2 tablespoons roasted sunflower seeds

1. Melt butter in medium-size saucepan over medium-high heat. Add fennel seeds and, shaking pan constantly, let seeds sizzle 30 seconds, or until fragrant. Add raisins and toss until well coated with butter. Add rice, and about ½ teaspoon salt if desired. Reduce heat to medium-low and fry rice 30 seconds, or until well coated with butter but not browned. Add 1½ cups water, stir, and bring to a boil over high heat.

2. Reduce heat to medium and cook rice, partially covered, 8 to 10 minutes, or until most of water is absorbed.

3. Stir rice, tightly cover pan, and reduce heat to very low. Cook rice another 10 minutes, or until tender and fluffy.

4. Remove pan from heat and let pilaf rest, covered, 5 minutes.

5. To serve, fluff pilaf with fork and divide among 4 dinner plates. Sprinkle with roasted sunflower seeds.

Jean Anderson

MENU 1 (Right)
Minted Buttermilk and Radish Soup
Lemon-Marinated Swordfish Kabobs
Carrot and Coriander Pilaf Salad

MENU 2
Falafel Cutlets with Tahini Sauce
Cucumbers with Mint and Yogurt
Red Onion and Orange Salad with Fresh Basil

MENU 3
Sautéed Chicken Breasts with
Walnut-Yogurt Sauce
Tabbouleh Salad
Melon Kabobs with Honey and
Orange-Flower Water

After many trips through the Middle East, Jean Anderson has developed her own repertoire of Middle Eastern dishes. Although she alters and adapts traditional recipes to suit American ingredients, she manages to preserve authentic tastes. In Menu 1, she re-creates a refreshing cold soup, based on buttermilk and chopped radishes, that she once tasted in Beirut. The entrée—broiled lemon-marinated swordfish kabobs and an aromatic rice salad with carrots and coriander—is also Lebanese.

Inhabitants of the eastern Mediterranean love *falafel* in pita bread as much as Americans love hamburgers on buns. A popular fast food sold at sidewalk stands, *falafel* (traditionally made of ground chickpeas shaped into balls and deep fried) is the featured dish of Menu 2. Here, the cook shapes the *falafel* into cutlets, which she browns quickly, then tops with a nutty sauce made with *tahini* (sesame seed paste). Cucumber crescents with mint and yogurt and a light salad of red onions and oranges are the refreshing accompaniments.

Menu 3 presents a streamlined version of a Middle Eastern classic—chicken in walnut-yogurt sauce—that would normally take well over an hour to prepare. This recipe calls for boned and flattened chicken breasts, which are sautéed in a matter of minutes. With the chicken, Jean Anderson serves *tabbouleh* salad and, at the meal's end, jewel-like pieces of macerated melon threaded on skewers, a variation on a dessert she once enjoyed in Cairo.

To create a truly Middle Eastern atmosphere for this meal, serve the buttermilk and radish soup, swordfish kabobs, and rice pilaf salad on a colorful carpet.

214

Minted Buttermilk and Radish Soup
Lemon-Marinated Swordfish Kabobs
Carrot and Coriander Pilaf Salad

I f fresh swordfish is unavailable, the cook suggests substituting fresh salmon steaks rather than frozen swordfish; frozen fish tends to exude so much liquid that it dilutes the marinade.

WHAT TO DRINK

To complement this menu, try a very crisp, dry white wine, such as a French Sancerre or Muscadet.

SHOPPING LIST AND STAPLES

Four 1¼-inch-thick swordfish steaks (about 1½ pounds total weight)
Large bunch radishes
Small head romaine lettuce
2 medium-size carrots
1 medium-size plus 1 small yellow onion
1 large plus 1 small clove garlic
Small bunch fresh coriander, if available
Small bunch flat-leaf parsley, if not using coriander
Small bunch fresh mint, or 4 teaspoons dried
15 large bay leaves, preferably fresh, or dried
3 large lemons
1 quart buttermilk
5 cups chicken stock, preferably homemade (see page 13), or canned
5 tablespoons good-quality olive oil
1 cup converted white rice
1 teaspoon dried basil
½ teaspoon dried thyme
¼ teaspoon ground coriander, plus ¼ teaspoon if not using fresh
⅛ teaspoon ground cumin
Salt and freshly ground pepper

UTENSILS

Food processor or blender
Large heavy-gauge saucepan with cover
Medium-size heavy-gauge saucepan
Large glass or ceramic dish
13 x 9 x 2-inch flameproof baking pan
2 large bowls
2 small bowls
Large strainer
Measuring cups and spoons

Chef's knife
Paring knife
2 wooden spoons
Four 15-inch metal skewers
Vegetable peeler

START-TO-FINISH STEPS

1. Peel onions. Quarter small onion for soup recipe. Coarsely chop enough of large onion to measure 1 cup for salad recipe; set aside. Crush and peel garlic. Set aside large clove for soup recipe and mince enough of small clove to measure 1 teaspoon for salad recipe; set aside. Wash and dry coriander or parsley, and fresh mint and bay leaves if using, and dry with paper towels. Mince enough coriander or parsley to measure ⅓ cup for salad recipe. Set aside 4 mint sprigs for garnish, if using, and mince enough remaining mint to measure ⅓ cup for soup recipe. Set aside.
2. Follow soup recipe steps 1 and 2 and swordfish recipe steps 1 through 3.
3. While swordfish marinates, follow soup recipe steps 3 and 4 and salad recipe steps 1 through 4.
4. Fifteen minutes before serving time, follow swordfish recipe steps 4 and 5.
5. While swordfish kabobs are broiling, follow soup recipe step 5 and salad recipe step 5.
6. Follow swordfish recipe step 6 and serve with soup and salad.

RECIPES

Minted Buttermilk and Radish Soup

3 cups chicken stock
Small yellow onion, quartered
Large clove garlic, crushed and peeled
1 teaspoon dried basil
¼ teaspoon dried thyme
¼ teaspoon salt
⅛ teaspoon freshly ground pepper
Large bunch radishes
1½ cups buttermilk
⅓ cup chopped fresh mint, or 4 teaspoons dried
4 mint sprigs for garnish (optional)

1. Heat stock in large heavy-gauge saucepan over medium heat until hot. Add onion, garlic, basil, thyme, salt, and pepper, and simmer, covered, 15 minutes.

2. Meanwhile, wash and dry radishes. Trim radishes and reserve 4 for garnish, if desired. Coarsely chop remaining radishes; you should have about 1⅓ cups. Place chopped radishes in small bowl; cover with plastic wrap. If using radishes for garnish, cut decoratively and immerse in small bowl of ice water; cover bowls and refrigerate until ready to serve.

3. Turn stock into large strainer set over large bowl. Transfer solids remaining in strainer to food processor or blender. Add 1 cup stock and process 15 seconds, or until mixture is puréed. Return purée to bowl with stock.

4. Stir in buttermilk and dried mint, if using. (Do not add fresh mint at this point.) Cover bowl with plastic wrap and place in freezer to chill until serving time.

5. To serve, divide soup among 4 bowls. Sprinkle each serving with chopped radishes, and chopped fresh mint if using, and garnish with a whole radish and a mint sprig, if desired.

Lemon-Marinated Swordfish Kabobs

3 large lemons
3 tablespoons good-quality olive oil
15 large bay leaves, preferably fresh, or dried
¼ teaspoon freshly ground pepper
Four 1¼-inch-thick swordfish steaks (about 1½ pounds total weight)

1. Wash and dry lemons. Using vegetable peeler, remove zest from 1 lemon in long, thin strips, avoiding white pith as much as possible. Halve peeled lemon and squeeze enough juice to measure ¼ cup. Cut remaining lemons into 12 wedges.

2. For marinade, combine lemon zest, lemon juice, olive oil, 3 bay leaves, and pepper in glass or ceramic dish large enough to hold swordfish steaks in one layer.

3. Rinse swordfish and dry with paper towels. Cut swordfish into approximately sixteen 1½-inch cubes. Add swordfish to marinade and toss to coat well. Cover dish with plastic wrap and refrigerate at least 30 minutes.

4. Preheat broiler. Thread swordfish cubes alternately with lemon wedges and remaining bay leaves on four 15-inch metal skewers. Balance skewers lengthwise on 13 x 9 x 2-inch flameproof baking pan. Drizzle kabobs with marinade.

5. Broil kabobs 4 inches from heat 5 minutes. Turn skewers over and broil another 5 minutes.

6. Divide kabobs among 4 dinner plates and serve.

Carrot and Coriander Pilaf Salad

2 medium-size carrots
Small head romaine lettuce
2 tablespoons good-quality olive oil
1 teaspoon minced garlic
1 cup coarsely chopped onion
¼ teaspoon ground coriander, plus ¼ teaspoon if not using fresh
¼ teaspoon dried thyme
⅛ teaspoon ground cumin
⅛ teaspoon freshly ground pepper

1 cup converted white rice
2 cups chicken stock
½ teaspoon salt
⅓ cup chopped fresh coriander or flat-leaf parsley

1. Wash and dry carrots. Coarsely chop carrots. Wash and dry 4 large romaine leaves. Place leaves in plastic bag and refrigerate until ready to use. Reserve remaining romaine for another use.

2. Heat oil over medium-high heat in medium-size heavy-gauge saucepan 1 minute. Add carrots, garlic, and onion, and sauté, stirring, 2 to 3 minutes, or until onion is golden.

3. Add ground coriander, thyme, cumin, pepper, and rice, and stir 30 seconds. Reduce heat to medium-low, add stock and salt, and simmer, uncovered, 18 to 20 minutes, or until rice is tender and all liquid is absorbed.

4. Transfer rice to large bowl. Add fresh coriander or parsley and toss lightly to combine. Cover salad loosely and let stand at room temperature until ready to serve.

5. To serve, place 1 romaine leaf on each of 4 dinner plates and divide salad among leaves.

ADDED TOUCH

Adjust the amount of sugar to your taste in this tart and refreshing ruby-red dessert.

Cranberry-Tangerine Sorbet

¾ pound fresh cranberries, or 12-ounce bag frozen cranberries, partially thawed
3 medium-size tangerines (about 1 pound total weight)
⅓ cup sugar
1 cup light corn syrup

1. Place cranberries in colander and rinse. Remove and discard any stems or imperfect berries. Set cranberries aside to drain.

2. Wash and dry tangerines. Remove 4 long strips of rind from 1 tangerine, avoiding white pith as much as possible; set aside. Halve tangerines and squeeze enough juice to measure 1 cup.

3. Transfer cranberries to food processor fitted with steel blade; pulse 10 to 12 times to chop coarsely. Or, chop cranberries with chef's knife.

4. Combine cranberries and 2 cups water in medium-size heavy-gauge saucepan. Bring liquid to a boil over high heat, reduce heat to medium, and simmer berries 5 minutes.

5. Turn cranberries into fine sieve set over large bowl. Using wooden spoon or spatula, force as much cranberry pulp as possible through sieve.

6. Add tangerine juice, sugar, and corn syrup to bowl and stir until sugar dissolves.

7. Pour mixture into 9-inch square glass baking dish and freeze at least 3 hours, or until firm.

8. Remove sorbet from freezer 20 to 30 minutes before serving and let stand at room temperature to soften.

9. Spoon sorbet into stemmed goblets or dessert dishes and garnish each serving with a strip of tangerine rind.

Falafel Cutlets with Tahini Sauce
Cucumbers with Mint and Yogurt
Red Onion and Orange Salad with Fresh Basil

Filling falafel *cutlets, fragrant with Eastern spices, need only light salads and pita bread as accompaniments.*

Chickpeas are the foundation of *falafel*. Although the cook prefers dried chickpeas for most Middle Eastern recipes, she uses the canned variety for this one because they are soft and bind well with the other ingredients. For frying the *falafel* cutlets, use a mixture of dark sesame oil and peanut oil. If sesame oil is unavailable or seems too costly, use peanut oil only.

Tahini, a thick paste made of ground raw white sesame seeds, is a popular Middle Eastern condiment. It is readily available in most well-stocked supermarkets and in Middle Eastern markets and health food stores. Because *tahini* turns rancid quickly, refrigerate it after opening and use it within a month. When stored, the oil tends to separate from the paste, so stir the *tahini* to blend it before each use.

WHAT TO DRINK

Ice-cold beer or ale is the best beverage here, though you might prefer to serve a well-chilled Alsace Gewürztraminer or Riesling instead.

SHOPPING LIST AND STAPLES

3 medium-size cucumbers (about 2 pounds total weight)
Small head romaine lettuce
2 small red onions (about ½ pound total weight)
Small yellow onion
2 large cloves plus 1 small clove garlic
Small bunch parsley
Small bunch mint
Small bunch basil
3 large navel oranges
3 medium-size lemons
Large egg
¼ cup milk
1 pint sour cream
8-ounce container plain low-fat yogurt
20-ounce can chickpeas
4-ounce jar tahini
4-ounce bottle dark sesame oil
¼ cup good-quality olive oil
2 tablespoons peanut oil, approximately

218

2 tablespoons honey
5 slices firm-textured white bread
¾ cup fine dried bread crumbs
¾ teaspoon dried thyme
½ teaspoon dried marjoram
1¼ teaspoons paprika
¾ teaspoon ground cumin, approximately
½ teaspoon Cayenne pepper
½ teaspoon ground coriander
Salt and freshly ground black pepper

UTENSILS

Food processor or blender
Large heavy-gauge skillet
Large baking sheet
2 large bowls, 1 nonaluminum
2 medium-size bowls
Small bowl
Colander
Measuring cups and spoons
Chef's knife
Paring knife
Metal spatula
Vegetable peeler

START-TO-FINISH STEPS

1. Crush and peel 1 large and 1 small clove garlic for falafel and cucumbers recipes. Peel and quarter 1 large clove garlic for salad recipe; set aside. Halve 1 lemon and cut into 8 thin slices for falafel recipe. Halve remaining lemons and squeeze enough juice to measure 3 tablespoons for salad recipe and 4 teaspoons for tahini sauce recipe. Peel onions. Quarter yellow onion for falafel recipe and cut enough red onions into ½-inch-thick slices to measure 1½ cups for salad recipe. Wash and dry fresh herbs. Set aside 4 parsley sprigs for garnish and measure ⅓ cup loosely packed sprigs for falafel recipe. Set aside 12 mint sprigs for garnish and finely chop enough mint to measure ⅓ cup for cucumbers recipe. Coarsely chop enough basil leaves to measure ⅓ cup for salad recipe.
2. Follow falafel recipe steps 1 through 4 and rinse food processor or blender.
3. While falafel chills, follow salad recipe steps 1 and 2 and cucumbers recipe steps 1 and 2.
4. Follow tahini sauce recipe steps 1 and 2.
5. Follow salad recipe step 3 and falafel recipe steps 5 and 6.
6. Follow cucumbers recipe step 3 and salad recipe step 4.
7. Follow falafel recipe step 7 and serve with cucumbers and salad.

RECIPES

Falafel Cutlets with Tahini Sauce

20-ounce can chickpeas
5 slices firm-textured white bread
⅓ cup loosely packed parsley sprigs, plus 4 sprigs
    for garnish
½ teaspoon dried marjoram
¾ teaspoon salt
1¼ teaspoons paprika
¼ teaspoon dried thyme
¼ teaspoon ground coriander
¼ teaspoon Cayenne pepper
⅛ teaspoon ground cumin
⅛ teaspoon freshly ground black pepper
Small yellow onion, quartered
Large clove garlic, crushed and peeled
Large egg
1 tablespoon tahini
¾ cup fine dried bread crumbs
1 tablespoon dark sesame oil
2 tablespoons peanut oil, approximately
Tahini Sauce (see following recipe)
8 lemon slices for garnish

1. Rinse and drain chickpeas in colander and pat dry with paper towels.
2. Tear or cut bread into small pieces. In food processor fitted with steel blade, or in blender, combine bread, ⅓ cup parsley, marjoram, salt, ½ teaspoon paprika, thyme, coriander, Cayenne pepper, cumin, and black pepper. Process until bread is reduced to crumbs. Transfer mixture to large bowl.
3. In food processor or blender, combine chickpeas, onion, and garlic, and process until finely chopped. Add to bread-crumb mixture, and stir to combine. Add egg and tahini and stir until well blended.
4. Spoon falafel mixture onto large sheet of aluminum foil, flatten to 1 inch thick, and freeze, wrapped in foil, 20 minutes.
5. Spread dried bread crumbs on plate. Line large baking sheet with waxed paper. Divide falafel mixture into 4 equal portions. Flatten each portion into 6-inch oval cutlet about ¾ inch thick, and dredge each cutlet in dried bread crumbs, pressing to help them adhere. Using metal spatula, transfer cutlets to baking sheet.
6. Heat sesame oil and peanut oil in large heavy-gauge skillet over high heat 1 minute, or until almost smoking. Using spatula, carefully add cutlets and brown 3 minutes on one side. Turn cutlets and brown another 2 minutes, adding more peanut oil if necessary.
7. Divide cutlets among 4 dinner plates. Top with some tahini sauce and sprinkle with remaining paprika. Garnish with lemon slices and parsley sprigs. Serve remaining sauce separately.

Tahini Sauce

1¼ cups sour cream
⅓ cup tahini
¼ cup milk
4 teaspoons freshly squeezed lemon juice
½ teaspoon salt
¼ teaspoon ground coriander

¼ teaspoon ground cumin
¼ teaspoon dried thyme
¼ teaspoon Cayenne pepper

1. Combine all ingredients in container of food processor or blender and process until smooth.
2. Transfer sauce to medium-size bowl, cover with plastic wrap, and set aside at room temperature until ready to serve.

Cucumbers with Mint and Yogurt

3 medium-size cucumbers (about 2 pounds total weight)
1 cup plain low-fat yogurt
⅓ cup finely chopped mint, plus 12 sprigs for garnish
¼ teaspoon ground cumin
Small clove garlic, crushed and peeled
¼ teaspoon salt
⅛ teaspoon freshly ground pepper

1. Peel and trim cucumbers and halve lengthwise. Scoop out seeds with spoon and invert halves onto paper towels to drain.
2. Combine yogurt, chopped mint, cumin, garlic, salt, and pepper in medium-size bowl, and stir to blend. Cover with plastic wrap and set aside.
3. Just before serving, remove garlic clove from yogurt, if desired. Cut cucumber halves crosswise into ½-inch slices. Add slices to yogurt mixture and toss lightly. Divide cucumbers among 4 dinner plates and garnish each serving with 3 mint sprigs.

Red Onion and Orange Salad with Fresh Basil

Small head romaine lettuce
3 large navel oranges
¼ cup good-quality olive oil
3 tablespoons freshly squeezed lemon juice
2 tablespoons honey
⅓ cup coarsely chopped fresh basil
¼ teaspoon dried thyme
⅛ teaspoon freshly ground pepper
Large clove garlic, peeled and quartered
1½ cups sliced red onions

1. Wash romaine and remove any bruised or discolored leaves. Remove 8 leaves and pat dry with paper towels. Wrap leaves in plastic bag and refrigerate until ready to use. Reserve remaining lettuce for another use. Peel oranges, removing all of white pith, and cut crosswise into ¼-inch-thick slices.
2. Combine oil, lemon juice, honey, basil, thyme, pepper, and garlic in small bowl, and stir to blend. Set aside at least 10 minutes to allow flavors to meld.
3. Place one third of orange slices in large nonaluminum bowl and top with one third of onion slices. Discard garlic from dressing and drizzle one third of dressing over salad. Layer remaining oranges, onion, and dressing in same manner. Set aside until ready to serve.
4. To serve, divide lettuce among 4 dinner plates and top with salad.

220

This bright-yellow pudding, which is studded with pistachios and candied fruits, is well worth the lengthy preparation time. For the best flavor, make the pudding a day or two ahead, refrigerate it, and unmold it just before serving.

Saffron Rice Pudding with Wildflower Honey Sauce

2½ cups milk
¼ teaspoon saffron threads
½ cup long-grain white rice
¼ cup chopped mixed candied fruits
¼ cup chopped blanched pistachio nuts
1 envelope unflavored gelatin (1 tablespoon)
⅔ cup granulated sugar
4 egg yolks
½ teaspoon vanilla extract
¼ teaspoon almond extract
1 cup plain low-fat yogurt

Wildflower Honey Sauce:
⅓ cup wildflower honey
1 tablespoon freshly squeezed lemon juice
Pinch of cinnamon

1. Pour 1½ cups milk into small heavy-gauge saucepan. Crush saffron threads and add to milk. Bring mixture to a boil over medium heat. When milk boils, reduce heat to low and stir in rice. Cook rice, uncovered, 10 minutes. Cover pan and cook another 10 to 15 minutes, or until rice is tender and all milk is absorbed.
2. Transfer rice to large bowl and stir in candied fruits and 3 tablespoons pistachios.
3. In same small saucepan, combine remaining 1 cup milk, gelatin, and sugar. Cook mixture over low heat, stirring constantly, 5 minutes, or until gelatin dissolves completely. Remove from heat and set aside.
4. In small bowl, beat egg yolks lightly. Whisk a little hot-milk mixture into yolks, pour yolk mixture back into pan, and whisk until combined. Cook over low heat, stirring, 3 to 5 minutes, or until mixture becomes slightly thickened.
5. Remove pan from heat and stir milk mixture into rice. Add vanilla, almond extract, and yogurt, and stir to combine. Set pudding aside to cool 30 minutes. Meanwhile, butter 2-quart melon-shaped mold or other decorative 2-quart mold.
6. When cooled, stir pudding well and spoon into prepared mold. Cover mold with plastic wrap and chill 3 to 4 hours, or until pudding is firm.
7. Meanwhile, prepare wildflower honey sauce: Combine honey, lemon juice, and cinnamon in small bowl. Stir to combine and set aside.
8. To unmold pudding, dip mold briefly in hot water and invert over small serving platter. Top pudding with some sauce and sprinkle with remaining 1 tablespoon pistachios. Serve remaining sauce separately.

Sautéed Chicken Breasts with Walnut-Yogurt Sauce
Tabbouleh Salad
Melon Kabobs with Honey and Orange-Flower Water

Let everyone help themselves to chicken with walnut-yogurt sauce, tabbouleh *salad, and skewered melon pieces.*

Every Middle Eastern country has its own version of *tabbouleh*, a cracked-wheat salad with chopped tomato, parsley, mint, and olive oil. This Jordanian recipe calls for bulgur, a type of wheat that has been steamed and dried. Because of the processing, bulgur needs only brief soaking in boiling water to be ready for the salad.

WHAT TO DRINK

An acidic or full-bodied white wine would make a good foil for these dishes. If you like acidic liveliness, choose an Italian Pinot Grigio or Verdicchio; for fuller body, select a California Chardonnay or Pinot Blanc.

SHOPPING LIST AND STAPLES

2 whole skinless, boneless chicken breasts, pounded thin (about 1¼ pounds total weight)
5 medium-size plum tomatoes (about 1 pound total weight)
Medium-size carrot
1 small plus 2 medium-size yellow onions
Medium-size clove garlic
Large bunch parsley
Small bunch mint
Small cantaloupe (about 2 pounds)
Small honeydew melon (about 2½ pounds)
2 lemons
8-ounce container plain low-fat yogurt
1 cup chicken stock, preferably homemade (see page 13), or canned
⅓ cup good-quality olive oil, approximately
⅓ cup honey
4-ounce bottle orange-flower water
8-ounce package bulgur
3-ounce can walnut pieces
1 slice firm-textured white bread
2 teaspoons sweet paprika
½ teaspoon dried marjoram
¼ teaspoon dried thyme
Salt and freshly ground pepper

UTENSILS

Food processor or blender
Large heavy-gauge skillet
2 small saucepans, 1 heavy-gauge

2 large nonaluminum bowls
Large heatproof bowl
Medium-size nonaluminum bowl
3 small bowls
Large fine sieve
Measuring cups and spoons
Chef's knife
Paring knife
2 wooden spoons
Rubber spatula
Citrus juicer (optional)
Ladle
Whisk
Metal tongs
Four 12-inch skewers
Melon baller

START-TO-FINISH STEPS

1. Peel onions. Quarter small onion for chicken recipe. Coarsely chop medium-size onions for salad recipe; set aside. Halve lemons and squeeze enough juice to measure 2 tablespoons for salad recipe, 2 tablespoons for melon recipe, and 1½ teaspoons for chicken recipe. Wash and dry parsley and mint. Coarsely chop enough parsley to measure ⅓ cup for salad recipe and finely chop enough to measure 1 teaspoon for chicken recipe. Reserve 10 mint sprigs for melon recipe and coarsely chop enough mint to measure ¼ cup for salad recipe.
2. Follow chicken recipe steps 1 through 3.
3. While stock simmers, follow salad recipe steps 1 through 4 and melon recipe steps 1 and 2.
4. Follow chicken recipe steps 4 and 5 and salad recipe step 5.
5. Follow chicken recipe steps 6 and 7.
6. Follow salad recipe step 6, chicken recipe step 8, and serve.
7. Follow melon recipe step 3 and serve for dessert.

RECIPES

Sautéed Chicken Breasts with Walnut-Yogurt Sauce

Medium-size clove garlic
Medium-size carrot
1 cup chicken stock
Small yellow onion, quartered

½ teaspoon dried marjoram
¼ teaspoon dried thyme
1 slice firm-textured white bread
¾ cup walnut pieces
2 teaspoons sweet paprika
1½ teaspoons freshly squeezed lemon juice
¼ teaspoon salt
⅛ teaspoon freshly ground pepper
½ cup plain low-fat yogurt
2 whole skinless, boneless chicken breasts, pounded
   thin (about 1¼ pounds total weight)
4 teaspoons good-quality olive oil
1 teaspoon finely chopped parsley for garnish

1. Crush and peel garlic. Peel, trim, and thinly slice carrot into rounds.
2. Combine stock, garlic, carrot, onion, marjoram, and thyme in small heavy-gauge saucepan. Bring mixture to a boil over high heat, reduce heat to medium-low, and simmer 25 minutes.
3. Meanwhile, tear bread into small pieces and place in food processor or blender with ½ cup walnuts and paprika. Process until bread is reduced to fine crumbs; transfer to small bowl and set aside.
4. After stock mixture has cooked, remove ½ cup liquid from saucepan and set aside in another small bowl.
5. Transfer remaining stock mixture to food processor or blender. Add bread-crumb mixture, lemon juice, salt, pepper, and yogurt, and process until well combined. Transfer walnut-yogurt sauce to medium-size nonaluminum bowl, cover loosely with plastic wrap, and set aside.
6. Rinse chicken breasts and dry with paper towels. Heat oil in large heavy-gauge skillet over high heat 1 to 1½ minutes, or until almost smoking. Add chicken breasts, reduce heat to medium-high, and sauté chicken 3 to 4 minutes on one side, or until browned. Using tongs, turn chicken and sauté another 3 to 4 minutes. Transfer chicken to serving platter and keep warm on stove top.
7. Add reserved ½ cup stock to skillet and boil over high heat 1 minute, scraping up browned bits from bottom of pan. Pour into walnut-yogurt sauce and stir to combine.
8. To serve, spoon sauce over chicken and sprinkle with remaining ¼ cup walnut pieces and finely chopped parsley.

Tabbouleh Salad

5 medium-size plum tomatoes
   (about 1 pound total weight)

¾ cup bulgur
⅓ cup coarsely chopped parsley
¼ cup coarsely chopped mint
2 medium-size yellow onions, coarsely chopped
¼ cup good-quality olive oil
2 tablespoons freshly squeezed lemon juice
1½ teaspoons salt
⅛ teaspoon freshly ground pepper

1. Bring 1½ cups water to a boil in small saucepan over high heat.
2. Meanwhile, wash tomatoes and dry with paper towels. Coarsely chop 4 tomatoes; cut remaining tomato lengthwise into wedges. Set aside.
3. Place bulgur in large heatproof bowl. Add boiling water, stir, and let mixture stand 20 minutes.
4. Meanwhile, combine chopped tomatoes, parsley, mint, onions, olive oil, lemon juice, salt, and pepper in large nonaluminum bowl.
5. After 20 minutes, turn bulgur into large fine sieve and drain very well. Add bulgur to tomato mixture and toss to combine; set aside until ready to serve.
6. To serve, toss salad again and mound on serving platter. Garnish with tomato wedges.

Melon Kabobs with Honey and Orange-Flower Water

Small cantaloupe (about 2 pounds)
Small honeydew melon (about 2½ pounds)
⅓ cup honey
2 tablespoons freshly squeezed lemon juice
1 tablespoon orange-flower water
10 mint sprigs for garnish

1. Halve melons and discard seeds. Cut cantaloupe lengthwise into 1½-inch-wide wedges; trim off and discard rind. Cut cantaloupe wedges into 1½-inch cubes and place in large nonaluminum bowl. Using large end of melon baller, scoop flesh of honeydew melon into balls; add to bowl with cantaloupe.
2. Place honey, lemon juice, and orange-flower water in small bowl and whisk to combine. Pour over melon and toss well. Cover bowl and refrigerate until shortly before serving.
3. To serve, skewer cantaloupe cubes and honeydew balls alternately on four 12-inch skewers. Place skewers on serving dish and garnish with mint.

Rowena M. Hubbard

MENU 1 (Left)
Moroccan Couscous
Harissa
Orange and Olive Salad

MENU 2
Braised Lamb with Apricots
Parslied Rice
Cucumber Salad with Pickled Beets
and Black Olives

MENU 3
Spicy Chicken with Olives
Cracked-Wheat Pilaf
Zucchini and Tomato Salad with Almonds

After many years of cooking professionally—and sampling the cuisines of many countries—Rowena Hubbard has found the vibrant and aromatic foods of Morocco to be especially delicious. "I love well-seasoned food," she says, "and I admire the way Moroccan cooks know how to use spices so that the basic ingredients in a dish are not overpowered."

In her first menu, she presents *couscous*, an elaborate and spicy dish that is found throughout the Maghreb (a region that includes the northern parts of Morocco, Algeria, Tunisia, and Libya). Of Berber origin, *couscous* exists in as many versions as there are cooks. Although it can be made with grains such as millet and barley, it is most often prepared with *couscous* grains, for which the dish is named. In North Africa, a cook may spend several hours steaming and tenderizing *couscous* grains in a special two-tiered pot called a *couscousière*. Rowena Hubbard shortens this lengthy process by simmering the grains in chicken stock. The accompanying stewed lamb with vegetables, and fiery *harissa*, a sauce made of chilies, garlic, olive oil, and spices, should be spooned over the *couscous* grains.

Menu 2 contrasts spicy-sweet lamb and apricots with a cucumber-yogurt salad. Both dishes are complemented by parslied rice. In the easy-to-prepare Menu 3, chicken breasts are baked with lemons, olives, and a typically Moroccan mixture of spices. With the chicken, the cook serves a flavorful zucchini and tomato salad and cracked-wheat pilaf.

This lavish meal is great for a party. The lamb and vegetable stew is spooned on top of the golden couscous *grains, then sparked with red-hot* harissa *sauce. Temper the spices with a refreshing orange and olive salad.*

225

Moroccan Couscous
Harissa
Orange and Olive Salad

Golden grains of *couscous*, made from finely ground semolina wheat, are sold in bulk in Middle Eastern markets and health food stores, or packaged in many supermarkets and specialty food shops. Avoid instant *couscous*; it is an inferior substitute for the real thing. Store any extra uncooked *couscous* in an airtight container in a cool dry place, where it will keep indefinitely.

The *harissa* recipe calls for tiny, very hot Mexican *pequín* chilies. Sold in some southwestern supermarkets, *pequíns* are commonly found in Mexican groceries. If you prefer, you can use red pepper flakes, or purchase ready-made *harissa* in sauce or paste form. *Harissa* should be stored in a tightly sealed container in the refrigerator.

WHAT TO DRINK

With this spicy main dish, you can choose from several beverage options: ice-cold beer, especially dark beer; a light red wine, such as chilled Beaujolais or California Gamay; a spicy white wine such as California or Alsace Gewürztraminer; or a lightly sweet German Riesling.

SHOPPING LIST AND STAPLES

2 pounds boneless leg of lamb, cut into 1-inch cubes
3 large zucchini (about 2¼ pounds total weight)
2 large ripe tomatoes (about 1½ pounds total weight)
2 medium-size yellow onions (about 1 pound total weight)
4 medium-size carrots (about ¾ pound total weight)
2 medium-size cloves garlic
Small bunch coriander (optional)
Small bunch parsley
3 large navel oranges (about 2 pounds total weight)
2 medium-size lemons
4 tablespoons unsalted butter
2 cups chicken stock, preferably homemade (see page 13), or canned (optional)
15½-ounce can chickpeas
4¾-ounce jar pimiento-stuffed olives
½ cup good-quality olive oil, approximately
1 pound medium-grain couscous
15-ounce box golden raisins
2 teaspoons dried pequín chilies, or 2 teaspoons dried red pepper flakes
2¼ teaspoons ground cumin
1 teaspoon caraway seeds (optional)

¼ teaspoon powdered saffron
½ teaspoon ground ginger
Salt and freshly ground black pepper

UTENSILS

Food processor (optional)
Large heavy-gauge nonaluminum skillet with cover
Medium-size saucepan with cover
Small saucepan
Large heatproof platter
Large heatproof serving bowl
Large bowl
Small bowl
Strainer
Measuring cups and spoons
Chef's knife
Paring knife
2 wooden spoons
Mortar and pestle (optional)

START-TO-FINISH STEPS

1. Follow Moroccan couscous recipe steps 1 through 5 and couscous grains recipe step 1.
2. While lamb cooks, follow salad recipe steps 1 through 4 and harissa recipe steps 1 through 3.
3. Follow couscous grains recipe steps 2 and 3.
4. Follow Moroccan couscous recipe step 6 and harissa recipe step 4.
5. Follow salad recipe step 5, couscous grains recipe step 4, Moroccan couscous recipe step 7, and serve with harissa.

RECIPES

Moroccan Couscous

2 pounds boneless leg of lamb, cut into 1-inch cubes
2 medium-size yellow onions (about 1 pound total weight)
3 large zucchini (about 2¼ pounds total weight)
4 medium-size carrots (about ¾ pound total weight)
15½-ounce can chickpeas
1 cup golden raisins
2 tablespoons unsalted butter
½ teaspoon ground ginger
½ teaspoon salt

½ teaspoon freshly ground black pepper
¼ teaspoon powdered saffron
2 large ripe tomatoes (about 1½ pounds total weight)
Small bunch parsley
Couscous Grains (see following recipe)

1. Preheat oven to 200 degrees. If butcher has not done so already, cut lamb into 1-inch cubes. Set aside.
2. Peel onions; cut into ½-inch-thick wedges. Wash and dry zucchini and trim ends. Wash, peel, and trim carrots. Using food processor fitted with medium slicing blade, or chef's knife, cut zucchini and carrots into ¼-inch-thick rounds. Rinse and drain chickpeas in strainer.
3. In large bowl, combine onions, zucchini, carrots, chickpeas, and raisins. Toss to mix well; set aside.
4. Melt butter in large heavy-gauge nonaluminum skillet over medium-high heat. Stir in ginger, salt, pepper, and saffron and cook until butter foams. Add lamb and cook, tossing to coat with seasonings, 2 to 3 minutes, or until browned.
5. Stir in vegetable mixture and ½ cup water. Cover, reduce heat to low, and simmer 20 to 25 minutes, or until lamb and vegetables are tender. Place large heatproof serving platter in oven to warm.
6. Wash tomatoes and dry with paper towels. Core tomatoes and chop coarsely. Wash and dry parsley. Trim stems and discard. Finely chop enough sprigs to measure ⅓ cup.
7. Fold tomatoes and parsley into lamb mixture and turn onto warmed serving platter. Serve with couscous grains. Or, if you prefer, serve the lamb and vegetables over the grains in serving bowl.

Couscous Grains

2 cups chicken stock (optional)
2 tablespoons unsalted butter
½ teaspoon salt
2 cups medium-grain couscous

1. Place large heatproof serving bowl in 200-degree oven to warm.
2. Combine stock or 2 cups water, butter, and salt in medium-size saucepan over high heat and bring to a boil.
3. When water boils, add couscous grains, stirring until grains are well moistened. Cover pan, remove from heat, and let grains stand for 5 minutes.
4. Turn couscous grains into warmed serving bowl.

Harissa

1 teaspoon caraway seeds (optional)
2 teaspoons dried pequín chilies or dried red pepper
  flakes
2 medium-size cloves garlic
3 tablespoons good-quality olive oil
2 teaspoons ground cumin
½ teaspoon salt

1. If using caraway seeds, grind seeds using mortar and pestle. Crush chilies, if using, in mortar with pestle or under flat blade of chef's knife. Crush and peel garlic.

2. Combine ground caraway seeds, crushed chilies and garlic, and remaining ingredients in small saucepan and sauté, stirring constantly, over medium-high heat, about 2 minutes, or until garlic is light brown.
3. Remove pan from heat and set harissa aside to cool.
4. Pour harissa into small serving bowl. You will have about ¼ cup.

Orange and Olive Salad

3 large navel oranges (about 2 pounds total weight)
2 medium-size lemons
Small bunch coriander (optional)
4¾-ounce jar pimiento-stuffed olives
¼ cup good-quality olive oil
¼ teaspoon ground cumin

1. Peel oranges, removing as much white pith as possible. Cut oranges crosswise into ½-inch-thick slices. Arrange slices in overlapping pattern on large serving platter.
2. Halve lemons and squeeze enough juice to measure ⅓ cup. Wash and dry coriander, if using. Reserving 4 sprigs for garnish, chop enough remaining coriander to measure 2 tablespoons. Drain olives and chop enough to measure ½ cup.
3. Combine chopped olives, olive oil, lemon juice, chopped coriander, and cumin in small bowl. Stir briefly and spoon sauce over oranges.
4. Cover oranges with plastic wrap and refrigerate until serving time.
5. Just before serving, garnish salad with coriander sprigs, if desired.

___

ADDED TOUCH

These pastries are popular throughout Morocco. You can assemble them ahead and freeze them until needed.

Gazelle Horns

8-ounce package almond paste (1 cup)
1 cup confectioners' sugar
1 tablespoon rose water
17¼-ounce package frozen puff pastry sheets, thawed

1. Preheat oven to 450 degrees. Using food processor or heavy-duty electric mixer, combine almond paste, sugar, and rose water and mix well.
2. Using about 2 tablespoons for each, roll almond paste mixture into twenty-four 4-inch logs.
3. Unfold pastry sheets and cover with damp towel. Cut 24 rectangles of pastry, each 1½ by 4½ inches.
4. Wrap one piece of pastry around each almond log. Brush water over long edges and ends of pastry, and press together to seal. Form each log into crescent shape.
5. Place horns on ungreased baking sheets and prick tops with fork.
6. Bake 10 minutes, or until horns are lightly browned.
7. Using metal spatula, transfer gazelle horns to wire rack to cool. Serve when cool.

Braised Lamb with Apricots
Parslied Rice
Cucumber Salad with Pickled Beets and Black Olives

Lamb with apricots and almonds, served with parslied rice and cucumbers, beets, and olives, will surely delight guests.

The lamb dish is a variation on a traditional Moroccan *tagine* (stew), which requires lengthy cooking because tough cuts of lamb are generally used. Here the cook uses round-bone lamb chops, which are tender and cook in less than an hour. This quick method retains all the flavors of the original dish with much less fuss.

Whole roasted salted almonds are added to the lamb dish toward the end of the cooking time. If you purchase whole natural almonds instead, roast them as follows: Spread the almonds in a single layer on a baking sheet. Place the sheet in a cold oven, then turn the oven to 350 degrees and bake 12 minutes, or until the almonds are golden. Remove the almonds from the oven, sprinkle with a teaspoon of salt, and allow them to cool. The nuts will continue to brown slightly as they cool.

The orange-flower water used to perfume the lamb is made by distilling orange blossoms. This fragrant water is sold in liquor stores, well-stocked supermarkets, and Middle Eastern and Indian markets. The dish can be made without orange-flower water; it will be slightly less authentic but no less delicious.

WHAT TO DRINK

The lamb and its accompaniments need a full-bodied red wine such as a Margaux or similar wine from one of the other Bordeaux communes.

SHOPPING LIST AND STAPLES

Four 1-inch-thick round-bone lamb chops
(about 1½ pounds total weight)
4 medium-size cucumbers (about 2½ pounds total weight)
Large onion
2 large cloves garlic
Small bunch each mint, coriander, and parsley
½ pint plain yogurt
4 tablespoons unsalted butter
3 cups chicken stock, preferably homemade
(see page 13), or canned
8¼-ounce jar sliced pickled beets
10-ounce jar salt-cured black olives
8-ounce jar honey

4-ounce bottle orange-flower water
1½ cups long-grain white rice
5 ounces whole roasted salted almonds
8-ounce package dried apricot halves
½ teaspoon ground ginger
½ teaspoon cinnamon
½ teaspoon powdered saffron
Salt and freshly ground pepper

UTENSILS

Food processor (optional)
Large deep heavy-gauge skillet with cover
Medium-size heavy-gauge saucepan with cover
Medium-size bowl
Strainer
Measuring cups and spoons
Chef's knife
Paring knife
2 wooden spoons
Grater (if not using food processor)
Metal tongs

START-TO-FINISH STEPS

1. Follow lamb recipe steps 1 through 5.
2. While lamb is cooking, follow salad recipe steps 1 through 3 and rice recipe steps 1 through 3.
3. Follow lamb recipe step 6 and rice recipe step 4.
4. Follow salad recipe step 4.
5. Follow rice recipe step 5, lamb recipe step 7, and serve with salad.

RECIPES

Braised Lamb with Apricots

Four 1-inch-thick round-bone lamb chops
   (about 1½ pounds total weight)
2 large cloves garlic
Large onion
2 tablespoons unsalted butter
½ teaspoon ground ginger
½ teaspoon cinnamon
½ teaspoon freshly ground pepper
⅛ teaspoon powdered saffron
1 cup dried apricot halves
1 cup whole roasted salted almonds
¼ cup honey
½ teaspoon orange-flower water

1. Pat lamb chops dry with paper towels.
2. Crush garlic under flat blade of chef's knife; remove and discard peels. Peel onion and cut into ½-inch wedges.
3. Melt butter over medium-high heat in large deep heavy-gauge skillet. Stir in garlic, ginger, cinnamon, pepper, and saffron, and cook 2 minutes.
4. Add lamb chops and turn to coat both sides with seasonings. Sauté about 3 minutes on one side, or until slightly

browned. Turn with tongs and sauté another 3 minutes, or until browned.
5. Add onion, apricots, and ¼ cup water. Cover skillet, reduce heat to low, and cook lamb mixture 25 minutes.
6. After 25 minutes, remove cover, turn chops over, and add almonds. Drizzle in honey and sprinkle with orange-flower water. Cook chops, uncovered, another 15 minutes, or until tender.
7. Place 1 chop on each dinner plate and top with onion, apricots, almonds, and any remaining cooking liquid.

Parslied Rice

2 tablespoons unsalted butter
1½ cups long-grain white rice
3 cups chicken stock
¼ teaspoon salt
Small bunch parsley

1. Melt butter over medium-high heat in medium-size heavy-gauge saucepan.
2. Add rice and stir to coat thoroughly with butter.
3. Add chicken stock and salt, cover pan, and reduce heat to low. Cook rice 20 to 25 minutes, or until stock is completely absorbed and rice is fluffy.
4. Wash and dry parsley. Trim stems and discard. Finely chop enough sprigs to measure ¼ cup; set aside.
5. Just before serving, add parsley to rice and toss until evenly distributed. Divide rice among 4 dinner plates and serve.

Cucumber Salad with Pickled Beets and Black Olives

4 medium-size cucumbers (about 2½ pounds total weight)
Small bunch mint
Small bunch coriander
¾ cup plain yogurt
½ teaspoon salt
8¼-ounce jar sliced pickled beets
¼ pound salt-cured black olives (about ⅔ cup)

1. Wash and dry cucumbers. Halve lengthwise and scoop out seeds using teaspoon; do not peel. Wash and dry mint and coriander; trim stems and discard. Reserving 4 mint sprigs for garnish, finely chop enough mint to measure ¼ cup. Finely chop enough coriander to measure ¼ cup. Set aside.
2. Using food processor fitted with medium shredding disk, or grater, shred cucumbers. You should have about 2 cups shredded cucumbers. Squeeze out excess liquid from cucumbers in double thickness of paper towels.
3. Combine chopped mint and coriander, yogurt, and salt in medium-size bowl. Add cucumbers and stir to coat with dressing. Set aside at room temperature until ready to serve.
4. Just before serving, drain beets in strainer and dry with paper towels. Divide cucumber mixture, pickled beets, and olives among 4 salad plates and garnish each plate with a mint sprig.

Spicy Chicken with Olives
Cracked-Wheat Pilaf
Zucchini and Tomato Salad with Almonds

The essence of Moroccan cooking is captured in the main-course chicken dish, with its intriguing blend of seasonings. The side dishes are a pilaf made with cracked wheat, and zucchini sticks with cherry tomatoes and slivered almonds.

This light chicken dish balances the contrasting flavors of green olives, lemon, and cinnamon. In Morocco, special lemons preserved in salt and their own juice would be used, but here salty olives, lemon juice, and lemon zest are substituted.

WHAT TO DRINK

Choose either a spicy Gewürztraminer from Alsace or California or an acidic Sauvignon Blanc from California, Italy, or the French Loire.

SHOPPING LIST AND STAPLES

4 large boneless chicken breasts, halved, with skin intact (about 2¼ pounds total weight)
6 small zucchini (about 2 pounds total weight)
1 pint cherry tomatoes
Small bunch scallions
3 large cloves garlic
Small bunch coriander
4 medium-size lemons
6 tablespoons unsalted butter
3½ cups chicken stock, preferably homemade (see page 13), or canned
6-ounce can pitted green olives
15½-ounce can chickpeas
½ cup mild olive oil
10 ounces cracked wheat
4-ounce bag slivered almonds
1 teaspoon ground ginger
½ teaspoon cinnamon
¼ teaspoon ground cumin
¼ teaspoon Cayenne pepper, approximately
Salt and freshly ground black pepper

UTENSILS

2 medium-size heavy-gauge saucepans with covers
Small nonaluminum saucepan
14 x 7 x 2-inch nonaluminum baking dish
Small baking sheet
Medium-size nonaluminum bowl
Colander
Large strainer
Measuring cups and spoons
Chef's knife

Paring knife
3 wooden spoons
Grater
Zester (optional)

START-TO-FINISH STEPS

1. Wash and dry lemons. Thinly slice 1 lemon for chicken recipe. Using zester or fine side of grater, grate enough zest from 1 lemon to measure 1 teaspoon for chicken recipe. Squeeze enough lemon juice to measure ¼ cup for chicken recipe and ⅓ cup for salad recipe.
2. Follow chicken recipe steps 1 through 7 and salad recipe steps 1 through 4.
3. Follow cracked-wheat recipe steps 1 through 3.
4. While cracked wheat cooks, follow chicken recipe step 8 and salad recipe steps 5 through 7.
5. Follow cracked-wheat recipe step 4, chicken recipe step 9, salad recipe step 8, and serve.

RECIPES

Spicy Chicken with Olives

3 large cloves garlic
4 large boneless chicken breasts, halved, with skin intact (about 2¼ pounds total weight)
4 tablespoons unsalted butter
1 teaspoon grated lemon zest
1 teaspoon ground ginger
½ teaspoon cinnamon
½ teaspoon freshly ground black pepper
⅛ teaspoon Cayenne pepper
6-ounce can pitted green olives
15½-ounce can chickpeas
Small bunch scallions
Small bunch coriander
¼ cup freshly squeezed lemon juice
1 lemon, thinly sliced
¼ cup mild olive oil

1. Preheat oven to 400 degrees. Crush garlic under flat blade of chef's knife; remove and discard peels. Set aside.
2. Wash and dry chicken breasts. If butcher has not done so already, halve breasts. Place breast halves, skin-side up, in 14 x 7 x 2-inch nonaluminum baking dish.
3. Melt butter over medium heat in small nonaluminum saucepan. Add lemon zest to butter. Stir in garlic, ginger, cinnamon, black pepper, and Cayenne pepper, and mix well. Drizzle sauce over chicken.
4. Bake chicken, uncovered, in lower half of oven 30 minutes.
5. Meanwhile, drain olives. Place chickpeas in large strainer, rinse under cold running water, and set aside to drain.
6. Wash and dry scallions and coriander. Trim ends and discard. Thinly slice enough scallions to measure ½ cup. Finely chop enough coriander to measure ¼ cup.
7. Combine lemon juice, lemon slices, scallions, coriander,

and olive oil in medium-size nonaluminum bowl. Add drained olives and chickpeas and stir to combine. Set aside, stirring occasionally.
8. After chicken has baked 30 minutes, reduce oven temperature to 350 degrees. Spoon olive mixture over chicken and bake another 15 minutes, or until juices run clear when chicken is pierced with a knife.
9. Transfer chicken to serving platter and top with olive mixture and pan juices.

Cracked-Wheat Pilaf

2 tablespoons unsalted butter
1½ cups cracked wheat
3½ cups chicken stock
Salt and freshly ground pepper

1. Melt butter over high heat in medium-size heavy-gauge saucepan.
2. Add cracked wheat and cook, stirring, about 1 minute, or until all kernels are coated and wheat is lightly toasted.
3. Add chicken stock, cover pan, and reduce heat to low. Cook cracked wheat 35 to 40 minutes, or until tender but still firm to the bite.
4. Add salt and pepper to taste and turn pilaf into large serving bowl.

Zucchini and Tomato Salad with Almonds

6 small zucchini (about 2 pounds total weight)
⅓ cup freshly squeezed lemon juice
¼ cup mild olive oil
¼ teaspoon ground cumin
¼ teaspoon freshly ground black pepper
¼ teaspoon salt
Dash of Cayenne pepper
¼ cup slivered almonds
1 pint cherry tomatoes

1. Wash and dry zucchini; trim but do not peel. Cut zucchini into ¼-inch-thick by 2-inch-long sticks.
2. Place zucchini sticks in medium-size heavy-gauge saucepan and add ⅓ cup water. Cover and cook over high heat 1 to 2 minutes, or until crisp-tender.
3. Turn zucchini into colander and drain well. Transfer zucchini to large serving bowl and toss with lemon juice, oil, cumin, black pepper, salt, and Cayenne.
4. Cover bowl with plastic wrap and refrigerate zucchini at least 30 minutes.
5. Spread almonds on small baking sheet and toast in 350-degree oven 5 to 7 minutes, or until golden, shaking pan occasionally to prevent scorching.
6. Meanwhile, wash and dry tomatoes. Remove stems, if necessary, and cut tomatoes in half; set aside.
7. Remove almonds from oven and turn out onto paper towels to cool briefly.
8. Just before serving, add tomatoes to zucchini and toss to combine. Sprinkle toasted almonds over salad and serve.

Joyce Goldstein

A n ardent world traveler, Joyce Goldstein attributes her eclectic cooking style to her fascination with international cuisines, particularly the foods of the Mediterranean. Unlike many of her contemporaries, who prefer to experiment with recipes, she sticks to tradition. "I am a classicist and a scholar," she says. "I research dishes in numerous cookbooks, and from seven versions of the same recipe I will pick the one that seems truest and then follow it exactly." As a consequence, when you sample her dinners—two from Portugal and one from Turkey—you will have eaten as the natives do.

The dramatic Portuguese main dish of clams and sausage (*amêijoas na cataplana*) in Menu 1 is from the Algarve region. Traditionally it is cooked in a *cataplana*, a clam-shaped copper cooking vessel with a tight-fitting lid, which you open at the table for an appetizing burst of aromas. However, as Joyce Goldstein shows, you can prepare this dish just as successfully in a covered sauté pan.

Menu 3, also from Portugal, begins with a lusty garlic and bread soup, followed by sweet-tart pork with peppers and onions from the Alenteja region. The fried new potatoes—a ubiquitous Portuguese dish—may be served on one side of the plate or, more traditionally, arranged in a ring around the meat.

For the Turkish dinner of Menu 2, the cook presents a spinach soup with yogurt, then offers broiled marinated chicken, and a pilaf enlivened with currants and toasted pistachios. The marinade for the chicken, a mixture of olive oil, lemon juice, onion, garlic, and cinnamon, may be used on cubed lamb as well.

This Portuguese meal begins with a rich chicken soup flavored with lemon and mint. Follow the soup with spicy clams and sausage and a light tossed salad.

Portuguese Chicken Soup
Steamed Clams and Sausage in Spicy Sauce
Mixed Green Salad

Littlenecks are hard-shelled clams native to the coastal waters off New England and Long Island. If you cannot get littlenecks, use whatever small clams are available in your local fish market. Select only those clams with tightly closed shells. After you bring the clams home, scrub them with a stiff brush under cold water, and discard any with cracked or broken shells. Once cooked, discard any that do not open.

Spicy, garlicky Portuguese *linguiça* sausage—or the similar Spanish *chorizo*—is often added to cooked dishes for a flavor accent. Look for these sausages in Latin American or Caribbean markets or in well-stocked supermarkets. Smoked and dry-cured *linguiça* keeps well at room temperature for several days; made of fresh pork, *chorizo* requires refrigeration. If you like, serve the clams and sausage with a loaf or two of crusty bread, or spooned over white rice.

WHAT TO DRINK

You could drink a white or a red wine with this meal, but in either case, your first choice should be Portuguese. Try a Dão for the red; a crisp, clean Vinho Verde for the white. If Portuguese wine is not available, serve a white or red Spanish Rioja.

SHOPPING LIST AND STAPLES

24 to 36 littleneck clams
1 whole skinless, boneless chicken breast (about 1 pound)
¾ pound linguiça or chorizo sausage
⅓ pound prosciutto (6 to 7 medium-thin slices)
Small head romaine lettuce
1 head Boston or small head red leaf lettuce
1 bunch watercress
1 small plus 2 medium-size red onions
6 medium-size cloves garlic
Small bunch parsley
Small bunch mint
Small bunch coriander (optional)
2 large lemons
35-ounce can Italian plum tomatoes
4 cups chicken stock, preferably homemade (see page 13), or canned
1 cup fruity olive oil
6-ounce can pitted black olives

1 cup long-grain white rice
2 teaspoons paprika
1 teaspoon dried oregano
1 teaspoon red pepper flakes, approximately
3 bay leaves
Salt and freshly ground black pepper
1 cup dry white wine

UTENSILS

Large sauté pan with cover
Medium-size saucepan
Small heavy-gauge saucepan with cover
Salad bowl
Medium-size nonaluminum bowl
Small nonaluminum bowl
Salad spinner (optional)
Strainer
Measuring cups and spoons
Chef's knife
Paring knife
2 wooden spoons
Slotted spoon
Ladle
Whisk
Citrus juicer (optional)

START-TO-FINISH STEPS

1. Wash parsley, mint, and coriander if using, and dry with paper towels. Trim stems and discard. Chop enough parsley to measure ½ cup for clams recipe. Chop enough mint to measure 6 tablespoons for soup recipe. If using coriander, chop enough to measure ⅓ cup for salad recipe. Reserve remaining herbs for another use. Squeeze enough lemon juice to measure ¼ cup each for soup and salad recipes; set aside.
2. Follow salad recipe steps 1 through 4.
3. Follow soup recipe step 1.
4. While rice simmers, follow clams recipe steps 1 through 5.
5. Follow soup recipe step 2 and clams recipe steps 6 through 11.
6. While onions are cooking, follow soup recipe steps 3 through 5.
7. While chicken simmers, follow clams recipe steps 12 and 13.

8. While sauce simmers, follow soup recipe steps 6 and 7 and serve as first course.

9. Follow clams recipe steps 14 and 15.

10. While clams are steaming, follow salad recipe step 5.

11. Follow clams recipe step 16 and serve with salad.

RECIPES

Portuguese Chicken Soup

4 cups chicken stock
1 cup long-grain white rice
1 whole skinless, boneless chicken breast (about
    1 pound)
¼ cup lemon juice
Salt and freshly ground black pepper
6 tablespoons chopped mint

1. Combine 1 cup stock and 1 cup water in small heavy-gauge saucepan and bring to a boil over high heat. Stir in rice, cover pan, and reduce heat to low. Simmer rice gently, undisturbed, about 20 minutes, or until all liquid is absorbed.

2. When rice is cooked, remove from heat and set aside, covered.

3. Pour remaining 3 cups chicken stock into medium-size saucepan and bring to a simmer over medium-high heat.

4. Meanwhile, rinse chicken breast under cold running water and dry with paper towel. Cut chicken into 1-inch-long by ½-inch-wide strips.

5. Add chicken to stock, reduce heat to medium, and simmer gently, uncovered, 3 minutes.

6. Stir in rice, lemon juice, and salt and pepper to taste.

7. Add mint, pour soup into large serving bowl, tureen, or 4 individual soup bowls, and serve immediately.

Steamed Clams and Sausage in Spicy Sauce

24 to 36 littleneck clams
2 medium-size red onions
6 medium-size cloves garlic
35-ounce can Italian plum tomatoes
¾ pound linguiça or chorizo sausage
½ cup fruity olive oil
⅓ pound prosciutto (6 to 7 medium-thin slices)
2 teaspoons paprika
1 teaspoon red pepper flakes, approximately
1 cup dry white wine
3 bay leaves
1 teaspoon dried oregano
Salt and freshly ground black pepper
½ cup chopped parsley

1. Wash clams well. Keep cold until ready to steam.

2. Peel onions and cut enough crosswise into ⅛-inch-thick slices to measure about 2 cups; set aside.

3. Crush and peel garlic and mince enough to measure 2 tablespoons; set aside.

4. Turn tomatoes into strainer set over medium-size non-aluminum bowl to drain. Reserve juice, and chop enough tomatoes to measure about 2 cups; set aside.

5. Remove casings from linguiça or chorizo and crumble meat; set aside. You should have about 2½ cups.

6. For sauce, heat 3 tablespoons olive oil in large sauté pan over medium-high heat.

7. While oil is heating, line plate with double thickness of paper towels; set aside.

8. Add sausage to pan and fry, stirring occasionally, about 3 minutes, or until fat is released.

9. Meanwhile, stack prosciutto slices and cut into 1-inch-long julienne strips; set aside.

10. Using slotted spoon, transfer sausage to paper-towel-lined plate to drain; set aside. Drain fat from pan.

11. Add remaining 5 tablespoons oil to pan and heat over medium heat until hot. Add onions and sauté, stirring occasionally, 5 minutes.

12. Add garlic, paprika, and red pepper flakes to taste to pan and stir to combine. Cook another minute.

13. Stir in sausage, prosciutto, tomatoes and their juice, wine, bay leaves, and oregano. Increase heat to medium-high and bring liquid to a boil. Lower heat to medium and simmer, uncovered, about 20 minutes.

14. Taste and adjust seasoning, adding salt and pepper to taste, and additional red pepper flakes if desired.

15. Place clams on top of simmering sauce, cover pan, and steam clams 3 to 6 minutes, or until they open.

16. Remove and discard any unopened clams. Gently turn mixture into serving dish, sprinkle with chopped parsley, and serve.

Mixed Green Salad

Small head romaine lettuce
1 head Boston or small head red leaf lettuce
1 bunch watercress
Small red onion
12 pitted black olives
½ cup fruity olive oil
¼ cup lemon juice
Salt
Freshly ground black pepper
⅓ cup chopped coriander (optional)

1. Wash greens and dry in salad spinner or with paper towels. Remove and discard any bruised or discolored leaves. Trim stems from watercress and discard. Tear greens into bite-size pieces and place in salad bowl; set aside.

2. Peel onion and cut crosswise into ⅛-inch-thick slices; add to bowl with greens.

3. Drain olives and add to salad. Cover bowl with plastic wrap and refrigerate until ready to serve.

4. For dressing, combine oil, lemon juice, and salt and pepper to taste in small nonaluminum bowl and whisk until blended; set aside.

5. Just before serving, whisk dressing to recombine and pour over salad. Toss salad until evenly coated and sprinkle with coriander, if desired.

Spinach Soup with Yogurt
Turkish Broiled Chicken
Pilaf with Currants and Pistachios

The marinated chicken can be grilled over a charcoal or wood fire, if you prefer cooking outdoors. Place the grill about 4 inches above the coals and cook the chicken quarters skin-side up for the first 10 minutes so the underside cooks through and there is less likelihood of fire flare-up from dripping fat. During the final 10 minutes of grilling, baste the chicken with the marinade. The chicken is done when the juices run clear when it is pierced with the tip of a knife. You may want to prepare the marinade in the morning (or the night before) and let the chicken marinate, covered, in the refrigerator as long as possible.

For a festive Middle Eastern meal, first offer spinach soup with yogurt, then broiled marinated chicken and a delectable rice pilaf studded with currants and pistachios.

WHAT TO DRINK

A medium-bodied white wine, especially one with an assertive flavor, goes well with this menu. A California or Alsace Gewürztraminer would be ideal.

SHOPPING LIST AND STAPLES

2½-pound broiling chicken, quartered
1 pound spinach
1 large plus 3 medium-size yellow onions
Small bunch scallions (optional)
3 large cloves garlic
Small bunch parsley (optional)
Small bunch dill

2 large lemons, plus 1 lemon for garnish (optional)
5 cups chicken stock, preferably homemade (see page 13), or canned
1 stick unsalted butter
1-pint container plain yogurt
1½ cups fruity olive oil
1 cup long-grain white rice
10-ounce box currants
2¼-ounce package shelled pistachio nuts
2 teaspoons cinnamon
Salt
Freshly ground black pepper
1 tablespoon coarsely ground black pepper

UTENSILS

Food processor (optional)
Blender
Broiler pan with rack
Small baking sheet
13 x 9 x 2-inch glass or ceramic dish
Medium-size saucepan
Small heavy-gauge saucepan with cover
Small bowl
Salad spinner (optional)

Measuring cups and spoons
Chef's knife
Paring knife
2 wooden spoons
Ladle
Rubber spatula
Metal tongs
Citrus juicer (optional)
Kitchen scissors (optional)

START-TO-FINISH STEPS

1. Follow chicken recipe steps 1 through 9.
2. While chicken is marinating, follow pilaf recipe steps 1 through 9.
3. While pilaf simmers, follow chicken recipe step 10 and soup recipe steps 1 through 7.
4. Follow chicken recipe step 11.
5. While chicken is broiling, follow pilaf recipe steps 10 through 14.
6. Follow soup recipe step 8 and chicken recipe step 12.
7. While chicken continues to broil and pilaf rests, follow soup recipe step 9 and serve as first course.
8. Follow chicken recipe step 13 and pilaf recipe step 15 and serve.

Spinach Soup with Yogurt

1 pound spinach
2 medium-size yellow onions
4 tablespoons unsalted butter
Small bunch dill
3 cups chicken stock
1½ cups plain yogurt
Salt
Freshly ground black pepper

1. Wash spinach thoroughly in several changes of cold water. Remove and discard tough stems. Dry leaves in salad spinner or with paper towels; set aside.
2. Peel onions and cut enough crosswise into ¼-inch-thick slices to measure 2 cups.
3. Heat butter in medium-size saucepan over medium heat. Add onions and sauté, stirring occasionally, about 2 minutes, or until translucent.
4. Meanwhile, rinse dill and dry with paper towels. Snip enough dill to measure 1 teaspoon; set aside.
5. Increase heat under saucepan to medium-high, add chicken stock, and bring to a boil.
6. Add spinach, stirring and pushing leaves down into stock, and simmer 1 minute.
7. Remove pan from heat and set aside to cool.
8. When cool, combine stock, spinach, onions, and 1 cup yogurt in food processor or blender, and purée.
9. Return soup to saucepan and reheat briefly. Add salt and pepper to taste. Divide soup among 4 bowls, top each serving with a dollop of yogurt, and sprinkle with dill.

Turkish Broiled Chicken

2 large lemons, plus additional lemon for garnish
    (optional)
3 large cloves garlic
1 large yellow onion
2 teaspoons cinnamon
1 teaspoon salt
1 tablespoon coarsely ground black pepper
1½ cups fruity olive oil
2½-pound broiling chicken, quartered
4 sprigs parsley for garnish (optional)

1. Squeeze enough lemon juice to measure ½ cup; set aside.
2. Peel and mince enough garlic to measure 3 tablespoons; set aside.
3. Peel and quarter onion and purée in food processor or blender.
4. Add lemon juice, garlic, cinnamon, salt, and pepper, and process until blended.
5. Turn onion mixture into 13 x 9 x 2-inch glass or ceramic dish. Add olive oil and stir to combine.
6. Rinse chicken and dry with paper towels. Remove and discard any cartilage or excess fat.
7. Add chicken to marinade and turn to coat. Set aside to marinate at least 15 minutes, turning chicken occasionally.
8. Wash lemon for garnish, if using, and dry with paper towel. Halve lemon and cut one half into quarters; set aside. Reserve remaining half for another use.
9. Wash parsley sprigs, if using, and dry with paper towel; set aside.
10. Preheat broiler.
11. Place chicken, skin-side down, on broiler rack set 6 inches from heating element and broil 10 to 12 minutes.
12. Using tongs, turn chicken and broil other side about 10 minutes, or until juices run clear when chicken is pierced with tip of knife.
13. Transfer chicken to dinner plates and garnish each serving with a lemon wedge and a sprig of parsley, if desired.

Pilaf with Currants and Pistachios

¼ cup currants
¼ cup shelled pistachio nuts
Medium-size yellow onion
4 tablespoons unsalted butter
1 cup long-grain white rice
2 cups chicken stock
Small bunch scallions (optional)

1. Preheat oven to 350 degrees.
2. Place currants in small bowl and add ½ cup warm tap water; set aside to plump.
3. Spread pistachios on small baking sheet and toast in oven, shaking occasionally to prevent scorching, 5 to 7 minutes, or until lightly toasted.
4. Meanwhile, halve and peel onion. Finely chop enough onion to measure ½ cup; set aside. Reserve remaining onion for another use.
5. Remove pistachios from oven and set aside to cool.
6. Heat butter in small heavy-gauge saucepan over medium heat. Add onion and sauté, stirring occasionally, about 2 minutes, or until translucent.
7. Add rice to onion and sauté, stirring, about 3 minutes, or until rice is opaque.
8. Add chicken stock and stir to combine. Increase heat to medium-high and bring to a boil.
9. Cover pan, reduce heat to medium-low, and simmer 15 minutes.
10. Coarsely chop pistachios.
11. Drain currants.
12. Add drained currants and toasted pistachios to rice, and cook another 5 minutes.
13. Meanwhile, if using scallions, wash under cold running water and dry with paper towels. Trim ends and discard. Chop enough scallions to measure ¼ cup; set aside. Reserve remainder for another use.
14. Turn off heat under pan and allow pilaf to rest, covered, at least 10 minutes before serving.
15. To serve, divide pilaf among 4 dinner plates and sprinkle each serving with chopped scallions, if desired.

Garlic and Bread Soup
Pork with Peppers and Onions
Portuguese-style Fried Potatoes

Garlic soup crowned with a poached egg, sautéed pork with roasted peppers, and fried potatoes are a traditional Portuguese meal.

This garlic soup is one of the Portuguese bread-based soups known as *açordas*. In this version, from the province of Minho, the soup is topped with poached eggs and sparked with pungent coriander. When you poach eggs, you cook them in liquid that is barely simmering; this keeps the whites from becoming rubbery. Add the eggs to the poaching liquid one at a time. If desired, you can poach the eggs up to 24 hours in advance. After simmering, put them immediately into a bowl of ice water to stop the cooking process and to keep them moist, then refrigerate. To reheat, dip them briefly in hot water; they will taste just as good in the soup.

WHAT TO DRINK

Dāo, a red Portuguese wine, is a fine accompaniment for these dishes, but a California Zinfandel or an Italian Barbera would also be good.

SHOPPING LIST AND STAPLES

Eight ½-inch-thick slices boneless pork loin (about 1½ pounds total weight)
1½ pounds small new red potatoes
2 medium-size yellow onions

239

1 medium-size yellow bell pepper
2 medium-size red bell peppers
5 large cloves garlic
Large bunch parsley
Small bunch coriander
Large lemon
3 cups chicken stock, preferably homemade (see page 9), or canned
4 eggs
4 tablespoons unsalted butter
1½ cups fruity olive oil
½ teaspoon white wine vinegar
Small baguette
3 tablespoons sugar
1 teaspoon dried thyme
½ teaspoon ground coriander
2 bay leaves
Salt
Freshly ground black pepper
3 whole black peppercorns

UTENSILS

Large heavy-gauge skillet
Medium-size skillet or egg poacher
Large sauté pan
Small saucepan
13 x 9 x 2-inch glass or ceramic baking dish
2 platters, 1 heatproof
Small bowl, plus additional small bowl (if not using mortar and pestle)
Measuring cups and spoons
Chef's knife
Serrated bread knife (optional)
Paring knife
Wooden spoon
Slotted spoon
Ladle
Metal spatula
Long-handled two-pronged fork
Metal tongs
Stiff-bristled brush
Meat pounder or rolling pin
Citrus juicer (optional)
Mortar and pestle (optional)
Brown paper bag

START-TO-FINISH STEPS

One hour ahead: Set out eggs to come to room temperature for soup recipe.

1. Wash parsley and coriander and pat dry with paper towels. Trim stems and discard. Finely chop enough parsley to measure ¼ cup for soup recipe, 2 tablespoons for pork recipe, and 1 teaspoon for potatoes recipe if desired. Finely chop enough coriander to measure ¼ cup for soup recipe. Reserve remaining herbs for another use. Crush garlic cloves under flat blade of chef's knife. Remove peels

and discard. Set aside 1 whole clove for soup recipe. Mince enough remaining garlic to measure 2 tablespoons for soup recipe and 2 tablespoons for pork recipe.
2. Follow pork recipe steps 1 through 8.
3. Follow soup recipe steps 1 through 7.
4. Follow potatoes recipe steps 1 and 2.
5. While potatoes are cooking, follow pork recipe steps 9 through 14.
6. Follow potatoes recipe step 3.
7. Follow soup recipe steps 8 through 12 and serve as first course.
8. Follow pork recipe step 15, potatoes recipe step 4, and serve.

RECIPES

Garlic and Bread Soup

Small baguette
½ cup fruity olive oil
1 large clove garlic, peeled, plus 2 tablespoons minced garlic
¼ teaspoon salt
¼ cup finely chopped parsley
¼ cup finely chopped coriander
½ teaspoon white wine vinegar
3 cups chicken stock
4 eggs, at room temperature

1. Cut bread crosswise into eight ½-inch-thick slices; set aside.
2. Heat ¼ cup oil over medium heat in sauté pan large enough to accommodate bread slices in a single layer. Add peeled garlic clove and sauté 1 minute.
3. Meanwhile, line platter with double thickness of paper towels; set aside.
4. Add bread slices to sauté pan and fry 1 to 2 minutes per side, or until golden brown.
5. Using tongs, transfer bread slices to paper-towel-lined platter to drain; set aside.
6. Combine minced garlic and salt in mortar and mash to a fine paste with pestle. Or, combine in small bowl and mash with back of spoon.
7. Divide garlic paste, parsley, and coriander among 4 soup bowls. Add 1 tablespoon olive oil to each bowl and stir to combine; set aside.
8. Bring 1 quart water and ½ teaspoon white wine vinegar barely to a simmer in medium-size skillet over medium-low heat. Or, bring water to a simmer in egg poacher.
9. Meanwhile, in small saucepan, heat chicken stock over medium-low heat until hot.
10. One by one, crack eggs into a small cup, then slide gently into simmering water. Or, if using egg poacher, crack eggs and slide into poacher cups. Poach eggs 3 minutes.
11. Meanwhile, divide toasted bread slices among soup bowls.
12. Using slotted spoon, place poached eggs on top of bread. Ladle hot stock into bowls and serve immediately.

Pork with Peppers and Onions

Marinade:

3 tablespoons sugar
1 tablespoon salt
3 whole black peppercorns
2 bay leaves
1 teaspoon dried thyme
½ teaspoon ground coriander

Eight ½-inch-thick slices boneless pork loin (about 1½
    pounds total weight)
1 medium-size yellow bell pepper
2 medium-size red bell peppers
2 medium-size yellow onions
Large lemon
¾ cup fruity olive oil
1 to 2 tablespoons minced garlic
Salt
Freshly ground black pepper
2 tablespoons finely chopped parsley

1. For marinade, combine sugar, salt, and 2 tablespoons warm tap water in small bowl and stir until dissolved.
2. Under flat blade of chef's knife, bruise peppercorns.
3. Add crushed peppercorns, bay leaves, thyme, coriander, and 1 cup warm water to bowl, and stir to combine; set aside.
4. Trim excess fat from pork and discard. Arrange pork slices in a single layer in 13 x 9 x 2-inch glass or ceramic baking dish.
5. Pour marinade over pork, making sure that marinade covers meat. If not, add a bit more warm water. Set aside to marinate at least 15 minutes.
6. One by one, pierce bell peppers through top with long-handled two-pronged fork and hold directly over gas flame, turning to char skins evenly. Or, place on broiler rack set 3 inches from heating element and broil, turning peppers to char skins evenly. Transfer peppers to brown paper bag, close bag, and set peppers aside to steam.
7. Meanwhile, peel onions and cut enough into ¼-inch-thick slices to measure 2 cups; set aside.
8. Halve lemon and squeeze enough juice to measure ¼ cup; set aside.
9. Preheat oven to 200 degrees.
10. When peppers are cool enough to handle, hold under cold running water and rub gently to remove skins; pat dry with paper towels. Halve and core peppers. Cut peppers lengthwise into ½-inch-wide strips and arrange in single layer on shallow platter. Drizzle with ½ cup olive oil and set aside at room temperature.
11. Meanwhile, heat 2 tablespoons olive oil in large sauté pan over medium heat. Add onions and garlic and sauté, stirring occasionally, 2 minutes, or until translucent but not soft. Add onions and garlic to roasted peppers, season with salt and pepper to taste, and sprinkle with 2 tablespoons lemon juice; toss and set aside.
12. Drain marinade from pork and pat meat dry with paper towels. Place each slice between 2 sheets of waxed paper and pound to ¼-inch thickness with meat pounder or rolling pin. Sprinkle pork with salt and pepper.
13. Add 2 tablespoons olive oil to sauté pan and heat over medium-high heat. Add pork slices and sauté 2 to 3 minutes per side, or until golden brown.
14. Add peppers and onions to pan and sprinkle with remaining lemon juice. Cook 1 to 2 minutes, or just until peppers are heated through. Transfer pork and vegetables to heatproof platter, cover loosely with foil, and keep warm in oven until ready to serve.
15. To serve, divide pork slices among 4 dinner plates, top with equal portions of vegetables, and sprinkle with some chopped parsley.

Portuguese-style Fried Potatoes

1½ pounds small new red potatoes
4 tablespoons unsalted butter
4 tablespoons fruity olive oil
Salt
Freshly ground black pepper
1 teaspoon chopped parsley (optional)

1. Using stiff-bristled brush, scrub potatoes under cold running water, rinse, and dry with paper towels. Do *not* peel. Cut potatoes crosswise into ¼-inch-thick slices; set aside.
2. Combine butter and oil in large heavy-gauge skillet over medium-high heat. When hot, add potatoes and cook, turning occasionally with metal spatula, 15 to 20 minutes, or until potatoes are golden brown and cooked through.
3. Add salt and pepper to taste, cover loosely, and keep warm on stove top until ready to serve.
4. Just before serving, reheat potatoes briefly. Divide potatoes among dinner plates and sprinkle each serving with parsley, if desired.

ADDED TOUCH

A perfectly ripe pineapple is needed for this light dessert. Select a heavy one with a golden rind and deep-green crown leaves.

Pineapple with Port

1½- to 2-pound pineapple
½ cup sugar, approximately
¼ to ½ cup tawny port

1. Trim crown and stem end from pineapple and cut pineapple lengthwise into quarters. Remove core from each quarter and discard. Trim rind and remove any remaining eyes with paring knife. Cut each quarter crosswise into 1-inch chunks and place in large glass bowl.
2. Sprinkle pineapple with sugar to taste, and toss to coat.
3. Sprinkle with port and toss again.
4. Cover bowl with plastic wrap and refrigerate at least 1 hour before serving.

Stevie Bass

W hen cooking for company, Stevie Bass likes to tantalize her guests with the unexpected and dramatic. She finds that serving ethnic food is a good way to please a crowd. Here, all three of her menus feature Greek main courses well known to Americans. Each menu balances color, flavor, and texture, and all are easy to prepare.

In Menu 1, the showstopper is *spanakopita*, or spinach pie, which here consists of layers of flaky filo pastry wrapped around a spinach and cheese filling. Although this dish may appear difficult, it is easy once you master handling the filo dough. With the spinach pie, Stevie Bass offers baked tomatoes with garlic, cheese, and oregano. The pear and lettuce salad can be served before, with, or after the main course.

Originally a Middle Eastern dish, the *moussaka* of Menu 2 has been adopted by the Greeks. The principal ingredient is eggplant, which is subtly flavored with cinnamon and red wine. Green beans sparked with fennel and a simple tomato and cucumber salad are the refreshing side dishes.

In Menu 3, a number of popular Greek seasonings—oregano, bay leaves, rosemary, and garlic—flavor the lamb kabobs. Parslied almond rice and a Greek salad that includes feta cheese and Kalamata olives are the traditional accompaniments.

For this festive Greek meal, offer the spanakopita, *tossed salad, and baked tomatoes on typical Mediterranean pottery, and add a bowl of assorted Greek olives, if you wish.*

242

Pear and Lettuce Salad with Olives and Anchovies
Spanakopita
Baked Tomatoes

The spinach filling for the *spanakopita* is wrapped in filo, a tissue-thin pastry that is sold frozen in sheets in half-pound or one-pound boxes. To prevent the sheets from cracking when you separate them, thaw the entire block of dough in the refrigerator overnight; then, shortly before you need them, set out seven sheets. Never refreeze the extra dough or the sheets may stick together; refrigerate it and use it within a week.

Because filo can dry out and crumble when overexposed to air, you should work quickly and keep the pastry sheets moist. Unroll the dough and lay the seven sheets, unseparated, on waxed paper on a damp kitchen towel; cover them with a second sheet of waxed paper and a damp towel. Work with one sheet of dough at a time, leaving the rest covered. The butter you brush on the sheets helps to separate the layers, keeps them moist, and turns the pastry a golden brown as it bakes.

WHAT TO DRINK

These Greek dishes require an acidic white wine. Try either a French Muscadet or an Italian Pinot Grigio or Verdicchio, served well chilled.

SHOPPING LIST AND STAPLES

¾ pound fresh spinach
Medium-size head romaine lettuce
2 medium-size tomatoes (about 1¼ pounds total weight)
3 medium-size cloves garlic
1 lemon
Large ripe pear, preferably Bartlett
Small bunch fresh oregano, or 1½ teaspoons dried
Small bunch fresh basil, or 1 teaspoon dried
5 tablespoons unsalted butter
1 egg
8-ounce container ricotta cheese
¼ pound Parmesan cheese
6 ounces feta cheese
½-pound package frozen filo dough
⅓ cup good-quality olive oil, preferably extra-virgin
2 tablespoons red wine vinegar
11-ounce jar Kalamata or other Greek olives
2-ounce tin anchovy fillets
3 tablespoons all-purpose flour
Freshly grated nutmeg
Salt and freshly ground pepper

UTENSILS

Food processor or grater
Large heavy-gauge skillet
9-inch springform pan
8-inch square baking dish
Small heavy-gauge saucepan or butter warmer
Large bowl
Large strainer
Measuring cups and spoons
Chef's knife
Paring knife
Wooden spoon
Metal spatula
Rubber spatula
Pastry brush
Kitchen scissors
Small jar with tight-fitting lid

START-TO-FINISH STEPS

Twenty minutes ahead: Set out 7 sheets of filo dough for spanakopita recipe.

1. Peel and mince 3 cloves garlic for salad and tomatoes recipes. Using food processor fitted with steel blade, or grater, grate enough Parmesan to measure ⅓ cup for spanakopita recipe and ¼ cup for tomatoes recipe; reserve remainder for another use. Crumble feta for spanakopita recipe. Prepare fresh herbs if using, or crush dried herbs.
2. Follow spanakopita recipe steps 1 through 10.
3. Follow salad recipe steps 1 through 6.
4. Follow tomatoes recipe steps 1 and 2.
5. While tomatoes and spanakopita are baking, follow salad recipe step 7 and serve as first course.
6. Follow tomatoes recipe step 3, spanakopita recipe step 11, and serve.

RECIPES

Pear and Lettuce Salad with Olives and Anchovies

Medium-size head romaine lettuce
8 flat anchovy fillets
12 Kalamata or other Greek olives
1 lemon
Large ripe pear, preferably Bartlett

⅓ cup good-quality olive oil, preferably extra-virgin
2 tablespoons red wine vinegar
1 teaspoon minced garlic
1 tablespoon finely chopped fresh basil, or 1 teaspoon
   dried, crushed
¼ teaspoon freshly ground pepper

1. Wash and dry lettuce. Tear into bite-size pieces and place in serving bowl.
2. Rinse and dry anchovy fillets; add to bowl with lettuce.
3. Drain olives; add to lettuce and anchovies.
4. Squeeze enough lemon juice to measure 1 tablespoon; set aside. Reserve remaining lemon for another use.
5. Wash pear and dry with paper towel. Halve pear lengthwise; remove core and stem and discard. Cut each half lengthwise into 4 slices and place on plate. Sprinkle with lemon juice to prevent discoloration and turn to coat evenly with juice. Add pear slices to salad; set aside.
6. For dressing, combine oil, vinegar, garlic, basil, and pepper in small jar with tight-fitting lid and shake until well blended; set aside.
7. Just before serving, shake dressing to recombine and pour over salad.

Spanakopita

5 tablespoons unsalted butter
7 sheets frozen filo dough, thawed
¾ pound fresh spinach
6 ounces feta cheese, crumbled
1 cup ricotta cheese
⅓ cup freshly grated Parmesan cheese
3 tablespoons all-purpose flour
1 egg
1 tablespoon minced fresh oregano, or 1 teaspoon dried,
   crushed
¼ teaspoon salt
¼ teaspoon freshly ground pepper
Pinch of freshly grated nutmeg

1. Preheat oven to 400 degrees.
2. Melt butter in small heavy-gauge saucepan or butter warmer over low heat.
3. Meanwhile, butter bottom and sides of 9-inch spring-form pan; set aside.
4. Fit 1 sheet of filo dough into prepared pan, pressing it against sides and allowing it to overlap edge of pan. Brush filo lightly with melted butter. Repeat, one sheet at a time, with 3 more sheets, brushing each layer with butter before adding the next. Using scissors, trim filo so dough hangs over sides of pan only about 1½ inches. Place trimmings in bottom of pan, brush with butter, and set pan aside.
5. Wash spinach in several changes of cold water; do not dry. Remove tough stems and discard.
6. Place spinach in large heavy-gauge skillet and cook, stirring, over high heat 2 to 3 minutes, or until limp.
7. Turn spinach into large strainer, pressing with back of spoon to remove excess moisture. Coarsely chop spinach. You will have about ⅔ cup.

8. Combine spinach and remaining ingredients in large bowl, and stir with wooden spoon until blended. Turn mixture into filo-lined pan and smooth.
9. Fold overhanging filo layers over filling. Brush 1 of the remaining sheets of filo with butter and fold in half, buttered-side in. Place dough on top of filling, tucking edges under to roughly form a round; brush lightly with melted butter. Repeat with remaining 2 sheets of filo.
10. Bake spanakopita 40 minutes, or until golden.
11. Transfer spanakopita to serving platter and carefully remove sides of pan. To serve, cut into wedges.

Baked Tomatoes

2 medium-size tomatoes (about 1¼ pounds total weight)
2 teaspoons minced garlic
¼ cup freshly grated Parmesan cheese
1½ teaspoons minced fresh oregano, or ½ teaspoon dried,
   crushed

1. Wash and dry tomatoes. Core and halve crosswise. Cut thin slice from bottom of halves so they will rest flat.
2. Place tomato halves cut-sides up in 8-inch square baking dish and sprinkle each with garlic, Parmesan, and oregano. Cover pan with foil and bake in 400-degree oven 20 minutes, or until tomatoes are heated through.
3. Using spatula, transfer tomatoes to platter and serve.

ADDED TOUCH

This popular soup is known in Greece as *avgolemono*. It is a tangy blend of eggs and lemon juice.

Egg-Lemon Soup

4 tablespoons unsalted butter
2 lemons
¼ cup all-purpose flour
4 cups chicken stock
2 eggs
Salt

1. Melt butter in medium-size nonaluminum saucepan over medium heat.
2. While butter is melting, squeeze enough lemon juice to measure ¼ cup; set aside.
3. Add flour to melted butter and whisk until blended.
4. Whisking continuously, add chicken stock and whisk until blended and smooth. Cook over medium-high heat, stirring occasionally, just until mixture comes to a boil.
5. Meanwhile, separate eggs, placing yolks in small bowl and reserving whites for another use. Whisk yolks just until blended.
6. Whisking continuously, gradually add ¼ cup hot stock mixture to yolks and whisk until blended.
7. Whisk yolk mixture into remaining hot stock mixture and cook over medium-high heat, whisking continuously, about 2 minutes, or just until mixture returns to a boil.
8. Remove pan from heat. Add lemon juice, and salt to taste, and whisk until blended. Divide soup among 4 bowls and serve.

Moussaka
Green Beans with Fennel Seeds
Tomato and Cucumber Salad

An ample portion of moussaka *paired with fennel-flavored green beans and a light salad makes ideal summer fare.*

The *moussaka*, with its custardy topping, is an excellent company meal. Be sure the eggplant you choose has smooth dark-purple skin that is free of blemishes. It should be firm and feel heavy for its size, an indication that it is fresh and moist. A shriveled eggplant is old and probably bitter. Refrigerate the eggplant wrapped in a plastic bag, and use it within two or three days.

WHAT TO DRINK

A medium-bodied and fruity red wine, such as a young Dolcetto or Chianti from Italy, a French Côtes du Rhône, a young Spanish Rioja, or a California Zinfandel, would be the right choice for this meal.

SHOPPING LIST AND STAPLES

1 pound lean ground beef or lean ground lamb
1 eggplant (1 to 1¼ pounds)
1 pound fresh green beans
2 large or 3 small tomatoes (about 1¼ pounds total weight)
Medium-size cucumber
Medium-size onion
Small bunch scallions
2 medium-size cloves garlic
Small bunch fresh oregano, or ½ teaspoon dried
1 lemon
1 cup milk
1 stick plus 2 tablespoons unsalted butter
2 ounces Parmesan cheese
6-ounce can tomato paste
3 tablespoons good-quality olive oil, preferably extra-virgin
2 tablespoons all-purpose flour
1 teaspoon fennel seeds
½ teaspoon cinnamon
Salt
Freshly ground pepper
⅛ teaspoon whole peppercorns
⅓ cup dry red wine

UTENSILS

Food processor or grater
Large heavy-gauge skillet
Steamer unit or medium-size covered saucepan large enough to accommodate collapsible steamer
Collapsible vegetable steamer (if not using steamer unit)
Small heavy-gauge nonaluminum saucepan
15 x 10-inch baking pan
Shallow 2-quart casserole
Medium-size bowl
Small nonaluminum bowl
Colander

Measuring cups and spoons
Chef's knife
Paring knife
2 wooden spoons
Metal spatula
Whisk
Pastry brush
Mortar and pestle (optional)
Rolling pin (if not using mortar and pestle)

START-TO-FINISH STEPS

1. Follow salad recipe steps 1 through 7.
2. Follow moussaka recipe steps 1 through 11.
3. While moussaka is baking, follow green beans recipe steps 1 through 4.
4. Follow salad recipe step 8, green beans recipe step 5, moussaka recipe step 12, and serve.

RECIPES

Moussaka

1 stick unsalted butter
1 eggplant (1 to 1¼ pounds)
Medium-size onion
2 medium-size cloves garlic
2 ounces Parmesan cheese
1 pound lean ground beef or lean ground lamb
3 tablespoons tomato paste
⅓ cup dry red wine
½ teaspoon cinnamon
Salt
Freshly ground pepper
2 tablespoons all-purpose flour
1 cup milk

1. Preheat oven to 425 degrees.
2. In small heavy-gauge nonaluminum saucepan, melt 6 tablespoons butter over low heat.
3. Meanwhile, wash eggplant and dry with paper towels. Trim ends and discard. Halve eggplant lengthwise, then cut each half crosswise into ¼-inch-thick slices. Arrange slices in single layer in 15 x 10-inch baking pan and, working quickly, brush slices with half of melted butter. Turn slices and brush other sides with remaining melted butter. Bake 20 minutes.
4. Meanwhile, halve and peel onion. Mince enough onion to measure 1 cup; set aside.
5. Peel garlic and mince enough to measure 1½ to 2 teaspoons; set aside.
6. Using food processor fitted with steel blade, or grater, grate enough Parmesan cheese to measure ½ cup; set aside.
7. Heat large heavy-gauge skillet over medium-high heat. Add beef or lamb and onion and sauté, stirring and breaking up any lumps, 4 to 5 minutes, or until meat is browned.
8. Remove skillet from heat. Using metal spatula, scrape up any browned particles clinging to bottom of skillet and

stir to combine. Stir in garlic, tomato paste, red wine, cinnamon, and salt and pepper to taste; set mixture aside.

9. Melt remaining 2 tablespoons butter in small heavy-gauge nonaluminum saucepan over medium-low heat. Whisk in flour. Whisking continuously, gradually add milk and whisk until blended. Cook sauce, stirring, over medium heat 1 to 2 minutes, or until it thickens and comes to a boil.

10. Remove sauce from heat, add Parmesan, and stir until blended; set aside.

11. Remove baked eggplant from oven. Arrange enough eggplant slices in a single layer to cover bottom of shallow 2-quart casserole. Top with half of meat mixture. Add another layer of eggplant and remaining meat mixture. Top with remaining eggplant and pour cheese sauce over casserole. Bake moussaka, uncovered, 20 minutes, or until heated through.

12. Using metal spatula, divide moussaka among 4 dinner plates and serve.

Green Beans with Fennel Seeds

1 pound fresh green beans
1 teaspoon fennel seeds
2 tablespoons unsalted butter
Salt
Freshly ground pepper

1. Place beans in colander and rinse under cold running water. Trim ends and discard.

2. Bring 2 cups water to a boil over medium-high heat in steamer unit or in medium-size saucepan large enough to accommodate collapsible vegetable steamer. Add beans to steamer basket, cover pan, and steam about 8 minutes, or just until crisp-tender.

3. Meanwhile, using mortar and pestle, crush fennel seeds, or place seeds between 2 sheets of waxed paper and crush with rolling pin; set aside.

4. Cut butter into several small pieces; set aside.

5. Drain beans, remove steamer basket, if necessary, and return beans to pan. Add butter, crushed fennel seeds, and salt and pepper to taste, and toss to combine. Divide beans among 4 dinner plates and serve.

Tomato and Cucumber Salad

2 large or 3 small tomatoes (about 1¼ pounds total
    weight)
Medium-size cucumber
Small bunch scallions
1 lemon
Small bunch fresh oregano, or ½ teaspoon dried
⅛ teaspoon whole peppercorns
3 tablespoons good-quality olive oil, preferably extra-
    virgin

1. Wash tomatoes and dry with paper towels. Core tomatoes and cut lengthwise into wedges. Place wedges in medium-size bowl and set aside.

2. Wash cucumber and dry with paper towels. Trim ends and discard; do *not* peel. Using fork, score cucumber lengthwise. Cut cucumber crosswise into ⅛-inch-thick slices and add to bowl with tomatoes.

3. Wash scallions and dry with paper towels. Trim ends and discard. Cut enough scallions crosswise into ¼-inch-thick slices to measure ⅔ cup and add to tomatoes and cucumber. Cover bowl with plastic wrap and refrigerate until ready to serve.

4. Squeeze enough lemon juice to measure 1 tablespoon; set aside.

5. Wash fresh oregano, if using, and dry with paper towel. Chop enough to measure 1½ teaspoons, or crush dried oregano.

6. Crush peppercorns under flat blade of chef's knife.

7. Combine oil, lemon juice, oregano, and pepper in small nonaluminum bowl and whisk until blended; set aside.

8. Just before serving, whisk dressing to recombine. Pour dressing over vegetables and toss until evenly coated. Divide vegetables among 4 salad plates and serve.

ADDED TOUCH

For these light flaky cookies, finely chop the nuts in the container of a food processor fitted with a steel blade or in a blender.

Butter Crescents

2 sticks unsalted butter or margarine, at room
    temperature
1¼ cups confectioners' sugar
1 egg yolk
1 teaspoon almond extract
¼ teaspoon salt
2 cups all-purpose flour
1 cup finely chopped pecans, almonds,
    or walnuts

1. Preheat oven to 350 degrees.

2. Combine butter and 1 cup confectioners' sugar in large mixing bowl and cream together with wooden spoon until well blended and fluffy.

3. Add egg yolk, almond extract, and salt, and beat until blended.

4. Gradually add flour and chopped nuts, beating until they are totally incorporated and dough is formed. If necessary, knead dough until smooth.

5. Break off small handfuls of dough and roll between your palms into ½-inch-thick ropes.

6. Cut each rope into 2-inch lengths and shape into crescents, placing each crescent on ungreased baking sheet as you form it. You should have about 7 dozen.

7. Bake crescents 10 to 12 minutes, or until bottoms are light brown. Tops of cookies should remain pale.

8. Using wide metal spatula, transfer cookies to wire racks. Sift remaining confectioners' sugar over warm cookies and set aside to cool.

Lamb Kabobs with Parslied Almond Rice
Greek Salad

Arrange the lamb kabobs decoratively on a bed of almond-studded rice, and accompany the main course with a Greek salad.

When buying the lamb for this recipe, ask the butcher for cubes cut from the upper portion of the leg, where the meat is lean and free of gristle. Meat from the shank portion is too tough for this recipe. If your budget allows, purchase cubes cut from the loin, which is the tenderest part of the lamb. Marinate the lamb longer than 30 minutes, if possible.

To be sure the onion cooks through by the time the lamb is ready, do not skewer whole wedges; rather, pull the wedges apart into layers, then thread them on the skewers alternately with the lamb cubes.

Despite advance soaking, the bay leaves may char a bit during broiling. Threading the leaves between the meat and onions keeps them from blackening too much. Caution your family and guests against eating these sharp-edged leaves, which can cause intestinal damage if swallowed.

WHAT TO DRINK

An austere red shipper's Saint-Émilion from France, a California Merlot, or an Italian Barbera would be excellent with the lamb.

SHOPPING LIST AND STAPLES

1½ pounds lean boneless lamb, cut into 1-inch cubes
1 head Boston lettuce
Medium-size tomato
Medium-size green bell pepper
Small cucumber
2 medium-size onions (about 1 pound total weight), plus 1 small onion
Medium-size clove garlic
Small bunch fresh parsley
Small bunch fresh oregano, or 3 teaspoons dried
Small bunch fresh rosemary, or ¼ teaspoon dried
1 lemon
4 tablespoons unsalted butter
¼ pound feta or mozzarella cheese
7 tablespoons good-quality olive oil, preferably extra-virgin
¼ cup red wine vinegar
11-ounce jar Kalamata or other Greek olives
1 cup long-grain white rice
2½-ounce package whole almonds
2 teaspoons sugar
16 bay leaves
Salt
Freshly ground pepper
⅓ cup dry white wine

UTENSILS

Medium-size heavy-gauge saucepan with cover
Broiler pan with rack
Shallow baking pan, plus 1 additional if using bamboo skewers

250

Salad bowl
Large glass or ceramic bowl
Measuring cups and spoons
Chef's knife
Paring knife
Whisk
Basting brush
Small jar with tight-fitting lid
Eight 10- to 12-inch metal or bamboo skewers

START-TO-FINISH STEPS

One hour ahead: If using bamboo skewers for kabobs, place in shallow baking dish with enough cold water to cover and set aside to soak.

1. Wash parsley, and fresh oregano and rosemary if using. Trim stems and discard. Mince enough parsley to measure 2 tablespoons for rice recipe. Mince enough oregano to measure 1 tablespoon each for lamb and salad recipes. Mince enough rosemary to measure ½ teaspoon for lamb recipe. Reserve remaining herbs for another use.
2. Follow lamb recipe steps 1 through 6.
3. While lamb is marinating, follow rice recipe steps 1 and 2.
4. While nuts are toasting, follow salad recipe steps 1 through 3.
5. Follow rice recipe steps 3 and 4, and lamb recipe step 7.
6. While rice cooks, follow salad recipe steps 4 through 10.
7. Follow lamb recipe steps 8 and 9.
8. When lamb is nearly finished broiling, follow salad recipe step 11 and rice recipe steps 5 and 6.
9. Follow lamb recipe step 10 and serve with salad.

RECIPES

Lamb Kabobs with Parslied Almond Rice

Medium-size clove garlic
1 lemon
1 tablespoon minced fresh oregano, or 2 teaspoons dried
½ teaspoon minced fresh rosemary, or ¼ teaspoon dried
⅓ cup dry white wine
3 tablespoons good-quality olive oil, preferably extra-virgin
2 tablespoons red wine vinegar
¼ teaspoon salt
¼ teaspoon freshly ground pepper
1½ pounds lean boneless lamb, cut into 1-inch cubes
2 medium-size onions (about 1 pound total weight)
16 bay leaves
Parslied Almond Rice (see following recipe)

1. Peel garlic and mince enough to measure 1½ teaspoons; set aside.
2. Squeeze enough lemon juice to measure 2 tablespoons; set aside.
3. Crush dried oregano and rosemary, if using.
4. For marinade, combine lemon juice, wine, olive oil,

vinegar, garlic, oregano, rosemary, salt, and pepper in large glass or ceramic bowl and whisk until blended.

5. Trim any fat and gristle from lamb, if necessary, and pat lamb dry with paper towels.

6. Add lamb to marinade and set aside to marinate at least 30 minutes.

7. Preheat broiler.

8. Halve and peel onions. Cut lengthwise into wedges and separate wedges into sections of 2 or 3 layers each.

9. Rinse and dry skewers, if necessary. Thread skewers alternately with lamb, onions, and bay leaves and arrange skewers in single layer on broiler rack. Brush generously with remaining marinade and broil meat 3 inches from heating element, turning once, about 6 minutes for rare, 7 for medium-rare, or 8 for well done.

10. Remove kabobs from broiler and serve on bed of parslied almond rice.

Parslied Almond Rice

2½-ounce package whole almonds
1 cup long-grain white rice
¼ teaspoon salt
4 tablespoons unsalted butter
2 tablespoons minced fresh parsley

1. Preheat oven to 350 degrees.

2. Chop enough almonds to measure ¼ cup. Spread almonds in shallow baking pan and toast in oven, shaking pan occasionally to prevent scorching, 5 to 6 minutes, or until golden.

3. Remove almonds from oven and set aside to cool.

4. Combine rice with 2 cups water and salt in medium-size heavy-gauge saucepan and bring to a boil over medium-high heat. Cover pan, reduce heat to low, and simmer 25 minutes, or until rice is tender and water is absorbed.

5. Just before serving, cut butter into small pieces.

6. Remove rice from heat. Add almonds, butter, and parsley, and toss with fork to combine. Turn onto platter.

Greek Salad

1 head Boston lettuce
Small cucumber
Medium-size tomato
Medium-size green bell pepper
Small onion
¼ pound feta or mozzarella cheese
12 Kalamata or other Greek olives
1 tablespoon minced fresh oregano, or 1 teaspoon dried
¼ cup good-quality olive oil, preferably extra-virgin
2 tablespoons red wine vinegar
2 teaspoons sugar
½ teaspoon salt

1. Wash and dry lettuce. Remove and discard any bruised or discolored leaves. Line salad bowl with lettuce; set aside. Reserve remaining lettuce for another use.

2. Wash and dry cucumber; trim ends and discard. Cut enough cucumber crosswise into ⅛-inch-thick slices to

measure 1 cup; set aside.

3. Wash and dry tomato. Core tomato and cut into wedges.

4. Wash and dry bell pepper. Core, seed, and derib; cut pepper crosswise into ¼-inch-thick rings; set aside.

5. Peel onion and cut enough crosswise into ⅛-inch-thick slices to measure ½ cup; set aside.

6. Cut cheese into ¼-inch-thick 1-inch squares; set aside.

7. Drain olives.

8. Crush dried oregano, if using.

9. Add cucumber slices, tomato wedges, bell pepper rings, onion slices, and olives to lettuce-lined bowl. Top with cheese and sprinkle with oregano. Cover bowl with plastic wrap and refrigerate until ready to serve.

10. Meanwhile, combine oil, vinegar, sugar, and salt in small jar with tight-fitting lid and shake until well blended; set aside.

11. Just before serving, shake dressing to recombine and pour over salad.

ADDED TOUCH

These buttery shortbread-type cookies are typically Greek and have a mild citrus-spice flavor. They may be frozen after baking, if desired.

Honey Rounds

2 sticks unsalted butter, at room temperature
½ cup granulated sugar
¼ cup honey
2 teaspoons freshly grated orange peel
1½ teaspoons vanilla extract
¼ pound almonds
2½ cups all-purpose flour
1 teaspoon baking powder
½ teaspoon baking soda
3 dozen whole cloves, approximately
¼ cup confectioners' sugar

1. Preheat oven to 350 degrees.

2. Combine butter and granulated sugar in large mixing bowl and cream together until well blended and fluffy.

3. Beat in honey, orange peel, and vanilla extract.

4. Grind enough almonds to measure 1 cup. When ground, almonds should have texture of coarse flour.

5. Combine almonds, flour, baking powder, and baking soda in medium-size bowl and stir with fork to blend.

6. Add dry ingredients to butter mixture, one half at a time, stirring after each addition until a smooth dough is formed.

7. Pinch off walnut-size pieces of dough and shape into balls. Place on ungreased cookie sheet and flatten into ¾-inch-thick 2-inch rounds. You will have about 3 dozen rounds.

8. Press clove into center of each round and bake 10 to 15 minutes, or until bottoms are golden. Tops should be pale.

9. Remove cookies from oven and sift confectioners' sugar over them. Using wide metal spatula, transfer to wire rack to cool.

Beatrice Ojakangas

MENU 1 (Right)
Finnish Summer Soup
Smoked Salmon and Egg Smörrebröd
Tomato and Enoki Mushroom Salad

MENU 2
Red and White Soup
Pasties with Mustard Butter
Creamy Havarti and Vegetable Salad

MENU 3
Hearty Beef, Barley, and Wild Rice Stew
with Finnish Raisin Dumplings
Scandinavian Salad

A resident of a Scandinavian community in Minnesota, Beatrice Ojakangas is proud of her Finnish heritage. Not surprisingly, her favorite cuisine is from Scandinavia, and she has traveled there to master traditional recipes and techniques. The three menus she presents here span the seasons. Menu 1 features a delicate Finnish summer soup known as *kesäkeitto*, which is made with baby carrots, new potatoes, and young green beans. "In Finland, this produce is in abundance only during the intense summers, when the sun shines 24 hours a day," she says. She is delighted that many American markets now carry baby vegetables all year round.

The thick red and white soup of Menu 2 is more autumnal, using red bell pepper, fresh tomatoes, potatoes, and leeks. An attractive vegetable and cheese salad and flaky turnovers called pasties (pronounced *past*-ees), filled with a savory mixture of sausage, beef, and seasonings, are served with the soup.

Menu 3 is a hearty winter meal reflecting both Swedish and Finnish influences. Beef, onions, mushrooms, barley, and wild rice simmer in a stock, melding to create a rich flavorful stew. Finnish raisin dumplings, an old-country classic, steam with the stew, and a colorful vegetable salad is the refreshing accompaniment.

Celebrate summer with a large bowl of hot Finnish soup made with a variety of colorful vegetables. An open-faced sandwich of smoked salmon topped with cheese soufflé, and a simple tomato and mushroom salad, are appealing partners for the soup.

Finnish Summer Soup
Smoked Salmon and Egg Smörrebröd
Tomato and Enoki Mushroom Salad

The *smörrebröd*, which literally means "buttered bread" in Danish, has as its base slices of pumpernickel, which should be buttered thickly and evenly to seal the bread from the juices in the toppings. Toppings for *smörrebröd* can consist of almost any foods that look and taste good together. For this version, the cook uses colorful smoked salmon and a simple soufflé containing Danish Edam cheese. Purchase top-quality salmon and use it as soon as possible, since it deteriorates quickly. If desired, you can add two chopped hard-boiled eggs to the salmon mixture.

The sliced tomatoes are crowned with *enoki* (or *enokitaki*) mushrooms—slender, ivory-colored stalks that look like tiny umbrellas. These mushrooms are increasingly available in well-stocked supermarkets, specialty food stores, and Oriental groceries. Refrigerate them in the original package or wrapped in paper towels for a day or two. You can substitute fresh button mushrooms or chanterelles for the *enoki*.

WHAT TO DRINK

In Scandinavia, this summer soup would be accompanied by a well-chilled light beer, but crisp white wine is also appropriate. Consider a California Sauvignon Blanc or a French Sancerre.

SHOPPING LIST AND STAPLES

¾ pound smoked salmon, in one piece
Medium-size head cauliflower (about 2 pounds)
2 large ripe tomatoes (about 1½ pounds total weight)
8 small new red potatoes (about ¾ pound total weight)
¾ pound baby carrots, or 3 medium-size carrots
¾ pound fresh green peas, or 9-ounce package frozen
¼ pound fresh snow peas
2 ounces small fresh green beans
Large head butter lettuce
Small bunch fresh spinach (optional)
¼ pound fresh enoki mushrooms
Small white onion (about ¼ pound)
Small bunch chives
Small bunch parsley
Large lemon
2 eggs
1 pint half-and-half
½ pint sour cream

6 tablespoons unsalted butter, approximately
¼ pound Danish Edam cheese
4 cups chicken stock, preferably homemade (see page 13), or canned
¼ cup vegetable oil
2 tablespoons white wine vinegar
3 tablespoons mayonnaise
2 teaspoons Dijon mustard
2 tablespoons all-purpose flour
2 teaspoons sugar
Small loaf pumpernickel bread
Salt and freshly ground white pepper

UTENSILS

Electric mixer (optional)
Large stockpot with cover
Small deep saucepan
15 x 10-inch baking sheet
Medium-size bowl
3 small bowls, 1 nonaluminum
Colander
Measuring cups and spoons
Chef's knife
Paring knife
2 wooden spoons
Grater
Whisk
Metal spatula
Rubber spatula
Vegetable peeler
Ladle

START-TO-FINISH STEPS

Thirty minutes ahead: Set out eggs and 4 teaspoons butter to come to room temperature for smörrebröd recipe.

1. Follow soup recipe steps 1 through 3 and smörrebröd recipe steps 1 through 5.
2. Follow salad recipe step 1 and soup recipe steps 4 through 6.
3. Follow salad recipe steps 2 and 3 and smörrebröd recipe steps 6 and 7.
4. While smörrebröd bake, follow salad recipe steps 4 through 6 and soup recipe step 7.
5. Follow smörrebröd recipe step 8, soup recipe step 8, and serve with salad.

Finnish Summer Soup

Medium-size head cauliflower (about 2 pounds)
¾ pound baby carrots, or 3 medium-size carrots
8 small new red potatoes (about ¾ pound total weight)
Small white onion (about ¼ pound)
2 teaspoons salt
4 cups chicken stock or water, approximately
¾ pound fresh green peas, or 9-ounce package frozen
¼ pound fresh snow peas
2 ounces small fresh green beans
2 cups half-and-half
2 tablespoons all-purpose flour
4 tablespoons unsalted butter
1 teaspoon sugar
⅛ teaspoon freshly ground white pepper
Small bunch fresh spinach for garnish (optional)

1. Trim and discard stem and leaves from cauliflower. Wash cauliflower and separate into florets; cut florets into 1-inch pieces. You should have about 8 cups. Peel and trim carrots; cut carrots crosswise, if necessary, into 2½- to 3-inch pieces. Wash and peel potatoes; cut into quarters. Peel onion and cut into 8 wedges.
2. In large stockpot, combine cauliflower, carrots, potatoes, onion, salt, and enough stock or water to barely cover vegetables. Cover and bring to a boil over high heat. Reduce heat and simmer vegetables 15 minutes, or until just tender but not mushy.
3. Meanwhile, shell enough fresh peas, if using, to measure 1½ cups. If using frozen peas, remove from freezer and separate enough peas to measure 1½ cups; do not thaw first. Wash, trim, and string snow peas. Wash and trim green beans; cut into 1-inch pieces.
4. Add peas, snow peas, green beans, and 1 cup half-and-half to stockpot. Simmer over low heat 3 minutes.
5. Meanwhile, in small bowl, combine remaining 1 cup half-and-half with flour and beat until smooth. Stir mixture into simmering soup and cook, stirring occasionally, 1 to 2 minutes, or until soup is slightly thickened.
6. Cut butter into small pieces and add to soup along with sugar and pepper. Keep soup warm over very low heat until ready to serve; do not let soup boil.
7. Wash enough spinach, if using, to measure ⅓ cup; reserve remaining spinach for another use. Trim stems and cut spinach leaves into ½-inch-wide ribbons. Set aside for garnish.
8. To serve, divide soup among 4 bowls and top with spinach leaves, if desired.

Smoked Salmon and Egg Smörrebröd

¾ pound smoked salmon, in one piece
3 tablespoons mayonnaise
3 tablespoons sour cream
Large lemon
Small loaf pumpernickel bread
4 teaspoons unsalted butter, at room temperature
¼ pound Danish Edam cheese
2 eggs, at room temperature
Small bunch parsley

1. Preheat oven to 375 degrees.
2. Remove skin and bones, if necessary, from salmon. Flake fish into small bowl. Add mayonnaise and sour cream and stir with fork until well blended.
3. Wash lemon. Using vegetable peeler or paring knife, remove four 2-inch-wide strips of lemon peel and reserve for garnish. Halve lemon and squeeze enough juice to measure ¼ cup; stir juice into salmon mixture.
4. Cut four ½-inch-thick slices of pumpernickel and spread each slice with 1 teaspoon softened butter.
5. Spread pumpernickel slices with salmon mixture. Place slices on 15 x 10-inch baking sheet; set aside.
6. Using grater, finely shred cheese. Separate eggs, placing whites in medium-size bowl and reserving yolks for another use. Using electric mixer or whisk, beat egg whites until stiff. Using rubber spatula, fold in shredded cheese. Spread mixture equally over salmon.
7. Bake smörrebröd 10 to 15 minutes, or until topping is golden.
8. Just before serving, wash and dry parsley. Cut 4 sprigs for garnish and reserve remainder for another use. Place 1 smörrebröd on each of 4 dinner plates and garnish each with a parsley sprig and a strip of lemon peel.

Tomato and Enoki Mushroom Salad

Large head butter lettuce
Small bunch chives
2 large ripe tomatoes (about 1½ pounds total weight)
2 teaspoons Dijon mustard
2 tablespoons white wine vinegar
1 teaspoon sugar
¼ teaspoon salt
¼ cup vegetable oil
¼ pound fresh enoki mushrooms

1. Bring 1 quart water to a boil in small deep saucepan over high heat.
2. Wash and dry lettuce and chives. Wrap lettuce in paper towels or plastic bag and refrigerate until needed. Finely chop enough chives to measure ¼ cup; set aside.
3. Immerse tomatoes in boiling water 30 seconds. Turn tomatoes into colander and refresh under cold running water. Peel tomatoes and set aside.
4. In small nonaluminum bowl, whisk together mustard, vinegar, sugar, and salt. Stir in chopped chives. Whisking constantly, add oil in a slow, steady stream, and whisk until smooth.
5. Wipe mushrooms with damp paper towel and trim stem ends. Add to dressing and toss gently to coat. Core tomatoes and cut each crosswise into 4 slices.
6. To serve, line 4 salad plates with lettuce leaves. Place 2 tomato slices on each plate and top with mushrooms and dressing.

Red and White Soup
Pasties with Mustard Butter
Creamy Havarti and Vegetable Salad

Serving two contrasting soups in one bowl is a sure way to delight guests. Offer the pasties before, with, or after the soup and salad.

The unusual cold soup is actually two soups in one. To ensure that they remain separate, use shallow bowls and pour both soups carefully into the bowls at the same time. The soup is as good hot as cold.

When baking the pasties, line the baking pans with kitchen parchment (available in kitchen supply stores) to aid in even browning. Brown wrapping paper makes an adequate substitute. The pasties can be served hot or at room temperature.

WHAT TO DRINK

Beer, ale, or a California Zinfandel or Petite Sirah would be a good choice for this light supper.

SHOPPING LIST AND STAPLES

½ pound lean ground beef
¼ pound seasoned pork sausage
3 large ripe tomatoes (about 1½ pounds total weight)
3 medium-size boiling potatoes (about 1 pound total weight)
Large head butter, Boston, or Bibb lettuce
Small head red cabbage
Small head cauliflower
Large leek
Large red bell pepper
Medium-size yellow onion
Medium-size clove garlic
Small bunch fresh basil, or 1 teaspoon dried
1 cup milk
½ pint heavy cream
2 sticks unsalted butter, approximately
¼ pound creamy Havarti cheese
½ pint creamed small curd cottage cheese
4 cups chicken stock, preferably homemade (see page 13), or canned
¼ cup plus 2 tablespoons vegetable oil
2 tablespoons white wine vinegar
¼ cup coarse-grain mustard
2 teaspoons Dijon mustard
1¼ cups all-purpose flour
1 teaspoon sugar
2 tablespoons cornstarch
¼ cup walnut or pecan pieces
1 tablespoon fine dry bread crumbs
½ teaspoon dried thyme
¼ teaspoon ground allspice
Salt
Freshly ground white pepper

UTENSILS

Food processor or blender
2 large heavy-gauge saucepans with covers
Small saucepan
17 x 11-inch baking sheet
3 large bowls, plus 1 bowl (optional)
Medium-size bowl
Small nonaluminum bowl
Measuring cups and spoons
Chef's knife
Paring knife
2 wooden spoons
Metal spatula
Rubber spatula
Whisk
Rolling pin
Pastry blender (if not using food processor)
Vegetable peeler
Parchment paper or brown wrapping paper

START-TO-FINISH STEPS

1. Follow soup recipe steps 1 through 4.
2. While soups are simmering, follow pasties recipe steps 1 through 3.
3. While dough is chilling, follow salad recipe steps 1 through 3.
4. Follow soup recipe steps 5 and 6.
5. While soups are chilling, follow pasties recipe steps 4 through 9.
6. While pasties are baking, follow salad recipe steps 4 through 6.
7. Follow pasties recipe step 10, soup recipe step 7, and serve with salad.

RECIPES

Red and White Soup

Medium-size yellow onion
Medium-size clove garlic
Large leek
Large red bell pepper
3 medium-size boiling potatoes (about 1 pound total weight)
3 large ripe tomatoes (about 1½ pounds total weight)
Small bunch fresh basil, or 1 teaspoon dried
3 tablespoons unsalted butter
4 cups chicken stock
2 tablespoons cornstarch
Salt
Freshly ground white pepper
1 cup milk
½ cup heavy cream

1. Peel onion and garlic; coarsely chop both and set aside. Cut off and discard dark green leaves of leek. Trim root end, split leek lengthwise, and wash well under cold running water; dry with paper towel. Coarsely chop leek and set aside. Wash and dry red bell pepper. Halve, core, and seed pepper; chop coarsely and set aside. Peel potatoes and cut into coarse dice; set aside. Wash, core, and coarsely chop tomatoes; set aside.
2. Wash and dry fresh basil, if using. Set aside 4 sprigs for garnish and coarsely chop enough basil to measure 1 table-

spoon; set aside. Reserve remaining basil for another use.

3. In large heavy-gauge saucepan, melt 2 tablespoons butter over medium heat. Add onion and garlic and sauté 1 minute, or until soft but not browned. Add bell pepper and tomatoes and sauté 2 to 3 minutes, stirring once or twice, until heated through but not browned. Add 2 cups stock, cover, and simmer about 20 minutes, or until vegetables are tender.

4. Meanwhile, in another large heavy-gauge saucepan, melt remaining tablespoon butter over medium heat. Add leek and sauté 1 minute, or until soft but not browned. Add potatoes and sauté 2 to 3 minutes, stirring once or twice, until heated through but not browned. Add remaining 2 cups stock, cover, and simmer about 20 minutes, or until vegetables are tender.

5. Pour bell pepper and tomato mixture into food processor fitted with steel blade, or blender, and purée until almost smooth. Add cornstarch and continue processing until smooth. Return soup to pan, bring to a simmer over medium heat, and cook, stirring, 2 to 3 minutes, or until soup thickens. Stir in chopped or dried basil, and salt and pepper to taste. Transfer soup to large bowl and chill in refrigerator at least 20 minutes, or until ready to serve.

6. Rinse out processor or blender and turn potato mixture into it. Process until puréed and smooth (the potato soup should be of the same consistency as the pepper soup). Stir in milk and cream, and salt and pepper to taste. Transfer soup to large bowl and chill in refrigerator at least 20 minutes, or until ready to serve.

7. To serve, stir each chilled soup to ensure smoothness. Taste, and adjust seasonings. Using 2 cups, simultaneously pour 1 cup of each soup into shallow soup bowl so that red soup is on one side and white soup is on the other side. (The equal density of the two soups keeps them from running together.) Fill remaining 3 soup bowls in same manner. Garnish each with a basil sprig.

Pasties with Mustard Butter

1¼ cups all-purpose flour
1 stick plus 4 tablespoons unsalted butter, well chilled
½ cup creamed small curd cottage cheese
¼ pound seasoned pork sausage
½ pound lean ground beef
1 tablespoon fine dry bread crumbs
½ teaspoon salt
½ teaspoon dried thyme
¼ teaspoon ground allspice
¼ cup coarse-grain mustard

1. Prepare pastry: Place flour in food processor fitted with steel blade. Cut 1 stick butter into small pieces and add to flour. Process, pulsing on and off 8 to 10 times, until mixture is in pea-size pieces. Add cottage cheese and pulse 10 to 15 times, or until dough holds together in a ball. (If mixture is too dry to form a ball, add 1 tablespoon cold water.) To make pastry by hand, add cut-up butter to flour in large bowl and blend with pastry blender or 2 knives until mixture is in pea-size pieces. Add cottage cheese and

stir with wooden spoon until dough holds together, adding 1 tablespoon cold water, if necessary. Remove dough from processor or bowl and flatten into a disk. Wrap dough in plastic and refrigerate 10 minutes.

2. Meanwhile, in medium-size bowl, combine sausage, beef, bread crumbs, salt, thyme, and allspice, and stir until well blended.

3. Preheat oven to 450 degrees.

4. Lightly dust rolling pin with flour. Place dough on lightly floured surface and roll out pastry to ¼-inch thickness. Trim dough to 10 x 20-inch rectangle and cut into eight 5-inch squares.

5. Divide meat mixture into eight equal portions. Spread one portion on one triangular half of each square, leaving a narrow border.

6. Fold pastry squares diagonally in half to make triangular pasties, pressing down to flatten slightly. Crimp edges with tines of fork. Cut 3 slits on top of each pasty with tip of knife to allow steam to escape.

7. Line 17 x 11-inch baking sheet with parchment paper or brown wrapping paper. Using metal spatula, transfer pasties to parchment.

8. Bake pasties 15 minutes, or until golden.

9. Meanwhile, melt remaining 4 tablespoons butter in small saucepan. Add mustard and stir to blend. Pour into 4 small ramekins or one small serving bowl.

10. Using metal spatula, transfer 2 pasties to each of 4 plates and serve with mustard butter on the side.

Creamy Havarti and Vegetable Salad

Small head red cabbage
Small head cauliflower
¼ pound creamy Havarti cheese
Large head butter, Boston, or Bibb lettuce
2 teaspoons Dijon mustard
1 teaspoon sugar
2 tablespoons white wine vinegar
¼ cup plus 2 tablespoons vegetable oil
Salt and freshly ground pepper
¼ cup walnut or pecan pieces

1. Wash, halve, and core cabbage. Cut enough cabbage into medium-size shreds to measure about 6 cups; place in large bowl. Reserve remaining cabbage for another use.

2. Trim stem and leaves from cauliflower. Wash cauliflower and break enough into ½-inch florets to measure about 2 cups; add to bowl.

3. Cut cheese into ¼-inch-thick by 2-inch-long pieces and add to bowl; set aside.

4. Wash lettuce and dry with paper towels. Arrange 3 or 4 leaves on each of 4 dinner plates or line 4 salad plates with leaves.

5. For dressing, in small nonaluminum bowl, whisk together mustard, sugar, and vinegar. Whisking constantly, add oil in a slow, steady stream and whisk until smooth. Season with salt and pepper to taste.

6. To serve, pour dressing over vegetables and cheese and toss to coat. Spoon onto lettuce and sprinkle with nuts.

Hearty Beef, Barley, and Wild Rice Stew
with Finnish Raisin Dumplings
Scandinavian Salad

A colorful vegetable salad with creamy dressing is an attractive complement to the beef stew with dumplings.

The substantial stew calls for an American native—wild rice. The seeds of a wild grass, wild rice is painstakingly harvested by hand, hence it is costly, but well worth the price. Fortunately, a little goes a long way.

The cook also uses whole allspice berries to flavor the stew. These dried unripe berries of the West Indian allspice tree taste like a combination of cloves, cinnamon, and nutmeg and are most flavorful in their unground state.

WHAT TO DRINK

This cold-weather meal demands a sturdy drink: Select a dark ale or a young California Zinfandel.

SHOPPING LIST AND STAPLES

1 pound boneless sirloin or top round steak, trimmed
3 medium-size beets (about 1¼ pounds total weight)
3 medium-size carrots (about ½ pound total weight)
3 medium-size boiling potatoes (about 1 pound total weight)
½ pound fresh mushrooms
2 large onions (about 1½ pounds total weight)
Small bunch scallions
Small bunch fresh parsley
Small bunch fresh dill, or 1 teaspoon dried
2 medium-size Granny Smith apples (about 1 pound total weight)
Small lemon
1 egg
½ cup milk
½ pint heavy cream
4 tablespoons unsalted butter
4 cups beef stock, preferably homemade, or canned
16-ounce jar dill pickles
1 tablespoon vegetable oil
4-ounce package wild rice
¼ cup pearl barley
1 cup all-purpose flour
1 teaspoon baking powder
2 teaspoons sugar
½ cup dark raisins
3 whole allspice berries
¼ teaspoon ground allspice
Salt

UTENSILS

Electric mixer
Large stockpot with cover
Medium-size saucepan
Small saucepan
Large bowl
Medium-size bowl
Small bowl
Colander
Strainer
Measuring cups and spoons
Chef's knife
Paring knife
2 wooden spoons
Ladle

START-TO-FINISH STEPS

1. Follow salad recipe steps 1 and 2.
2. While vegetables cook, follow stew recipe steps 1 through 6.
3. While stew simmers, follow salad recipe steps 3 through 8.
4. Follow stew recipe steps 7 through 10 and salad recipe step 9.
5. Follow stew recipe step 11 and serve with salad.

RECIPES

Hearty Beef, Barley, and Wild Rice Stew with Finnish Raisin Dumplings

⅓ cup wild rice
2 large onions (about 1½ pounds total weight)
4 tablespoons unsalted butter
¼ cup pearl barley
1 pound boneless sirloin or top round steak, trimmed
3 whole allspice berries
4 cups beef stock
½ pound fresh mushrooms
Small bunch parsley

Finnish Raisin Dumplings:
1 egg
1 tablespoon vegetable oil
½ cup milk
1 cup all-purpose flour

260

1 teaspoon baking powder
½ teaspoon salt
¼ teaspoon ground allspice
½ cup dark raisins

1. Place wild rice in small bowl. Add hot tap water to cover and stir; drain in strainer. Repeat until soaking water is clear. Drain.
2. Peel onions and slice ¼-inch thick; set aside.
3. Melt butter in large stockpot over medium heat. Add\ wild rice and barley and stir to coat with butter.
4. Add onions to rice and barley and stir to separate onion slices into rings. Simmer 3 to 5 minutes, or until onions begin to soften.
5. Meanwhile, cut steak into ¼-inch-thick slices. Cut slices crosswise into 1-inch pieces. Add steak and allspice berries to stockpot and increase heat to high. Cook, stirring, 5 minutes, or until meat is no longer pink.
6. Add stock and bring to a boil. Reduce heat, cover, and simmer 30 minutes, or until meat is tender and rice and barley are cooked.
7. Wipe mushrooms clean with damp paper towel. Cut mushrooms into ¼-inch-thick slices; set aside. Wash and dry parsley. Chop enough parsley to measure 2 teaspoons; set aside. Reserve remainder for another use.
8. Combine all raisin dumpling ingredients in large bowl. Stir until dry ingredients are just moistened.
9. Dip a tablespoon into stew cooking liquid to moisten, then scoop up a rounded spoonful of dumpling batter. Drop batter into stew; repeat for remaining batter. You should have about 15 dumplings.
10. Add mushrooms to stew, cover, and simmer 5 minutes. Stir gently, cover, and cook another 5 to 7 minutes, or until dumplings are fluffy and no longer doughy underneath.
11. Sprinkle stew with parsley and serve directly from stockpot. Or, ladle stew into 4 soup bowls.

Scandinavian Salad

3 medium-size beets (about 1¼ pounds total weight)
3 medium-size carrots (about ½ pound total weight)
3 medium-size boiling potatoes (about 1 pound total weight)
4 large dill pickles
Small lemon
2 medium-size Granny Smith apples (about 1 pound total weight)

4 scallions
Small bunch fresh dill, or 1 teaspoon dried
1 cup heavy cream
2 teaspoons sugar
½ teaspoon salt

1. Place medium-size bowl and beaters in freezer to chill.
2. Wash beets, being careful not to damage skin. Trim stems, if any, no closer than 2 inches; do not trim bottoms. Wash carrots and potatoes. Place beets in small saucepan and add water to cover. Place carrots and potatoes in medium-size saucepan and add water to cover. Bring water in both pans to a boil over high heat. Reduce heat to low and simmer vegetables 15 to 20 minutes, or until slightly tender but still firm.
3. Cut dill pickles into ½-inch dice and arrange in one corner of large platter. Halve lemon and squeeze enough juice to measure at least 4 teaspoons; set aside. Core, but do not peel, apples. Cut apples into ½-inch dice and sprinkle with 1 teaspoon lemon juice. Arrange apples in diagonal row next to pickles. Wash and trim scallions. Cut scallions crosswise into ¼-inch slices; set aside. Wash and dry fresh dill, if using. Set aside 1 sprig for garnish, and finely chop enough dill to measure 1 tablespoon; set aside. Reserve remaining dill for another use.
4. For dressing, in chilled medium-size bowl, whip cream. Add remaining tablespoon lemon juice, sugar, salt, and chopped or dried dill. Blend in 2 teaspoons beet cooking liquid to tint dressing slightly. (If dressing seems pale, add ¼ teaspoon finely chopped beet after beets are cooked to tint it more deeply.) Turn dressing into small serving bowl.
5. When beets are tender, drain in colander, return to pan, and cover with cold water. Let stand 2 to 3 minutes, or until cool enough to handle.
6. Meanwhile, drain carrots and potatoes, return to pan, and cover with cold water.
7. When beets are cool, trim tops and root ends and slip off skins. Cut beets into ½-inch dice and arrange in diagonal row next to apples on platter.
8. When carrots and potatoes are cool, peel and cut both into ½-inch dice. Arrange potatoes in diagonal row next to beets on platter, and arrange carrots in same manner next to potatoes.
9. Sprinkle narrow band of chopped scallions between rows of vegetables. Garnish dressing with dill sprig and serve with salad.

Jenifer Harvey Lang

MENU 1 (Left)
Sauerkraut-Bean Soup
Viennese-style Turkey Cutlets
Mushroom and Bell Pepper Salad

MENU 2
Hungarian Turkey Terrine
Sautéed Squash with Sour Cream
Baked Stuffed Apples

MENU 3
Sautéed Turkey Cutlets
Lecsó
Rice and Peas

Over the years, Jenifer Harvey Lang has come to prefer honest, uncomplicated food. After marrying restaurateur George Lang and traveling with him in his native Hungary, she discovered that the cuisine of that country suited her taste. All three of her menus typify meals you might eat in eastern European homes. "This is down-to-earth cooking," she says, "that will leave your guests full and immensely satisfied."

Menu 1 starts with a sauerkraut and bean soup, followed by Viennese-style turkey cutlets (*Wienerschnitzel*). *Schnitzel* is a thin slice of boneless meat, usually veal. Here, pounded scallops of turkey are dipped into beaten egg, then into bread crumbs, and are sautéed quickly—just as the classic veal dish is prepared. An easy-to-assemble mushroom and bell pepper salad completes the meal.

A Hungarian terrine, or *fasirt* (pronounced fash-*eert*), made of turkey is the main course of Menu 2, an ideal lunch for company. Sautéed squash complements this lightly seasoned dish.

Menu 3 features turkey cutlets topped with *lecsó,* a Hungarian vegetable sauté resembling *ratatouille.* The cook also serves the *lecsó* on the side.

Bright flowers and a rustic table setting underscore the informality of this Viennese meal. Serve the browned turkey cutlets with slices of tomato and lemon on a large platter, the sauerkraut-bean soup in a lidded tureen, and the mushroom and pepper salad in a wooden bowl.

263

Sauerkraut-Bean Soup
Viennese-style Turkey Cutlets
Mushroom and Bell Pepper Salad

The rich soup contains sauerkraut, lard, and paprika—three common Hungarian ingredients. Sauerkraut, or salted shredded cabbage fermented in its own juice, is best when purchased fresh—you can usually find it at a German delicatessen. A good second choice is sauerkraut sealed in plastic bags, which is available in most supermarkets. Because sauerkraut is pickled, it lasts for a month or longer when stored in a nonmetallic container in the refrigerator. Taste it before using: If it seems too strong, rinse it under cold running water.

Lard, or rendered pork fat, is sold in one-pound blocks at most supermarkets. It refrigerates well for a month and can be frozen for up to a year. The easiest way to measure lard is to cut the block lengthwise into quarters, like sticks of butter, then mark off eight equal sections along each quarter (each section is equal to roughly 1 tablespoon).

For an authentic flavor in the soup, use only imported sweet Hungarian paprika, sold in tins or occasionally in bulk at specialty food stores. The finest paprika is from the town of Szeged and is labeled as such. Spanish paprika (the usual supermarket variety) is not a substitute. Fresh paprika is bright red; brown or faded powder is flavorless. Because paprika loses its delicate flavor quickly, store it in a tightly closed container in the refrigerator.

WHAT TO DRINK

Beer or light ale is the best choice here. A light lager, also called pilsner, would be the most authentic accompaniment for this meal.

SHOPPING LIST AND STAPLES

Eight ¼-inch-thick turkey cutlets (about 2 pounds total weight), pounded to ⅛-inch thickness
¾ pound medium-size or large fresh cultivated mushrooms
Small head Boston lettuce
Large tomato
Small red bell pepper
Small green bell pepper
Small onion
Small bunch thyme or parsley
2 large lemons
16-ounce can red kidney beans
2 large eggs
1 pound fresh sauerkraut, or 16-ounce package
10 tablespoons lard (about ⅓ pound)

½ cup vegetable or peanut oil
1 cup plus 2 tablespoons all-purpose flour
4 slices fresh or stale white bread, approximately
2 teaspoons mild sweet Hungarian paprika
Salt and freshly ground pepper

UTENSILS

Food processor or blender
Large heavy-gauge skillet
Large heavy-gauge saucepan
Wire rack or platter
Ovenproof serving platter
Salad bowl
Large mixing bowl
3 shallow bowls
Colander
Strainer
Measuring cups and spoons
Chef's knife
Paring knife
2 wooden spoons
Juicer
Metal tongs

START-TO-FINISH STEPS

1. Follow salad recipe steps 1 through 4.
2. Follow soup recipe steps 1 through 4.
3. Follow turkey recipe steps 1 through 5.
4. Follow soup recipe step 5.
5. Follow turkey recipe step 6.
6. Follow soup recipe step 6 and serve as first course.
7. Follow salad recipe step 5 and turkey recipe step 7, and serve.

RECIPES

Sauerkraut-Bean Soup

1 pound fresh sauerkraut, or 16-ounce package
Small onion
2 tablespoons lard
2 tablespoons all-purpose flour
2 teaspoons mild sweet Hungarian paprika
1 teaspoon salt
Freshly ground pepper
16-ounce can red kidney beans

1. Place sauerkraut in strainer to drain. Peel and chop enough onion to measure ¼ cup.

2. In large heavy-gauge saucepan, melt lard over medium heat. Stir in flour and cook, stirring continuously, until mixture begins to turn a pale golden brown, about 3 minutes.

3. Add chopped onion and cook, stirring, about 3 minutes, or until onion begins to wilt.

4. Add paprika and cook, stirring, 15 seconds. Add sauerkraut, 4 cups cold water, salt, and pepper to taste, and bring to a boil. Reduce heat to low and simmer, uncovered, 20 minutes, stirring occasionally.

5. Drain kidney beans in colander and rinse under cold running water. Add beans to soup and simmer another 5 minutes.

6. Turn soup into tureen or large serving bowl.

Viennese-style Turkey Cutlets

Large lemon
Large tomato
4 slices fresh or stale white bread, approximately
1 cup all-purpose flour
1 tablespoon salt
1 teaspoon freshly ground pepper
2 large eggs
Eight ¼-inch-thick turkey cutlets (about 2 pounds total weight), pounded to ⅛-inch thickness
8 tablespoons lard
1 sprig fresh parsley for garnish (optional)

1. With paring knife, remove peel and as much white pith as possible from lemon. Cut lemon crosswise into nine ¼-inch-thick slices; set aside. Wash tomato, dry, core, and cut crosswise into eight ¼-inch-thick slices; set aside.

2. Trim crusts from bread. In food processor fitted with steel blade, or in blender, process enough bread to measure about 1 cup crumbs.

3. Combine flour, salt, and pepper in shallow bowl and stir with fork to blend. Crack eggs into another shallow bowl and beat with fork until blended. Turn bread crumbs into third shallow bowl.

4. Preheat oven to 200 degrees.

5. One at a time, dip cutlets into flour, shaking off excess, then into beaten eggs, and then into bread crumbs, coating thoroughly. As coated, place cutlets on wire rack or platter.

6. In large heavy-gauge skillet, melt 4 tablespoons lard

over medium-high heat until quite hot. Add only as many cutlets to skillet as will fit in a single layer and sauté until golden brown, about 30 seconds per side. Reduce heat to medium if lard begins to smoke. When cutlets are cooked, transfer to ovenproof serving platter and keep warm in oven. Add remaining lard and repeat for remaining cutlets.

7. Top each cutlet with 1 slice of tomato and 1 slice of lemon. Garnish platter with remaining slice of lemon and a sprig of parsley, if desired, and serve.

Mushroom and Bell Pepper Salad

¾ pound medium-size or large fresh cultivated
  mushrooms
Small head Boston lettuce
Small bunch thyme or parsley
Small red bell pepper
Small green bell pepper
Large lemon
1 teaspoon salt
Freshly ground pepper
½ cup vegetable or peanut oil

1. Fill large bowl with cold water and add mushrooms. Bounce mushrooms up and down with your fingers for about 15 seconds to dislodge dirt. With paper towel, gently wipe any mushroom caps that still appear dirty. Remove mushrooms from water, pat dry with paper towels, and cut into halves or quarters. Rinse and dry bowl.

2. Wash lettuce and thyme or parsley, and dry with paper towels. If using thyme, strip enough leaves to measure 1 tablespoon; if using parsley, chop enough to measure 2 tablespoons. Wash and dry bell peppers. Halve, core, and seed peppers; cut lengthwise into 1-inch-long julienne. Squeeze enough lemon juice to measure about ¼ cup. Line salad bowl with lettuce leaves, cover, and refrigerate until ready to serve.

3. In blender or food processor, combine thyme leaves or chopped parsley, 2 tablespoons lemon juice, salt, pepper to taste, and oil, and blend about 15 seconds, or until dressing is smooth and thick. Taste and add more lemon juice if desired.

4. In large mixing bowl, combine mushrooms and peppers. Add dressing and toss to combine. Set aside at room temperature, and stir occasionally.

5. When ready to serve, transfer mushrooms and peppers to lettuce-lined salad bowl.

Hungarian Turkey Terrine
Sautéed Squash with Sour Cream
Baked Stuffed Apples

Slices of turkey terrine and a helping of squash are the entrée for this Hungarian meal, with baked stuffed apples as dessert.

A terrine is an earthenware dish or mold in which a seasoned blend of chopped meat, fish, or vegetables cooks—and it lends its name to the resultant pâté-like loaf. In this Hungarian adaptation of a classic terrine, the turkey mixture cooks freestanding on a greased baking sheet. If you wish to create an elegant mosaic pattern when the cooked terrine is sliced, put half the ground turkey mixture on the baking sheet, place a row of hard-cooked eggs or sections of kielbasa sausage lengthwise down the center, and cover with the remaining turkey. Bake as indicated in the recipe. This terrine can be served hot, cold, or at room temperature.

WHAT TO DRINK

A crisp, flavorful white wine with a touch of spiciness makes an excellent partner for these dishes. Try an Alsatian or California Gewürztraminer, or, if you want a red wine, perhaps a lightly chilled Beaujolais.

SHOPPING LIST AND STAPLES

2 pounds ground turkey
4 slices bacon (about ¼ pound)
2 medium-size yellow crookneck or zucchini squash (about 1 pound total weight)
Medium-size onion plus 1 small onion
Small bunch parsley
Small bunch dill
4 firm apples
1 lemon for garnish (optional)
1 lime for garnish (optional)
2 large eggs
½ cup milk
½ pint sour cream
1½ tablespoons unsalted butter
1 tablespoon white vinegar
12-ounce jar currant jelly
2 slices fresh or stale white bread
1 tablespoon all-purpose flour
3-ounce can walnut or pecan pieces, or 4-ounce can slivered almonds
1 teaspoon mild sweet Hungarian paprika
Salt and freshly ground pepper

UTENSILS

Food processor or blender
Large heavy-gauge skillet
11 x 17-inch baking sheet with sides
8 x 8-inch baking pan
Large mixing bowl
Shallow bowl
Small mixing bowl
Measuring cups and spoons
Chef's knife
Wooden spoon
2 large metal spatulas
Apple corer
Grater (if not using processor)
Nut grinder (if not using processor)

START-TO-FINISH STEPS

1. Follow turkey recipe step 1.
2. Follow apples recipe steps 1 through 4.
3. While apples are baking, follow turkey recipe steps 2 through 6.
4. Follow squash recipe step 1 and apples recipe steps 5 and 6.
5. Follow turkey recipe step 7 and squash recipe steps 2 through 6.
6. Follow turkey recipe step 8 and serve with squash.
7. Follow apples recipe step 7 and serve as dessert.

RECIPES

Hungarian Turkey Terrine

2 slices fresh or stale white bread
½ cup milk
Medium-size onion
Small bunch parsley
4 slices bacon (about ¼ pound)
2 large eggs
1 teaspoon mild sweet Hungarian paprika
1 teaspoon salt
Freshly ground pepper to taste
2 pounds ground turkey

1. Preheat oven to 375 degrees.
2. Place bread in a shallow bowl; pour milk over bread and set aside to soak 5 to 10 minutes.
3. Meanwhile, peel onion and cut into 8 pieces. Wash parsley and dry with paper towels; chop enough to measure ⅓ cup.
4. Place soaked bread (discarding any unabsorbed milk), onion, parsley, and all remaining ingredients except ground turkey in food processor fitted with steel blade, or in blender, and process just until combined.
5. In large mixing bowl, combine ground turkey and ingredients from food processor and mix with your hands until well blended.
6. Generously oil large rectangular baking sheet with sides. Turn terrine mixture out onto prepared sheet and shape into rounded 12 x 4-inch loaf that is about 3 inches high. Smooth top and bake 20 minutes.
7. Increase oven temperature to 450 degrees and bake loaf another 10 minutes, or until juices are clear (not pink).
8. Using 2 large metal spatulas, transfer terrine to cutting surface. Cut into ¾-inch-thick slices and divide among dinner plates.

Sautéed Squash with Sour Cream

2 medium-size yellow crookneck or zucchini squash (about 1 pound total weight)
Small onion
Small bunch dill

1½ tablespoons unsalted butter
1 tablespoon all-purpose flour
1 tablespoon white vinegar
1 teaspoon salt
¼ cup sour cream

1. In food processor fitted with grating disk, or on coarse side of grater, grate squash. Peel and mince onion. Wash dill and dry with paper towel; chop enough to measure 1 tablespoon.

2. In large heavy-gauge skillet, melt butter over medium heat. Stir in flour to make a smooth paste and cook, stirring, until mixture begins to turn light brown, about 2 minutes.

3. Add onion and sauté, stirring, 3 minutes, or until onion begins to wilt.

4. Add grated squash, vinegar, and salt, and sauté, stirring, another 2 minutes.

5. Add sour cream and cook, stirring, 30 seconds.

6. Divide squash among 4 dinner plates and sprinkle with chopped dill.

Baked Stuffed Apples

4 firm apples
3-ounce can walnut or pecan pieces, or 4-ounce can
    slivered almonds
¼ cup currant jelly
1 lemon for garnish (optional)
1 lime for garnish (optional)

1. Wash apples and dry with paper towels. With apple corer, core apples without cutting through bottoms; do not peel. Using food processor or nut grinder, grind enough nuts to measure ½ cup.

2. Oil an 8 x 8-inch baking pan. Fit apples snugly into the pan.

3. Combine ground nuts and currant jelly in small bowl. Spoon one-quarter of mixture into each apple.

4. Bake apples in 375-degree oven 30 minutes.

5. Wash lemon and lime, if using, and dry with paper towels. Slice four ¼-inch-thick slices from lemon and reserve remaining lemon for another use. Cut four ⅛-inch-thick rounds from lime; stack rounds and cut a notch halfway through diameter, so that lime will stand up when twisted.

6. Remove apples from oven, cover loosely with foil, and set aside until ready to serve.

7. When ready to serve, transfer apples to dessert plates and garnish each serving with a lemon slice and a lime twist, if desired.

ADDED TOUCH

Use fresh or frozen chicken or turkey carcasses to make the stock for this flavorful soup. For maximum flavor, select deep red and firm fresh beets of small or medium size; large beets tend to be coarse.

Beet Soup

5 medium-size fresh beets (about 1½ pounds total weight)
1 lemon
1½ tablespoons lard
2 tablespoons all-purpose flour
4 cups chicken or turkey stock, preferably homemade
    (see page 13), or canned
1 teaspoon caraway seeds
½ teaspoon salt
Freshly ground pepper
2 or 3 sweet Italian sausages or frankfurters (about 6
    ounces total weight)
½ cup sour cream
2 tablespoons milk

1. Trim off tops of beets and reserve for another use. Wash and peel beets and cut enough into ½-inch dice to measure about 4 cups. Cut lemon in half, squeeze juice from one half, and set aside. Reserve remaining half for another use.

2. In large heavy-gauge saucepan, melt lard over medium heat. Stir in flour and cook, stirring, until mixture begins to turn pale golden brown, about 3 minutes.

3. Add chicken or turkey stock, beets, lemon juice, caraway seeds, salt, and pepper to taste, and bring to a boil over high heat. Reduce heat to low and simmer, uncovered, 15 minutes, or until beets are cooked.

4. Meanwhile, cut sausages into ¼-inch-thick slices. In medium-size skillet, sauté sausages over medium-high heat, stirring, 8 to 10 minutes, or until browned on both sides; transfer to paper towels to drain.

5. When beets are cooked, add browned sausages to soup and stir just to combine.

6. Combine sour cream and milk in small bowl and stir until blended. Divide soup among 4 individual bowls and top each serving with a generous spoonful of sour cream mixture.

Sautéed Turkey Cutlets
Lecsó
Rice and Peas

Spoon some lecsó *over the cutlets, then offer the rest in a separate bowl. Rice and peas provide additional texture.*

I n Hungary, *lecsó* is served hot or cold, spicy or mild. It can also be a topping for cutlets, as in this menu; an accompaniment to omelets; or a meal in itself with the addition of sausage, meat, or eggs. If you are fond of piquant foods, you can add extra fire by chopping up and stirring in a hot Mexican jalapeño or serrano chili pepper. Or, you can add 1 tablespoon of chopped dried chili pepper, ½ teaspoon of Cayenne pepper, or some hot pepper sauce, along with the paprika in step 5 of the recipe. *Lecsó* should be stewed slowly so that all the flavors meld.

The cook recommends garnishing the *lecsó* with cracklings (the crisp pieces that remain after rendering the skin and fat of poultry or pork). If you make the cracklings ahead and refrigerate them, you can recrisp them by moistening with a few drops of water and cooking them in a covered skillet.

WHAT TO DRINK

Red wine is appropriate with the cutlets, and the cook suggests the Hungarian favorite Egri Bikavér. If it is not available, try a California Zinfandel.

SHOPPING LIST AND STAPLES

Eight ½-inch-thick turkey cutlets (about 2 pounds total weight)
4 green, red, or yellow bell peppers, or 1½ pounds long Italian frying peppers

1 pound very ripe plum tomatoes, or 16-ounce can Italian
   plum tomatoes
3 large onions (about 2¼ pounds total weight)
Small hot chili pepper (optional)
2 large lemons
⅓ cup beef stock (optional)
2 cups chicken stock, preferably homemade (see page 13),
   or canned, plus ⅓ cup additional (if not using
   beef stock)
4 tablespoons lard
10-ounce package frozen peas
¾ cup vegetable oil, approximately
1 cup long-grain white rice
1 teaspoon sugar
1 tablespoon mild sweet Hungarian paprika
1 bay leaf
Salt
Freshly ground pepper

UTENSILS

Food processor or blender
2 large heavy-gauge skillets, 1 ovenproof and 1 with cover
Large heavy-gauge saucepan with tight-fitting cover
Ovenproof serving platter
Ovenproof serving bowl
Strainer
Measuring cups and spoons
Chef's knife
2 wooden spoons
Metal tongs
Juicer

START-TO-FINISH STEPS

1. Peel and slice enough onions to measure 3 cups for lecsó
recipe. Mince enough onion to measure 1 cup for rice and
peas recipe.
2. Follow lecsó recipe steps 1 through 4.
3. While vegetables are cooking, follow rice and peas
recipe steps 1 through 3.
4. Follow turkey recipe steps 1 and 2, and lecsó recipe
step 5.
5. Follow rice and peas recipe steps 4 and 5.
6. Follow lecsó recipe step 6.
7. Follow turkey recipe steps 3 through 6, rice and peas
recipe step 6, and serve with lecsó.

RECIPES

Sautéed Turkey Cutlets

2 large lemons
½ cup vegetable oil, approximately
Eight ½-inch-thick turkey cutlets (about 2 pounds
   total weight)
Salt
Freshly ground pepper
⅓ cup chicken or beef stock
Lecsó (see following recipe)

1. Preheat oven to 200 degrees.
2. Squeeze enough lemon juice to measure ⅓ cup.
3. Heat enough oil to cover bottom of large ovenproof
heavy-gauge skillet over medium-high heat. Add only as
many cutlets to pan as will fit in a single layer, and sauté
until light brown, 2 to 3 minutes per side. Reduce heat to
medium if oil begins to smoke.
4. When cutlets are cooked, transfer to ovenproof serving
platter and sprinkle with salt and pepper. Keep warm in
oven. Repeat for remaining cutlets. Pour off all but 2
tablespoons oil from skillet.
5. Add stock and lemon juice to skillet and bring to a boil
over high heat. Cook, scraping up browned bits that cling
to bottom of pan, until liquid is reduced by half, about
5 minutes.
6. Spoon sauce over cutlets and top with some of the lecsó.

Lecsó

4 tablespoons lard
3 cups sliced onions
4 green, red, or yellow bell peppers, or 1½ pounds long
   Italian frying peppers
Small hot chili pepper (optional)
1 pound very ripe plum tomatoes, or 16-ounce can Italian
   plum tomatoes
1 tablespoon mild sweet Hungarian paprika
2 teaspoons salt
1 teaspoon sugar

1. In large heavy-gauge skillet, melt lard over medium
heat. Add onions and sauté, stirring occasionally, 5 to 8
minutes, or until very soft and translucent.
2. Meanwhile, wash peppers and dry with paper towels.
Halve, core, and seed bell peppers; cut into ¼-inch-wide
strips. If using chili pepper, wearing rubber gloves, halve

lengthwise; remove seeds with tip of knife for less fiery flavor, if desired. Dice chili.

3. When onions are cooked, stir in bell peppers, and chili pepper if using. Reduce heat to low, cover, and cook, stirring occasionally, 15 to 20 minutes, or until peppers are very soft.

4. Meanwhile, if using fresh tomatoes, wash, and dry with paper towels. Remove stem ends from tomatoes and discard. Quarter fresh tomatoes and purée in food processor fitted with steel blade, or in blender. If using canned tomatoes, do not drain; purée in food processor or blender.

5. Add paprika, salt, and sugar to peppers and onions and cook, stirring, about 1 minute. Stir in puréed tomatoes, increase heat to medium, and simmer, stirring occasionally, about 8 minutes, or until mixture is medium-thick.

6. Turn lecsó into ovenproof serving bowl and keep warm in 200-degree oven until ready to serve.

Rice and Peas

¼ cup vegetable oil
1 cup minced onion
1 cup long-grain white rice
2 cups chicken stock
1 bay leaf
¾ teaspoon salt
Freshly ground pepper
1 cup frozen peas

1. In large heavy-gauge saucepan, heat oil over medium heat. Add onion and sauté, stirring, 3 to 5 minutes, or until soft and translucent.

2. Add rice and stir until evenly coated with oil.

3. Stir in stock, bay leaf, salt, and pepper to taste. Increase heat to high and bring to a boil. Reduce heat to very low, cover tightly, and simmer 15 minutes.

4. Place peas in strainer and rinse under cold water to separate. Remove bay leaf from rice and discard. Stir in peas, cover, and cook another 3 minutes.

5. Turn off heat and keep rice and peas warm, covered, until ready to serve.

6. Fluff rice and peas with fork and turn into serving bowl.

ADDED TOUCH

This steamed pudding cooks for several hours in a coffee can. After steaming, you can serve it immediately, let it cool to room temperature, or chill it. The colder the pud-ding, the denser and more chocolaty it becomes. Be sure to top it with whipped cream.

Steamed Chocolate-Almond Pudding

3 eggs, at room temperature
1 ounce (1 square) semisweet chocolate
5 tablespoons unsalted butter
⅓ cup plus 1 tablespoon sugar
2 tablespoons bread crumbs, preferably homemade
1 tablespoon rum
5 tablespoons ground unblanched almonds
Vegetable cooking spray or butter for greasing coffee can
1 cup heavy cream
1 teaspoon vanilla extract

1. Separate eggs into 2 small bowls. With electric mixer at high speed, beat whites until stiff.

2. Place chocolate in top of double boiler set over, not in, barely simmering water. Cover double boiler and remove from heat. Bring a kettle of water to a boil.

3. Combine butter and ⅓ cup sugar in large bowl and beat with electric mixer at medium speed about 3 minutes, or until light and fluffy.

4. While beating, gradually add egg yolks to mixture and continue to beat until totally incorporated.

5. In small bowl, combine bread crumbs and rum. Add crumb mixture and ground almonds to pudding and beat 30 seconds.

6. Stir chocolate to make sure it has melted completely. Add to pudding and beat until incorporated.

7. Using rubber spatula, fold in egg whites until totally incorporated and no streaks of white remain.

8. Coat inside of clean 1-pound coffee can with vegetable cooking spray or small amount of butter. Pour in pudding batter and tightly cover coffee can with a quadruple layer of foil tied around the top.

9. Place coffee can in saucepan or Dutch oven at least 5½ inches deep. Add enough boiling water to reach halfway up the sides of can. Place pan over medium-low heat, cover, and steam pudding 1 hour and 20 minutes.

10. To test for doneness, remove foil and press top of pudding with your finger. If the top springs back, pudding is cooked. Invert can to unmold pudding.

11. When ready to serve, cut pudding crosswise into four equal slices and place each slice on a dessert plate.

12. Beat heavy cream with vanilla and remaining sugar until very thick but not stiff. Top each slice of pudding with a generous spoonful of whipped cream and serve.

Laurie Goldrich

MENU 1 (Left)
Beef Grillades
Garlic-Cheese Grits
Chicory and Red Onion Salad with
Pumpernickel Croutons

MENU 2
Chicken and Okra Gumbo
Creole Rice
Chocolate Praline Pôts de Crème

MENU 3
Blackened Seafood Stew
Asparagus Vinaigrette
Jalapeño Biscuits

Although Laurie Goldrich has prepared many ethnic meals in her lifetime, she favors southern cooking—particularly the one-pot dishes of Louisiana's Creole cuisine—over all. Inspired by French, Spanish, and African cuisines, Creole cooking consists largely of highly seasoned yet subtle and elegant seafood and vegetable dishes.

To showcase this original and eclectic way of cooking, Laurie Goldrich offers three well-known Creole main courses, beginning in Menu 1 with beef *grillades*, a traditional New Orleans dish generally served at breakfast or brunch and accompanied by grits. *Grillade* is a French word meaning "grilled meat." *Grillades* are generally made with tougher cuts of beef or veal, which become tender when braised at length in a thick sauce. This menu calls for beef tenderloin tips and quick-cooking grits to save time.

Gumbo is the featured dish of Menu 2. Although there is no hard and fast recipe for gumbo, this soup-stew usually contains a variety of meats, seafood, and vegetables. Here chicken parts, spicy *andouille* sausage, and fresh okra (used for thickening) are the principal ingredients. Creole rice flecked with bits of red bell pepper and scallion is served with the gumbo, and chocolate praline *pôts de crème* are the finale.

In Menu 3, the cook offers a seafood stew that combines elements of a popular Creole pan-blackened (not burned) fish dish and the French seafood stew *bouillabaisse*. Asparagus vinaigrette and *jalapeño* biscuits go well with the flavorful entrée.

Beef grillades, *here cubes of tenderloin braised in a seasoned sauce, served over garlicky cheese grits, make a delicious brunch or dinner. The crisp salad of chicory, pumpernickel croutons, and onion rings can be presented on the same plate or served separately.*

273

Beef Grillades
Garlic-Cheese Grits
Chicory and Red Onion Salad with Pumpernickel Croutons

When dried and hulled corn kernels (hominy) are finely ground, the resultant particles are known as grits. In the South, grits are served in one form or another at almost every meal. Look for quick-cooking grits (which take only about 5 minutes to prepare) in any well-stocked supermarket, and store them in an airtight container, where they will keep indefinitely.

WHAT TO DRINK

A good beverage here would be dark beer, particularly stout. If you prefer wine, serve a simple red California Zinfandel, French Côtes du Rhône, or Italian Dolcetto.

SHOPPING LIST AND STAPLES

1½ pounds beef tenderloin tips, cut into ¾-inch cubes
Large head chicory
2 medium-size tomatoes (about 1 pound total weight)
Medium-size red onion
Medium-size yellow onion
Large bunch scallions
3 medium-size cloves garlic
Small bunch fresh thyme, or ½ teaspoon dried
½ cup milk
4 tablespoons unsalted butter
6 ounces sharp yellow Cheddar cheese
2 cups beef stock, preferably homemade
    or canned
¾ cup good-quality olive oil
2 tablespoons red wine vinegar
4 tablespoons Worcestershire sauce
2 tablespoons tomato paste
½ teaspoon hot pepper sauce
24-ounce box quick-cooking grits
1 loaf pumpernickel bread
1 cup all-purpose flour
1 bay leaf
Salt and freshly ground pepper

UTENSILS

Food processor (optional)
Medium-size heavy-gauge skillet
Large heavy-gauge saucepan
Medium-size heavy-gauge saucepan
Large bowl
Small bowl
Measuring cups and spoons
Chef's knife
Paring knife
2 wooden spoons
Slotted spoon
Grater (if not using food processor)

START-TO-FINISH STEPS

1. Peel and mince garlic for grillades and grits recipes. Peel onions. Slice red onion for salad recipe. Coarsely chop yellow onion for grillades recipe.
2. Follow grillades recipe steps 1 and 2 and salad recipe step 1.
3. Follow grillades recipe steps 3 through 6.
4. About fifteen minutes before grillades are done, follow grits recipe steps 1 and 2 and salad recipe steps 2 through 6.
5. Follow grits recipe steps 3 through 5, grillades recipe step 7, and serve with salad.

RECIPES

Beef Grillades

8 scallions
2 medium-size tomatoes (about 1 pound total weight)
Small bunch fresh thyme, or ½ teaspoon dried
2 cups beef stock
1 cup all-purpose flour
¼ cup good-quality olive oil
1½ pounds beef tenderloin tips, cut into ¾-inch cubes
Medium-size yellow onion, coarsely chopped
2 medium-size cloves garlic, minced
2 tablespoons tomato paste
4 tablespoons Worcestershire sauce
½ teaspoon hot pepper sauce
1 bay leaf
1 teaspoon freshly ground pepper
Salt
Garlic-Cheese Grits (see following recipe)

1. Wash and dry scallions, tomatoes, and fresh thyme if using. Mince 2 scallions and reserve for garnish. Coarsely chop remaining scallions. Core tomatoes and chop coarsely. Mince enough fresh thyme to measure 1½ teaspoons.
2. In medium-size saucepan, heat stock over low heat until hot.

3. Spread flour on sheet of waxed paper. Heat 2 tablespoons oil in large heavy-gauge saucepan over medium-high heat until almost smoking.

4. Dredge beef in flour and brown in oil 8 to 10 minutes. Using slotted spoon, transfer beef to plate.

5. Add remaining 2 tablespoons oil to large saucepan with fat from beef and heat until hot. Add chopped scallions, tomatoes, onion, and garlic and cook over medium heat 3 to 4 minutes, or until onion is translucent.

6. Return beef to saucepan and add hot stock, fresh or dried thyme, tomato paste, Worcestershire sauce, hot pepper sauce, bay leaf, pepper, and salt to taste. Stir to combine. Bring liquid to a simmer and cook beef over low heat 40 to 45 minutes, or until tender.

7. Discard bay leaf. Serve grillades over garlic-cheese grits and garnish with minced scallions.

Garlic-Cheese Grits

6 ounces sharp yellow Cheddar cheese
½ teaspoon salt
Medium-size clove garlic, minced
1 cup quick-cooking grits
4 tablespoons unsalted butter
½ cup milk

1. In food processor fitted with steel blade, or with grater, grate enough cheese to measure 1½ cups; set aside.

2. Bring 3 cups water and salt to a boil in medium-size heavy-gauge saucepan over medium-high heat.

3. Add garlic and slowly stir in grits. Return to a boil, reduce heat to low, and simmer 5 minutes, stirring constantly.

4. Cut butter into small pieces. Add butter, milk, and all but 2 tablespoons cheese to grits and stir until smooth.

5. Divide grits among 4 dinner plates and sprinkle with reserved cheese.

Chicory and Red Onion Salad with Pumpernickel Croutons

Large head chicory
½ cup good-quality olive oil
2 thick slices pumpernickel bread
2 tablespoons red wine vinegar
Salt and freshly ground pepper
Medium-size red onion, cut into ¼-inch-thick rings

1. Wash and dry chicory and tear into bite-size pieces; place in plastic bag and refrigerate until needed. Line plate with double thickness of paper towels.

2. In medium-size heavy-gauge skillet, heat 2 tablespoons oil over medium-high heat until hot.

3. Meanwhile, cut pumpernickel slices into 1-inch cubes.

4. Add bread cubes to oil and cook 2 to 3 minutes, or until evenly browned. Using slotted spoon, transfer croutons to paper-towel-lined plate to drain.

5. For dressing, combine remaining 6 tablespoons oil, vinegar, and salt and pepper to taste in small bowl, and beat with fork until combined.

6. In large bowl, combine chicory, onion rings, and croutons. Pour dressing over salad and toss to coat. Divide salad among 4 dinner plates.

ADDED TOUCH

Because crabmeat is delicate and can be ruined by overcooking, sauté the fritters quickly and remove them from the skillet promptly once they have browned.

Crab Fritters with Salsa

¾ pound fresh crabmeat, or two 6-ounce packages frozen, thawed
2 medium-size ripe tomatoes
1 each small red and green bell pepper
Small jalapeño chili
Small yellow onion
1 tablespoon unsalted butter
¼ cup all-purpose flour
1 teaspoon baking powder
¼ cup milk, approximately
2 eggs, lightly beaten
½ teaspoon Worcestershire sauce
½ teaspoon salt
¼ teaspoon hot pepper sauce
Dash of Cayenne pepper
¼ teaspoon freshly ground black pepper
¼ cup vegetable oil

1. Preheat oven to 200 degrees. Line heatproof platter with paper towels. Place crabmeat in large bowl. Carefully pick over crabmeat, discarding any cartilage or bits of shell. Flake crabmeat with fork and set aside.

2. Wash and dry tomatoes and bell peppers. Core and coarsely chop tomatoes. Core and seed peppers. Coarsely chop enough peppers to measure ¼ cup each. Finely chop enough remaining peppers to measure ¼ cup each; set aside. Wash and dry jalapeño chili. Wearing rubber gloves, seed, derib, and mince jalapeño.

3. Peel onion. Coarsely chop enough onion to measure ¼ cup and finely chop enough onion to measure ¼ cup; set aside.

4. For salsa, combine *coarsely* chopped vegetables and jalapeño in serving bowl; set aside.

5. In large heavy-gauge skillet, heat butter over medium heat until hot. Add *finely* chopped vegetables and sauté 2 minutes, or until soft.

6. Add sautéed vegetables to bowl with crabmeat. Add flour, baking powder, milk, eggs, Worcestershire sauce, salt, hot pepper sauce, Cayenne, and black pepper and mix well. (Add more milk if needed to make batter of dropping consistency.)

7. Heat oil in large heavy-gauge skillet over medium-high heat until hot. Add enough crab mixture by tablespoonful to fit in skillet without crowding and cook 2 to 3 minutes on each side, or until browned. Remove fritters to paper-towel-lined platter and keep warm in oven. Repeat for remaining batter. You should have about 36 fritters.

8. Transfer fritters to serving platter. Serve with salsa.

Chicken and Okra Gumbo
Creole Rice
Chocolate Praline Pôts de Crème

Chicken and okra gumbo is served with a bowl of appetizing Creole rice and a rich dessert of chocolate praline pôts de crème.

The hearty gumbo contains okra, a popular southern vegetable brought to America by African slaves in the eighteenth century. A tapered green or white seed pod, okra exudes a thick liquid while cooking that gives substance to sauces. Buy tender pods that are no longer than 4 inches and that snap easily.

WHAT TO DRINK

The cook suggests serving a flavorful white wine, such as a Gewürztraminer, with this meal. Or try a Riesling from California, the Pacific Northwest, or Alsace.

SHOPPING LIST AND STAPLES

2½- to 3-pound chicken, cut into 8 pieces
¼ pound andouille sausage or kielbasa
1 each small green and red bell pepper
Small bunch celery
¼ pound fresh okra, or 10-ounce package frozen
Small yellow onion
Small bunch scallions
2 eggs
¾ cup milk
2 tablespoons unsalted butter
4 cups chicken stock, preferably homemade (see page 13), or canned
¼ cup vegetable oil
½ cup all-purpose flour
1 cup long-grain white rice
3-ounce can pecan halves
6-ounce package semi-sweet chocolate pieces
½ teaspoon instant coffee powder or espresso powder
½ teaspoon Cayenne pepper
1 bay leaf
Salt and freshly ground pepper
¼ cup hazelnut or praline liqueur

UTENSILS

Blender
Large heavy-gauge flameproof casserole with cover
Small heatproof casserole with cover

3 small saucepans
Large bowl
Medium-size metal bowl
Measuring cups and spoons
Chef's knife
Paring knife
2 wooden spoons
Metal tongs
Four 8-ounce ramekins or custard cups

START-TO-FINISH STEPS

One hour ahead: Set out frozen okra, if using, to thaw for gumbo recipe.

1. Wash, dry, core, and seed bell peppers. Coarsely chop enough green and red pepper for gumbo recipe. Mince enough red pepper for rice recipe.
2. Follow pôts de crème recipe step 1 and gumbo recipe step 1.
3. Follow rice recipe steps 1 through 3.
4. Follow pôts de crème recipe steps 2 through 6.
5. Follow rice recipe step 4.
6. While rice is cooking, follow gumbo recipe steps 2 through 7.
7. Follow rice recipe step 5 and gumbo recipe step 8.
8. Follow rice recipe step 6, gumbo recipe step 9, and serve.
9. Follow pôts de crème recipe step 7 and serve for dessert.

RECIPES

Chicken and Okra Gumbo

1 stalk celery
¼ pound fresh okra, or 10-ounce package frozen, thawed
Small yellow onion
½ cup all-purpose flour
½ teaspoon Cayenne pepper, approximately
Salt and freshly ground pepper
2½- to 3-pound chicken, cut into 8 pieces
2 cups chicken stock
¼ cup vegetable oil
1 tablespoon unsalted butter
½ cup each coarsely chopped green and red bell pepper
1 bay leaf
¼ pound andouille sausage or kielbasa

1. Wash celery, and fresh okra if using. Coarsely chop celery. Cut enough okra into 1-inch pieces to measure ½ cup; dice remaining okra to measure ¼ cup. Peel and coarsely chop onion.
2. In paper bag, combine flour, ½ teaspoon Cayenne, and salt and pepper to taste. Add chicken and shake to coat.
3. Heat stock in small saucepan over high heat until hot.
4. Meanwhile, line platter with paper towels; set aside. Heat oil in large heavy-gauge flameproof casserole over medium-high heat until very hot. Add chicken and cook, turning once, 5 to 7 minutes, or until well browned.

5. Using tongs, transfer chicken to paper-towel-lined platter to drain. Pour off oil from casserole and add butter, celery, 1-inch okra pieces, onion, and chopped bell peppers. Cook over medium-high heat, stirring, 3 to 5 minutes, or until okra is tender.
6. Return chicken to casserole and add hot stock and bay leaf. Partially cover pan. Bring gumbo to a simmer and cook over low heat 30 minutes.
7. Meanwhile, cut sausage into ¼-inch dice; set aside.
8. When gumbo has cooked 30 minutes, add sausage and season with salt, pepper, and additional Cayenne if desired. Simmer, uncovered, another 10 minutes.
9. Just before serving, discard bay leaf. Stir in diced okra and divide gumbo among 4 individual bowls.

Creole Rice

Medium-size scallion
2 cups chicken stock
1 cup long-grain white rice
2 tablespoons minced red bell pepper
1 tablespoon unsalted butter
1 teaspoon salt

1. Preheat oven to 375 degrees.
2. Wash and dry scallion and mince enough white and green parts to measure 2 tablespoons; set aside.
3. Heat stock in small saucepan over medium-high heat until hot.
4. Place scallion, hot stock, rice, bell pepper, butter, and salt in small heatproof casserole and stir to combine. Bake, covered, 40 to 45 minutes, or until rice is tender and stock is absorbed.
5. Turn off heat and keep rice warm in oven until ready to serve.
6. Divide rice among 4 individual bowls.

Chocolate Praline Pôts de Crème

¾ cup milk
⅓ cup pecan halves
1 cup semi-sweet chocolate pieces
2 eggs
½ teaspoon instant coffee powder or espresso powder
¼ cup hazelnut or praline liqueur

1. Place four 8-ounce ramekins or custard cups in freezer.
2. Scald milk over medium heat in small saucepan.
3. Meanwhile, reserving 4 pecan halves for garnish, place remaining pecans, chocolate, eggs, coffee powder, and liqueur in blender.
4. Add hot milk to blender and blend mixture at high speed 1 to 2 minutes, or until smooth.
5. Fill large bowl with ice cubes and 1 cup cold water. Pour milk mixture into medium-size metal bowl and place medium-size bowl in large bowl. Stir mixture 2 to 3 minutes, or until slightly cooled.
6. Pour mixture into chilled ramekins or custard cups and refrigerate at least 20 minutes, or until ready to serve.
7. Just before serving, garnish with pecan halves.

Blackened Seafood Stew
Asparagus Vinaigrette
Jalapeño Biscuits

Celebrate spring with a wholesome dinner of asparagus vinaigrette and Creole-style seafood stew. The homemade biscuits flecked with slivers of jalapeño should be kept warm in a napkin-lined basket.

The peak season for asparagus is April through late June; however, some fine greengrocers stock asparagus at other times of the year. Select plump, nicely rounded spears with compact tips.

WHAT TO DRINK

The seafood stew goes well with a crisp white wine, such as an Italian Verdicchio or a French Muscadet.

SHOPPING LIST AND STAPLES

2 pounds firm-fleshed fish fillets, such as salmon, halibut, or swordfish, or any combination
16 medium-size fresh shrimp, shelled and deveined, or 16 oysters or clams
1 pound asparagus
Small bunch celery
Medium-size green bell pepper
2 ears fresh corn, or 10-ounce package frozen kernels
2 medium-size tomatoes
Small jalapeño chili
Medium-size yellow onion
Small bunch fresh dill, or 2 teaspoons dried
1 cup milk
2 tablespoons unsalted butter
2½ cups fish stock, preferably homemade (see page 13), or three 8-ounce bottles clam juice
2-ounce jar imported capers
½ cup good-quality olive oil
2 tablespoons vegetable oil
2 tablespoons red wine vinegar
1 teaspoon Dijon mustard
5 tablespoons vegetable shortening
2 cups unbleached flour
1 tablespoon baking powder
½ teaspoon Cayenne pepper
Salt and freshly ground black pepper

UTENSILS

Large cast-iron skillet
Large saucepan with cover
Large flameproof casserole
17 x 11-inch baking sheet
Large bowl
Small nonaluminum bowl

Colander
Small strainer
Measuring cups and spoons
Chef's knife
Paring knife
Metal spatula
Metal tongs
Flour sifter or sieve
Rolling pin
2½- or 3-inch round biscuit cutter
Stiff-bristled brush

START-TO-FINISH STEPS

One hour ahead: Set out frozen corn, if using, to thaw.

1. Prepare bell pepper, and jalapeño (see page 15).
2. Follow asparagus recipe step 1 and stew recipe steps 1 through 3.
3. Follow biscuits recipe step 1 and asparagus recipe steps 2 through 6.
4. Follow stew recipe steps 4 through 6.
5. Follow biscuits recipe steps 2 through 6.
6. While biscuits bake, follow stew recipe steps 7 and 8 and asparagus recipe step 7.
7. Follow biscuits recipe step 7, stew recipe step 9, and serve with asparagus.

RECIPES

Blackened Seafood Stew

16 medium-size fresh shrimp, shelled and deveined, or 16 oysters or clams
1 stalk celery
2 medium-size tomatoes
Small bunch fresh dill, or 2 teaspoons dried
2 ears fresh corn, or 10-ounce package frozen corn kernels, thawed
Medium-size yellow onion
2 tablespoons unsalted butter
Medium-size green bell pepper, coarsely chopped
2 tablespoons vegetable oil
2 pounds firm-fleshed fish fillets
½ teaspoon Cayenne pepper
Salt and freshly ground black pepper
2½ cups fish stock or clam juice

1. If using oysters or clams, scrub and rinse thoroughly.
2. Wash and dry celery, tomatoes, and fresh dill if using. Cut celery diagonally into ½-inch-thick slices. Core tomatoes and cut into 8 wedges. Chop enough dill to measure 2 tablespoons plus 1 teaspoon.
3. Shuck fresh corn, if using. With chef's knife, cut off kernels. Peel and coarsely chop onion.
4. Heat butter in large flameproof casserole over medium-high heat until foam subsides. Add celery, onion, and green pepper and cook 10 to 12 minutes, or until tender.
5. Meanwhile, heat oil in large cast-iron skillet over high

heat until smoking.
6. Sprinkle fish fillets on both sides with Cayenne, salt, and black pepper. Sear fish in skillet 2 minutes on each side, or until dark golden brown. Using metal spatula, transfer fish to large plate. If using shrimp, sear 1 minute on each side. Transfer shrimp to small plate.
7. Add stock, tomatoes, and fresh or frozen corn to vegetables in casserole, reduce heat, and simmer 5 minutes.
8. Cut seared fish into 2-inch pieces and add to casserole with 2 tablespoons fresh dill or all of dried dill. Add shrimp, oysters, or clams. Simmer 4 to 5 minutes, or until fish is firm and oysters or clams have opened.
9. Sprinkle stew with remaining fresh dill, if using, and serve.

Asparagus Vinaigrette

1 pound asparagus
1 teaspoon capers
½ cup good-quality olive oil
2 tablespoons red wine vinegar
1 teaspoon Dijon mustard
Salt and freshly ground pepper

1. Bring 3 quarts water to a boil in large saucepan over high heat.
2. Trim asparagus. Peel stalks, if desired, and rinse.
3. Drain capers in small strainer.
4. Combine capers, oil, vinegar, and mustard in small nonaluminum bowl; beat with fork until well blended.
5. Add asparagus to boiling water. Simmer, covered, 3 to 5 minutes, or until asparagus is tender.
6. Using tongs, gently transfer asparagus to colander and refresh under cold running water. Set aside to drain.
7. To serve, arrange asparagus on serving platter. Beat dressing to recombine and pour over asparagus. Sprinkle with salt and pepper to taste, and serve.

Jalapeño Biscuits

2 cups unbleached flour
1 tablespoon baking powder
1 teaspoon salt
5 tablespoons vegetable shortening
1 cup milk
1 tablespoon thinly sliced jalapeño chili

1. Preheat oven to 400 degrees.
2. Sift together flour, baking powder, and salt into large bowl. Add shortening and blend mixture with 2 knives until it resembles coarse cornmeal.
3. Add milk and jalapeño and mix with fork until mixture forms a dough.
4. Gather dough into a ball and knead on lightly floured surface 1 minute.
5. Roll out dough to ½-inch thickness. With floured 2½- or 3-inch round cutter, cut out biscuits.
6. Place biscuits on ungreased 17 x 11-inch baking sheet and bake 12 to 15 minutes, or until golden brown.
7. Transfer biscuits to napkin-lined basket and serve.

Meet the Cooks

Susan DeRege spends summers traveling throughout the Italian countryside collecting recipes. She teaches Italian cooking at the New School in New York City and at the Kings Cookingstudio in Short Hills, New Jersey.

Nancy Verde Barr, who specializes in southern Italian cooking, is executive chef to Julia Child at *Parade* magazine. She has taught cooking in France and in Italy.

Bernice Hunt is an ardent amateur cook with a particular interest in the cooking of northern Italy. She is the author of two cookbooks, *Easy Gourmet Cooking* and *Great Bread!*

Felice and **Lidia Bastianich** were born in Istria, but met and married in New York City. They now own and operate Felidia in Manhattan, a restaurant featuring authentic Italian regional food with a focus on Istrian dishes.

Evelyne Slomon specializes in French cooking and pizza workshops at her cooking school in Manhattan. She is the author of *The Pizza Book: Everything There Is to Know About the World's Greatest Pie*.

Warren V. Mah teaches the course "Introduction to Hot Foods" at the Culinary Institute of America. He was also chef-instructor in Oriental cooking at the Institute for several years.

Connie Handa Moore has been a caterer, cooking teacher, food consultant, and sushi chef. She is the owner of Handa Food Management, Inc., in Princeton, New Jersey.

Barbara Tropp, who reads, writes, and speaks fluent Mandarin, is a scholar turned Chinese cook. She is the author of the highly acclaimed *Modern Art of Chinese Cooking* and the owner of the China Moon Café, a Chinese bistro in San Francisco.

Karen Lee has been a Chinese cooking teacher and caterer for over 15 years. She is the author of *Chinese Cooking for the American Kitchen* and *Chinese Cooking Secrets*, and is at work on two new cookbooks.

Dennis Gilbert combines two careers: cooking and writing. His short stories have appeared in numerous publications and he is now the *chef de cuisine* at the Vinyard Restaurant in Portland, Maine.

Danièle Delpeuch created the Ecole d'Art et Traditions du Périgord in 1979. Recently she toured the United States demonstrating the traditional cooking techniques of that French region.

Maria and **Guy Reuge** specialize in country French cooking with regional American overtones at their Long Island restaurant, Mirabelle, where Guy is the classically trained chef and Maria develops the recipes.

Jill Van Cleave and **William Rice** live, work, and cook in New York City. Currently, she is the test kitchen supervisor at the Ketchum Food Center, a public relations firm specializing in food accounts. He trained at Le Cordon Bleu in Paris and was editor in chief of *Food & Wine* magazine. Currently he is a freelance food consultant and writer.

Elizabeth Schneider writes for *Food & Wine* and other magazines. She is the author of *Ready When You Are: Make-Ahead Meals for Entertaining* and *Uncommon Fruits and Vegetables: A Commonsense Guide*.

Jane Butel worked as a home economist in New Mexico before moving to New York to head the Pecos Valley Spice Company, which sells ingredients for Mexican cooking. She is the author of five cookbooks, including *Chili Madness*.

Sue Huffman was food and equipment editor for *Ladies' Home Journal* and is now director of consumer affairs at Best Foods. She is a member of Les Dames d'Escoffier and the New York Women's Culinary Alliance.

Rick Bayless learned traditional southwestern cooking at his family's Oklahoma restaurant. He has been a caterer, cooking instructor, chef, and restaurant consultant, and is currently writing a book on regional Mexican cooking.

Lucinda Hutson frequently travels throughout Mexico, gathering authentic recipes. She teaches traditional Mexican recipes and techniques as well as her own style of Mexican cooking in her home town of Austin, Texas.

Julie Sahni was born in India and is now a resident of New York City. She writes regularly for many national food magazines and is the author of *Classic Indian Vegetarian and Grain Cooking*.

Jean Anderson is the author of more than ten cookbooks, including *Unforbidden Sweets*. She was the food editor at *Ladies' Home Journal* and a contributing editor at *Family Circle*. She now writes for *Food & Wine* and *Gourmet*.

Rowena M. Hubbard is a home economist and nutritionist and a managing partner of Anderson, Miller, and Hubbard, food publicists in San Francisco. She has written hundreds of recipe leaflets and cookbooks.

Joyce Goldstein founded the California Street Cooking School in 1965, then worked as a head chef and recipe planner. Today she cooks at her own restaurant, Square One, in San Francisco, which features Mediterranean, Latin American, and American foods.

Stevie Bass, a food stylist and recipe developer, runs her own consulting firm, Food Concepts, which works with advertising and public relations agencies, photographers, filmmakers, and food companies in the San Francisco area.

Beatrice Ojakangas has been food editor at *Sunset* magazine and contributes regularly to *Woman's Day*, *Bon Appétit*, and *Gourmet*. She has written several books, among them *The Finnish Cookbook* and *Scandinavian Cooking*.

Jenifer Harvey Lang is a food writer and professional cook and a graduate of the Culinary Institute of America. She is the author of *Tastings*, a rated guide to the forty most important staples in the American pantry.

Laurie Goldrich, who trained at the Culinary Institute of America, has owned a catering business in Vermont and cooked at leading New York City restaurants. At present she is a freelance food stylist.

Acknowledgments

Cover photo: John Burwell. *Frontispiece:* tiles—Country Floors; copper basin, jugs, small bowls—Amigo Country; Kilim—La Chambre Perse; baskets, box—Be Seated; square plate—Julien Mousa-Oghli; carafe—Pottery Barn. **ITALIAN MENUS.** *Pages 22–23:* tiles—Nemo Tile; casserole—Pottery Barn; servers—Gorham; platters, napkins, plates—Frank McIntosh at Henri Bendel. *Pages 26–27:* napkins—Pierre Deux; underplates—Frank McIntosh at Henri Bendel; tablecloth—Laura Ashley; flatware, glasses—Gorham; plates—Ad Hoc Housewares. *Page 29:* napkin, tablecloth—Laura Ashley; plate—Frank McIntosh at Henri Bendel. *Pages 32–33:* tiles—Elon Tiles, Inc.; platters—Mud, Sweat & Tears. *Pages 36–37:* plates—The Mediterranean Shop. *Page 39:* plates—Conran's; flatware—The Lauffer Co. *Pages 42–43:* glass salad bowl, ceramic casserole, wooden cheese board—Conran's; hand thrown platter—Feu Follet; tabletop—Formica® Brand Laminate by Formica Corp. *Page 46:* soup bowl, pasta plate—Buffalo China; flatware—Supreme Cutlery; tabletop—Formica Brand Laminate by Formica Corp. *Pages 50–51:* plates—MacKenzie-Childs, Ltd.; utensils—Gorham. *Page 54:* dishes—Villeroy & Boch; servers—The Lauffer Co.; tablecloth—Conran's; napkin—Leacock & Co. *Pages 58–59:* marble, napkin—Pottery Barn. *Page 62:* tiles—Country Floors, Inc.; plate—Wolfman-Gold & Good Co. *Page 65:* basket—Be Seated, Inc.; salad bowl—Wolfman-Gold & Good Co.; platter—Villeroy & Boch; tiles—Country Floors, Inc. **ORIENTAL MENUS.** *Pages 70–71:* paper surface—Four Hands Bindery; bowl, spoon, chopsticks—Five Eggs; plates—The Museum Store of the Museum of Modern Art. *Page 74:* flatware—Gorham; plate—Dan Levy. *Page 77:* dishes, napkin, tablecloth—Pierre Deux. *Pages 80–81:* tiles—Country Floors, Inc.; plate—Haviland & Co.; flatware—Gorham; rice bowl—Japan Interiors Gallery. *Pages 84–85:* sake cups, sake pot, small bowls—Japan Interiors Gallery; screen—Four Hands Bindery. *Page 87:* platter, white bowl—Eigen Arts; tabletop—Formica® Brand Laminate by Formica Corp. *Pages 90–91:* china—Richard Ginori; flatware—Reed & Barton Silversmiths; glass—Pierre Deux; tablecloth—Leacock & Co. *Pages 94–95:* dinnerware, tablecloth, placemats, napkins—Pierre Deux; glassware—Simon Pierce; flatware—Wallace Silversmiths. *Page 98:* china—Richard Ginori; serving pieces—Reed & Barton Silversmiths; tablecloth, napkin—Pierre Deux.

Pages 102–103: pottery—Far Eastern Antiques; tile—Country Floors, Inc. *Page 106:* lacquer tray—Far Eastern Antiques; napkin—Leacock Co.; dinner plate, teapot—Georges Briard Designs, Inc. *Page 109:* dinner plate—Pottery Barn. **FRENCH MENUS.** *Pages 114–115:* napkin—Fabindia; salad bowl—Feu Follet; knife—Linda Campbell Franklin Collection. *Page 118:* flatware, glass—Gorham; plate—Dan Levy. *Page 121:* cloth—Ad Hoc Softwares; platters—Phillip Mueller, NYC. *Pages 124–125:* utensils—Gorham; tablecloth, glass, dishes, napkin—Pierre Deux. *Pages 128–129:* plates—Dan Bleier; napkin—Conran's. *Page 131:* plate, glass—Haviland & Co.; utensils—Wallace Silversmiths; tablecloth—Pierre Deux. *Pages 134–135:* plates—Haviland & Co.; tablecloth—Pierre Deux; fork—Gorham; plates—Feu Follet. *Page 138:* plates, tablecloth, napkins—Pierre Deux; pan—Charles Lamalle. *Pages 144–145:* flatware—Gorham; napkins—Leacock & Company; plates—Columbus Avenue General Store; cloth—Ad Hoc Softwares. *Page 148:* dishes, glasses—Conran's; copper casserole, ladle, pots de crème—Charles Lamalle. *Page 151:* flatware—Frank McIntosh at Henri Bendel; plate—Bennington-Potteries. **MEXICAN MENUS.** *Pages 156–157:* flatware—Haviland Limoges; plates—Dan Bleier, courtesy of Creative Resources; tablecloth—Four Hands Bindery; napkin—Leacock & Company. *Pages 160–161:* flatware—The Lauffer Company; glass—Conran's; cloth—Primitive Artisans. *Page 163:* spoon, rug, bowl—Bowl & Board. *Pages 166–167:* glasses—Conran's; dishes—Gorky Gonzales, courtesy of Amigo Country, Brooklyn, NY; vase, table, chair—Amigo Country. *Page 170:* glass, tablecloth—Conran's; bowl, plates—Rose Gong; napkin—Marimekko. *Page 172:* bowls, rug—Amigo Country. *Pages 174–175:* flatware—Wallace Silversmiths; glasses, dishes, napkin rings—Haviland Limoges; napkins—Leacock & Company; service plates—Conran's. *Page 178:* flatware—Wolfman-Gold & Good Co.; mug—Conran's; dishes, tablecloth—Pan American Phoenix. *Page 180:* servers—Dean & DeLuca; large bowl—Julien Mousa-Oghli; pie plate, small bowl, tablecloth—Conran's; napkin—Leacock & Company. *Pages 182–183:* flatware—L.L. Bean; dishes—Mark Anderson. *Page 186:* leather mat—The Tulip Tree Collection, New Milford, CT. *Page 189:* platters, leather—Terrafirma. *Pages 192–193:* plates—Fitz & Floyd. *Page 196:* servers—Robert Murray; casserole, fruit bowl—Rubel

& Co.; lace cloth—Ad Hoc Softwares. **MORE INTERNATIONAL MENUS.** *Pages 204–205:* dessert glasses, plate—Pan American Phoenix; tablecloth—Handloom Batik Importers. *Page 208:* plate—Gear; napkin—Pan American Phoenix. *Page 211:* plate—Pan American Phoenix. *Pages 214–215:* rug—Conran's; underplates—Pottery Barn; plates, bowls—Dan Levy; glasses, flatware—Gorham. *Page 218:* plates, platter—Mad Monk; napkin, tablecloth—Stevie Bass. *Page 221:* rug, white platters—City Life. *Pages 224–225:* platters, bowl—ceramic designer Claire Des Becker; baskets, copper plate—Be Seated. *Page 228:* mat—Be Seated; plates—Pottery Barn; flatware—Gorham. *Page 230:* platters—ceramic designer Claire Des Becker; runner—Stevie Bass. *Pages 232–233:* cataplana pan—Williams Sonoma; salad bowl, thermos, mugs, vase—Wolfman-Gold & Good Co.; napkins, blue bowl—Broadway Panhandler, NYC. *Pages 236–237:* rug—Al Della Fera; flatware, glasses—Gorham; pitcher—Young Collection. *Page 239:* underplate—City Life; plate—Japan Interiors Gallery; flatware—Camilla Toniola and Eric Beason. *Pages 242–243:* dishes—Ceramica Mia; tiles—Country Floors. *Page 246:* tablecloth—Conran's; fork—Gorham; dinner plate, napkin—Broadway Panhandler, NYC. *Page 249:* tiles—Country Floors; platters, servers—Amigo Country; skewers—Charles Lamalle. *Pages 252–253:* dishes—Gear; spoon—Gorham. *Page 256:* mat, bowl, plate, glass—Gear; tabletop—Formica® Brand Laminate by Formica Corp. *Page 259:* platter, bowls—Ad Hoc Housewares; copper pan, spoon—Charles Lamalle; tablecloth—Gear. *Pages 262–263:* tureen, platter—Louis Lourioux; wooden bowl—Bowl & Board. *Page 266:* vase, dishes—Conran's; utensils—Wallace Silversmiths. *Page 269:* platter, casserole—Conran's. *Pages 272–273:* plates, glasses, coasters—Pottery Barn; flatware—Gorham; tiles—Country Floors. *Page 276:* plates—Wilton Armetale; fork—Gorham. *Page 278:* tureen, platter—Mad Monk; tiles—Country Floors; basket—Be Seated. *Kitchen equipment courtesy of:* White-Westinghouse, Commercial Aluminum Cookware Co., Robot-Coupe, Caloric, Kitchen-Aid, J.A. Henckels Zwillingswerk, Inc., and Schwabel Corp. Microwave oven courtesy of Litton Microwave Cooking Products.

Illustrations by Ray Skibinski.

Index